CAMPUS RECREATIONAL SPORTS

Managing Employees, Programs, Facilities, and Services

Library of Congress Cataloging-in-Publication Data

Campus recreational sports : managing employees, programs, facilities, and services / NIRSA.
p. cm.
Includes bibliographical references and index.
ISBN 978-0-7360-6382-1 (hard cover) -- ISBN 0-7360-6382-X (hard cover)
1. College students--Recreation--United States. 2. Intramural sports--United States--Management. 3.College sports--United States--Management. 4.Recreation centers--United States--Management. 5.Sports facilities--United States--Management.I. National Intramural-Recreational Sports Association (U.S.)

LB3608.C36 2012
796.04'30973--dc23

2011046144

ISBN-10: 0-7360-6382-X (print)
ISBN-13: 978-0-7360-6382-1 (print)

The web addresses cited in this text were current as of May 2012, unless otherwise noted.

NIRSA Managing Editor: Mary Callender, CRSS, Sr. Director of Professional Development & Leadership

Acquisitions Editor: Gayle Kassing, PhD; **Developmental Editor:** Jacqueline Eaton Blakley; **Assistant Editor:** Anne Rumery; **Copyeditor:** Tom Tiller; **Indexer:** Dan Connolly; **Permissions Manager:** Dalene Reeder; **Graphic Designer:** Joe Buck; **Graphic Artist:** Dawn Sills; **Cover Designer:** Cory Granholm; **Photographer (cover):** Photos of official and supervisor and pool and canoes courtesy of Stephen F. Austin State University, photo of outdoor field courtesy of the University of Texas at San Antonio, and photo of food service courtesy of Florida International University; **Photographer (interior):** © Human Kinetics, unless otherwise noted; **Art Manager:** Kelly Hendren; **Associate Art Manager:** Alan L. Wilborn; **Illustrations:** © Human Kinetics; **Printer:** Edwards Brothers Malloy

Printed in the United States of America 10 9 8 7 6 5 4 3 2 1

The paper in this book is certified under a sustainable forestry program.

Human Kinetics
Website: www.HumanKinetics.com

United States: Human Kinetics
P.O. Box 5076
Champaign, IL 61825-5076
800-747-4457
e-mail: humank@hkusa.com

Canada: Human Kinetics
475 Devonshire Road Unit 100
Windsor, ON N8Y 2L5
800-465-7301 (in Canada only)
e-mail: info@hkcanada.com

Europe: Human Kinetics
107 Bradford Road
Stanningley
Leeds LS28 6AT, United Kingdom
+44 (0) 113 255 5665
e-mail: hk@hkeurope.com

Australia: Human Kinetics
57A Price Avenue
Lower Mitcham, South Australia 5062
08 8372 0999
e-mail: info@hkaustralia.com

New Zealand: Human Kinetics
P.O. Box 80
Torrens Park, South Australia 5062
0800 222 062
e-mail: info@hknewzealand.com

NIRSA
4185 S.W. Research Way
Corvallis, OR97333
www.nirsa.org

E3724

Contents

Preface ix

CHAPTER 1 Evolution of Campus Recreational Sports: Adapting to the Age of Accountability 1

Douglas Franklin

Defining Campus Recreational Sports in a Changing World. 1
Learning and the Age of Accountability 4
Evolution in Campus Recreational Sports: Adaptation in a Changing World 5
Organizational Fit and Location 14
Issues and Trends 16
Summary 18
Glossary. 18
References 18

CHAPTER 2 A Career in Campus Recreational Sports 25

Sarah E. Hardin

Growth of the Profession 25
Campus Recreational Sports as a Career 26
Professional Preparation 28
Educational Credentials 33
Opportunities to Attain Professional Skills 35
Lifelong Learning: Professional Development Opportunities 39
Principles of the Profession 43
Summary 44
Glossary 44
References 44

CHAPTER 3 Relationships in Campus Recreational Sports: Professional, Institutional, and Community 47

Douglas Franklin

Interpersonal Relationships 47
Intradepartmental Relationships. 54

Interdepartmental and Intra-Institutional Relationships . . . 55
Community Relationships . . . 60
Professional Relationships . . . 61
Summary . . . 62
Glossary . . . 63
References . . . 63

CHAPTER 4 Budgeting and Internal Controls . . . 65
Maureen McGonagle
What Is a Budget? . . . 65
Budget Development . . . 66
Budget Submission and Approval . . . 72
Budget Management . . . 72
Internal Controls . . . 79
Summary . . . 81
Glossary . . . 81

CHAPTER 5 Marketing . . . 85
Evelyn Kwan Green, Aaron Hill, and Bradley Hunt
Program Promotion . . . 85
Marketing Plan . . . 88
Sponsorship Solicitation . . . 92
E-Marketing . . . 96
Branding . . . 96
Summary . . . 103
Glossary . . . 103
Resources . . . 104
References . . . 104

CHAPTER 6 Assessment in Campus Recreational Sports . . . 105
Jacqueline R. Hamilton
Defining Terms . . . 105
The Practice of Assessment—How and Why . . . 106
Contemporary Issues in Assessment . . . 108
Standards of Comparison . . . 111
Types and Areas of Assessment . . . 113
Methodology and Research Design . . . 115
Dissemination of Information . . . 117
Assessment Resources . . . 118

Summary 118
Glossary 119
References 120

CHAPTER 7 Risk Management 123
Jeff Sessine
Principles of Risk Management 123
Managing Risk 126
Training 127
Response 129
Environment 135
Equipment 137
Documentation 140
Summary 140
Glossary 141
References 143

CHAPTER 8 Technology for the Recreation Practitioner 145
Robert L. Frye and José H. Gonzalez
Making the Right Selection 145
New Technology in Facility Management 148
New Technology in Sports and Fitness Equipment 154
Using Marketing Technology 156
Using Technology in Staff Development 158
Summary 161
Glossary 161
References 162

CHAPTER 9 Human Resources 163
Stephen Kampf
Types of Recreation Employees 163
Hiring 166
Employee Training 171
Evaluation 174
Motivation 174
Certification 177
Summary 180
Glossary 181
References 181

CHAPTER 10 Program Planning Using a Student Learning Approach . . 183
Julia Wallace Carr
Step 1: Determine Priorities . . . 184
Step 2: Develop Outcomes . . . 188
Step 3: Develop Initiatives and Interventions . . . 192
Step 4: Develop Measureable Outcomes . . . 194
Step 5: Conduct Initiatives and Interventions . . . 194
Steps 6 and 7: Conduct Assessment and Evaluation and Then Revise, Maintain, or Terminate . . . 195
Summary . . . 195
Glossary . . . 195
References . . . 196

CHAPTER 11 Facilities . . . 199
Gordon M. Nesbitt
Facility Types . . . 199
Standards and Guidelines . . . 203
Scheduling . . . 208
Staffing . . . 209
Maintenance . . . 210
Summary . . . 213
Glossary . . . 213
References . . . 213

CHAPTER 12 Services . . . 215
William F. Canning and Jennifer R. de-Vries
Membership . . . 215
Equipment Checkout and Rentals . . . 221
Child Care and Babysitting . . . 226
Food Service . . . 227
Athletic Training . . . 229
Massage . . . 230
Summary . . . 230
Glossary . . . 230

CHAPTER 13 Special Events 231

Gordon M. Nesbitt

Feasibility Study 231
Financial Planning. 233
Staffing Plans 234
Rules and Officials Plans 236
Risk, Emergency, and Crisis Plans 236
Registration Plans 238
Scheduling Facilities 239
Equipment, Uniforms, and Supplies 239
Awards 239
Food Service Plans 239
Transportation Plans 240
Housing Plans 242
Promotion Plans 242
Communication Plans 242
Event Evaluation Plan 242
Summary 244
Glossary. 244
References 244

Index 245
About NIRSA: Leaders in Collegiate Recreation 250
About the Contributors 251

Preface

The process of designing, funding, and constructing a multimillion-dollar campus recreational sports facility can take years if not decades to complete. That shiny new space is just space without a well-managed department that can maximize the attributes of any facility by providing high-quality staff, programs, and services.

Campus Recreational Sports: Managing Employees, Programs, Facilities, and Services is a professional resource that provides practical information relating to the overall management of a campus recreational sports program. These facilities and programs not only create opportunities for students and faculty to engage in physical activity but also provide a place for meeting friends, establishing relationships, and being a part of the larger university community.

The first part of this book focuses on the evolution of campus recreational sports, the profession, and university and community relationships. Chapter 1 defines campus recreational sports in a changing world and how it has evolved into what it is today. Chapter 2 discusses careers in campus recreational sports and how professional preparation, credentialing, and lifelong learning develop well-rounded professionals. Chapter 3 explores the importance of relationships—collegial relationships within a department as well as the broader institution, relationships with community members and leaders, and professional relationships outside of the university or community.

Campus Recreational Sports then delves into the nuts and bolts of managing a campus recreational sports department, including budgeting, marketing, assessment, risk management, and integrating technology. Chapter 4 introduces the stages of development, submission, and approval of a budget and then managing that budget through a series of internal controls. While some may think students are a captive audience, ensuring recreational programs and services are top of mind can be a marketing challenge. Chapter 5 highlights program promotion through e-marketing and effective branding of programs, facilities, and services. In a university setting where data and research are integral components of academic life, assessment of campus recreational sports programs, facilities, and services is often expected. Chapter 6 presents a thorough introduction to assessment in campus recreational sports and the importance of disseminating the information to a broad audience. By the simple nature of sport and recreation, professionals work within the parameters of risk management on a daily basis. Chapter 7 discusses the methodologies for developing programs, renting space and equipment, offering services, and all business and operating practices through the lens of risk management. Chapter 8 outlines the process of selecting technology as well as a review of technologies that recreation practitioners can consider in improving facility operations, programs, marketing, and staff development.

The final chapters bring it all together by introducing the human resources aspect, program planning, facilities and facility management, member or user services, and special events. Chapter 9 presents the background for the variety of employee types most often seen in a campus recreational sports program, because no two are alike. As one of the largest employers of students, campus recreational sports programs need to constantly hire, train, and motivate their student and professional staff. Program planning is introduced in chapter 10. This chapter discusses the nuts and bolts of programming in order to help administrators make good decisions in creating activities and services in campus recreational sports. Facility management is a core component in the administration of any campus recreational sports program, whether the department controls its own facility or shares it with other departments. Chapter 11 highlights facility types (indoor and outdoor) as well as how to schedule, staff, and maintain those facilities. Chapter 12 presents the options in services to provide in a campus recreational sports facility (such as memberships, equipment checkout, child care, and food service) and what those services entail. Special events are covered in chapter 13, the final chapter. Special events can be distinguished from other events in that they do not occur on a regular basis. Most students and professionals can expect to have responsibility for other functions outside of their job descriptions; therefore, they should be ready to handle any and all events that could possibly be held in their facilities.

Managing a campus recreational sports program or facility encompasses many aspects, and *Campus Recreational Sports: Managing Employees, Programs, Facilities, and Services* presents a variety of best practices to help students and professionals alike accomplish all goals.

This text is dedicated to Jennifer de-Vries

CHAPTER

1

Evolution of Campus Recreational Sports

Adapting to the Age of Accountability

Douglas Franklin
Ohio University

The modern campus recreational sports program is the product of an evolution brought about by changes in student life and by diversification in the field of physical culture and physical education that was prevalent in colleges and universities in the late 19th and early 20th centuries. The field's origins and original purposes shed light on its present state and can exert a powerful effect on future programs. In addressing the roots of the field, this chapter defines campus recreational sports in the 21st century, offers examples of program terminology, identifies common program elements, clarifies organizational purposes, and explores learning in the age of accountability. The chapter also provides historical context, including the development of college life, **physical culture** and physical education, muscular Christianity, and the intramural movement. Other points of discussion include organizational fit (i.e., where campus recreational sports programs best fit within the institution) and suggestions for developing strong relationships both on campus and in the larger community. The discussion also addresses current issues and trends facing the campus recreational sports professional, including the arms race among colleges and universities.

DEFINING CAMPUS RECREATIONAL SPORTS IN A CHANGING WORLD

Campus recreational sports departments bear different names reflecting a myriad of services. The original programs were called intramurals—that is, activities conducted "within the walls" (Mitchell, 1929) of the institution—and grew out of physical education programs in the early 20th century. Some programs continue to use this name (e.g., at Brigham Young, Gonzaga, and Brown Universities), and they exist as separate entities within the broader program of athletic and recreational activities. Other departments (e.g., those at the Universities of Arkansas, Virginia, and Louisville, as well as that at Guilford College in North Carolina) have added recreational sports or activities to the title in order to more clearly define program offerings. The original intramural programs at the University of Michigan and Ohio State University simply use the term recreational sports to describe their offerings. Some programs opt for a unique name, such as intramural and recreative services at Michigan State University, while other programs focus on specific functions, such as recreation and fitness (e.g., Allegany and Mercer Colleges) or student recreation, fitness, and wellness (e.g., Lewis University). Still other programs go by the name of their recreational facility, such as Stone Recreation Center at Alma College in Michigan and the Oberlin College Recreation Center in Ohio. Other terms provide a more inclusive description, as is the case with campus recreation services (e.g., Northern Arizona and Western Washington Universities) and campus recreation (used by many schools, including Florida State and Ohio Universities, and the Universities of Maryland and Illinois). Campus recreation and intramurals (e.g., Georgia Southern University) maintains the autonomy of the intramural program while acknowledging the changes in the field.

Modern campus recreational sports programs integrate diverse activities and offerings into the curricular and co-curricular fabric of the institution in order to provide opportunities for social integration, healthy behaviors, and fun. The term campus recreational sports most aptly describes the totality of the endeavor and provides the fewest limitations on the descriptor. Campus, of course, indicates the grounds and buildings associated with the college or university, whereas recreation indicates a time for renewal and re-creation (Franklin & Hardin, 2008). Sport was first introduced into the lexicon in the mid-15th century and was defined as "pleasant pass time" and was first recorded as a "game involving physical exercise" in the 1520s (Online Etymology Dictionary, 2012). Current definitions include "an athletic activity requiring skill or physical prowess and often of a competitive nature, as racing, baseball, tennis, golf, bowling, wrestling, boxing, hunting, fishing, etc.; a diversion, recreation or pleasant pastime" (Dictionary.com, 2012) and "an activity involving physical exertion and skill that is governed by a set of rules or customs and often undertaken competitively and an active pastime such as recreation" (The Free Dictionary, 2012). Thus the term campus recreational sports suggests that the field now encompasses any physical activity held on the grounds of an institution of higher education that renews the person.

Promotional taglines and branding efforts often provide a glimpse of the focus of the modern campus recreational sports program. Statements like "stay active" (University of North Carolina, 2010), "where recreation meets learning" (Ohio University, 2010), and "a place for everyone" (University of Illinois) clarify program intent. In an apparent takeoff from the original IM (intramural) abbreviation (Mitchell, 1929), the University of California, Davis, has adopted an "I am" program focused on developing active, healthy, community-minded students (University of California, Davis, 2010). For a more in-depth view of purpose, mission statements reflect the general state of campus recreational sports. For example, the University of South Florida's campus recreation mission statement describes the department's intent to enrich the educational experience by providing opportunities for students, faculty, and staff to develop lifelong wellness skills through diverse programs, services, and facilities that allow for learning in safe, challenging, and supportive environments (University of South Florida, 2010). The University of Idaho's campus recreational sports department states that it "provides . . . programs, services, facilities and equipment to enrich the ... learning experience . . . [and] foster a lifetime appreciation and involvement in recreation and wellness activities for our students, faculty, [and] staff and the community . . . [thus] contribut[ing] to the physical, social, intellectual and cultural development of those we serve (2010)."

Common Program and Facility Elements

Modern campus recreational sports departments typically include intramural and sport clubs, fitness and wellness programs, aquatics, outdoor and adventure pursuits, informal recreation, instructional and adaptive programs, and community programs. Many departments operate student recreation facilities that may include gymnasiums, racquetball or squash courts, fitness centers and weight rooms, wellness centers, group exercise rooms, instructional spaces, climbing walls, outdoor centers, swimming pools, lounges, locker rooms, and office spaces. A few also operate golf courses, driving ranges, tennis facilities, ice rinks, and bowling alleys. As budget constraints have grown, departments have even created profit centers, such as retail shops and food venues, to generate funds—for example, the Cleveland State University Recreation Center and the University of Wisconsin Oshkosh Student Recreation and Wellness Center (Athletic Business, 2010).

Organizational Purpose

The purpose of the modern campus recreational sports program does not differ greatly from the original purpose of physical education and intramural programs. Early college physical culture and education programs were thought to improve conduct and develop character (Sargent, 1908) and enable worthy use of one's leisure time (Draper, 1930; Mitchell, 1939). Elmer Mitchell, considered the father of intramurals, suggested that intramural sports also help participants develop social contacts, group spirit, better health, permanent interest in sport, bodily prowess, and more effective scholarly performance (1939). Intramural programs in the middle of the 20th century pursued the goals of physical and mental health and fitness, development of lifelong appreciation for recreation, personal growth according to social values, group cooperation and spirit, and coordination and skill development (Means, 1973; Mueller, 1971).

As the field progressed and matured, the list grew to include fun and enjoyment, fair play, safety, and equality (Bayless, 1983). A recent study, commissioned by the National Intramural-Recreational Sports Association, found that participation in campus recreational sports programs improves students' emotional well-being, improves happiness and self-confidence, reduces stress, builds character and community, facilitates interaction with diverse sets of people, teaches team-building skills, aids in time management, improves leadership skills, and constitutes an important part of the learning experience and college social life (National Intramural-Recreational Sports Association, 2004). The goals of campus recreational sports programs align well with those of community-based recreation programs designed to enrich citizens' quality of life, contribute to personal development, make the community a more attractive place to live and visit, prevent antisocial uses of free time, improve intergroup relations, strengthen institutional ties, meet the needs of special populations, enrich community culture, and promote health and safety (Mclean, Hurd, & Rogers, 2008).

These goals and objectives focus on participants, but college physical culture, intramural sports, and recreation programs have also long advocated student involvement in administration of these activities as a method for growth and development. Early proponents included Forrest Craver, the first director of physical training at Dickinson College in Pennsylvania. In writing to the college's president and faculty, Craver asked for "a suitable number of [student] assistants" (Mackey, 2012, p. 1) to help manage the school's gymnasium and classes; in a perhaps self-serving addendum, he asked that these positions be given to his best track athletes (Mackey, 2012). In his first book, *Intramural Athletics*, Mitchell (1929) discusses the use of student committees in handling the unpleasant duties of "eligibility, protests and forfeits" (p. 27).

As student involvement in intramural programs progressed, Mitchell (1939) later warned that rather than being totally responsible for an intramural program, students should assist in its operation by providing advice only. Some years later, speaking at the 23rd annual conference of the National Intramural-Recreational Sports Association (NIRSA), Harvey Miller (1972) offered that "student help and student workers play a vital role in the organization and administration of intramural activities" (p. 120), and McGuire (1976) called intramurals the "great arena of student service" (p. 116). More recently, the general concept is that "student employees

Photo courtesy of Aztec Recreation, San Diego State University.

Student employment reflects the historical value that campus recreation programs have placed on growth and development.

form the foundation of success for most collegiate recreational sports programs" (Gaskins, 1996, p. 46) and that professional staff serve as educators of student employees (DeRozario and Witt, 1996). Keiser (1996) focused on the student employee as an internal customer in the total quality management (TQM) model.

As the academic discipline of physical education diversified into more specific areas (e.g., recreation and leisure services, outdoor recreation and education, exercise physiology, and fitness), campus recreational sports programs could offer student majors an opportunity to work on campus in their specific area of their academic discipline—a realization of John Dewey's experiential learning model (Westbrook, 1993).

LEARNING AND THE AGE OF ACCOUNTABILITY

In 1972, the American Association for Higher Education raised the issue of accountability from three perspectives: managerial accountability, accountability versus evaluation, and accountability versus responsibility (Mortimer, 1972). In the ensuing years, accountability in higher education has been the topic of numerous books and articles and the focus of commissions including the National Commission on Accountability in Higher Education (State Higher Education Executive Officers, 2010) and the United States Department of Education Secretary's Commission on the Future of Higher Education (United States Department of Education, 2006). The general thrust of these studies is that institutions of higher education need to be more accountable for what they produce for society, and this focus has resulted in a **sea change** for many colleges and universities. In this context, NIRSA has aligned with the Council for the Advancement of Standards in Higher Education (CAS), the Student Affairs in Higher Education Consortium (SAHEC), the Council of Higher Education Management Associations (CHEMA), and other higher education groups. With these groups NIRSA plays a major role in positioning the profession of campus recreational sports to address issues of accountability and in particular to advance the position that learning occurs throughout the entirety of the college experience, including out-of-class activities.

One major contribution of the association lies in its participation in the seminal *Learning*

Reconsidered publications. In 2004, the National Association of Student Personnel Administrators (NASPA) and the American College Personnel Association (ACPA) published *Learning Reconsidered*, which cast learning as a "comprehensive, holistic, transformative activity that integrates academic learning and student development" and suggested that out-of class experiences are as central as academic classes to the process of learning (NASPA & ACPA, 2004, p.1). In 2006, NIRSA partnered with NASPA, ACPA, and other professional associations to publish *Learning Reconsidered 2: A Practical Guide to Implementing a Campus-Wide Focus on the Student Experience* (ACPA et al.). *Learning Reconsidered 2* provided context and method for the college learning described in *Learning Reconsidered* and posited the educational theory of **constructivism** as central to out-of-class learning. Constructivism holds that meaning comes from questioning, communication, and relationship building; it recognizes that individual perspective and life experience shape how one interprets information (Thirteen.Org, 2012). *Learning Reconsidered 2* calls for and provides guidance in how to develop learning outcomes and learning goals for all co-curricular areas. It is available for download on the members-only portion of the NIRSA website.

EVOLUTION IN CAMPUS RECREATIONAL SPORTS: ADAPTATION IN A CHANGING WORLD

The term evolution has been used for nearly 40 years to describe the changes in campus recreational sports terminology, programming, and facility management. The term first appeared in this sense in the fourth edition of Mueller's *Intramurals: Programming and Administration* (1971), in which he described the "evolution of intramural terminology" (p. 3). He used the term again in the book's fifth edition to describe the evolution of intramural-recreational sports terminology (Mueller & Reznik, 1979, p. 1). The issue was also addressed in 1978 by McKinley Boston of Montclair State College, when he referred to "the evolution of an intramural-recreational program from athletics to physical education to student activities" (Boston, 1978, p. 28). The term evolution has also been used to describe a change in focus within recreation facilities from academics to self-generating amenities (Taylor, Canning, Brailsford, & Rokosz, 2003) and to describe growth and change in American sport as a basis for the development of campus recreational sports (Wilson, 2008). Blumenthal (2009) used evolution when describing the exponential growth of campus recreational sports and the changes leading to the construction of modern recreational facilities. Recreation departments often use the idea of evolution to demonstrate attitudes and criteria necessary for establishing programmatic change. For example, Barry University states that "for recreation to evolve, the students must be active and voice their opinions concerning what they want from recreation" (Barry University, 2010). Even the student newspaper at the University of West Georgia used the term evolution to describe a name change from intramural department to campus recreation (Elrod, 2010).

So, what exactly is evolution, and how should it be defined in the context of campus recreational sports?

Defining Evolution

Evolution can refer to something as simple as a pattern of change or as complex as the biological adaptation first suggested by Charles Darwin in *On the Origin of Species*. Using the term simply to describe change over time, as is often the case, lessens the complexity of the concept. This section of the chapter presents the case that the evolution of campus recreational sports is about adaptation and mutation as much as it is about simple change. Charles Darwin once wrote that there will come a time "when we shall have very fairly true genealogical trees of each great kingdom of nature" (Darwin, 1857, p. 456). The image of a tree—made up of roots, stems, and branches—provides a powerful metaphor for viewing the evolution of campus recreational studies.

Roots of Involvement and Learning

Tension has existed between student life and institutional control of physical culture since the beginning of American higher education. Colonial colleges founded by, affiliated with, or influenced by the dominant religions of the time demonstrated the diversity of colonial religious thought. Those with Puritan affiliation included Harvard College (founded in 1636 and now called Harvard University, the oldest institution of higher education in the United States) and the Collegiate School (founded in 1701 and now called Yale University). The College of William and Mary (1693), chartered by King William III and Queen Mary II of England, and Kings College in New York (1754), now called Columbia University, were both Anglican. The College of New Jersey (1746), now called Princeton University, was affiliated with the New Light Presbyterians, whereas the College of Rhode Island (1764), now Brown University, was Baptist. Queens College in New Jersey (1770), now Rutgers University, was Dutch Reform. Dartmouth College (1769) of New Hampshire, a wilderness at the time, was Congregational (Rudolph, 1990, p. 11). The College of Philadelphia (1740), the predecessor of the University of Pennsylvania, was originally not religion based but was later controlled by the Anglicans (Brubacher & Rudy, 2002, p. 7).

The conflict between various religious norms of the period—whether Puritan, Anglican, Baptist, or other—and young men's "natural urge to play" (Dulles, 1965, p. 20) created conflict from the outset and served as one of the key sources of tension between students and institutions. Students faced with puritanical views of exercise as wasteful and with the egalitarian analysis best described in a statement by officials at Rensselaer Polytechnic Institute that "running, jumping, climbing, scuffling, and the like . . . detract from that dignity of deportment which becomes a man of science" (Rudolph, 1990, p. 151) often found themselves at odds with institutional authority.

Early College Life: Roots of Involvement

Students have long exercised influence on the development of the field, beginning even slightly

Photo courtesy of Stephen F. Austin State University Campus Recreation.

Students have always been the center of campus recreational sports programs.

prior to institutional control of physical culture. Put another way, student recreation has been around significantly longer than has the academic discipline of physical education. Indeed, student involvement is the one aspect of campus recreational sports that has remained constant throughout the history of American higher education. From the earliest informal student competition of running and wrestling to the student-managed campus recreational sports programs of the 21st century, students have remained at the center of the endeavor.

The concept of college recreation in the United States arose more than 300 years ago with the appearance of the first colonial colleges. Though we have only limited information about student recreational pursuits during that period, we can easily imagine that young men attending colleges possessed and acted upon Dulles' "natural urge to play." In order to understand how the modern campus recreational sports program has grown and evolved, we must know and appreciate the context in which it was born and the factors that have affected its development.

As with any view of history, events and culture should be viewed from the perspective of what remains similar and what has changed. Though technology and information management are drastically different now from their state in the 18th century, students and their actions may be more similar than one might expect. Student life in the 18th and early 19th centuries was a mix of the formal curricular culture and the informal "extracurriculum" (Thelin, 2004, p. 136) made up of first literary and debating societies, fraternities, student clubs, and athletic associations.

It was during these early days that the first recorded collegiate sporting events occurred. As might be expected of boys, who were the predominant attendees of the early colleges, the first competitive events involved challenges of speed and strength. The University of Pennsylvania, for example, cites a footrace in 1760 involving a Penn student, Alexander Graydon, as its first sporting event (University of Pennsylvania, 2012a). Harvard University suggests that an interclass wrestling match in 1780 and quasi-football games in 1827 were their first sporting activities (Harvard, 2006).

Participation in these and other more informal activities often resulted in students running afoul of institutional rules and cultural mores. However, as is the case for contemporary college students, "compliance with the formal curriculum was merely the price of admission into college life" (Thelin, 2004, p. 65). As activities became more prevalent and disruptive, institutions attempted to formalize them in order to gain control.

Physical Culture and Education: Roots of Learning

In the period from 1820 to 1890, religious affiliation and the dominance the church had on the colonial colleges came together with the growing focus on nationalism, and the need to field a physically fit military. The result was a nexus of conflicting theories of physical training. Reviewing institutions that existed in the 18th and 19th centuries reveals similarities in how college students engaged in out-of-class experiences, in the physical culture on campus, and in how institutions wrestled with students and exercise. At the beginning of the 19th century, several factors converged—changes in societal views of physical activity, continued conflicts between institutions and students, and the felt need to harden men in order to build a nation—to create a new view of physical culture in American higher education. For the first time since the inception of colleges, students would engage in both compulsory and optional physical activity. During this period, institutions began to investigate the effect of physical activity as a method to promote moral development, control student behavior, and prepare young men for military service and nation building.

In forming the University of Virginia in 1818, Jefferson acknowledged the importance of exercise by establishing two gymnasiums in the campus plans for the purpose of "gymnastics and exercises for students" (Kiracofe, 1931, p. 3). Jefferson favored a directed exercise program related to military preparation that would benefit national defense (Jefferson, 1818). Unfortunately, the gymnasiums were "unserviceable" and never used for student health and exercise but rather fell into disrepair and were converted into public halls in 1830 (Kiracofe, 1931, p. 3). Jefferson's views on the importance of exercise were well articulated in his statement "leave all the afternoon for exercise and recreation, which are as necessary as reading. I will rather say more necessary because health is worth more than learning" (Think Exist.com, 2012).

One of the first institutionally sponsored formal exercise programs in an American college was the gymnastics program at Harvard College, created in 1826 by Karl Follen, who was a protégé of Friedrich Ludwig Jahn, the father of the German gymnastics movement. Follen was a professor of German but also led exercises for students. The faculty supported Follen's attempt to "work the devil out of the students" (Brubacher & Rudy, 2002, p. 49) through strict and rigorous physical exercise. Though not widely popular with students, Follen's program led Harvard and others to construct the first collegiate gymnasiums in the United States. Outdoor gymnasiums based on the German model were developed at Yale, Amherst, Williams, Brown, Bowdoin, and Dartmouth colleges from 1826 to 1828 but ran afoul of the Puritan ethic, fell into disrepair, and ceased operation (Rudolph, 1990, p. 151).

19th-Century College Life: Campus Involvement Grows a Stem

Physical recreation in colonial days was limited by work-related time constraints and a return to the Puritan ethic of the 17th century. American thought in the 1830s and the 1840s was focused on mental and spiritual things, not physical frivolities (Dulles, 1965, p. 91). Even so, the concept of physical well-being as aligned with religion and morality, though not mainstream, was beginning to take hold, and it would be a driving force in the development of physical education and athletic and recreation programs.

From the middle to the close of the 19th century, "college life"—those functions and activities outside of the classroom and beyond institutional control—were organized and controlled by students. Organizations and activities focused on Greek-letter fraternities, literary and debating societies, and interclass and intercollegiate athletic teams, particularly in the growing sports of track and field, crew, football, and baseball. Thus college life conformed and adapted to societal interests and to the growth of sport.

The development of student organizations such as the Junior Club (1832) at the University of Pennsylvania, the Yale Boat Club (1843), and the Harvard Boat Club (1844) signaled changes in the landscape of student life in American higher education. Many of the first competitions for these clubs were interclass (thus predecessors to intramural sports) or pitted college students against local citizen-based clubs. The first intercollegiate sporting event was a boat race in 1852 between the Yale and Harvard boat clubs. In 1859, the first intercollegiate baseball game was played by Amherst College and Williams College. Students began to rally around their sport teams, form athletic associations, and work with alumni to fund and field more competitive teams. Because students were responsible for organizational finances, it was not uncommon for only those students with financial means to participate in any aspect of sport (Welch, 2004, p. 196). Student control of interclass and intercollegiate athletics continued until around 1880. Institutions were supportive of intercollegiate competition because it stopped the student unrest and disruption (Welch, 2004) that Follen and the Harvard faculty had sought to quell in the early part of the century.

The 19th century ended with more scrutiny being placed on intercollegiate athletics, particularly on football finances and safety. In fact, intercollegiate sport had become such a dominant feature of American higher education that many faculty sought ways to regulate or eliminate it. The paradox for new colleges and land grant universities lay in the fact that the public acceptance and prestige the schools received through intercollegiate athletics often outweighed the need for control (Welch, 2004, p. 197). As the new century began, student control of intercollegiate athletics and institutional control of gymnastics, physical culture, and hygiene programs were on a collision course, and they would soon come under the control of a single entity.

Today, intercollegiate athletics is an enormous business, far evolved from its roots as a means of ensuring student health and recreation.

19th-Century Physical Culture, Education, and Muscular Christianity: Competing Branches and Stems

As America developed, it was influenced by European thought regarding physical culture and morality, which suggested that men were made in the image of God and as such should be seen as strong and masculine. The movement began in Britain and was presented in the United States with an *American Quarterly* article Physical Culture, the Result of Moral Obligation, written by a Boston physician John Jeffries in 1833 (Park, 2007) The idea of "sound body, sound soul" became foundational to the development of physical culture in both high schools and colleges, and it lasted throughout the 19th century. The relationship between physical development and morality became so strong that gymnasiums were built and programs developed to ensure the character development of college students. In an address to the 10th meeting of the American Association for the Advancement of Physical Education, Edward Hitchcock, a medical doctor and the founder and head of the physical culture department at Amherst College, stated that "body and heart and soul must go hand in hand. What God has joined together let not man put asunder. . . . [W]e are all beginning to ask what was the ideal form and proportion in the mind of the Creator when he said, Let man be formed in our image. . . . [T]he supreme work of creation has been accomplished that you might possess a body—the sole erect—of all animal bodies the most free, and for what?—for the service of the soul" (Hitchcock, 1877, p. 47). Dudley Alan Sargent, medical doctor and director of physical culture at Harvard, was of the same mind when he suggested that muscular activity should be designed to improve conduct and develop character and that physical training was a "fundamental basis for higher education" (Sargent, 1908, p.10).

Hitchcock and Sargent were two of the most influential supporters of the physical education movement in the United States. Hitchcock, an early advocate of anthropometrical measurement, held several areas of responsibility, including managing the gym and giving gymnastics instruction, overseeing student health, teaching elocution, physical training, lecturing on hygiene, and overseeing physical culture (Hitchcock, 1877). Sargent was one of the last true generalists in the field of physical culture and possessed a scope of knowledge spanning secondary and collegiate physical education, anthropometric measurement, intercollegiate sports, exercise for women, and health education (Bennett, 1974).

Sargent is important to the field for bridging physical education and intercollegiate athletics, and in doing so was one of the first casualties of the conflict between the two. Sargent served as a gymnasium director at Bowdoin College in 1868, where he began his formal schooling. He attended medical school at Yale in 1878 and soon after graduation accepted a position at Harvard as assistant professor of physical education and director of Hemenway Gymnasium. While serving on the Harvard athletic committee, Sargent lost his professorship after 10 years because of his attempts to control and regulate athletics. He served as director of the gymnasium for the next 30 years but was never again permitted to serve on the athletic committee.

Both Hitchcock and Sargent were considered to be supporters of the **muscular Christianity** movement. The Amherst College hygiene and physical education department sought to maintain the health of its students, and the underlying purpose of student health was articulated as follows: "Keep thyself pure: the body is the temple of the Holy Ghost" (Rudolph, 1990, p.153).

Based on concern about feminization of the church, muscular Christians suggested that passivity and compassion should be replaced by physical strength and power. Supporters of the movement, President Theodore Roosevelt among them, created and supported new physical ventures in sport and recreation, such as the Young Men's Christian Association (YMCA). Women soon joined the muscular Christians and created organizations such as the Young Women's Christian Association (YWCA) and the Girl Scouts (Putney, 2001). YMCA and YWCA chapters were found on many college campuses at the turn of the century and along with athletics played a critical role in providing recreational pursuits for students and in playing an important role in the evolution of college recreation.

The Intramural Movement: The Stem Becomes a Tree

As college athletics became more prominent and commercial, the original focus on social and health benefits was displaced by the desire to win and generate money (Welch, 2004, p.199) and while this focus generated public interest in the institution and its athletes, the general male student population was left with a choice between doing boring gymnastics and watching their classmates perform on the athletic field. As one student claimed, "athletics as conducted now in our larger universities is but for the few picked teams while the very students who most need physical development become stooped-shouldered rooting from the back of the bleachers" (unknown student from the University of California in 1904, Rudolph, 1990, p. 387).

The term intramural sport, or sport "within the walls" (Mitchell, 1929, p. 1), refers to team and dual or individual activities, tournaments, meets, and special events that are limited to participants and teams who come from within a specific school or institutional setting (Mitchell, 1939; Mueller, 1971; Means, 1973; Hyatt, 1977; National Intramural Sports Council, 1986). Mitchell (1929) describes the early state of "intramurals" to delineate "a distinct division within the Department of Physical Education" (p. 2). As stated previously, interclass competition had been a staple of college life for many years, and numerous authors have claimed that the first true intramural contest was a baseball game held between first- and second-year students at Princeton in 1857 (Stein, 1985; Mueller, 1971; Means, 1973; Hyatt, 1977). More recent information suggests that intramural events date back as far as 1780, when the first- and second-year classes at Harvard participated in a wrestling match and the first football game in 1827 (Harvard University, 2006). The University of Pennsylvania considers the intersquad games played by the Junior (Cricket) Club in 1842 to be its first intramural activity (University of Pennsylvania, 2012b). Yale claims to have been home to an annual football game between first-year and second-year students beginning in the early 1840s (Welch & Camp, 1899, p. 513). While these examples of early intramural play provide a brief view into early college life, it is unlikely that anyone will be able to identify the exact moment at which two groups of students from the same institution got together and for the first time said, "We challenge you."

As institutional control of physical education and athletics expanded, so did the opportunity for students to participate in formalized intramural events. Leaders in the field of physical education began to realize that physical fitness could be achieved through exercise derived from sport. In-house leagues were developed and served the functions of both physical education and intercollegiate athletics. Intramural programs were used as farm systems for varsity athletics (Draper, 1930; Mitchell, 1939; Means, 1973; Welch, 2004), and Mitchell suggested that "intramural sports should stand at the base of a well-founded athletic pyramid of which the varsity is the peak" (Mitchell, 1939, p. 15). One of the most famous examples of this practice was the system created at the University of Chicago by Amos Alonzo Stagg, the institution's football coach (Lawson & Ingham, 1980; University of Chicago, 2010). A proponent of muscular Christianity and moral athletics, Stagg was hired by university president William Rainey Harper in 1892 to serve as physical director. Stagg was a former Walter Camp All-American football player, and was hired with the purpose of building a football powerhouse and answering to the physical needs of the general student. In doing so, Stagg created one of the first institutionally controlled intramural sport programs to serve student health needs while also enhancing football recruitment. Similar positions and attitudes toward intramural sport were held by John Corbett, athletic instructor at Ohio University and protégé of Dudley Allen Sargent, and Forrest Craver, director of physical training at Dickinson College. The use of intramural sport to recruit varsity talent remained a common practice until the 1920s.

The University of Michigan and Ohio State University created the first true college intramural departments in 1913 and other large state universities, including Texas, Illinois, and Oregon State, began their programs in 1916 (Mueller, 1971; Means, 1973). Intramural programs were spurred to exponential development by the growth of sport in the early 20th century and by the effect of veterans returning from World War I (Hyatt, 1977; Colgate, 1978).

The University of Michigan is seen as a key innovator of the day and is credited with many intramural firsts including naming the first intramurals director, Elmer Mitchell in 1919. Mitchell wrote the first book about intramural sports *Intramural Athletics* in 1929 and operated the first intramural facility in 1928. Mitchell and the intramural directors from the Western Athletic Conference (the predecessor of the Big 10) also helped form the first meetings in the early 1920s to discuss issues related to the administration of intramural programs (Mueller & Reznik, 1979).

Over the next 30 years, the growth of intramural sport programs followed the development of sport and recreation in America. During this time the construction of sport and recreational facilities as part of public works projects made the public more aware of leisure programming (Welch, 2004) and profoundly affected the scope of intramural offerings.

The 1930s also saw the first professional associations organized to support intramurals. The Committee on Women's Athletics was recognized as a section of the American Physical Education Association and advocated a wide range of intramural sports for women (Means, 1973). The National College of Physical Education Association for Men established a section for intramurals in 1933 (Colgate, 1978; Mueller & Reznik, 1979; Hyatt, 1977), and the American Association for Health, Physical Education and Recreation established one in 1938 (Mueller & Reznik, 1979).

Due to the Servicemen's Readjustment Act of 1944, commonly known as the GI Bill, World War II veterans enrolled in colleges in large numbers, and some disagreement exists regarding the effect that veterans had on campus recreational sports. Hyatt (1977) suggests that veterans were more focused on doing schoolwork

Photo courtesy of University of Illinois Campus Recreation.

The University of Illinois has one of the oldest college intramural departments, begun in 1916.

and starting families than participating in out-of-class activities, whereas Mueller & Reznik (1979) and Colgate (1978) propose that veterans participated in sport and physical training programs while in the service and expected similar programs to be available when they enrolled in college. Colgate also offers that increased funds from the influx of veterans provided money for equipment and for the expansion of college intramural programs and facilities.

As the golden age of intramurals drew to a close, recreation took hold on campuses and reached the verge of another change that would begin the period of professionalization and adaptation by creating a national professional organization—the National Intramural Association.

Professionalization: The Tree Takes Shape

The field of campus recreational sports began to be professionalized in earnest in 1950, when Dr. William Wasson, intramural director at Dillard University, brought together 22 male and female intramural directors from 11 black colleges and universities to form the National Intramural Association (NIA), which would eventually become NIRSA. Topics addressed at this original meeting included the philosophy and objectives of the association, co-recreation intramurals, organization and staff, activities, welfare of participants, regulations and governing documents, and maintenance of records (National Intramural Association, 1950). An in-depth biography of Wasson and the history of NIRSA is available on the NIRSA website (NIRSA, 2012).

The NIA became affiliated with the American Association of Health, Physical Education and Recreation (AAHPER) in 1959. AAHPER provided much to the NIA and to the field of intramurals during this early association. Contributions included journal articles, conference sponsorship, presentations, and professional preparation (Means, 1973). In 1961, the NIA declined an offer to merge, and in 1975 it changed its name to the National Intramural-Recreational Sports Association, reflecting the diversification of services provided by its members. AAHPER maintained the National Intramural Sports Council, which focused primarily on K–12 intramural programs until it was disbanded in 2001.

See chapter 2 for more on the professionalization of campus recreational sports.

Adaptation: The Changing Tree

From the formation of the NIA in 1950 to the present, changes in campus recreational sports reflect the ability of the profession to adapt and respond to its environment. Even before 1950, the field had demonstrated its ability to adapt to the increasing societal interest in sport. From baseball to football and then basketball, sport competition was conducted through intramurals and later in intercollegiate form. Intramurals also adapted to meet the physical fitness needs of the military in both world wars, which in turn expanded the collegiate programs. Current societal pressures focus on college accountability and affordability, and the profession is well positioned to meet these demands. Through participation in the CAS consortium and as partners in the *Learning Reconsidered* publications, NIRSA and its members have established learning as the center of its mission and are developing assessment tools to measure achievement of these goals.

The profession has also adjusted to meet the challenges posed by scientific discoveries associated with cardiovascular exercise (Cooper, 1968) by developing aerobic dance and group exercise classes, fitness centers, and personal training. When the concept of wellness became synonymous with health promotion and holistic balance, campus recreational sports programs around the country added wellness to their portfolio or partnered with campus wellness programs. When mandatory college physical education programs began to disappear, campus recreational sports programs took their place as instillers of healthy behaviors. As physical culture diversified, intramural sports and later campus recreational sports programs adjusted to adopt or work with new college recreational pursuits. Programs in outdoor education and adventure recreation are now staples of many campus recreational sports programs. Aquatics programs have also become part of campus recreational sports and are now considered an essential element in many new facilities.

In meeting campus needs, campus recreational sports programs continue to adapt to institutional requirements and lead the way in establishing collaborative partnerships. Examples include first-year-student initiatives such as the New Foundations course at Dartmouth College (Lombardo, (2010), the New Adventures trip at Ohio University (Ohio University, 2012), and the First-Year Adventure trip at Kent State University (Kent State University, 2010). Other examples of campus partnerships include working with non-trip-based first-year experiences and other academic programs; supporting institutional service efforts such as Red Cross blood drives; facilitating team building and leadership in student organizations, departments, and community groups; providing noncredit and in some cases credit-generating courses in first aid, CPR, and learn-to programs; partnering with health and wellness programs, counseling centers, and housing and residence life offices in promoting alternatives to high-risk behaviors; assisting in institutional sustainability efforts, including participating in recycling programs, reducing energy consumption, generating energy through devices such as the ReRev systems, and building green; and employing cost sharing for costly tools and systems that support institutional assessment efforts. In addition, campus recreational sports programs provide community support by allowing access to facilities not available in the private sector; by using facilities to support emergency response efforts; and by working with students to support community service initiatives.

Campus recreational sports programs have also been very successful at adapting to changes in student populations in order to address the specific needs generated by GI bills, Title IX, the Americans with Disabilities Act, and initiatives to promote universal access, institutional diversity, and globalization. Indeed, one of the great strengths of modern campus recreational sports programs is their ability to diversify and expand program offerings for returning veterans and other nontraditional students, women, minorities and other underserved populations, students with disabilities, and international students.

The University of Texas at San Antonio, Department of Campus Recreation.

Modern campus recreational sports programs are adept with accommodating a wide variety of needs.

ORGANIZATIONAL FIT AND LOCATION

Many institutionally controlled intramural programs originated as part of physical education. One major exception is the University of Texas, whose intramural athletics program started in the department of intercollegiate athletics in 1916 and moved to student affairs 19 years later. A separate women's intramural program was started in 1918 as part of the academic department of physical training for women. In 1973, these two departments were consolidated in the division of recreational sports as an independent unit within student affairs (University of Texas, 2010).

Though the University of Texas was not alone in locating intramurals in student affairs, it was in the minority. In that same year, 1973, a survey was conducted to investigate the reporting sequences of 1,955 colleges and universities in the United States and Canada. The study found that the majority of all intramural programs were located in the institution's physical education department but programs in large colleges were based in student affairs (Maas, Mueller, & Anderson, 1974). These findings formed the basis for a round-table presentation titled "Intramurals: Where Does It Belong, in Physical Education or Student Affairs?" at the 26th annual NIRSA conference. Carolyn Hewatt from the University of Texas spoke to the importance of establishing the department as an "autonomous unit" (p. 29), having a "broader base" (p. 30), and being involved in all aspects of student services (Harms, 1975). Bill Ellis from Colorado State University noted that benefits of being located in the physical education department included ease of facility scheduling and the ability to share academic equipment; one disadvantage was funding insecurity caused by intramurals being a lower priority than academics. Jill Williams indicated intramurals at Arizona State University was under the direction of Associated Students (p. 32), a student-fee-based organization with an executive manager reporting to the head of student affairs. She suggested that student fee funding was a benefit when the department was associated with student affairs. One concern for Williams was the scheduling of facilities. Bill Quayle, speaking on behalf of Phillips University, a small liberal arts institution, was supportive of his location within physical education and cited the importance of instruction and economics on the funding of his program. Kent Bunker of Oklahoma State University reflected on being in the more encompassing department of health, physical education, and recreation and indicated that the primary problem with this organizational structure was competition for access to physical space. Raydon Robel from Kansas State University indicated that his department was moved into student affairs at the request of students and that the name of the program was changed from the intramural and recreation department to recreational services to demonstrate the program's scope. Robel stressed the importance of maintaining a relationship with physical education. Speakers at the session agreed that as long as the department enjoyed some autonomy, it did not really matter where it was housed (Harms, 1975). Twenty years later, the topic was raised again in the *Rationale for Independent Administration* (NIRSA, 1994) a NIRSA white paper on organizational location.

Rationale for Independent Administration

In October 1994, Bryant, Anderson, and Dunn co-authored the NIRSA-sponsored white paper *Rationale for Independent Administration of Collegiate Recreational Sports Programs: A Position Paper*, which provided a rationale for separating campus recreational sports programs from academic and intercollegiate athletic units. The paper cited a 1992 survey that found 61 percent of campus recreational sports programs were located in student affairs, 18 percent in athletics, and 16 percent in academics. The primary reason for the change in organizational location from academics and athletics to student affairs as cited in the Maas, Mueller, & Anderson (1974) study was the changing missions of academic, athletic, and campus recreational sports programs. The rise of campus recreational sports, the increased societal awareness of aerobic fitness, the reduction in mandatory physical education programs, and the increase in women on campuses as a result of the Title IX education amendments of 1972 created a new demand for fitness programs. These forces fundamentally changed program focus from supporting academic and athletic units to providing independent recreation and fitness services. New expansive facilities, necessary for institutions to remain competitive in recruiting, were dedicated to student recreation and created opportunities for new programs.

In many cases the drive for independence from academic and athletic organizations appears to have derived from frustrations related to shared facilities and inadequate budgets. For example, Edward Londono, director of campus recreation at Florida International University, spoke of the relationship between athletics and recreation and stated that in an athletic department "athletics always comes first . . . and recreation is looked upon as the ugly stepchild" (Cohen, 1995, p. 32). This sense of frustration can be found among many campus recreational sports professionals. Programs located within academic units often encounter a similar attitude, since academic faculty are focused on their teaching and research facility needs and often do not value recreation programs that reduce facility availability (Cohen, 1995).

Home Is Where the Heart Is

In a recent survey, the most common locations for campus recreational sports programs were student affairs (72%), intercollegiate athletics (16%), academics (3%), and the institution's business and finance office (3%) (Franklin, 2007). The continued migration of departments to student affairs derives largely from the role that campus recreational sports programs play in providing student and student-directed recreational activities (Cohen, 1995). The second most common location, within intercollegiate athletics, is designed to facilitate the use of shared facilities and equipment between intercollegiate athletics, club sports, and intramurals. This is a popular model at small, liberal arts schools competing in NCAA Division III or in the NAIA, but some larger institutions (e.g., the University of Buffalo) also use this approach.

ISSUES AND TRENDS

Much of this chapter has dealt with the past and how the profession has adapted to the environment to achieve its current place within higher education. The remainder of the chapter focuses on selected major issues and trends that now face campus recreational sports professionals and how the profession might evolve in dealing with them.

The Arms Race and the Paradox of the Recreational Facility

Recreational sport facilities and programs are viewed as important assets for institutions of higher education and are presumed to help attain institutional goals, such as recruitment and retention of students (Taylor, Canning, Brailsford, & Rokosz, 2003). At issue is the lack of funding to operate these facilities and programs in the face of public perception that they unnecessarily drive up the cost of higher education and resulting issues of college affordability.

To some, recreation facilities—along with student unions, enhanced housing environments, and intercollegiate athletics—are part of a growing arms race within higher education (Hersh, & Merrow 2005). Richard K. Vedder, an emeritus professor at Ohio University calls the issue "the country-clubization of the American University" and has stated that "...in the zeal to get students, they [college and universities] are going after them on the basis of recreational amenities" (Dillon, 2010). This perception is heightened by articles such as *Fancier Perks for Higher Education* (Dennis, 2004), "*Jacuzzi U.?: A Battle of Perks to Lure Students*" (Winter, 2003), *Colleges Replace Drab Gyms With Sleek Playful Facilities* (Reisburg, 2001), and *The Ivory Climbing Wall*" (Frield, 2003), as well as the PBS documentary *Declining by Degrees: Higher Education at Risk* (Hersh & Merrow, 2005).

Despite these concerns, construction, renovation, and expansion of student recreational facilities continue unabated. Data from NIRSA's

Photo courtesy of University of Cincinnati.

Despite challenges to obtaining funding, many campus recreational sports programs continue to build and renovate today.

Collegiate Recreational Sports Facilities Construction Report for 2010-2015 (NIRSA, 2012) reveal that during the reporting period 82 colleges and universities were involved in 129 projects of facility construction, expansion, or renovation at a total cost of nearly $1.7 billion dollars. The average project expenditure was $13.2 million, which constituted an increase of $1.3 million over the 2006 average amount.

Adapting to the Changing Needs of Professional Preparation

From the first meeting of Elmer Mitchell and the intramural directors from the Western Athletic Conference in the early part of the 20th century, people working in the field of campus recreational sports have long desired to associate their work with a profession. The formation of the National Intramural Association (NIA) in 1950 was a major step in the professionalization of the field. As the NIA progressed the topic of professional preparation soon made its way into association discussions.

In 1970, while at the twenty-first meeting of the NIA, Jim Wittenauer, intramural director at Indiana State called for intramural directors to engage in professional preparation beyond the field of physical education and suggested a curriculum including leadership in recreation and intramurals, first aid, report and news writing, audiovisual preparation, and field experiences. He also called for the NIA to create a committee to recommend minimum standards and qualifications for certification of professionally trained intramural leaders (Wittenauer, 1973). In 1973, Lawrence Preo conducted a study of intramural directors that identified key skills for professional preparation, including intramural administration, facilities and equipment expertise, finance, budgeting, and recreation administration (Preo, 1973). Preo also called for the development of professional standards and proposed a model for professional preparation that included formal study and reflection, practical work experience, and the skill to conceptualize theory into practice (Preo, 1976). Beardsley and Mull (1977) supported an interdisciplinary approach to professional preparation and suggested a curriculum incorporating topics in teaching, coaching, training, physiology, recreation, outdoor education, parks, management, and cultural social programming. Jamieson (1987) and Regier and Boucher (1990) called for a competencies approach to the preparation of campus recreational sports professionals. The NIRSA curriculum guide (1992) provided a broad range of topics for undergraduate preparation: foundations and philosophy, programming techniques, management, risk management and legal concepts, facility supervision, governance, public relations, exercise science and fitness management, officiating, and computer applications. For graduate studies, the guide listed budget and finance, governance, marketing and public relations, facility management and design, philosophy, psychology and sociology of sport, and research. Using the Competencies of Sport Managers Instrument, a study of 457 recreational sports managers, revealed competencies in management, programming, administration, and understanding relevant theories (Barcelona & Ross, 2004).

The culmination of all of these discussions and the solution to the lack of academic preparation in campus recreational sports was the development of the Registry of Collegiate Recreational Sports Professionals. Established in 2011 the Registry "guides, encourages and recognizes purposeful and continuous professional development" in the profession's body of knowledge (NIRSA, 2012c). The Registry's competency areas, built from a validation study published by the NIRSA National Research Institute include philosophy and theory; programming; management techniques; business procedures; facility management, planning and design; research and evaluation, legal liability and risk management; and personal and professional qualities (NIRSA, 2012c).

Adapting in a Struggling Fiscal Environment

The earliest faculty athletic committees saw the need for special fees for athletics and intramurals. As the intramural and campus recreational sports field progressed, and particularly as programs migrated to student affairs, fees continued in some form or fashion for participation. These fees have increased considerably over the years in order to fund the construction of new facilities, the subsequent bond debt, and the associated operational costs, including staffing. As professional and student staffing grows, systems become complex and more personnel intensive, the need increases for supplies, equipment, and support services. Balancing cost containment efforts and revenue generation from other income sources, including fees for personalized services and memberships to faculty and community, are often used to offset expenses associated with campus recreational sports operations.

Technological solutions can help departments increase operational efficiency, increase revenue, reduce cost, and contribute to improved customer satisfaction. Several software technologies are available to support program management objectives. In selecting a package, campus recreational sports professionals should take the following steps: (1) define and prioritize departmental requirements, including elements for membership and program management, online registration, establish processes for transactions at the point-of-sale reporting needs, and so on; (2) identify and include partners in the process; and (3) establish cost parameters (including ongoing maintenance) and choose features based on critical need. Your selection criteria should also include the vendor's experience, system stability and customer service as experienced by peers, and overall cost.

SUMMARY

The field of campus recreational sports has demonstrated its ability to evolve and adapt to college students' changing needs. Modern departments, with their massive facilities and diverse programs, have grown from roots in the simplest of activities, such as a wrestling match or baseball game between classes at the colonial colleges. As physical health and leisure drew increasing societal interest, the campus recreational sports profession gathered into communities of practice, formed professional associations, and participated in scholarly work to assess its effect on students in higher education. The profession has adapted and grown from the roots of involvement and physical culture into a strong and mature tree with branches in intramural and club sports, fitness and wellness, aquatics, outdoor education and recreation, challenge course and experiential education, and informal recreation. Aligning with other professional associations in higher education helps the profession to adapt to new challenges of accountability and make learning the central focus of the modern campus recreational sports program.

Glossary

constructivism—Learning theory suggesting that meaning is created from the interface between one's experiences and one's thoughts (Thirteen.org, 2012).

muscular Christianity—Mid-19th-century religious movement that stressed vigorous physical activity to build the human body as a testament to God. One good example of an entity born out of muscular Christianity is the YMCA, where basketball and volleyball were invented (Putney, 2001).

physical culture—"Philosophy, regimen, or lifestyle seeking maximum physical development through such means as weight (resistance) training, diet, aerobic activity, athletic competition, and mental discipline. Specific benefits include improvements in health, appearance, strength, endurance, flexibility, speed, and general fitness, as well as greater proficiency in sport-related activities." (Fair, 2012).

sea change—Term associated with the change from calm to rough seas that is used to indicate a striking change or transformation.

References

American College Personnel Association, Association of College and University Housing Officers–International, Association of College Unions–International, National Academic Advising Association, National Association for Campus Activities, National Association of Student Personnel Administrators, et al. (2006). *Learning reconsidered 2*. Washington, DC: Author.

Athletic Business. (2010). 2009 facilities of merit. Retrieved from www.athleticbusiness.com/galleries/FacilitiesOfMerit.aspx?year=2009.

Barcelona, B., and Ross, C.M. (2004). An analysis of the perceived competencies of recreational sport administrators. *Journal of Park and Recreation Administration, Volume 22, Number 54 Winter*, pp. 25-42.

Barry University. (2010). Intramural and recreational sports policies and procedures. Retrieved from www.barry.edu/hpls/recreation/policies.htm.

Bayless, K.G. (1983). *Recreational sports programming*. North Palm Beach, FL, Athletic Institute.

Beardsley, K.P., and Mull, R.F. (1977). *Professional preparation of the intramural-recreational sports specialist*. Washington, DC: American Alliance for Health, Physical Education and Recreation.

Bennett, B.L. (1974, December). *Dr. Dudley Sargent: A sterling example of commitment, communication, and cooperation*. Paper presented at the annual meeting of the Tennessee Association for Health, Physical Education, and Recreation, Chattanooga, TN.

Blumenthal, K.J. (2009). Collegiate recreational sports: Pivotal players in student success. *Planning for higher education* v37(2). Society of College and University Planners.

Boston, M. (1978). The evolution of an intramural-recreational program from athletics to physical education to student activities. In, *Operational and theoretical aspects of intramural-recreational sports*, edited by Thomas P. Sattler, Peter J. Graham, and Don.C. Bailey, p. 28-33. West Point, NY: Leisure Press.

Briel, B. (2001). The ivory climbing wall. *National Journal*, 11/15/2003, Vol. 35 Issue 46, p3488, 6p.

Brubacher, J.S., and Rudy, W. (2002). *Higher education in transition: A history of American colleges and universities, 4th ed*. New Brunswick, NJ: Transaction Publishers.

Bryant, J., Anderson, B., and Dunn, M.J. (1994). *Rationale for independent administration of collegiate recreational sports programs: A position paper*. National Intramural-Recreational Sports Association.

Cohen, A. (1995). Separate but equal. *Athletic Business, 19*, 29-38.

Colgate, J.A. (1978). *Administration of intramural and recreational activities: Everyone can participate*. New York: Wiley.

Cooper, K. (1968). *Aerobics*. Philadelphia: Lippincott.

Darwin, C. (1857). From a letter to T.H. Huxley. In F. Darwin (ed.), *The life and letters of Charles Darwin, including an autobiographical chapter* (Vol. 2, p. 456). London: Murray.

Dennis, B. (2004). Fancier perks of higher ed. *St. Petersburg Times. On campus: A new monthly feature*. St. Petersburg, FL: Feb 3, 2004. pg. 1.B.

DeRozario, F., and Witt, J. (1996). Student staff development: Exploring its potential. In, *Practices, issues & challenges in recreational sports: A collection of papers submitted for the 47th NIRSA annual conference-1996*, Joel L. Fitch, Editor. Corvallis, OR: National Intramural-Recreational Sports Association.

Dillon, S. (2010). Share of college spending for recreation is rising. New York Times. Retrieved from www.nytimes.com/2010/07/10/education/10education.html.

Draper, E.M., and Smith, G.M. (1930). *Intramural athletics and play days*. New York, NY: A.S. Barnes and Company.

Dulles, F.R. (1965). *The history of recreation: America learns to play*. Englewood Cliffs, NJ: Prentice Hall.

Elrod, A. (2010). The evolution of UWG intramurals. *The West Georgian.* Retrieved from http://thewestgeorgian.com/mobile/the-evolution-of-uwg-intramurals-1.1086906.

Fair, J.D. (2012). Physical culture. Retrieved from www.britannica.com/EBchecked/topic/1100468/physical-culture.

Franklin, D.S. (2007). Student development and learning in campus recreation: Assessing recreational sports directors' awareness, perceived importance, application of and satisfaction with CAS standards. Unpublished dissertation. Retrieved from http://etd.ohiolink.edu/view.cgi/Franklin%20Douglas%20S.pdf?ohiou1177514055.

Franklin, D.S., and Hardin, S.E. (2008). Philosophical and theoretical foundations of campus recreation: Crossroads of theory. In NIRSA, *Campus recreation: Essentials for the professional*, pp. 3-20. Champaign IL: Human Kinetics.

Gaskins, D. (1996). A profile of recreational sports student employees. *NIRSA Journal*, v20(3), pp. 43-47. National Intramural-Recreational Sports Association.

Harms, B. (1975). Intramurals: Where does it belong; physical education or student affairs? In W. Hollsberry (ed.), *Twenty-sixth annual conference proceedings*. Corvallis, OR: National Intramural-Recreational Sports Association.

Harvard University. (2006). Harvard athletics: A timeline of tradition. Retrieved from www.gocrimson.com/information/history/traditiontimeline.

Hersh, R.H., and Merrow, J. (2005). *Declining by degrees: Higher education at risk*. New York, NY: Palgrave.

Hitchcock, E. (1877). Hygiene at Amherst College: Experience of the department of physical education and hygiene in Amherst College for the past sixteen years. In, *The American Association for the Advancement of Physical Education, Third Annual Meeting at Brooklyn, NY.* New York: Rome Brothers, Steam Printers.

Hyatt, R.W. (1977). *Intramural sports: Organization and administration*. Maryland Heights, MO: Mosby.

James Madison University. (2012). Masters degree in kinesiology: Campus recreation leadership track. Retrieved from www.jmu.edu/recreation/URECTeam/CRL%20MKTG.pdf.

Jamieson, L.M. (1987). Competency-based approaches to sport management. *Journal of Sport Management, 1*(1), 48-56.

Jefferies, J. (1833). Physical culture, the result of moral obligation. *American Quarterly Review*, 1833.

Jefferson, T. (1818). The Rockfish Gap Report: Report of the commissioners for the University of Virginia. Retrieved from www2.lib.virginia.edu/exhibits/rotunda/prefire/rockfish2.html.

Keeling, R.P. (2006). *Learning reconsidered 2: A practical guide to implementing a campus-wide focus on the student experience.* Washington, DC: American College Personnel Association, Association of College and University Housing Officers-International, Association of College Unions-International, National Academic Advising Association, National Association of Campus Activities, National Association of Student Personnel Administrators and National Intramural-Recreational Sports Association.

Keeling, R.P. (2004). *Learning reconsidered: A campus-wide focus on the student experience.* Washington, DC: American College Personnel Association and National Association of Student Personnel Administrators.

Keizer, S. (1996). Student employees: Focusing on the internal customer. *NIRSA Journal*, v24(2).

Kent State University. (2010). First year adventure. Retrieved from www.kent.edu/recservices/adventurecenter/index.cfm.

Kiracofe, E.S. (1931). An historical study of athletics and physical education in the standard four year colleges of Virginia.

Unpublished dissertation, University of Virginia. UMI No. DP14383.

Lawson, H.A., and Ingham, A.G. (1980). Conflicting ideologies concerning the university and intercollegiate athletics: Harper and Hutchins at Chicago, 1892–1940. *Journal of Sports History,7*(3), 37-67.

Lombardo, M.S. (2010). Freshman year success via outdoor orientation programs: A brief history. *New Foundations.* Retrieved from www.newfoundations.com/History/Outdoor.html.

Maas, G.M., Mueller, C.E., and Anderson, B.D. (1974). Survey of administrative reporting sequences and funding sources for intramural-extramural programs in two-year and four-year colleges in the United States and Canada. In, *1974 Twenty-fifth annual conference proceedings.* National Intramural Association.

Mackey, C. (2012). Forrest E. Craver, 1875-1958. Retrieved from http://chronicles.dickinson.edu/encyclo/c/craverbio.html.

McGuire, R.J. (1976). Student leadership: The student manager program. In J.A. Peterson (ed.), *Intramural administration: Theory and practice.* Englewood Cliffs, NJ: Prentice Hall.

McLean, D.D., Hurd, A.R., & Rogers, N.B. (2008). *Kraus' recreation and leisure in modern society* (8th ed.). Sudbury, MA: Jones and Bartlett.

Means, L.E. (1973). *Intramurals: Their organization and administration, 2nd ed.* Englewood Cliffs, N.J.; Prentice-Hall.

Miller, H. (1972). Student administered intramural programs. In, *the 23rd annual conference proceedings of the National Intramural Association*, pp. 120-121. Champaign, IL; University of Illinois.

Mitchell, E.D. (1939). *Intramural sports.* New York, NY: A.S. Barnes and Company.

Mitchell, E.D. (1929). *Intramural athletics.* New York, NY: A.S. Barnes and Company.

Mortimer, K.P. (1972). *Accountability in higher education.* Washington, DC: American Association for Higher Education.

Mueller, P. (1971). *Intramurals: Programming and administration, 4th ed.* New York, NY: The Ronald Press Company.

Mueller, P., and Reznik, J.W. (1979). *Intramural-recreational sports: Programming and administration, 5th ed.* New York: Wiley.

National Association of Student Personnel Administrators & American College Personnel Association. (2004). *Learning reconsidered.* Washington, DC: Author.

National Intramural Association. (1950). Proceedings of the National Intramural Association: Maximum participation. New Orleans, LA: Dillard University.

National Intramural-Recreational Sports Association. (2012a). *Collegiate recreational sports facilities construction report 2010-2015.* Retrieved from www.nirsa.org/AM/Template.cfm?Section=Research_Central&Template=/MembersOnly.cfm&ContentFileID=10403.

National Intramural-Recreational Sports Association. (2012b). *Dr. William N. Wasson.* Retrieved from www.nirsa.org/Content/NavigationMenu/AboutUs/History/WilliamWasson/Dr_William_Wasson.htm.

National Intramural-Recreational Sports Association. (2012c). *Registry of collegiate recreational sports professionals presented by Cybex.* Retrieved from www.nirsa.org/Content/NavigationMenu/Education/RegistryofCollegiateRecreationalSportsProfessionals/professionalregistr.htm.

National Intramural-Recreational Sports Association. (2004). *The value of recreational sports in higher education: Impact on student enrollment, success, and buying power.* Champaign, IL: Human Kinetics.

National Intramural-Recreational Sports Association. (1992). *Recreational sports curriculum: A resource guide.* Corvallis, OR: Author.

National Intramural Sports Council. (1986). *Intramurals and club sports: A handbook.* Reston, VA: American Alliance for Physical Education, Recreation and Dance.

Ohio University. (2012). *New adventures*. Retrieved from www.ohio.edu/recreation/outdoorpursuits/newAdventures.cfm.

Park, R.J. (2007). Biological thought, athletics and the formation of a 'Man of Character': 1830-1900. *The International Journal of the History of Sport*, v 24 (12), pp. 1543-1569.

Preo, L.S. (1976). Professional preparation of administrators of intramural and physical recreation programs. In J.A. Peterson (ed.), *Intramural administration: Theory and practice*. Englewood Cliffs, NJ: Prentice Hall.

Preo, L.S. (1973). A comparative analysis of current status and professional preparation of intramural directors. In, *1973 Twenty-Fourth Annual Conference Proceedings of the National Intramural Association*, pp. 150-155.

Putney, C. (2001). *Muscular Christianity:Manhood and sports in Protestant America, 1880–1920*. Cambridge: Harvard University Press.

Regier, K.A., & Boucher, R.L. (1990). Professional preparation competencies of recreational sport administrators. *NIRSA Journal, 14*(2), 46–54.

Reisberg, L. (2001). Colleges replace drab gyms with sleek, playful facilities. *Chronicle of Higher Education v* 47 (22), pA38, 2p, 2c.

Rudolph, F. (1990). *The American college & university: A history*. Athens, GA: The University of Georgia Press.

Sargent, D.A. (1908). Physical education training in school and college. Shall it be compulsory? *American Physical Education Review*. V13(1). Springfield, MA: The American Physical Education Association.

State Higher Education Executive Officers (SHEEO). (2010). *National commission on accountability in higher education*. Retrieved www.sheeo.org/account/comm-home.htm.

Stein, E. (1985). The first organized intramural event (1869): Princeton University's cane spree. NIRSA Journal, V. 9, No. 2: 42-43.

Taylor, H., Canning, W.F., Brailsford, P., and Rokosz, F. (2003). Financial issues in campus recreation. *New Directions for Student Services*, No. 103, Fall, pp. 73-86.

Thelin, J.R. (2004). *A history of American higher education*. Baltimore, MD: Johns Hopkins University Press.

Think Exist.com. (2012). Jefferson quote on the importance of exercise. Retrieved from http://thinkexist.com/quotation/leave_all_the_afternoon_for_exercise_and/226072.html.

Thirteen.Org. (2012). Concept to Classroom. *Constructivism as a paradigm to teaching and learning*. Retrieved from www.thirteen.org/edonline/concept2class/constructivism/index.html.

United States Department of Education. (2006). *A test of leadership: Charting the future of U.S. higher education*. A report of the commission appointed by Secretary of Education Margaret Spellings. Retrieved from www2.ed.gov/about/bdscomm/list/hiedfuture/reports/final-report.pdf.

University of California, Davis. (2010). Home page. Retrieved from http://campusrecreation.ucdavis.edu/cms/.

University of Chicago. (2010). *Physical education and athletics: History: Amos Alonzo Stagg*. Retrieved from http://athletics.uchicago.edu/history/history-stagg.htm.

University of Idaho. (2010). Campus recreation mission statement. Retrieved from www.campusrec.uidaho.edu/Mission.

University of North Carolina. (2010). Fitness. Retrieved from http://campusrec.unc.edu/fitness/.

University of Pennsylvania. (2012a). *Penn athletics in the 19th century: The origins of Penn athletics*. Retrieved from www.archives.upenn.edu/histy/features/sports/sports1800s.html.

University of Pennsylvania. (2012b). *Cricket: Penn's first organized sport*. Retrieved from www.archives.upenn.edu/histy/features/sports/cricket/jrclub.html.

University of South Florida. (2010). Campus recreation. Retrieved from http://usfweb2.usf.edu/camprec/rec.html.

University of Texas. (2010). History of rec-sports. Retrieved from www.utrecsports.org/about/history/history.php.

Welch, L.S., and Camp, W. (1899). *Yale: Her campus, class-rooms, and athletics*. pp 449-631. Boston: L.C. Page and Company. Retrieved from http://books.google.com/books?id=V8wWAAAAIAAJ&pg=PA451&source=gbs_toc_r&cad=4#v=onepage&q&f=true.

Welch, P.D. (2004). *History of American physical education* (3rd ed.). Springfield, IL: Charles C Thomas.

Westbrook, R.B. (1993). John Dewey, 1859–1952. *Prospects: The Quarterly Review of Comparative Education, 23*(1/2), 277–291.

Wilson, P. (2008). History and evolution of campus recreation. In NIRSA, *Campus recreation: Essentials for the professional,* pp. 21-32. Champaign, IL; Human Kinetics

Winter, G. (2003). Jacuzzi U.?: A battle of perks to lure students. *The New York Times*. October 5, 2003. Retrieved from www.nytimes.com/2003/10/05/us/jacuzzi-u-a-battle-of-perks-to-lure-students.html?pagewanted=all&src=pm.

Wittenauer, J. (1970). Professional preparation. In NIRSA, *Twenty-first annual conference proceedings*. Macomb, IL: Yeast.

CHAPTER

2

A Career in Campus Recreational Sports

Sarah E. Hardin

Centers LLC at DePaul University

Campus recreational sports is a unique field of work that incorporates many disciplines into its preparation and encompasses a wide variety of recreational offerings. Those who choose careers in this field come from a wide variety of backgrounds and preparation areas; the rallying point that unifies campus recreational sports administrators lies in their dedication to student growth and development. This chapter helps you explore career opportunities in the field and outlines the competencies, education, and certifications necessary for success, as well as the various disciplines influencing the body of knowledge that underpins the profession.

GROWTH OF THE PROFESSION

The **mission**, or primary goal, of most current campus recreational sports departments focuses on encouraging wellness and lifelong learning within the university community through a variety of recreational offerings. These comprehensive offerings typically include many recreational endeavors—for example, group exercise programs; individual fitness pursuits; aquatic activities; outdoor adventures; and intramural and sport club activities. The profession's emphases on lifelong activity and holistic wellness evolved from its foundations, which focused on **intramural sport** competition, in which organized sport and competitive activities were provided for those who did not participate in intercollegiate athletic teams.

Collegiate intramural and recreational sport pursuits have existed on American college and university campuses since the early 19th century. Related programming by university administrative staff was first offered in 1913, when the University of Michigan and Ohio State University both established departments of intramural athletics. According to Wilson (2008), other pivotal points in this evolutionary process include the appointments of Dr. Elmer Mitchell as the first director of intramurals at the University of Michigan in 1919 and of Anna Hiss as director of intramural sports for women at the University of Texas at Austin in 1920. Mitchell published the first book on intramurals, *Intramural Athletics*, in 1925, and the first facility "dedicated primarily to intramural sport activities" was built at the University of Michigan in 1928 (Wilson, p. 27). In 1957, Purdue University opened the Co-Rec, the "first university building in the United States created solely to serve students' recreational sports needs" (2012).

The profession's organizational origins lie in a meeting held at Dillard University in 1950, during which the National Intramural Association (NIA) was created by a gathering of 22 intramural administrators from 11 historically black colleges and universities (HBCUs). The organization grew steadily, and its membership soon expanded to include administrators from military installations, correctional institutions, and park and recreation programs. These administrators worked to expand recreation programming beyond activities focused on competition, thus creating more complete campus recreational sports program. Offerings included fitness and exercise programs, facilities for drop-in exercise, noncredit classes that taught lifetime activity skills, and outdoor trips (e.g., backpacking, kayaking, and climbing). In order to reflect this evolution from a focus on intramural sports to a more comprehensive offering of recreational opportunities, the organization changed its name in 1975 to the National Intramural-Recreational Sports Association (NIRSA).

CAMPUS RECREATIONAL SPORTS AS A CAREER

As the activity offerings grew and more campus facilities were dedicated specifically to recreational pursuits, institutions also needed more full-time administrators. As a result, what started as a group of physical educators, teachers, and coaches helping students plan sporting events eventually emerged as a profession in its own right—one that now includes a myriad of positions.

Scope of Employment

While the primary function of all campus recreational sports professionals is of course to provide recreation programs and services, the field now encompasses a diversity of positions, many of which require unique capabilities and skill sets. Career paths or areas of specialization include, but are not limited to, the following:

- **Aquatics** generally involves overseeing pool operations, maintenance, scheduling, risk management, and lifeguard training and scheduling. The aquatics administrator may be responsible for a number of pools—both indoor and outdoor—and for planning and administering programs in aquatic facilities.

- **Facility operations** work involves supervising daily operations of facilities that provide activity areas, classrooms, and support areas (e.g., offices, locker rooms, and service or storage spaces). Depending on the institution, such facilities may include multiple indoor and outdoor areas. Supervision usually includes, among other responsibilities, daily and annual maintenance of facilities and equipment, logistical operations, risk management planning, scheduling of space usage, staffing, and activity set-up.

- **Fitness and wellness** has grown so much in recent years that it may end up splitting into two sections, and the meaning of the term varies across campuses. Most campuses offer a formal group exercise program for students, as well as an informal or drop-in fitness or workout area for self-directed exercise. Other fitness services may include fitness testing, personal training, and nutrition planning or counseling. Wellness may encompass all of these endeavors and involve outreach or campus collaborations related to **holistic wellness**. Administration of such programs includes staffing, training, scheduling, and handling the logistical details of delivering the varied services.

- **Intramural sports** is a term derived from a combination of two Latin words: *intra*, meaning "within," and *muralis*, meaning "wall" (Mull, Bayless, Ross, & Jamieson, 1997, p. 84). Intramural sports, in turn, are competitive activities in which teams and individuals compete against others from within the same institution. Intramural sports administrators must create policies, develop appropriate rules for successful competitive events, train and evaluate sport officials, schedule the contests, and handle player conflicts.

- **Instructional programs** provide knowledge and skill instruction to participants. Activities vary widely—from martial arts to cooking classes to children's programming to dance. The administrator recruits and hires instructors with relevant expertise to teach specific classes within each topic area.

• **Marketing** responsibilities involve developing a set of communications for the department to use in its delivery of programs and services. These administrators take part in campus outreach, establish a marketing plan for the department, conduct research to obtain information for program planning, and supervise staff efforts to prepare and disseminate publicity materials.

• **Membership services** professionals develop membership policies, monitor information flow, administer program registration, and handle financial operations.

• **Programming for special populations** addresses the fact that many campuses have significant populations with particular needs—for example, students with disabilities, graduate students with families, international students, and students of nontraditional age. Such students may be involved in mainline programs, but some campuses also conduct activities tailored specifically to a certain group (e.g., sports unique to a certain country, adaptations of traditional activities to remove barriers for people with a disability or for those with certain time or family constraints).

• **Outdoor recreation** usually includes developing and administering trips and expeditions to wilderness areas, as well as providing instruction in outdoor endeavors such as camping, backpacking, cycling, rock climbing, and paddling. It may also involve overseeing experiential education, use of climbing walls or challenge courses, and outdoor equipment rental.

• **Sport clubs** are student groups organized around a common activity interest. Group interests range from more traditional sports (e.g., ice hockey, volleyball) to less common activities such as martial arts, break dancing, and skiing. Groups develop a constitution, govern themselves, and use the campus recreational sports department for guidance in decision making and risk management.

• **Student development** focuses on the intentional design of programs, services, and student staff positions to enhance learning and growth among student participants and student employees in campus recreational sports.

• **Youth programming and summer camp** administrators develop summer (and perhaps year-round) programming for children and families. This type of programming is also likely to include outreach to the general community. This area of work may interrelate with programming for special populations (e.g., to serve nontraditional-aged students with children).

Climbing walls are sometimes included in the responsibilities of an outdoor recreation administrator.

Though each of these areas involves unique preparation and expertise, they all require practitioners to apply management principles of planning, scheduling, communicating, budgeting, staffing, assessing risk, allocating resources, and implementing plans.

Job Titles and Responsibilities

Institutions often use their own unique titles to indicate specific levels of responsibility on their particular campus. **Organizational structure**—which establishes the reporting lines of the organization—also varies widely across the country. It is based on many factors: the structure of the institution itself; the institution's population (e.g., the total number of students; the mix of undergraduate, graduate, and professional students; and other characteristics such as student age and residency); and the placement of the campus recreational sports program, which may be located in student affairs, auxiliary services, athletics, or another administrative area. For example, though this is not always the case, an institution with a large undergraduate population is more likely than a smaller one to establish a large campus recreational sports department that includes many levels of staff and offers a myriad of programs and services.

As a result, when pursuing job opportunities in the field, you are well advised to explore the unique characteristics of each position and institution. Pay close attention to the **job description** and list of responsibilities. A position listed as coordinator at one school may be comparable to a director position at another school or assistant director at a third school. Some assistant director positions are considered to be **entry-level**—that is, jobs for someone with little experience—whereas others require several years of professional experience. One important distinction between even entry-level recreation positions in the collegiate setting and those in other areas of recreation is that almost all campus recreational sports positions require in-depth experience (e.g., a graduate assistantship) and a degree beyond the bachelor's degree. The following overview lists various job titles found in university recreation departments and outlines general duties and responsibilities commonly associated with various levels of responsibility. Remember, however, that the level of responsibility assigned to a title may vary between institutions.

- **Directors** provide organizational vision and direction, strategic leadership and planning, budget management, and positioning of the department on campus. The director reports to someone outside of the department at an upper administrative level.
- **Associate directors** frequently supervise other professional staff members, serve as a liaison between them and the director, guide their **direct reports** (i.e., staff supervised by the associate director) in implementing their programs and services, help with long-range planning, and assist the director in leading the organization. These are senior staff members. See figure 2.1 for a sample job description for an associate director position.
- **Assistant directors** usually oversee and are directly involved in implementing a specific program, facility, or service area. They may supervise other professional staff, and they supervise student staff involved in the delivery of a specific area. Depending on staff size and scope, this may be an entry-level position. See figure 2.2 for a sample job description for an assistant director position.
- **Coordinators** work in direct delivery of a program, facility, or service area and may supervise relevant student staff. This is usually an entry-level position.

PROFESSIONAL PREPARATION

Given that campus recreational sports requires competencies from several areas of study, how can a student develop this myriad of skills? There is no single method of preparation; rather, many career paths have been followed by successful campus recreational sports professionals. All of these routes involve acquiring educational credentials, engaging in professional development activities, and participating in experiential

JOB TITLE

Associate director of facilities

Reports To

Director of campus recreational sports

Position Summary

The associate director is a member of the department's senior leadership team. Responsibilities include overseeing all facility operations, leading department efforts in student learning and development, and supervising and mentoring full- and part-time staff.

Department Values

Campus recreational sports sets very high expectations. All staff are expected to be effective and efficient while maintaining balanced lives. The staff culture values excellence, continuous learning, respect, passion, teamwork, and integrity.

Responsibilities

Student Learning and Development

- Provide managerial and leadership experiences in facility management that supervises student employees. Create and promote professional development opportunities. Administer employee-related disciplinary action.
- Actively work to develop positive student development outcomes.

Facilities and Risk Management

- Coordinate space allocation, including internal and external reservations and rentals.
- Conduct contract negotiations with outside users of the facility.
- Develop and oversee policies and procedures related to facility use.
- Coordinate work with facility operations to ensure proper preventive maintenance and repair. Maintain records detailing work schedules. Initiate and supervise facility projects.
- Coordinate and oversee a department-wide risk management plan.
- Administer participant-related disciplinary action.

Supervision and Administrative Responsibilities

- Administer the informal sports program.
- Supervise the assistant director of facilities.
- Create, encourage, and support professional development opportunities for staff.
- Actively support and maintain an environment that inspires innovation and progress.
- Monitor operating budgets for facility-related expenditures.
- Manage biweekly payroll and maintain payroll records and reports.
- Assist with long-term planning budget planning.

Qualifications

- Master's degree (required)
- Five years of relevant full-time professional experience, preferably in campus recreational sports
- Demonstrated leadership skills and strong communication and organizational skills
- Crisis management and customer relations skills
- Ability to work independently and as part of a team

Figure 2.1 Example of associate director of facilities job description.

JOB TITLE

Assistant director of aquatics operations

Reports To

Associate director of facilities

Basic Function and Purpose

The assistant director of aquatics operations has functional responsibility for day-to-day operations of the natatorium and outdoor pools. This position involves significant staff, administrative, and programming responsibilities. The assistant director develops long-range plans, supervises ongoing aquatic programs and activities, and ensures that all appropriate water health and safety standards are maintained. This position requires a strong commitment to teamwork, customer service, and student development. Specific duties include but are not limited to the following:

Responsibilities

- Hire, train, schedule, supervise, and evaluate lifeguards, water safety instructors (WSIs), and swim meet staff.
- Develop and implement revenue-generating instructional programming (youth programs, swim and dive programs, masters swimming, and special events).
- Coordinate all facility rentals occurring in the natatorium and outdoor pool.
- Work cooperatively with other university groups.
- Coordinate operations during events (e.g., staffing, setup and teardown, technical and security issues).
- Coordinate purchasing, inventory, and maintenance of aquatic equipment.
- Develop and coordinate budget and policies and procedures for aquatic programming and rentals.
- Coordinate the group reservation calendar.
- Provide statistical data and other information for inclusion in monthly and annual reports.

Minimum Qualifications

- Master's degree with two (2) years of experience or bachelor's degree with five (5) years of experience.
- Experience in campus recreational sports or a related field, including one (1) year of supervising student personnel including swim instructors.
- Demonstrated experience and success in pool operations, aquatics programming, and facility management.
- Appropriate aquatic certifications, including water safety instructor (WSI), lifeguard instructor (LGI), lifeguarding and first aid, CPR/AED for professional rescuer or lifeguard, and American Red Cross CPR/AED instructor.
- Experience in administering swim lessons, a masters swim program, and swim meets.
- Excellent communication, organization, management, leadership, and professional skills.
- Proven commitment to student and staff development and customer service.
- Demonstrated ability to take initiative, solve problems, and meet deadlines.
- Working knowledge of Microsoft Office and Adobe products.

Preferred Qualifications

- Degree in recreation, physical education, sports administration, or a related field.
- Certification as a pool operator or aquatic facility operator, water safety instructor trainer (WSIT), and lifeguard instructor trainer (LGIT).

Figure 2.2 Example of assistant director of aquatics job description.

and on-the-job learning opportunities. Successful professionals strive to improve their current skills and gain new competencies throughout their careers. They are committed to promoting lifelong learning and development for those they serve—and for themselves.

Professional Body of Knowledge

Campus recreational sports is a multidisciplinary or **interdisciplinary** field. According to NIRSA (2008), "The complex nature of campus recreation and the influence of recreation and sport, student development, and business on the operations of programs greatly influence standard knowledge in the field" (p. 296). The body of knowledge required to be successful in the profession varies with one's chosen area of specialization. According to Dudenhoeffer (1990), a comprehensive study of competencies required for administrators in the field of campus recreational sports or intramural-recreational sports was completed by Young (1980) and listed the following basic elements: management, programming, governance, philosophical foundations, safety and accident prevention, sport psychology, physiology, business procedures, communication, legality, officiating, facilities and equipment, and research. Dudenhoeffer (1990) states that these skills relate to professionalism not in "that we learn specific skills alone but that we also learn the application of skill as ruled by the circumstances required" (p.12). In other words, basic skills are important, but a competent campus recreational sports administrator must also know how to apply those skills to the unique characteristics of a specific institution or population.

This sense of competency as more than a list of skills was echoed by Mull and colleagues (1997). They propose that, while "procedural knowledge—how to set up tournaments, run a club, design and operate a facility, schedule personnel, or publicize a program" (Mull, et al., 1997, p. 20)—is certainly important for a competent campus recreational sports administrator, the key to providing a high-quality campus recreational sports program is to use these skills to focus on **participant development**, so that participants grow as a result or outcome of their experience. Thus Mull and colleagues contend that campus recreational sports administrators must develop a basic understanding of the populations they serve in order to design programs and services that "encourage a positive sport experience, develop leadership, and contribute to the growth and development of an individual" (1997, p. 20). Administrators who subscribe to this line of reasoning seek knowledge in **student development theory**.

More recently, as higher education institutions have begun to focus on the **learning outcomes** of higher education and the specific experiences that occur within it, many campus recreational sports departments have studied the processes occurring in their environments in order to better understand how participants learn and grow through their campus recreational sports experiences. This growing focus demonstrates an expectation that administrators be able to design programs, facilities, and services in order to produce results or expected outcomes. In turn, this expectation leads to the integration of even more disciplines in the already crowded study of campus recreational sports competency—specifically, those of higher education and educational research. Table 2.1 shows the skills and competencies expected of campus recreational sports administrators and the corresponding academic programs in which they may be learned or attained.

If you are preparing for a career in campus recreational sports, simply pursuing one academic program will not enable you to fully develop the competencies required to be successful in the field. Furthermore, in addition to gaining certain hard skills and defined competencies, prospective campus recreational sports administrators must develop an understanding of various philosophical perspectives that influence program and service delivery.

Philosophical Foundations

The interdisciplinary field of campus recreational sports has been called a "crossroads of theory" (Franklin & Hardin, 2008, p. 4) and a "convergence of multiple theories" (p. 7). As a

Table 2.1 Competency and Corresponding Academic Preparation

Skill or competency	Degree program
Management; governance; leadership	Sport management Recreation administration or management Business administration Organizational leadership
Programming	Recreation administration or management
Philosophical foundations	Physical education or kinesiology Recreation administration or management Higher education Business administration
Safety and accident prevention; risk management	Sport management Recreation administration or management Physical education or kinesiology
Sport psychology	Psychology Physical education or kinesiology Sport management
Physiology; fitness and wellness	Health sciences or health and fitness management Nutrition Physical education or kinesiology
Business procedures	Business administration Sport management Recreation administration or management
Facilities; equipment	Physical education or kinesiology Sport management
Research; student learning; participant development	Educational research Higher education or student affairs Physical education or kinesiology

result, campus recreational sports professionals must examine the various fields that affect the profession. Practitioners who provide recreation and fitness facilities, programs, and services apply elements of theories from a variety of disciplines, including higher education and student development, administration and management, and recreation and leisure. Successful administrators explore multiple disciplines in order to understand the multiple aspects of their job and to help guide their approaches toward major responsibilities. For instance, in allocating resources, monitoring the department's budget, and developing staffing policies, the campus recreational sports administrator draws from management theory. However, since the department is part of an educational institution whose mission focuses on student growth and learning, the administrator must also have a working knowledge of student development theory to help him or her develop intentional learning environments with an understanding of students' approaches to both their work and leisure environments. In addition, those who work specifically with fitness and wellness must apply principles from kinesiology, those who program events draw from recreation and leisure theory, and those involved in challenge and adventure programming or outdoor pursuits draw from experiential education theory and practices.

The philosophical underpinnings of a field help guide practitioner behavior through systematically defined values, beliefs, and preferences (Edginton, et al., 2002). The next section touches on some of the philosophies and theories that should be explored by campus recreational sports professionals. However, a full understanding of the many theories affecting campus recreational sports requires one to directly explore literature from the fields themselves. Indeed, the opportunity to gain multidisciplinary understanding should be a consideration when choosing a graduate program; ideally, you will gain some theoretical knowledge in one area as an undergraduate student and seek knowledge of other disciplines in graduate school.

For an in-depth exploration of disciplines and theories affecting campus recreational sports, see the first chapter of *Campus Recreation: Essentials for the Professional* (Franklin & Hardin, 2008). The process of developing a professional philosophy of campus recreational sports delivery should involve study of leisure theory, play theory, student development theory, management theory, organizational theory, and human resources management. An excellent example of the need to apply several theories can be found in an administrator's supervision of student staff. When working with student employees, an administrator must identify elements of management theory and human resource theory that are relevant to the supervisory situation, as well as appropriate elements of student development theory.

The recent increase in university attention to learning outcomes makes it particularly important for administrators to understand theories of student change. As Pascarella and Terenzini (2005) discuss in *How College Affects Students*, their synthesis of the research exploring the impact of college on students, practitioners must have a grasp on developmental theories that take into account a student's current stage of development and how each stage can affect the student's perceptions of situations. Theories such as those proposed by Nevitt Sanford (1967), Erik Erikson (1968), Arthur Chickering (1969), and many others, while disagreeing upon details of developmental assimilation, "assume a general movement toward greater differentiation, integration, and complexity" in thoughts and behaviors of an individual (Pascarella and Terenzini, 2005, p. 19). More recent exploration by others, including Alexander Astin (1993), George Kuh (1995), and Ernest Pascarella (1985), explore the specific impact of the various aspects of college on a student's learning and development (Pascarella and Terenzini, 2005). The practitioner who gains insight and understanding of the potential effect that campus recreational sports may have on student growth, learning, and development will be likely to put into place intentional processes to foster that growth, learning, and development.

Management and organizational theories explore people's reaction to the work environment: "Understanding why people work within organizations and what motivates or inhibits optimal performance is critical for the recreation professional" (Franklin & Hardin, 2008, pp. 15 & 16). Leisure and play theory offer explanations of how individuals may approach recreational activities—their motivations, expectations, and ability to handle the environmental factors that surround the chosen activities. Research into participation in campus recreational sports can be found in the *Recreational Sports Journal*, published by NIRSA through Human Kinetics.

EDUCATIONAL CREDENTIALS

This section addresses potential educational endeavors for students interested in a career path in campus recreational sports.

Degree Programs

How should an aspiring campus recreational sports administrator choose a degree program? Your chosen area of specialization may affect your academic preparation, but you may also be able to combine any of a number of degree programs with your campus recreational sports experience to prepare adequately for a career in the field. Campus recreational sports is not usually chosen by first-year college students; indeed, many professionals in the field realized only late in their undergraduate career that they would like to pursue a career in campus recreational sports. As a result, those who have been successful in the field tend to have foundations in a variety of undergraduate academic programs, and many successful professionals hold a bachelor's degree in a major that might be considered unrelated to the field of campus recreational sports.

Majors may range, for example, from history to engineering to the more applicable disciplines of communication, business, and physical education. A few institutions offer what is called a "recreational sport management" degree at the undergraduate level, but a major specifically designed to prepare students for a campus recreational sports career is very uncommon, especially at the undergraduate level. However, major elements of academic preparation can be found at the undergraduate level in recreation administration, sport management, physical education, and kinesiology, business administration, and, more tangentially, communication, marketing, and human resource development.

Education at the master's level offers the previously mentioned programs, as well as preparation for higher education and student affairs. Table 2.1 shows competencies that might be found in the curricula within these programs. Students should choose programs that are most applicable to their chosen area of focus. Ideally, if a student has chosen an undergraduate degree that provides some major elements related to the field (e.g., physical education, kinesiology, recreation administration, or sport management), then a graduate program in another area (e.g., higher education) will round out his or her preparation for a career as a campus recreational sports administrator.

Specialty Certifications

In addition to attaining appropriate degrees, you should pursue certifications applicable to your chosen specialization within the field of campus recreational sports. Specialty certifications exist within many of the areas that make up a comprehensive campus recreational sports program, and you should be aware of the certifications for each area. Table 2.2 outlines the major certifications within each program or service area of campus recreational sports; three of the listed certifications—cardiopulmonary resuscitation (CPR), automated external defibrillator (AED), and first aid certification—are helpful, and often required, for many positions. The identified certifications are not always required for a position

Table 2.2 Relevant Certifications in Campus Recreational Sports

Area	Certification	Awarding organization*
All areas	First Aid/CPR/AED	ARC or AHA
Aquatics	Lifeguard instructor Water safety instructor Certified pool operator Aquatic facility operator	ARC or E&A NSPF NRPA
Experiential education	Challenge course facilitator	Many organizations. See ACCT, AEE for standards
Facilities	Certified facility manager Certified pool operator Certified aquatic facility operator	IFMA NSPF NRPA
Fitness and wellness	Group fitness instructor Personal trainer Health fitness specialist Strength and conditioning specialist	AFAA, ACE NSCA, ACSM, ACE ACSM NSCA
Intramural sports	Officiating	NFHS
Outdoor pursuits	Wilderness first responder or wilderness first aid	WMA

*ACCT = Association for Challenge Course Technology, ACE = American Council on Exercise, ACSM = American College of Sports Medicine, AED = automated external defibrillator, AEE = Association for Experiential Education, AFAA = Aerobics and Fitness Association of America, AHA = American Heart Association, ARC = American Red Cross, CPR = cardiopulmonary resuscitation, E&A = Ellis & Associates, IFMA = International Facility Management Association, NFHS = National Federation of State High School Associations, NRPA = National Recreation and Park Association, NSCA = National Strength and Conditioning Association, NSPF = National Swimming Pool Foundation, WMA = Wilderness Medical Associates.

in a given area, but they can help you secure a job in your chosen area by demonstrating your knowledge, experience, and commitment. As you explore individual job descriptions, you will see that each one will list the requirement status of each certification. Certification requirements will vary among institutions.

For some of the categories, several organizations are listed, and you should explore the various organizations and the certifications and training curricula offered by each one in order to determine what is most applicable for you. For instance, when looking at personal trainer certifications, you may find that one organization focuses on athletics, another on personal training in the corporate fitness setting, and yet another on educational settings.

OPPORTUNITIES TO ATTAIN PROFESSIONAL SKILLS

Many opportunities are offered for attaining professional skills in campus recreational sports. If you are an undergraduate, you might work within campus recreational sports or in park and recreation programs to gain basic skills—both the "hard" skills (e.g., creating, designing, and implementing programs; analyzing situations to minimize risk; completing basic budgeting in program planning) and the "soft" skills (e.g., facilitating groups, handling difficult and conflict situations, solving problems, and providing customer service). Graduate assistantship positions provide even more in-depth experiences in each of these areas, as well as in staff and facility supervision.

Opportunities also exist outside of paid roles—for example, volunteering to assist with local events such as nonprofit fundraisers, races, and park clean-ups. In addition, workshops and conferences provide arenas in which to gain new knowledge, network with current administrators, and gain information about their expectations of prospective employees and future staff members. NIRSA offers inexpensive introductory workshops called Lead On Conferences to introduce students to the field at several sites throughout the United States. The NIRSA Annual Conference and Recreational Sports Exposition provides another excellent way to gain information and meet current and future professionals. In particular, the preconference workshop on student professional development offers a day-long introduction to NIRSA and helps students prepare for entering the field through discussions of topics such as professional ethics and other current issues, as well as job search strategies. In addition, most U.S. states and several Canadian provinces hold a state or provincial workshop either every year or every other year, and the six regions of NIRSA in the United States and Canada often hold their own annual or biannual workshops. State, provincial, and regional workshops usually last 2 or 3 days and are affordable for students and young professionals.

Leadership development in the field is also available to professionals with a few years of full-time experience under their belts. NIRSA's National School of Recreational Sports Management provides a several-day seminar that is designed to explore leadership and management topics such as risk management, personnel development, budgeting, communication, and learning outcomes in a small-group setting. NIRSA also offers symposia specifically focused on content areas such as facilities, sport clubs, fitness, intramural sports, aquatics, and marketing. Professionals in the area of outdoor pursuits might attend the international conference of the Association of Outdoor Recreation and Education (AORE). NIRSA membership is not a requirement to attend these events, but it may make them more affordable.

Undergraduate Work Experiences

Few fields of study provide the inherent experiential learning opportunities in the workplace that campus recreational sports does. Delivering campus recreational sports facilities, programs, and services requires a large workforce, and that role is filled largely by students. Many of these students do not plan to pursue a career in campus recreational sports, but those who do are provided with a ready learning laboratory. Many current professionals began their careers at the undergraduate level by working as an intramural sport official, fitness instructor, weight-room supervisor, or entrance attendant. The experiences gained in such jobs not only provide an excellent foundation for a future in the field of campus recreational sports; it also allows students who pursue careers in other fields to develop useful skills and competencies in customer service, problem solving, decision making, personnel supervision, planning, organization, and coordination. Students who seek a career in business, administration, teaching, communication, marketing, and human relations may all find an excellent environment within campus recreational sports to develop and hone their skills.

Graduate Work Experiences

As early as the 1979 NIRSA Annual Conference, a large number of job postings required master's degrees in physical education or recreation for a candidate even to be considered for the position (Wells, 1980). This trend has continued, although the acceptable degree has broadened a bit. Most professional position listings in campus recreational sports now indicate that successful candidates will hold a master's degree in a related field; therefore, most campus recreational sports professionals have reached this advanced level of higher education. In addition, many director position listings indicate a preference, if not a requirement, for a doctorate. While some may find these standards pose an obstacle to pursuing a career in the field, few fields of study provide more of a built-in opportunity to develop skills while attaining a higher degree than that of campus recreational sports.

Indeed, many institutions offer positions known as graduate assistantships for students who are pursuing master's degrees. A **graduate assistantship** is a paraprofessional work experience in which the recompense includes a small annual stipend but is primarily paid through a scholarship to the institution or a waiver of graduate tuition. The responsibilities of graduate assistantships vary widely across university departments, but within the field of campus recreational sports they usually include duties that are somewhat advanced from those of undergraduates and typically require some supervision of undergraduate staff (see figure 2.3). Some positions are very specialized in that the graduate assistant works specifically in one administrative area (e.g., intramural or sport clubs, fitness, facilities), whereas others give graduate students broader experience across a wide range of administrative areas and responsibilities.

Both of these assistantship structures offer benefits, so when you explore graduate opportunities determine what is appropriate to your

JOB TITLE

Graduate assistant for intramural and club sports

Reports To

Assistant director of intramural and club sports

General Responsibilities

The graduate assistant's responsibilities include, but are not limited to, the following:

- Planning, developing, scheduling, and implementing a comprehensive intramural sport program consisting of all individual, dual, and team sport activities;
- Helping develop and conduct club sport officer training sessions;
- Recruiting, training, scheduling, and evaluating sport officials and supervisors;
- Updating club sport records;
- Processing student employee payroll; and
- Maintaining equipment inventory.

Figure 2.3 Example of graduate assistant for intramural and club sports job description.

needs. The more specialized position allows you to delve deeply into the skill set needed for a specific area of interest, thus helping you prepare for a career path in that particular area. A broader, more generalized assistantship that allows you to work in a variety of administrative areas gives you an overview of the field, thus helping you understand the differences between various areas and gain insight into where you might most successfully apply your individual strengths. This type of assistantship also prepares you to apply for positions in institutions in which the professionals work across a variety of administrative areas. As discussed in the first section of this chapter, the organizational structure of a campus recreational sports department can vary greatly from institution to institution. Some departments have small staffs of one to five professionals, while others move into the double digits, and still others (at institutions with large student populations) may include twenty-five or more individuals involved in delivering programs.

Here are some criteria to consider when exploring prospective graduate study options:

- Focus and mission of the department
- Scope of the assistantship
- Responsibilities of the assistantship
- **Networking** opportunities
- Size of the department
- Support system
- Geographic location

Focus and Mission of the Department

When exploring a position, the job seeker must take a look at the institution and the department (this is very easy to do online). Here are some questions to explore:

- What is the university's mission?
- What is the mission of the campus recreational sports department?
- How are these missions related?
- Is the campus recreational sports mission well aligned with that of the university?
- Can you even find the mission for the campus recreational sports department?

The mission statements indicate what is most important to the department and university. Is the focus on lifelong activity or leisure choices? Current or future fitness and wellness? Competition or sport? These are just a few of the many focuses that a mission might take in campus recreational sports. In addition, consider how well the mission ties in with your goals. This, of course, requires you to ask yourself, "What am I looking for in a department, and what focus is most important to me?" Your answer will give you an idea of whether the department's focus matches your philosophy and goals. You may also get an idea of the focus of the learning experience offered in a particular assistantship.

Scope of the Assistantship

Assistantship scope and responsibilities vary widely between universities. Some institutions define positions by program areas, whereas others give you responsibilities across areas. For instance, an assistantship might focus on fitness, intramurals, or facilities, or it might give you duties within each of these areas. Most assistantships carry a 2-year contract and include a tuition waiver with a monthly stipend, but you may come across other formats. Most entry-level professional positions in higher education require candidates to have completed a graduate assistantship prior to applying for the job.

Responsibilities of the Assistantship

Explore not only the focus of an assistantship but also the types of responsibilities included in it. Here are some responsibilities that help prepare you for professional positions and consequently make you more marketable: supervision of staff (including hiring, training, evaluation, and disciplinary functions) and scheduling of staff, facilities, and programs.

Networking Opportunities

Consider as well the opportunities for professional development and networking both within and outside of the institution. Most institutions encourage graduate assistants to attend workshops and conferences and provide them with time off (and perhaps even financial or travel assistance) to do so, but some do not; thus it is worth asking about before deciding to attend a specific institution. Institutions with a large number of graduate students may sponsor a club or organization of students who work together to raise funds to help them pay for conference attendance.

Size of the Department

Some of the previous considerations are influenced by this characteristic, but size is also a consideration in itself. Departments of all sizes have their positive factors. For example, a large department that serves a large student body can provide excellent experience in learning how to design programs or provide facilities for a large number of participants, whereas a smaller program can provide experiential opportunities in a broader range of program or service areas, thus making the candidate more marketable for a variety of positions.

Support System

Consider the supervision and mentoring that professional staff members provide to graduate assistants. This process may include financial support and encouragement to participate in professional development opportunities, but it also includes basic daily mentoring. Professional staff members who work with graduate assistants to solve problems and analyze approaches to various situations encountered on the job can be quite helpful as you prepare for a career in the field. Ask current and previous graduates of the program about their experiences in order to determine the type of support you can expect within a given program.

Geographic Location

This characteristic involves both professional and personal implications. Professional aspects include the effect of geographic location on programs and facilities. If, for example, your long-term goal is to work in a mountainous area, it may help you in your job search to have worked in a similar climate or place with similar

The University of Texas at San Antonio, Department of Campus Recreation.

Professional staff can offer valuable mentoring and support to graduate assistants.

facilities. More personal considerations might include distance from home and family or personal interest in gaining new experiences in a new location.

Undergraduate, Graduate, and Professional Internships

The responsibilities of an internship vary from institution to institution and may take different forms based on the individual's level of experience. Generally, however, internships involve duties and responsibilities similar to those of graduate assistantships. The differences lie in the duration and, frequently, the scope of the positions. Whereas an assistantship is usually contracted for a 2-year span, the internship may be for only 1 year or even for a semester or several months. The internship may therefore involve a more focused role—for instance, completing a specific project or special event. Internships are designed to be helpful to both student and employer. Some degree programs (e.g., recreation and sport management) require an internship, but many do not. If a student has not had the opportunity to work in a graduate assistant position, an internship may provide necessary job-related experience and training. Some prospective professionals who have already completed graduate school opt to gain additional skills or experience at a different type of institution through an internship. In addition, students who graduate at a time when there are few professional positions available may seek an internship as a way to use their job search period as a time for gaining additional experiences and skills.

LIFELONG LEARNING: PROFESSIONAL DEVELOPMENT OPPORTUNITIES

Campus recreational sports professionals can find many professional development opportunities sponsored through state, regional, and national organizations. Several organizations focus generally on recreation or higher education, whereas others focus more specifically on areas of specialization within campus recreational sports. In 2010, almost 4,000 campus recreational sports administrators were affiliated with NIRSA, and the next section outlines opportunities provided by that organization and its corresponding regions, states, and provinces. Subsequent sections present additional organizations through which students and professionals can seek other opportunities.

National Intramural-Recreational Sports Association (NIRSA)

Professionals who want to stay current in the field of campus recreational sports are well advised to join NIRSA. Founded in 1950 as the National Intramural Association, this organization has grown from its roots with 22 members from 11 historically black colleges and universities (HBCUs) to a group that serves more than 700 colleges and universities. NIRSA serves its membership through educational opportunities and workshops, development of field standards, publications, and advocacy. NIRSA members also seek to gain access to the large number of networking opportunities, through which they can gain information about best practices and use the expertise of colleagues to help them fulfill their roles on campus.

NIRSA is a leader in higher education and the advocate for the advancement of recreation, sport, and wellness by providing educational and developmental opportunities, generating and sharing knowledge, and promoting networking and growth for our members (NIRSA Know, February 2012). Its vision statement is as follows:

> *NIRSA is the premier association of leaders in higher education who transform lives and inspire the development of healthy communities world-wide (February, 2012 NIRSA Know).*

NIRSA has emerged as the premier organization for campus recreational sports professionals. In a study of 145 campus recreational sports directors by Ross and Schurger (2007), 99.3 percent of respondents indicated NIRSA as their primary professional affiliation.

Related Regional, State, and Provincial Organizations

Those involved in NIRSA have also organized within smaller geographic regions to provide more local opportunities and networking. Formal structures within NIRSA include six regions, around which regional, provincial, and state opportunities have been developed. Figure 2.4 shows the division of the United States and Canada into the six regions. Although these regions provide a loose structure for governance and the organization of some professional development opportunities, and though the regions are autonomous in some of their decision

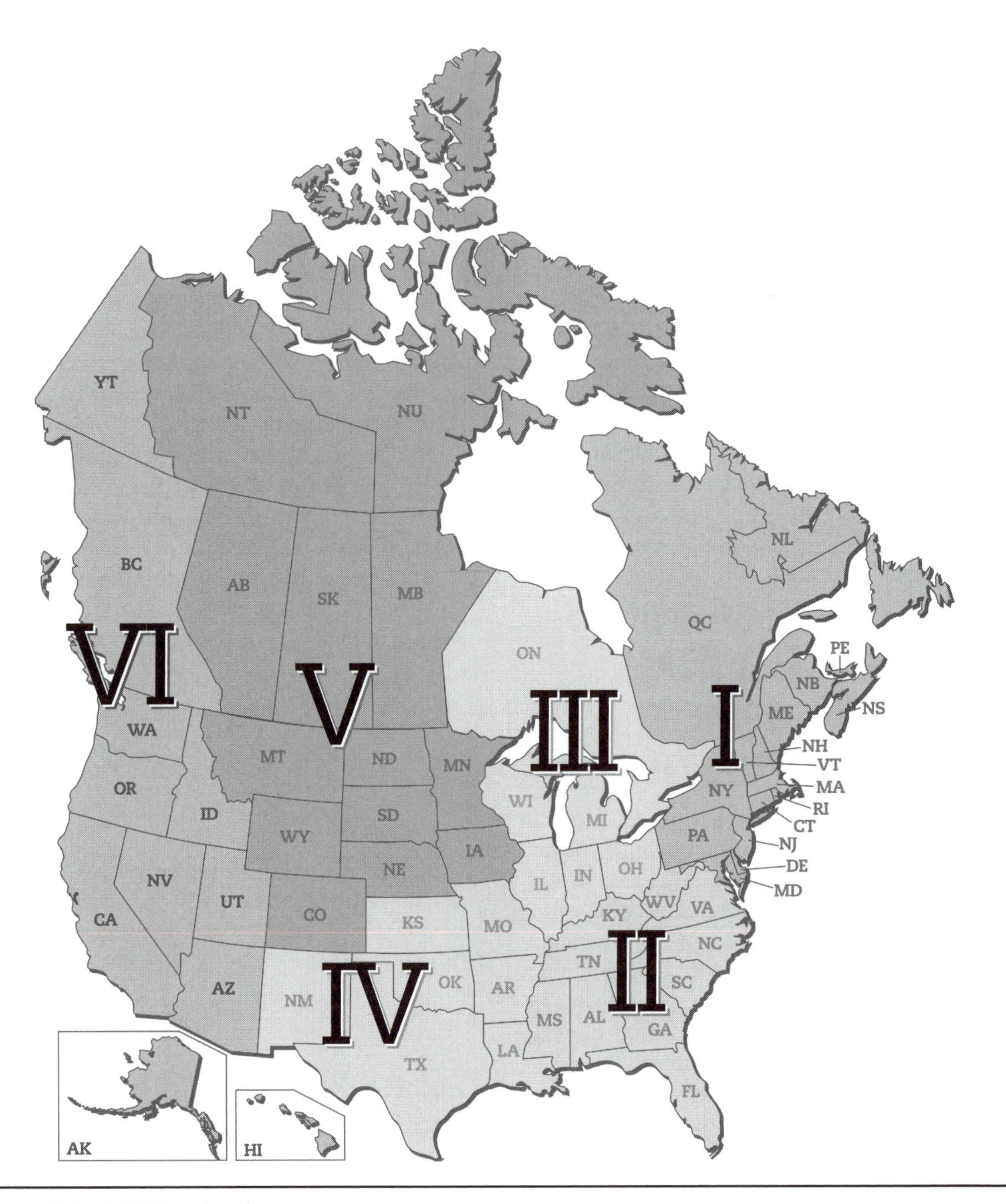

Figure 2.4 NIRSA regional map.

making, the regions look to the NIRSA organization for centralized guidance and resources. In addition, many states and provinces have developed their own state or provincial campus recreational sports associations. Most of these entities have names derived from that of the national NIRSA organization (e.g., the Michigan Intramural-Recreational Sports Association and the Indiana Recreational Sports Association) and are designed to function autonomously. Many of the professionals who belong to the state associations also belong to the national association, but membership in the state associations carries benefits of its own, including access to additional scholarship and professional development opportunities.

Workshops and Symposia

One key to ongoing professional development involves attending the variety of educational symposia provided through NIRSA. These include an annual NIRSA conference, several annual and biannual regional conferences, numerous state and provincial workshops, and leadership workshops designed specifically for students, such as the Lead On Conferences and the Emerging Recreational Sports Leaders Conference. In addition, specialty symposia are offered on a regular basis at which attendees can focus on a specific topic area, such as facilities management, sport clubs, intramural sports, marketing, and fitness. Advanced leadership and management competencies are explored through the annual National School of Recreational Sports Management, which provides an excellent small-group environment in which to consider current issues and trends in the field with experienced colleagues.

Additional Professional Organizations

Many practitioners belong to other organizations in addition to NIRSA. Membership in other organizations can help you keep abreast of trends in a more specialized area; for example, an assistant director of fitness might join the IDEA Health and Fitness Association. The following sections describe some organizations that may assist campus recreational sports professionals in fulfilling their responsibilities.

Recreation and Sport Organizations

The following recreation and sport organizations support professionals working in the management and leisure-related aspects of the field.

- North American Society for Sport Management (NASSM)—NASSM's purpose is "to promote, stimulate, and encourage study, research, scholarly writing, and professional development in the area of sport management"—both theoretical and applied aspects (2011). NASSM is actively involved in supporting and assisting professionals working in the fields of sport, leisure, and recreation.
- American Alliance for Health, Physical Education, Recreation and Dance (AAHPERD)—This organization's mission is "to promote and support leadership, research, education, and best practices in the professions that support creative, healthy, and active lifestyles. [Approved by the Alliance Assembly, April 2006]" (2011). A large number of AAHPERD's members focus on the pedagogy of physical education, but its diverse membership includes practitioners from a variety of fields.
- National Recreation and Park Association (NRPA)—"NRPA's mission is to advance parks, recreation, and environmental conservation efforts that enhance the quality of life for all people." Its purpose includes efforts to "educate professionals and the public on the essential nature of parks and recreation" as well as provide resources and advocate for the advancement of public parks and recreation (2012). In this capacity, it serves students and professionals in the recreation field with a focus on public parks and recreation organizations.

Higher Education Organizations

Both of the following organizations foster learning and development among university students through the support of student affairs professionals in institutions of higher learning. Each offers extensive opportunities for continued professional development and learning.

- NASPA (Student Affairs Administrators in Higher Education)—The mission of NASPA is "to be the principal source for leadership, scholarship, professional development, and advocacy for student affairs" (NASPA, 2012).
- American College Personnel Association (ACPA)—ACPA has recently added the tagline, *College Student Educators International,* to reflect its international focus. Its website describes the organization as "the leading comprehensive student affairs association that advances student affairs and engages students for a lifetime of learning and discovery." ACPA's mission is

to support and foster "college student learning through the generation and dissemination of knowledge, which informs policies, practices and programs for student affairs professionals and the higher education community" (2012).

Outdoor Recreation Organizations

For those interested in the specialty areas of outdoor adventure and challenge, the following organizations provide information and resources.

• Association of Outdoor Recreation and Education (AORE)—AORE's mission "is to provide opportunities for professionals and students in the field of outdoor recreation and education to exchange information, promote the preservation and conservation of the natural environment, and address issues common to college, university, community, military, and other not-for-profit outdoor recreation and education programs" (2011). The annual AORE conference allows for networking and information sharing with administrators and leaders in the field.

• Wilderness Education Association (WEA)—WEA's mission "is to promote the professionalism of outdoor leadership through establishment of national standards, curriculum design, implementation, advocacy, and research driven initiatives" (2011). The organization has developed national outdoor leadership standards, curriculum accreditation, and a database for professionals to be vetted and recognized as certified outdoor leaders.

• Association for Experiential Education (AEE)—AEE is "a nonprofit professional membership association dedicated to experiential education and the students, educators and practitioners who utilize its philosophy" (2011). AEE members include ropes course operators; school, college, and university staff and faculty; therapists; outdoor education practitioners; organizational development specialists; experience-based professionals working in nonprofit, private, and academic spaces; and members of many other areas of experiential education. AEE hosts an annual conference for members, as well as regional workshops throughout the year.

• National Outdoor Leadership School (NOLS)—This organization was founded in 1965 by Paul Petzoldt and was the first outdoor organization specifically focused on education and leadership development through outdoor recreation. "The mission of the National Outdoor Leadership School is to be the leading source and teacher of wilderness skills and leadership that serve people and the environment" (NOLS, 2012). It sponsors many expeditions and trips for the leisure participant as well as advanced skill-building trips for those interested in becoming trip or expedition leaders. NOLS also sponsors an annual wilderness risk management conference (2012).

Fitness, Wellness, and Exercise Science Organizations

The following organizations serve as resources and, in some cases, certifying bodies for professionals involved in the fitness and wellness specialization. This specialization can include various aspects of wellness; initiatives common to campus recreational sports include group exercise, mind–body classes, personal training, and wellness collaboration programs with other departments within an institution.

• American Council on Exercise (ACE)—The mission of this organization is to promote active, healthy lifestyles and their positive effects on the mind, body, and spirit. ACE's goal is to enable all segments of society to enjoy the benefits of physical activity and protect the public against unsafe and ineffective fitness products and instruction. The organization provides professional resources for the administrator as well as certifications including personal training, group exercise instruction, and health and fitness specialists (2011).

• Aerobics and Fitness Association of America (AFAA)—AFAA's mission is to deliver "comprehensive cognitive and practical education for fitness professionals, grounded in industry research, using both traditional and innovative modalities" (2012). This organization is primarily a certifying agency that provides study materials, courses, and certification exams for prospective personal trainers and group fitness instructors in general and specialty areas (2012).

• American College of Sports Medicine (ACSM)—This organization "promotes and integrates scientific research, education, and practical applications of sports medicine and exercise science to maintain and enhance physical performance, fitness, health, and quality of life" (2011). Its certifications include group exercise instructors, personal trainers, and clinical exercise specialists.

• IDEA Health and Fitness Association—Billing itself as the world's largest organization for fitness and wellness professionals, IDEA provides research, educational resources, certifications, and professional development opportunities. "IDEA and its members are passionately committed to improving the health and fitness of all people. We are focused on delivering compelling member value by imparting knowledge, credibility, inspiration, marketability and personal and professional growth opportunities" (2012).

PRINCIPLES OF THE PROFESSION

The profession of campus recreational sports was founded on principles that remain at its core today: professional development of practitioners, nurturing of student learning and development, and dedication to promoting lifelong learning and healthy lifestyles for students and other members of the university community. Successful prospective professionals demonstrate a commitment to and understanding of these core principles.

Dedication to Professional Development

Professional development is a core component of the field of campus recreational sports. Although the skills and competencies for program delivery bear many similarities to its sister field of parks and recreation, the fact that campus recreational sports practitioners are located in higher education institutions means that growth and development lie at the heart of their mission. This is true for practitioners and for those they serve. This mission is exemplified by the involvement of most professionals in professional organizations and the number of learning opportunities offered by these organizations. It is evident in any meeting of professionals across the country as they engage in learning and sharing through networking with each other. Anyone who wishes to be successful in the field must therefore be willing to share and borrow information, because doing so forms a key foundation of the field of campus recreational sports.

Commitment to Student Learning and Development

Another key aspect of campus recreational sports administration is a dedication to preparing students for their future, whether it lies within the field of campus recreational sports or elsewhere. Students who are involved in campus recreational sports programs grow and develop as a result of their involvement. In addition, campus recreational sports administrators work with students in delivering programs and services in order to prepare students for future success as professionals in the field. Encouraging, teaching, and providing intentional learning experiences for students encompasses every aspect of the responsibilities of a campus recreational sports professional. This historic effort to use recreation programs, facilities, and services to provide learning opportunities has been exemplified recently as practitioners have engaged in increased efforts to develop measurable learning outcomes for students who are staff members or participants in campus recreational sports organizations.

Promotion of Lifelong Learning and Healthy Lifestyles

The founders of NIRSA in the 1950s believed in helping students gain sports skills for lifelong fun and fitness. This original premise has been expanded within the more comprehensive campus recreational sports programs of today to include more offerings, such as programs specifically designed to promote health and wellness, and services and facilities that provide the opportunity to pursue growth and development in many areas. Campus recreational sports professionals also maximize these opportunities by collaborating with other departments on campus.

SUMMARY

Those who explore a career in campus recreational sports should seek out the various paths that are open to them. Because of the interdisciplinary nature of the profession, they will find valuable information and resources in many different courses of study, as well as through a variety of professional organizations and experiential learning opportunities. However, there are some basic skills and knowledge that can be gained only through experience in the field itself as undergraduate student employees or graduate assistants. It is vital for practitioners to be involved in professional development and networking with colleagues both within and outside of their home institutions in order to gain valuable insights into the field's various specialization areas and the fact that delivery systems of comprehensive campus recreational sports programs vary greatly between campuses.

It is imperative for anyone interested in a career in campus recreational sports to be motivated by a sense of purpose in enhancing and improving the health and wellness of the university community, to take a personal interest in continued professional development, and to be committed to student learning and development. These foundations define campus recreational sports and ensure congruence with the overall mission of the institution within which the department operates.

Glossary

direct reports—Staff positions which are supervised by a particular position; those staff members who answer directly to the person in that position.

entry-level job—Position requiring little or no full-time experience.

graduate assistantship—Paraprofessional campus work experience that accompanies pursuit of a graduate degree (in campus recreational sports, usually includes lower-level administrative responsibilities).

holistic wellness—Wellness approach addressing seven dimensions: social, emotional, spiritual, environmental, occupational, intellectual, and physical.

interdisciplinary—Involving interaction between various knowledge areas or academic disciplines.

intramural sport—Activity in which teams or individuals compete with others from within the same institution.

job description—List of responsibilities and expectations for a position; may include information about the hiring institution and department.

learning outcome—Measurable result of involvement in an activity or other experience.

mission—Overall purpose or primary objective of an organization.

networking—Interaction with colleagues intended to develop professional relationships.

organizational structure—Reporting lines of an organization that identify supervision responsibilities for personnel, programs, and services.

participant development—An individual's physical, mental, emotional, or civic growth due to involvement in specific experiences.

student development theories—Models explaining college student growth and change or readiness for change.

References

Aerobics and Fitness Association of America (AFAA). (2012). About AFAA. www.afaa.com/about_afaa.htm.

American Alliance for Health, Physical Education, Recreation and Dance (AAHPERD). (2011). Mission. www.aahperd.org/about/mission.cfm.

American College Personnel Association (ACPA). (2012). About ACPA. www2.myacpa.org/about-acpa/mission.

American College of Sports Medicine (ACSM). (2011). Who we are. www.acsm.org/about-acsm/who-we-are.

American Council on Exercise (ACE). (2011). About us. www.acefitness.org/aboutace/default.aspx.

Association for Experiential Education (AEE). (2011). About us. www.aee.org/about/.

Association of Outdoor Recreation and Education (AORE). (2011). Mission. www.aore.org/about-aore/default.aspx.

Astin, A. (1993). *What matters in college? Four critical years revisited.* San Francisco: Jossey-Bass.

Chickering, A. (1969). *Education and identity.* San Francisco: Jossey-Bass.

Dudenhoeffer, F. (1990). Genesis and evolution of the recreational sports profession. *NIRSA Journal, 14*(3), 12–13, 56.

Edginton, C., Jordan, D., DeGraaf, D., & Edginton, S. (2002). *Leisure and life satisfaction: Foundational perspectives.* Dubuque, IA: McGraw-Hill.

Erikson, E. (1968). *Identity: Youth and crisis.* New York: W.W. Norton.

Franklin, D., & Hardin, S.E. (2008). Philosophical and theoretical foundations of campus recreation: Crossroads of theory. In NIRSA, *Campus recreation: Essentials for the professional.* Champaign, IL: Human Kinetics, pp. 3-20.

IDEA Health & Fitness Association. (2012). About IDEA. www.ideafit.com/about.

Kuh, G. (1995). The other curriculum: Out-of-class experiences associated with student learning and personal development. *Journal of Higher Education*, 66, 123-155.

Mitchell, E. (1925). *Intramural athletics.* New York: Barnes.

Mull, R.F., Bayless, K.G., Ross, C.M., & Jamieson, L.M. (1997). *Recreational sport management* (3rd ed.). Champaign, IL: Human Kinetics.

National Intramural-Recreational Sports Association (NIRSA). (2008). *Campus recreation:Essentials for the professional.* Champaign, IL: Human Kinetics.

National Intramural-Recreational Sports Association (NIRSA). (2012). Mission statement. www.nirsa.org/Content/NavigationMenu/AboutUs/MissionVision/Mission_Vision.htm.

National Outdoor Leadership School (NOLS). (2011). About us. www.nols.edu/about/.

National Recreation and Park Association (NRPA). (2011). About NRPA. www.nrpa.org/About-NRPA/.

NIRSA. (2012). NIRSA Know. http://nirsa.informz.net/nirsa/archives/archive_2113572.html.

North American Society for Sport Management (NASSM). (2011). Purpose. www.nassm.com/InfoAbout/NASSM/Purpose.

Ross, C.M., & Schurger, T. (2007). Career paths of campus recreational sport directors. *Recreational Sports Journal, 31*, 146–155.

Pascarella, E. (1985). College environmental influences on learning and cognitive development: A critical review and synthesis. In J. Smart (Ed.), *Higher education: Handbook of theory and research* (Vol 1, pp. 1-64). New York: Agathon.

Pascarella, E.T., & Terenzini, P.T. (2005). *How college affects students: Volume 2. A third decade of research.* San Francisco: Jossey-Bass.

Purdue University Recreational Sports. (2012). History. www.purdue.edu/recsports/about_us/history/index.php.

Sanford, N. (1967). *Where colleges fail: A study of the student as a person.* San Francisco: Jossey-Bass.

Student Affairs Administrators in Higher Education (NASPA). (2012). About us. www.naspa.org/about/default.cfm.

Wells, J. (1980). Who are we? Current composition trends in the profession of intramural-recreational sports administrators. *NIRSA Journal*, 4(3), 44-45.

Wilderness Education Association (WEA). (2011). Mission and vision. www.weainfo.org/en/cms/188/.

Wilson, P. (2008). The history and evolution of campus recreation. In NIRSA, *Campus recreation: Essentials for the professional.* Champaign, IL: Human Kinetics, pp. 21-31.

Young, L. (1980). Competency areas in recreational sports. *Intramural-recreational sports: New directions and ideas.* Corvallis, OR: The National-Intramural Sports Association, pp. 65-93.

CHAPTER

3

Relationships in Campus Recreational Sports

Professional, Institutional, and Community

Douglas Franklin
Ohio University

A campus recreational sports director was guest-lecturing in a class of recreation management students when he was asked to identify the best and worst parts of his job. Without hesitation he said, "Working with people." That simple answer sums up the importance and complexity of establishing good relationships.

This chapter broadly defines areas of collaboration; clarifies what is necessary to establish effective cooperative partnership environments; and identifies offices, organizations, and associations where collaboration is most common and necessary for departmental and professional success. The chapter also explores interpersonal relationship building—including workplace relationships and group work—in terms of a 360-degree model with the campus recreational sports professional at the center. In addition, the discussion addresses reciprocity, organizational culture, and the process of seeking and building mutually beneficial relationships. To clarify how campus recreational sports professionals work within their organizations and with other departments in the university setting, the chapter also considers both intra- and interdepartmental relationships, as well as community and professional relationships.

INTERPERSONAL RELATIONSHIPS

Interpersonal relationships involve interactions and associations between people, and they are critically important in personal growth and development. They can also be either a boon or a detriment to the organization, and establishing good interpersonal relationships is foundational to successful campus recreational sports programs. Indeed, interpersonal relationships hold the power to define the recreational professional, the recreational program within an institution, and the profession itself.

Campus recreational sports professionals often enter the field because they have enjoyed the relationships they built during their own college experiences and feel a desire to help create that experience for others. So what makes a good interpersonal relationship, and how does one develop good relationship skills?

The basis for establishing good interpersonal relationships—the collaborative action of two or more independent partners who desire to develop a mutually beneficial relationship—resides in the strength and competence of the partners. Stephen Covey (1989) suggests that a person must establish independence before entering into an interdependent relationship, and he posits that such independence is gained by achieving a "private victory" (p. 63). This is done by establishing a proactive approach to life by creating and prioritizing goals, and developing effective time management skills. Competence underlies the concept of independence and is established when a person develops the knowledge, skills, and attitudes that produce capacity. For example, a positive attitude and a plan to develop an intramural sports tournament will get the professional only so far if he or she lacks knowledge of how to build a double elimination bracket and the skills to execute the tournament. With that said, it is also true that attitude, goal setting, and time management count heavily in the success of any program.

Covey (1989) also provides principles for establishing effective interpersonal—and interdependent—relationships. A relationship can be as simple as two people agreeing to go to dinner and as complex as the formation of teams, groups, and organizations. An interdependent relationship involves two or more people who are interconnected, hold common goals, and rely on each other to achieve success. Here the victory is public (Covey). Successful interdependent relationships involve creating mutually beneficial (i.e., "win-win") outcomes, establishing empathetic communication between partners, and making good use of synergy.

As interpersonal relationships become more complex, success also depends on additional elements such as shared values and philosophies. Strong marriages, for example, are created and maintained by establishing high standards manifested in the marriage vows taken at the beginning and in many cases restated at various moments along the way. Indeed, sharing the mutually beneficial values of loyalty, fidelity, and respect provides the foundation for good marriages and good relationships in general. In this type of relationship, each partner is responsible for maintaining dignity, exhibiting composure under pressure, acting selflessly, and focusing on the other person, or on the group, in order to create a mutually beneficial environment. Partners develop a sense that "we're in this together for the long run" by focusing on the big picture rather than on small incidents, thus eliminating mean-spiritedness, pettiness, and vulgarity and instead creating room for a healthy environment conducive to thoughtfulness, forgiveness, and decency. In this kind of environment, partners can transform insignificant and routine situations into enjoyable, stimulating, and memorable experiences. Doing so creates cultural waypoints by which people in a relationship can measure the cohesiveness of the association.

Workplace Relationships

In good working relationships—and, more generally, in effective organizations—participants agree to uphold established standards of behavior and shared values and to work toward creating an environment of honesty and trust. Productive working environments are also characterized by a goal-oriented, long-term, and big-picture perspective rather than a short-term, "get rich quick" approach, and these operational principles are useful as well in team and group work. A group is solidified when members relate to each other through shared values, standards, guidelines, plans, and mutually beneficial goals or desired results. This picture becomes more complex, of course, when we also consider the potential effects of participants' positions, degrees of power, roles, and functions.

Campus recreational sports professionals must also cultivate and demonstrate tolerance and acceptance of differences between individuals and develop the capacity to participate in mature and intimate relationships. Practicing tolerance helps professionals gain a clearer understanding of customs, values, stereotyping, and discrimination. Acceptance is facilitated when we are able to listen, understand, and empathize with others without needing to control or dominate. Healthy relationships are characterized by openness, trust, and reciprocity.

Figure 3.1 presents relationships likely to be experienced by the campus recreational sports professional and explains responsibilities and communication within the relationships. The center of the figure shows a circle cut into four segments depicting the keys to success for a campus recreational sports professional: knowledge, skills, attitudes, and actions. Professionals gain knowledge from a variety of sources, including academic preparation, student work experiences, worksite training, and other professional development opportunities. Skills involve applying one's knowledge, and they are often developed through many of the same sources; they are improved through experience. Attitudes are feelings, thoughts, and ways of viewing one's work. They are often described as an individual's positive or negative views of something. Finally, actions are manifested attitudes; they are what the professional does to demonstrate his or her thoughts and views. Thus a professional's knowledge, skills, attitudes, and actions are controllable, and they form the basis of professional competence.

The segmented circle in the figure is surrounded by rectangles representing potential relationships. Each professional has at least one supervisor, one subordinate, and one peer either in or outside of the organization. Most campus recreational sports programs use this traditional model with student employees in the lowest subordinate role. This is not to say that student employees are not a priority—merely that they are located on the lowest level of the **scalar chain** (chain of command).

A direct supervisor holds responsibility and administrative oversight for the professional. In small organizations, this role might be filled by the director; in large operations, there may be two or three levels of supervision. The

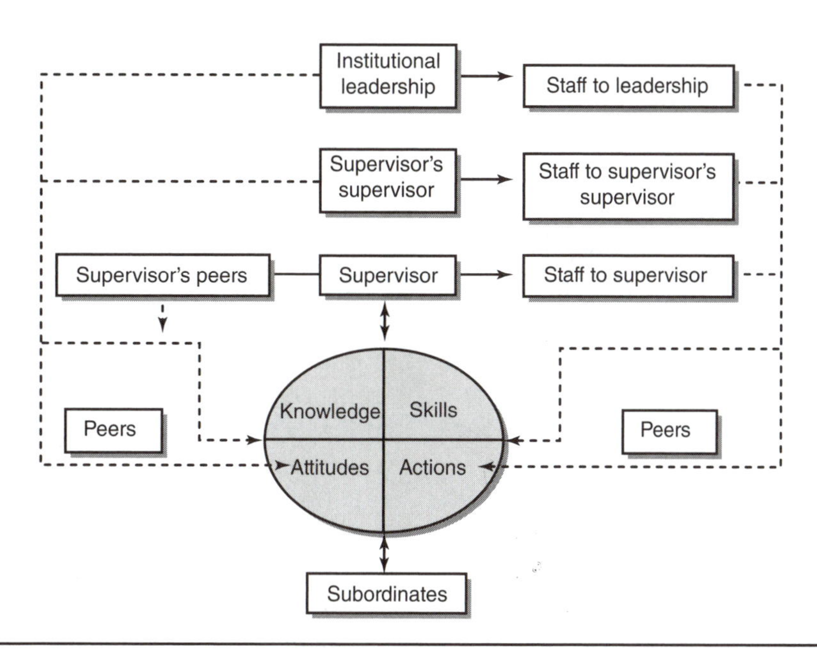

Figure 3.1 Particular knowledge, skills, attitudes, and actions are keys to success for the campus recreational sports professional.

professional's subordinates are those employees, including students, for whom he or she has direct responsibility and administrative oversight.

Peer relationships involve interactions between professionals at the same rank, or level, within or outside of the organization. Internal peer levels in large organizations may include multiple assistant or coordinator positions. Peers exist throughout the institution in the form of other professionals at similar pay grades and levels of authority. In theory, at least, peers are equal and hold the same level of organizational responsibility. Peer relationships are indirect and lack a dynamic of authority.

As relationships move further from the center of the circle, communication becomes more critical. Information flow becomes more complex and inconsistent and the chance for ambiguity increases. For example, institutional leadership may be considering developing a new research complex or parking garage on the intramural fields. If the campus recreational sports professional is not involved in the project planning or communication flow, the lack of information creates the potential for rumors and speculation to increase. The relationship between the supervisor's supervisor and the professional requires clear communication and some inclusion of the direct supervisor in order to avoid perceptions of favoritism or circumvention of the system. The same situation comes into play with the professional and his or her subordinates' subordinates.

Institutional leadership and upper management vary by institution. Some institutional leaders use a hands-on approach, while others operate through subordinates and staff members. It is essential for the campus recreational sports professional to know and understand how upper-level management works and communicates in order to contribute to organizational effectiveness.

An organizational structure includes two position types: line and staff. A **line position** holds direct responsibility within the organizational chain, whereas a **staff position** provides support to line personnel or other support functions within the institution. The solid lines in figure 3.1 represent line authority within the scalar chain. Note the solid line between institutional leadership and supervisors and their support staff. The dotted lines, on the other hand, represent communication between institutional leadership and their staff members and the campus recreational sports professional. Often, institutional leadership and middle management communicate through staff, and it is important for the campus recreational sports professional to know where he or she stands within the chain and to recognize and acknowledge this type of communication. The two-headed arrows indicate communication between supervisors and subordinates; effective interdepartmental communication goes both ways.

Working With Students: Young People in Transition

Transition is a three-phase, internalized psychological process that individuals go through when dealing with change (Bridges, 2003). Transition theory suggests that transition begins when something ends, stops when something starts, and is ambiguous in between (Bridges). Traditional-age college students (i.e., 18-24 years old) make up 41.3 percent of all undergraduates (National Center for Education Statistics, 2011), and these students are typically experiencing a variety of transitions. The most obvious one is the move from childhood to adulthood. This transition may occur when students move away from home, often for the first time, to attend college. In some cases, living in a residence hall may be a student's first experience of living with someone or sharing a bathroom. Another transition may take the form of having to work or play in an unscheduled and unsupervised manner for the first time. For example, intramural and sport club teams rarely have a coach to organize practices or manage games, and athletic directors are unavailable to schedule contests and ensure travel arrangements. Another transition occurs when a student begins to work, either on or off campus, and undergoes peer supervision and evaluation.

Helping students navigate these transitions is one of the central purposes of campus recreational sports professionals. They can help students move through the ambiguous phase, also known as the "neutral zone" by providing clearly defined expectations and creating challenging and rewarding opportunities. Professionals can find opportunities to support students' transitions—and help them learn and develop—during students' participation and employment in campus recreational sports. Participation in such programs is one of the most common experiences for college students; indeed, national research suggests that 75 percent of students use or participate in campus recreational sports programs, services, or facilities (National Intramural-Recreational Sports Association, 2003). Interaction with students often occurs during captains' meetings, organizational sessions, games and other activities, and disciplinary actions. The effect of the interaction may be limited by the duration and intensity of the contact.

Relationships between the professional and student employees present a much greater opportunity to exert a positive influence. Students often work as office, facility, or program assistants; officials; instructors; supervisors; and managers. The professional's relationships with these students are typically established over a considerable period of time, which means that they can have a greater effect on the students. In these environments, students often gain new knowledge, skills, and attitudes that help them make the transition from childhood to adulthood and from unemployed student to working adult citizen.

A unique dynamic often occurs when a professional works with students. The majority of professionals working in the field of campus recreational sports have less than 5 years of experience, which means that many of them are only a few years removed from the traditional student. This proximity creates both opportunities and risks. Opportunities include enhanced peer-type relationships, leading and modeling of positive behaviors, and mentoring for professionalism. Risks include crossing the student–professional social boundary and fracturing the student–professional relationship through immature behaviors; as a result, campus recreational sports professionals and

Photo courtesy of the University of Cincinnati.

Participating in campus recreational sports programs helps students navigate the many transitions they face in their years on campus.

graduate assistants must remember that they are no longer students and that they are held to a different standard of behavior.

Organizational Structure, Scalar Chain, and Power

Power exists when a person possesses or exercises authority or influence. It is "the potential to influence others for good or evil, to be a blessing or a scourge" (Lee, 1997, p. 7). **Positional or legitimate power** is used to maintain order and control within the institution. It is wielded by those in institutional leadership, senior management, and supervisory roles by virtue of their position within the organization. Other sources of influence are not restricted by position. **Expert or referent power**, for example, derives from knowledge, skills, and expertise; **instrumental power** is based on a positive attitude that results in getting things done; and **relation power** is created by interpersonal competence and the ability to maintain positive relationships (Lee, 1997). These types of power are particularly important for the campus recreational sports professional. The diverse knowledge and skills that form professional competence allow the professional to work with people serving in a wide variety of functions on campus. As the professional engages with others on campus, he or she gains respect and influence.

A campus recreational sports professional should be able to know and follow the chain of command from his or her position to the institution's head. The parameters of the relationship between supervisor and subordinate are established by the supervisor or the organizational director. It is critical for the professional to understand what operational parameters exist and how these boundaries often differ across institutions and organizations. Some directors are empowering and permit a great deal of latitude in operating and creating, whereas others are much more directive and limiting. Expectations between supervisor and subordinate should be established early in the relationship in order to avoid operational ineffectiveness. Supervisor–subordinate relationships are direct and always (even if it is left unstated) involve a power differential.

Group Work: Teams, Task Forces, and Committees

The concept of group work is not foreign to the recreational professional; in fact, many recreational professionals have experience in teamwork as a player, coach, or administrator. Teams come together to achieve a specific goal. To pursue that goal, they often divide into specialized positions, identify leaders, and develop mechanisms to effectively use their members' expertise. Teams in higher education attempt to capture the essence, if not the inherent competition, associated with sport teams, and they often involve specialized participants who represent various campus constituencies. Recreational professionals often participate on teams in student affairs because of their expertise and influence in student engagement or cocurricular learning and on teams in intercollegiate athletics because of their expertise in facility and program management. Team leadership is established by the team convener, who often holds a leadership position within the institution.

Recreational professionals may be less familiar with task forces unless they have served in the military, particularly in the Navy. A task force conjures up a vision of a flotilla of ships, grouped together by complementary functions in order to achieve a defined mission. As with teams, task forces are characterized by a mission, a set of members, and a leader or group of leaders selected by the tasking authority and based on the use of specialized skills. Both teams and task forces tend to be short-term entities driven by a specific goal or objective.

In contrast, a committee, though similar to a team or task force in some ways, is often created to work on a particular topic, activity, or issue for a longer period of time. Many committees hold "standing" (i.e., relatively fixed) status within the institution or play a role in institutional governance. Standing committees, such as the institution's intercollegiate athletic committee, may hold permanent standing yet consist of a fluid membership. Governance committees, such as an administrative senate or forum, may play a representative role in institutional leadership. Committees are so prevalent in some institutions that a "committee on committees" may be established to control the proliferation of these groups.

It is essential for the campus recreational sports professional to understand the role, scope, function, and tasking authority of any group in which he or she participates. Some groups are action based while others are established to advise or make recommendations to the convening authority. The professional can eliminate confusion and help the group achieve its goal by establishing its working parameters during the first session and then periodically reiterating them. The tasking authority decides how much power and autonomy the group can wield.

Reciprocity and Organizational Culture

In the film *A Beautiful Mind* (Howard, 2001), the character John Forbes Nash is a mathematician and winner of the Nobel Prize in Economic Sciences who provides a theory that is relevant to creating good group relationships. In challenging Adam Smith's economic philosophy that "in competition individual ambition serves the common good," Nash suggests that in fact "the best result comes from everyone in the group doing what is best for himself and for the group." By extension, relationships between people or departments need to be based on mutual benefit or reciprocity, and this is particularly important during difficult economic times.

Good relationships are built on fairness, trust, and mutually beneficial association. Part of the process involves knowing what each colleague or partner brings to the table. For example, a campus recreational sports professional may have access to or directly manage the student recreation center, whereas an intercollegiate athletic program manages some high-quality field space. If they share their facilities, both organizations benefit materially while also creating an environment that is conducive to a collaborative relationship. This type of relationship is especially important at institutions whose resources are limited. The partnership between campus recreational sports and intercollegiate athletics is advanced because each organization has something of equal value to bring to the table. This is called *reciprocity*—the process of mutual dependence—and it becomes more and more important to establish such mutually beneficial, or interdependent, relationships as budgets in higher education continue to tighten. More generally, any time a campus recreational sports professional enters into a relationship, his or her thought process should address personal and organizational expectations and how the collaboration will lead to success.

Resolving Workplace Relationship Issues

What happens when workplace relationships go wrong? The professional can mitigate potential negative effects by identifying the causes of potential problems before they occur and developing proactive solutions. When problems do occur—whether organizational or operational—they can be caused by systemic, structural, personal, or communication actions and attitudes.

Systemic issues are caused by processes or systems that unintentionally affect operations. For example, suppose the administrator of the student recreation center responds to a budget cut by closing the facility during low-use times. The direct effect on students is minimal, and the costs savings permit the department to address the drop in financial support. Imagine, however, that the admissions office, unaware that the center is closed, attempts to bring a recruitment tour through the building. Some of these students may decide not to attend the institution because they fear that the facility is often closed or because they did not have an opportunity to compare facilities with another institution of interest. The unintended consequence would be the loss of students. Many systemic issues involve and are controlled by policy and process, and organizations commonly establish policies and procedures to address such trouble before it begins—for example, limiting or precluding fraternization, nepotism, conflicts of interest, misuse or misappropriation of funds or resources, and other problems related to fraud, waste, and abuse.

Structural issues involve the definition of roles within the organization and tend to arise when job role, responsibilities, and reporting lines are left unclear. One example would be a job description that omits certain elements, thus creating ambiguity, overlapping areas of responsibility or gaps between two jobs, or a position that reports to two supervisors.

Personal issues appear when individuals within the organization do not live up to expectations of group congruity and conformity to organizational values. Personal issues associated with distrust and inequality include generating and spreading rumors or gossip, isolating or dividing employees, and withholding information or providing misleading information. Abusive behavior also undercuts positive interpersonal relationships—for example, bullying and harassment, as well as unethical and inappropriate use of technology, including the harmful use of social networking sites. Supervisory personal issues include favoritism and inequitable treatment of employees, violations of confidentiality, failure to resolve conflicts or address chronic personnel-related issues, abuse or misuse of power, micromanagement, and creation of an environment that inhibits employees' ability to interpret organizational rules. Whatever the specifics, personal issues can create a toxic environment that lowers employee morale and organizational ineffectiveness.

Communication issues result from both verbal and nonverbal actions that create ambiguity and inhibit and degrade relationships. Examples include failing to clearly articulate directions and expectations, assuming that the sender and receiver of a message share a mutual understanding, and demonstrating a closed-minded attitude. Relationship issues related to nonverbal communication include facial expressions, tone of voice, sense of touch, sense of smell, and body motions. Nonverbal communication is often a manifestation of passive aggression. One particularly troubling communication issue is that of saying one thing and doing another. The incongruence is created when the organization's stated theory of action conflicts with organizational actions (Argyris & Schon, 1974). The "gaps between espoused theories and theories-in-use might be cause for discouragement or even cynicism" (Senge, 2006, p. 177).

INTRADEPARTMENTAL RELATIONSHIPS

Intradepartmental relationships involve the ways in which professionals within a department work together to accomplish the unit's mission (see figure 3.2). Campus recreational

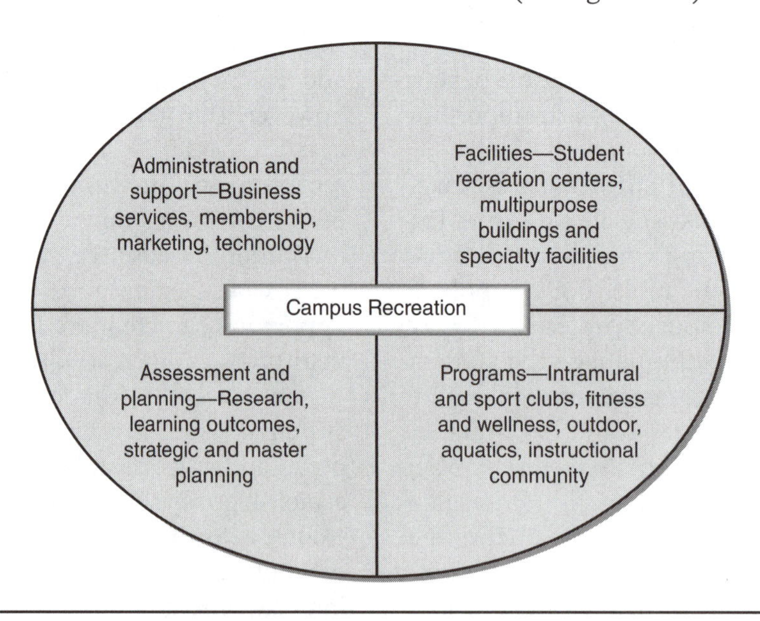

Figure 3.2 Intradepartmental relationships.

sports departments have become increasingly complex over the last half century due to the growth of recreational facilities and the diversification of programs. Typically, though not always, these departments are segmented into the following areas: administration and support, facility operations, program administration, and evaluation and assessment. The department can communicate and operate most effectively when each professional understands the role and function of each area and how he or she can best interact with other professionals and with student employees in the department. The following paragraphs summarize the four areas; for more information about a given area, see the appropriate chapter(s) in this book.

- **Administration and support**. These functions are handled by the organization's leadership, which usually includes the departmental director and executive director. In larger departments, associate directors may be considered part of departmental administration. Business services provide budget and financial support, including management and tracking of deposits, financial record keeping, and administration of business processes. In large departments, the business area may also handle membership services, including collecting membership dues and processing renewals. Another common administrative area handles marketing, promotions, and advertisement in order to present information consistently and in a unified fashion. Finally, technology services provide an integrated approach to systems management by means of usage tracking, point-of-sale software, and a file-sharing network.

- **Facility operations**. Campus recreational sports facilities have grown considerably in both size and complexity since the first intramural facility was built at the University of Michigan in 1923. This growth has led some campus recreational sports professionals to specialize in the areas of facility and operational management. Specific areas within facilities management include control and operations, scheduling, personnel supervision, risk management, maintenance, and, in some cases, custodial services.

- **Program administration**. Campus recreational sports programs vary by institution and are often limited by facility size and complexity. Primary program areas include informal activities such as pick-up basketball games, fitness, intramural sports, club sports or sport clubs, outdoor activities, instructional programs, and community outreach. Program activities are provided to individuals and groups and by varying levels of structure and complexity. Some activities, such as a fun run, might involve a thousand or more participants, while a service such as a fitness training session might be personalized to a single participant.

- **Evaluation and assessment**. As campus recreational sports programs become more closely tied to institutional accountability efforts, it has become increasingly important for professionals in the field to determine organizational effectiveness and efficiency. As a result, they have begun to routinely conduct internal and external program self-assessments and evaluations, customer satisfaction surveys, and research and assessment of learning outcomes. Some departments now assign these activities to campus recreational sports professionals who are hired specifically for their expertise in student development and assessment.

INTERDEPARTMENTAL AND INTRA-INSTITUTIONAL RELATIONSHIPS

The Council for the Advancement of Standards in Higher Education (CAS; 2009) helps define interdepartmental and intra-institutional relationships for recreational programs by setting the following standard: "maintain and promote effective relations with relevant individuals, campus offices, and external agencies" (p. 337). CAS stresses the importance of collaboration with many campus entities, "including student organizations, student union, clinical health services, health promotion services, counseling services, campus information visitor services, career services, student government, faculty and staff governance councils, conference services, residence halls and apartments, cultural centers, fraternity and sorority affairs, academic, campus police and public safety, athletics, alumni affairs, financial affairs, and physical plant" (p. 337)

Broadly speaking, an institution of higher education consists of three primary areas: academics, cocurricular units, and administrative support. Academics are divided into various disciplines and grouped by departments, schools, and colleges. The primary functions of an academic department are to provide instruction, conduct research, and engage in service to the discipline and institution. Cocurricular units provide learning outside of the classroom through service activities and student employment and may or may not be associated with academic units. Administrative and support units include departments and areas that directly or indirectly support the learning effort of academic and cocurricular units, as well as other institutional functions. Figure 3.3 provides a graphic representation of the most common units that have established relationships with campus recreational sports. Note the two-way

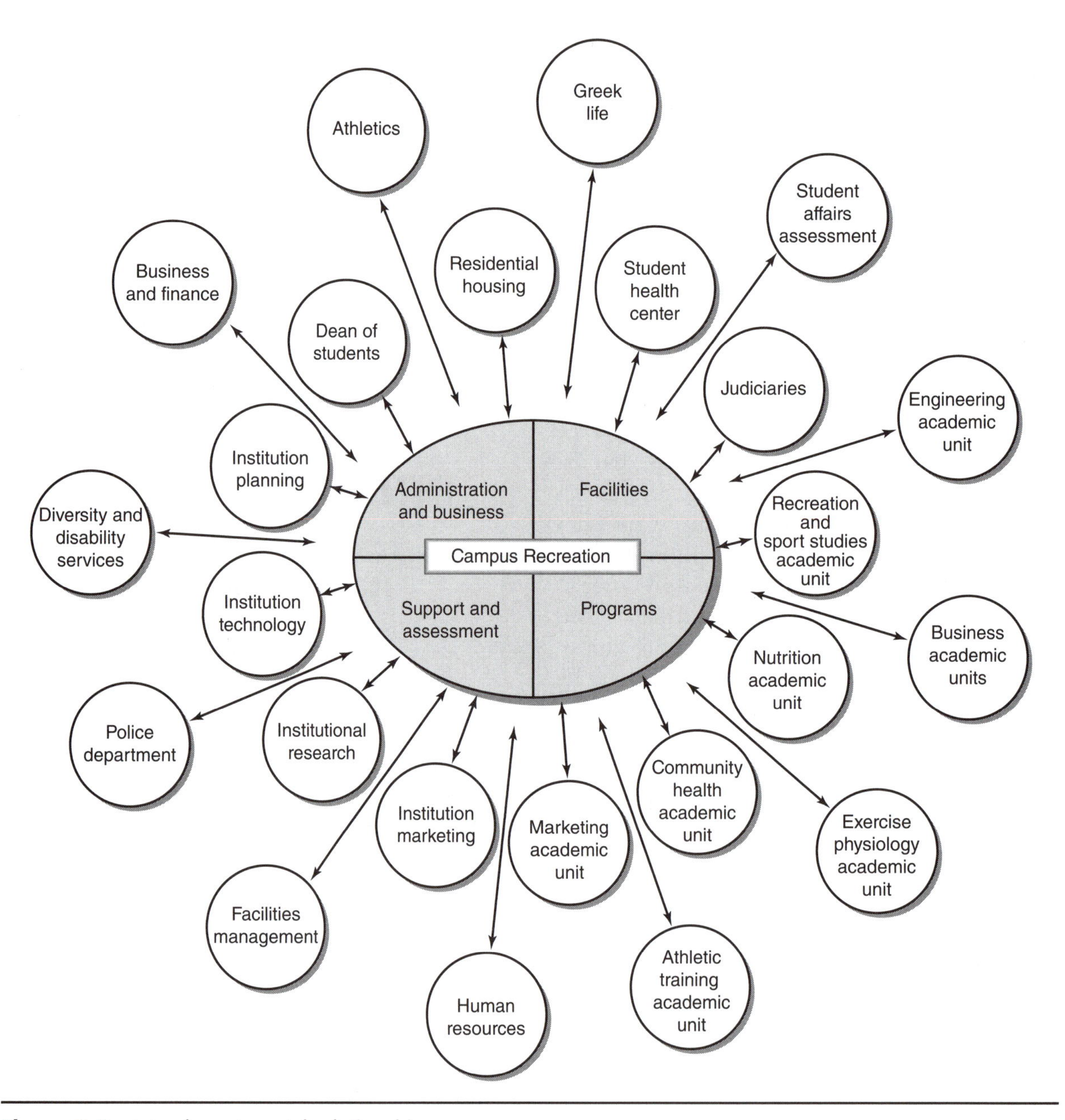

Figure 3.3 Interdepartmental relationships.

arrow between the campus recreational sports department and the institutional unit. This represents a collaborative relationship and emphasizes the importance of two-way communication.

Working With Academic Departments

The role of faculty in an institution of higher education is to manage classroom learning by developing and presenting the curriculum. Most college and university campuses are home to two kinds of faculty: tenured (or tenure-track) faculty and contingent faculty, which includes adjunct or part-time faculty, graduate teaching assistants, and guest lecturers. Tenure and tenure-track faculty, also called group 1 faculty, have three primary areas of responsibility: teaching, research, and service. Tenure is based on the concept of academic freedom, which establishes the premise that a faculty member is free to teach, conduct research, discuss, and publish without fear of reprisal or removal from his or her position. Tenure is often awarded on the basis of merit as determined by rigorous criteria weighted heavily in favor of scholarly publication. Contingent or part-time faculty members are not often afforded the benefit of tenure, though there remains an expectation of academic freedom. The primary responsibility of most contingent faculty members is teaching.

Faculty members possess varied levels of practical experience and maintain currency in the field by conducting research, examining discipline-specific literature, and observing operations relevant to their field of study. Thus campus recreational sports professionals provide unique opportunities for faculty—and, by extension, to students in related academic disciplines—to remain current. The diversity of the modern campus recreational sports program includes specializations related to many academic disciplines (see figure 3.3). Examples include recreation or sport studies, outdoor and adventure recreation, fitness and exercise physiology, nutrition, marketing and public relations, human resources, and mechanical engineering. College student personnel (CSP) and higher education (HE) academic programs are often associated with graduate level studies and can provide support for assistance with program planning, evaluation, assessment, and research.

Campus recreational sports professionals can establish relationships with faculty members directly, indirectly, or tangentially. Direct relationships can be created by using one's professional expertise in student academic development to serve as an instructor or guest lecturer or as a preceptor for experiential learning opportunities. Serving as an adjunct faculty member in an academic department may allow the professional to offer input into the development or refinement of curriculum or the general direction of the department. However, though faculty may invite the campus recreational sports professional to state his or her opinion, final curriculum decisions usually remain with tenured or tenure-track faculty members. It is also very common for modern campus recreational sports departments to provide experiential learning opportunities through internships, practicums, field experiences, and employment; indeed, practical experience often trumps theoretical discussion when it comes to student interest. To ensure a positive learning experience for students, it is essential that the professional and the faculty member communicate effectively in order to help students develop useful knowledge, skills, and attitudes. Faculty members may also be members of the campus recreational sports facility, participants in recreational programs, or advisors to clubs. In these cases, the professional relates to the faculty member as a service provider responding to a customer.

Working With Cocurricular Units

Working with or within the institution's division of student affairs often eliminates the power struggle that can occur between academic and cocurricular units. Cocurricular units are those departments that provide out-of-class learning experiences. They used to be referred to as extracurricular—that is, as activities outside of and disconnected from the classroom. However, the advent of holistic learning models championed a paradigm in which learning is viewed as occurring throughout the college experience, as expressed in such works as *The Student Learning Imperative: Implications for Student Affairs* (American College Personnel Association, 1996), *Powerful Partnerships: A Shared Responsibility for Learning* (American Association for Higher Education, American College Personnel Association, & National Association of Student Personnel Administrators, 1998), *Learning Reconsidered* (National Association of Student Personnel Administrators & American College Personnel Association, 2004), and *Learning Reconsidered 2* (American College Personnel Association et al., 2006). Because more than 70 percent of campus recreational sports programs are housed in student affairs, these units often work to build team and community in order to achieve the shared goal of student development and learning. Cocurricular units, usually housed within student affairs, include campus life, Greek life, judiciaries or community standards, culture and gender centers, student unions and centers, and, of course, campus recreational sports. Collaboration with and between cocurricular units can be accomplished through programming jointly, sharing facilities and resources, pooling funds, and combining assessment efforts.

Working with coaches and the department of intercollegiate athletics presents an interesting challenge for the recreational professional. Intercollegiate athletics tend to be externally focused and are often viewed as the "front porch" of the institution. These programs often provide direct services for athletes and indirect services for student spectators. The intercollegiate athletics director often answers directly to the institutional president and therefore wields political power not generally granted to campus recreational sports programs or professionals. Because recreational programs tend to be inwardly focused, their political power rests with the student leadership. Understanding where the power rests within the institution is often a key to achieving balance and a good working relationship between intercollegiate athletics and student recreation.

The amount of collaboration needed depends on the size and scope of the institution, the organizational location of the campus recreational sports and athletic departments, and the funding allocated to these functions. Large institutions from major athletic conferences often establish separate athletic facilities, and this type of athletic department may not interact with the campus recreational sports director any more than it does with any other institutional employee. Most institutions, however, are medium or smaller in size and possess limited funds to allocate to either intercollegiate athletics or recreation. In these institutions, sport and recreation facilities are often shared, thus requiring the professional to spend extensive time and effort in establishing a collaborative environment in which both the external and internal needs of the institution are met.

The most common shared facilities—and often the most costly—include aquatic centers, golf courses, court space, and multipurpose or practice facilities. Management of these facilities requires a careful assessment of use and usage needs. Professionals in this situation must clearly define user roles and needs, organizational responsibilities, operational funding sources, and short- and long-term maintenance responsibilities. When facilities are not designed to be shared, they might be handled through an exchange system, in which, for example, intramural sports programs often play championship games in athletic stadiums and arenas and intercollegiate athletic teams may use recreational facilities for practices and camps. Needs can be best clarified through a written memorandum of understanding (MOU), which provides a blueprint for operations and should be routinely reviewed and updated in order to address changing needs and requirements.

Working With Administrative and Institutional Support

Administrative and institutional support units are the entities that lead the institution, manage the academic and organizational infrastructure and processes, ensure equity and access, provide security, plan and assess institutional effectiveness, and promote the institution. These units include such areas as admissions and enrollment management, advising, academic help and assistance centers, student health services, psychological counseling, the registrar, facilities or physical plant management, business and finance, and human resources. When working with administrative and institutional support units, the campus recreational sports professional may relate to some units as both a data provider and a user and to other units as an information distributor. For example, an institution's enrollment management unit may well want to maximize the value of the high levels of student engagement experienced by most recreation departments and the effect of recreational facilities and programs on recruitment. The heavy traffic in recreational facilities also provides an excellent means for distributing information about academics and social services (human resource and personnel departments, for example, manage not only the hiring and compensation processes but also employee benefits and assistance programs).

The campus recreational sports professional will also come into contact with other administrative and institutional support units. Technology service offices, for example, manage the institution's network, technology backbone, and wireless system. It has become critically important for campus recreational sports professionals to work effectively with technology services as recreation programs have begun to collect and manage usage data, conduct sales operations, and use networked file sharing. Business and finance operations consist of accounting, budgeting, payroll, and purchasing. Many college recreation programs now generate considerable revenue and extensive operational expenses that necessitate routine communication with the institution's business office. These business needs derive from the fact that campus recreational sports offices operate some of the largest and most complex facilities on campus. While the recreational department is tasked with operational control of these facilities, the institution's department of facility management, sometimes known as the physical plant, is often charged with maintaining the building envelope (or enclosure) and systems. In some cases, facility management offices also manage the institution's custodial system. As the most common internal service providers, these units (technology services, finance, administration, and facility management) often establish service level expectations. Because campus recreational sports departments are seen as customers for these services, clear expectations must be established through MOUs or service level agreements (SLAs).

Another set of units—diversity, disability services, and international student offices—is tasked with ensuring equity, access, and fairness within the institution. Campus recreational sports professionals need to establish good working relationships with these units to help the recreation department fulfill its mission of engaging the campus community as a whole. For example, these units provide good information when the recreation professional is targeting programs and services to and for underrepresented populations.

The institution's office of public safety, or police department, is tasked with law enforcement and crime prevention on campus. Police departments work closely with campus recreational sports professionals when responding to altercations, developing and monitoring security systems to deter and prevent crimes, and assisting with various instructional programs focused on self-defense and sexual assault awareness.

Institutional research (IR) provides information and analytical support for university planning, management, and assessment activities. IR collects, analyzes, and interprets data about institutional performance and serves as an excellent source of information about student interest and participation in recreational and fitness activities. In order to avoid survey fatigue among students, IR also coordinates the campuswide survey process, including the institution's participation in national studies such as the National Survey of Student Engagement (NSSE), the Community College Survey of Student Engagement (CCSSE), and the Cooperative Institutional Research Program (CIRP). The campus recreational sports professional can find valuable information by reviewing existing IR reports, including treatment, engagement, and involvement studies.

COMMUNITY RELATIONSHIPS

The location of an institution of higher education affects the relationship between the community and the institution, which is known as the "town-and-gown" relationship. In many cases, the campus recreational sports department serves as a bridge between the institution and community. Residential colleges in small towns often develop synergistic relationships that are enhanced by the institution's recreational offerings. This is especially true in communities that possess only a limited tax base with which to support community centers and recreation programs, thus limiting their ability to provide the swimming pools, gymnasiums, fitness centers, ice rinks, and tennis facilities that are normally prevalent in large cities with robust suburban areas. Conversely, institutions housed in urban areas may find themselves in competition with private clubs, YMCAs, and community centers. These situations involve less of a need to create a bridge between town and gown but still may offer an opportunity to provide unique recreational experiences. In either case, community use of campus recreational sports facilities and programs can provide an extra source of revenue.

In offering opportunities to the community, the campus recreational sports professional must become well versed in the issues of unfair business practices and unrelated business income tax (UBIT). Unfair business practice involves the issue of competing interests between private businesses and nonprofit ventures. Because most colleges and universities operate as nonprofit or not-for-profit entities, they enjoy property tax and income tax advantages not afforded to private for-profit entities. This means that when the campus recreational sports program competes with a private corporation, it must ensure that it does not take unfair advantage of its tax status by undercutting the for-profit entity. UBIT, on the other hand, involves the fees (for services or

The University of Texas at San Antonio, Department of Campus Recreation.

A running event is one example of a way campus recreational sports programs can bridge the gap between the institution and the community in which it resides.

goods) generated as a result of the department's interactions with the community or unaffiliated customers. The growth and expansion of fee-for-service activities and retail operations within the modern campus recreational sports program creates the potential for generating UBIT. For example, some campus recreation programs provide services such as swimming lessons or facility memberships to the community which are considered unrelated to the primary academic mission of the institution. Unrelated funds are segregated from funds generated by institutionally related activities, such as faculty and staff memberships, and add to the institution's income tax liabilities.

Despite these financial complexities, many campus recreational sports programs interact with the community by providing services, such as individual memberships to fitness and recreational facilities, group and team facility rentals, participation in intramural and club sport teams, attendance at special events, and instructional classes provided for youth and adults. In some cases, campus recreational sports programs work with local schools to provide specialized recreation services for area youth, including youth sport leagues and learn-to programs.

The underlying principle when inviting the community into the campus recreational sports program is that students must remain at the center of the endeavor. The campus recreational sports professional must take care to ensure that students are not negatively affected by community involvement in what are essentially student recreation facilities. Some ways to do this are to monitor facility usage patterns by category, examine staff time, and observe community and student interactions.

In some cases, the campus recreational sports program is also a customer of services from the community—for example, local chapters of the American Red Cross, American Heart Association, or other organizations that provide training materials and certifications for staff members. The campus recreational sports professional may also work with local government officials and agencies, including health inspectors and the fire marshal, to help ensure that the institution's facilities and programs comply with state and local codes. It is also essential for the program to establish a relationship with the local emergency medical services and critical incident response personnel prior to an event to maximize the department's ability to respond effectively in a crisis.

Campus recreational sports professionals must also create and maintain good relationships with service providers and product vendors, such as vending suppliers, equipment maintenance and laundry companies, local or regional sporting goods vendors, and noninstitutional technology service providers.

PROFESSIONAL RELATIONSHIPS

The profession of campus recreational sports has been evolving for nearly a century. The historical background of that evolution is addressed in chapter 1 of this book, and chapter 2 covers specialized preparation, skill attainment, and professional development opportunities. The next portion of this chapter focuses on relationships and on how the professional engages with others in the profession. Engagement in the field of campus recreational sports can be demonstrated through active participation in the National Intramural-Recreational Sports Association (NIRSA) and other state, regional, and national professional organizations associated with the field.

The professional can formalize involvement by gaining acceptance to the Registry of Collegiate Recreational Sports Professionals. Members of the professional registry must demonstrate a well-rounded understanding of recreational sport management's body of knowledge through mastery of eight core competencies: philosophy and theory; programming; management techniques; business procedures; facility management, planning, and design; research and evaluation; legal liability and risk management; and personal and professional qualities. Entry into the registry and renewal both require that individuals participate in ongoing professional development by earning continuing education units (CEUs) and professional involvement credits (PICs) that indicate continued development of knowledge, skills, and abilities. CEUs are relatively straightforward and flexible and are awarded based on their relationship to competencies, the qualification of the instructor, identifiable and appropriate learning objectives, and a mechanism for evaluation and assessment that measures the success of learning outcomes.

PICs provide another important way for professionals to learn and stay current in the field. They come in two types—group A and group B. Group A activities include education, training, and scholarship. The education and training aspects include serving as a faculty member for the NIRSA National School of Recreational Sports Management, teaching an academic course for credit in a subject relevant to at least one of the eight professional core competencies, and teaching an online NIRSA course in a subject relevant to at least one of the core competencies. Qualifying scholarship and research activities include authoring an article published in the *Recreational Sports Journal* or another relevant refereed publication (e.g., *Journal for Leisure Research, Journal of College Student Development*) authoring an article published in a nonrefereed publication (e.g., *Athletic Business* or *Fitness Management*), or writing a chapter in a book related to campus recreational sports.

Other avenues of professional development might include acquiring a related specialty certification from associations such as the American College of Sports Medicine, American Council on Exercise, Aerobics and Fitness Association of American and the Association of Outdoor Recreation and Education. Giving a CEU presentation at a conference (state, regional, provincial, or national), symposium or institute, or non-NIRSA conference in a subject relevant to at least one of the core competencies; serving as a chair, director, or member of a thesis or doctoral committee for a graduate student in campus recreational sports; or serving as curricular or cocurricular advisor to undergraduate students pursuing a degree in a related field are also good methods of professional development.

Group B PICs involve leadership, governance, and service activities. Leadership and governance involvement includes serving on NIRSA-related boards of directors (e.g., the NIRSA Services Corporation and the NIRSA Foundation), on the NIRSA Member Network or in the assembly, as chair of a NIRSA committee or work team, or as a NIRSA state or provincial director. Other common forms of professional involvement include conducting or hosting a student Lead On session or Emerging Recreational Sports Leaders or specialty conference; hosting or serving on the host committee for a professional conference, symposium, or institute; and hosting or assisting with state, regional, provincial, or national extramural tournaments or sport club championships. Opportunities to extend professional relationships include serving on the board of directors of a related organization (e.g., American Alliance for Health, Physical Education, Recreation and Dance; Council for the Advancement of Standards in Higher Education; American College of Sports Medicine; Association of Outdoor Recreation and Education; Wilderness Education Association) and actively working at a campus recreational sports event or volunteering on behalf of a nonprofit organization to assist individuals or communities in need (e.g., through the American Red Cross, Special Olympics, Habitat for Humanity, or Big Brothers Big Sisters).

SUMMARY

Good relationships form the foundation for both the campus recreational sports profession and the individual professional. The professional's everyday working environment involves working with students, peers, supervisors, and subordinates and collaborating with academic, cocurricular, and administrative units to provide a learning-centered environment. Campus recreational sports professionals also work with the community to provide and receive services that enhance the town-and-gown relationship in both rural and urban settings. Professionals find opportunities for personal growth and help build the profession through professional involvement in local, regional, or national recreational associations. Overall, nurturing relationships cultivate effectiveness in campus recreational sports professionals, departments, and the profession as a whole so that professionals can provide high-quality services that produce great students.

Glossary

expert or referent power—Power created by special skills, knowledge, or expertise needed for group success (Lee, 1997, p. 82).

instrumental power—Results-based power created from a can-do attitude (Lee, 1997, p. 83).

interpersonal relationships—An association between two or more people that may range from fleeting to enduring.

line position—Position directly involved in daily operations that carries out primary activities and functions of the organization (Helms, 2006).

positional or legitimate power—Power "derived from a person's position in the group or organizational hierarchy" (Lee, 1997, p. 82).

relation power—Power derived from developing relationships with people who possess power (Lee, 1997, p. 84).

scalar chain—"Chain of superiors ranging from the ultimate authority to the lowest ranks" (Fayol, 1916/2000, p. 56).

staff position—Position that indirectly supports line functions, including those functions related to technical support, aides, and assistants to personnel and management; provides support, advice, and knowledge to other individuals in the scalar chain (Helms, 2006).

transition—"A three-phase psychological process that people go through as they internalize and come to terms with the details of the new situation that the change brings about" (Bridges, 2003, p.3).

References

American Association for Higher Education, American College Personnel Association, and National Association of Student Personnel Administrators. (1998). *Powerful partnerships: A shared responsibility for learning.* www.myacpa.org/pub/documents/taskforce.pdf.

American College Personnel Association. (1996). *The student learning imperative: Implications for student affairs.* www.acpa.nche.edu/sli/sli.htm.

American College Personnel Association, Association of College and University Housing Officers–International, Association of College Unions–International, National Academic Advising Association, National Association for Campus Activities, National Association of Student Personnel Administrators, et al. (2006). *Learning Reconsidered 2.* Washington, DC: Author.

Argyris, C., and Schon, D.A. (1974). *Theory in practice: Increasing professional effectiveness.* San Francisco: Jossey-Bass.

Bridges, W. (2003). *Managing transitions: Making the most of change* (2nd ed.). Cambridge, MA: DaCapo Press.

Council for the Advancement of Standards in Higher Education (CAS). (2009). *Recreational sports standards.* Washington, DC: Author.

Covey, S.R. (1989). *Seven habits of highly effective people: Restoring the character ethic.* New York: Simon & Schuster.

Fayol, H. (2000). General principles of management. In J.M. Shafritz & J.S. Ott (Eds.), *Classics of organization theory* (5th ed., pp. 48-60). Belmont, CA: Wadsworth. (Original work published 1916)

Helms, M.H. (Ed.). (2006). *Encyclopedia of management.* Farmington Hills, MI: Thomson Gale. www.enotes.com/management-encyclopedia/line-staff-organizations.

Howard, R. (Director). (2001). *A beautiful mind* [Motion picture]. Universal Studios.

Lee, B. (1997). *The power principle: Influence with honor.* New York: Simon & Schuster.

National Association of Student Personnel Administrators & American College Personnel Association. (2004). *Learning Reconsidered.* Washington, DC: Author.

National Center for Education Statistics (2011) Fast facts. Retrieved from http://nces.ed.gov/fastfacts/display.asp?id=372.

National Intramural-Recreational Sports Association (NIRSA). (2003). *The Value of Recreational Sports in Higher Education.* Champaign IL: Human Kinetics.

Senge, P. (2006) *The fifth discipline: The art and practice of the learning organization.* Double Day: New York.

CHAPTER 4

Budgeting and Internal Controls

Maureen McGonagle
Centers LLC at DePaul University

In today's campus recreational sports management environment, practitioners must use a diverse skill set in order to manage the increasing complexities and challenges of the workplace. More specifically, the *business* of recreation management has advanced considerably: the small sports program once run on borrowed fields and a shoestring budget is now often a multi-million dollar operation encompassing multiple program areas and expansive facilities. As recreation programs have grown in breadth and depth, their operations have increasingly been expected to generate more funds to make up for dwindling state appropriations and increasing costs. The landscape has also changed rapidly in the legal, technological, and human resource areas.

This set of changes has forced recreation professionals to become business savvy in order to excel—and even to survive. It is clear that in order to be both effective and efficient, recreation practitioners must fully understand the financial elements of their operations. To that end, this chapter is devoted to providing recreation professionals with a solid foundation for skillful financial management; specifically, it addresses financial management terms and concepts, budget development, budget management, and internal controls.

WHAT IS A BUDGET?

A **budget** is a plan of expected income and expenditures for an organization; it is used as a tool to help the organization reach its goals and objectives. The budget outlines how resources are allocated in order to achieve stated goals and can be used to help clarify priorities, guide decisions, and judge effectiveness. It should reflect the organization's values and mission.

Budgets are developed for a specified period of time, usually 12 months; this period is referred to as the **fiscal year**. While some organizations use a calendar year as their fiscal year, many institutions use a different time period; universities, for example, often use July 1 through June 30, whereas the federal government uses October 1 through September 30. The fiscal year is referred to by the ending year in the period; thus, if the fiscal year is defined as July 1, 2012, through June 30, 2013, then the period is referred to as FY2013 or FY13.

Recreation departments typically have at least two budgets: an **operating budget** and a **capital budget**. The operating budget addresses the organization's normal operating costs, whereas the capital budget (sometimes referred to as R&R—repair and replacement, or reserves) is typically a long-term plan for funding the replacement of fixed assets, such as equipment and facilities (i.e., capital expenditures). Sometimes the department controls an R&R budget that funds routine equipment replacements and modest facility repairs or renovations. The department may also have a separate capital fund for major repairs and construction projects, which may be funded either by the department or by the larger organization. If this capital account is funded by the department, the manager needs to carefully consider not only the annual budget cycle but also the cumulative effect of annual budgets over a 5- to 10-year period. Indeed, it is beneficial to view each annual budget as another step toward long-term financial health.

BUDGET DEVELOPMENT

The budget cycle includes four elements: development, submission and approval, execution, and review and audit (see figure 4.1). The first element—budget development—consists of estimating revenues and expenditures for a future fiscal year.

How Budgets Are Developed

Two ways of developing a budget are zero-based budgeting and incremental budgeting. In **zero-based budgeting**, the manager starts from zero and justifies every requested expense for each aspect of the operation. Thus zero-based budgeting provides a high degree of accountability, since every planned expense is fully explained and justified. Building a budget from the ground up, however, is also very time consuming; as a result, if a large portion of the operation remains routine from year to year, it may not be worth spending the additional time to justify every estimated expenditure.

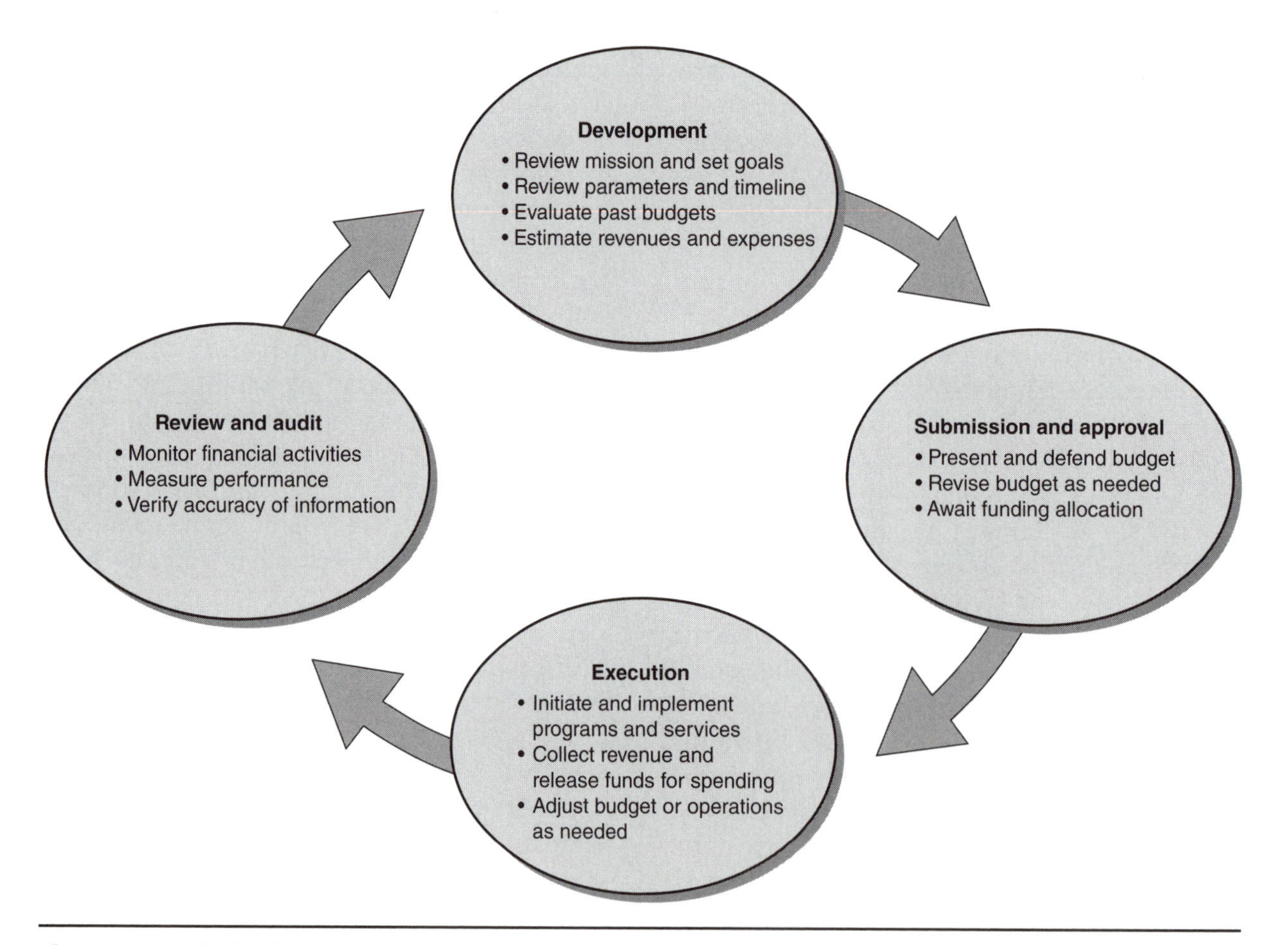

Figure 4.1 The budget cycle.

Incremental budgeting is a less time-consuming method in which the manager reviews previous fiscal year statements and makes adjustments based on anticipated changes in the operation. For example, let's assume that FY12 expected year-end spending for supplies is $30,000 and that no material (i.e., substantive) changes are anticipated in the operation for the next fiscal year. Supply costs, however, are expected to increase by 3 percent. In this case, the FY13 supply-line request would be $30,900 ($30,000 × 1.03).

Some organizations take a hybrid approach in which they use incremental budgeting for continuing operations and a zero-based approach for new projects and initiatives. All three of these options are considered **bottom-up budgeting** approaches since the manager develops a budget and submits it up the chain of command for approval. Other organizations use **top-down budgeting**, wherein a supervising authority dictates a dollar figure for the budget and the manager then creates a plan for making the operational elements fit within the stated financial parameters. For example, a manager might be told that the following fiscal year's bottom line must be 10 percent lower than the current year's bottom line, or a programmer might be given $2,000 to create a new special event.

The timing of the budget development phase varies greatly by organization, and the deadline for final budget submission might be anywhere from a few months to more than a year prior to the fiscal year in question. In any case, it is crucial to be aware of the deadline, determine how long it will take to gather the necessary input and construct the budget, and then work backward to establish a budget development timeline to meet the required date.

Constructing a budget requires pulling together a lot of information. Here are some questions to consider:

- What are the department's mission and priorities?
- What was the department's financial performance in prior periods?
- What modifications are staff proposing to the operating plan or programming mix?
- What projects, programs, and services will be funded?
- How much revenue can be expected from the various activities?
- What expenses are required to fund the desired programs and facility operations?
- Do any special circumstances need to be considered? (For example, if student fees are distributed to departments starting in late August but the operating year starts in July, where do operating funds come from in the interim?)

Budget Components

A budget comprises cash inflow and cash outflow. **Cash inflow** includes any funds coming into the organization, such as earned interest, incoming loans, and—most common in a recreation budget—**revenue**, which consists of funds earned through business operations. **Cash outflow**, also called expenditure or expense, includes charges incurred by the organization due to business operations.

Some of the many possible revenue sources for recreation operations include program fees, membership dues, student fees (for a university), tax dollars (for a municipal recreation center), service fees, sponsorship fees, donations, and

Whether a unit produces revenue determines whether it is considered a profit center or a cost center. A **profit center** controls the generation of revenues and expenses, whereas a **cost center** (e.g., human resources department) does not control revenue generation. In recreation departments, the mission dictates whether a program or service area is expected to generate a profit, break even, or be partially or completely subsidized. In the first three situations, it is a profit center; in the latter (completely subsidized), it is a cost center.

rental fees. Generated revenue is earned through specific activities of the organization, which can include everything in the preceding list except for student fees and tax dollars.

There are also many expense categories—for example, salaries and benefits, departmental (operating) expenses, and nondepartmental expenses. Departmental expenses include costs such as repairs, equipment, telecommunication, advertising, travel, entertainment, and supplies. Nondepartmental expenses include items such as depreciation, cost of goods sold (e.g., merchandise to be sold in a pro shop), taxes, physical plant overhead, and interest or rent payments.

Let's consider payroll as an example of an expense category. Universities typically use multiple payroll subcodes, which can include full-time staff (e.g., faculty; professional staff; clerical, trade, janitorial, and security staff), professional part-time staff, temporary staff, graduate assistants, and hourly student staff. Since payroll includes more than just staff salaries and hourly wages, institutions also use a separate subcode for employee benefits. Even so, the budgeting computation is often simple, since the manager is likely given a multiplier for determining the cost of living adjustment (COLA), the raise pool, and the benefit line. For example, the manager might be told to first determine the full-time salary line request for the upcoming year based on current-year dollars, then add a 3 percent COLA, a 2 percent raise, and 30 percent for benefits.

Although the benefits line is often determined by using a multiplier provided by the organization, it is still helpful to understand what additional costs are borne by the organization. These additional costs include the Federal Insurance Contributions Act tax (FICA), taxes from the State and Federal Unemployment Tax acts (SUTA and FUTA), workers' compensation insurance, and a variety of employer-sponsored benefits. Additional benefits costs might include employer contributions to health insurance, retirement contributions, short- and long-term disability (STD and LTD) insurance, paid time off, administrative costs of offering flexible spending accounts or transportation benefits, and the costs of providing tuition remission to staff and their dependents. Employment of professional part-time staff involves FICA, FUTA and SUTA, and workers' compensation but likely excludes many of the voluntary benefits provided to full-time staff. Student employment figures during the academic year most likely include only the wages earned, since college students are exempt from FICA taxes if they are enrolled at least half-time and working part-time for their university.

Here is an example of full-time labor costs for 1 month:

Salaries for full-time staff: $30,000
Social Security tax: $1,820
Medicare tax: $435
FUTA: $240
SUTA: $195
Workers' compensation insurance: $50
Health insurance contribution: $2,600
Retirement contribution: $2,400
STD and LTD: $250
Contributions to tuition remission program: $1,500
Monthly employer cost for full-time staff: $39,490

In 2010, the FICA-required employer contribution was 7.65 percent (6.2% for Social Security for up to the first $106,800 in wages and 1.45% for Medicare; these employer contributions match the required employee withholdings). In 2010, the FUTA rate was 6.2 percent on wages up to $7,000 (with a credit of up to 5.4% for SUTA, so FUTA is generally 0.8%). SUTA rates vary by state and by the organization's history of claims filed by terminated employees (this is analogous to the way in which car insurance rates are influenced by driver claims).

Financial Statements

Financial statements come in various types, each of which serves a useful purpose. A **profit and loss statement** (i.e., P&L or income statement) shows budgeted and actual revenues and expenses over a defined period of time. A P&L provides an easy way to quickly assess how well the organization is performing financially. Table 4.1 shows an example.

A **projected statement** (see table 4.2) estimates revenues and expenses for a fiscal period based on expected outcomes. A P&L statement is transformed into a projected statement by replacing the "actuals" column in the P&L with "year-end estimates."

A **pro forma statement** (see table 4.3) is based on assumptions that differ from the current reality. For example, if it is rumored during the fiscal year that the total expenses allowed may be reduced by 8 percent, the manager may need to manipulate the approved budget to see how the reduction might be accommodated should it become a reality.

A **comparative statement** (see table 4.4) includes more than one fiscal period. Since comparative statements make information from prior periods readily available and easy to compare,

Table 4.1 Profit and Loss Statement

	Approved budget	Actuals (through 3/31/12)	Percent received/ expended (%)
Total revenue	2,423,000	1,945,024	80.27
Total expenses	2,267,730	1,657,244	73.08
Net surplus (loss)	155,270	287,780	

This statement covers 9 months (July 1, 2011, through March 31, 2012) or 75 percent of the fiscal year. Only totals are shown for illustration.

Table 4.2 Projected Statement

	Approved budget	Year-end estimates	Variance favorable/ (unfavorable)
Total revenue	2,423,000	2,511,000	88,000
Total expenses	2,267,730	2,272,000	(4,270)
Net surplus (loss)	155,270	239,000	83,730

Fiscal year: July 1, 2011, through June 30, 2012. Statement date: March 31, 2012. Only totals are shown for illustration.

Table 4.3 Pro Forma Statement

Expenses	Approved budget	Adjusted budget
Student wages	125,000	119,100
Repairs	10,000	10,000
Equipment	12,000	9,000
Supplies	18,000	16,500
Telephone	2,000	2,000
Advertising	3,000	2,000
Travel	6,000	4,000
Uniforms	4,000	3,000
Total expenses	180,000	165,600

Fiscal year 2012. This adjusted budget represents one possible reaction to an 8 percent decrease in the total expense allocation. Only a portion of the statement is shown for illustration.

Table 4.4 Comparative Statement

	Actual FY10	Actual FY11	Proposed FY13
REVENUE			
Membership	2,235,228	2,278,125	2,380,000
Programs	417,833	415,938	425,000
Rentals	156,422	175,226	185,000
Total revenue	2,809,483	2,869,289	2,990,000
EXPENSES—SALARIES AND BENEFITS			
Full-time salaries	352,112	359,154	386,000
Part-time wages	201,089	205,111	221,000
Benefits	88,034	89,783	96,000
Total salaries and benefits	641,235	654,048	703,000
EXPENSES—DEPARTMENTAL			
Repairs	29,021	31,187	35,000
Equipment	25,188	28,094	26,000
Supplies	66,037	68,227	72,000
Telecommunication	4,842	4,955	5,100
Postage	2,583	2,681	2,750
Copying	8,921	9,225	9,300
Advertising	18,957	19,924	21,000
Travel	16,094	17,220	18,500
Dues	3,850	4,328	4,600
Other	5,211	3,382	2,500
Total departmental expenses	180,704	189,223	196,750
EXPENSES—NONDEPARTMENTAL			
Insurance	32,500	38,400	42,000
Overhead	1,102,049	1,135,193	1,192,000
Depreciation	312,873	318,900	318,000
Taxes	42,546	48,526	52,000
Interest payment	378,130	389,300	392,000
Total nondepartmental expenses	1,868,098	1,930,319	1,996,000
Total expenses	2,690,037	2,773,590	2,895,750
Account total	119,446	95,699	94,250

Budgets can either be **centralized** or **decentralized.** In a centralized process, the various units within an organization use the same budget (and the budget is controlled from the top); in a decentralized process, control of the budget is delegated down to the lowest level possible. A university recreation department has a centralized budget if it uses one department account for all revenues and operating expenses across all programs (i.e., one budget that covers facilities, intramural sports, club sports, group fitness classes, instructional programs, and outdoor adventures). It has a decentralized budget if each facility or program area has its own distinct budget account. A decentralized budget often provides more authority and accountability for the individual units, whereas a centralized budget often allows for more efficient use of resources since any budget savings can be pooled and reallocated within the same budget.

Unrelated business income tax (UBIT) is paid by tax-exempt organizations on revenue earned from activities considered to be unrelated business, which generally involves activity that is

- regularly carried on,
- a trade or business, and
- not substantially related to the organization's mission.

If a university recreation center generates revenue by serving the university population or otherwise in accordance with the mission of the university, that revenue is unlikely to be taxed. If it generates revenue not related to the university mission or from the university population, that revenue likely will be taxed. Here are some examples in a university setting, where the mission is education. Student, faculty, and staff facility membership sales are not taxable, since providing the university community with access to recreation and fitness facilities supports the university's mission, whereas facility membership sales to alumni and community members are taxable. Revenue generated from instructional programs would likely be exempt, regardless of whether the participants are students, faculty, staff, or nonaffiliated members, since instructional programs provide education and are thus mission-related for all audiences.

A tax-exempt organization is allowed to generate revenue from unrelated business, but it is imperative that the manager work closely with the university tax manager to ensure that the department is in compliance with the complex rules and regulations regarding unrelated business income, tax-exempt status, and the use of tax-exempt bonds.

they are often very helpful in the budget development phase.

Pricing Decisions

Pricing strategy is determined by whether a program is meant to generate a profit, break even, or be partially or completely subsidized. A recreation department's programming mix might use all four approaches: the personal training program might be priced to bring in a 20 percent profit, the babysitting service might be designed to cover costs (break even), intramural sport offerings might involve a nominal fee that defrays but doesn't completely cover costs (and thus is partially subsidized), and special events might be offered free of charge (and thus be completely subsidized). Organizations differ in what costs they use to calculate the break-even point for a program. Some consider only direct variable costs, others consider all direct costs, and still others calculate direct and indirect costs. There is no right or wrong in these approaches as long as the overall strategy supports the organization's mission and follows the budget approved by the organization's upper levels. The key is to be aware of, and follow, the organization's expectations.

As an example of the factors that inform pricing decisions, let's consider an arts and crafts program with direct costs of $300:

Supplies: $150

Social media ad and promotional flyers: $50

Labor (wages and taxes) for 2 hours/week at $10/hour for 5 weeks: $100

Total direct costs: $300

If this is a **break-even** program (i.e., revenue is equal to expenses), the registration fee could be set at $30 per person with a 10-participant minimum ($30 fee × 10 participants = $300 in revenue to match $300 in expenses).

If the program is designed to be **subsidized** (i.e., if revenue is less than expenses), the registration fee could be anything less than $30 per person—that is, anything that produces less revenue than the $300 amount of direct costs.

Costs: Direct and Indirect, Fixed and Variable

A **direct cost** can be attributed directly to a specific program or service, whereas an **indirect cost** cannot. For example, in regard to babysitting services, direct costs include the babysitters' wages and the cost of toys, children's videos, and promotional materials; indirect costs include heating, insurance, taxes, and administrative salaries.

A **variable cost** varies directly with the level of output—thus, in a program or service, with the level of participation. A semivariable cost, in contrast, is fixed up to a certain level of activity, and a **fixed cost** is not directly related to the level of output or participation. For example, when offering classes in CPR (cardiopulmonary resuscitation) and the use of an AED (automated external defibrillator), variable costs include the instruction book and face shield provided to each participant, the semivariable cost consists of the instructor's wages (the instructor-to-participant ration is 1:10, so the cost of wages jumps after every group of 10), and fixed costs include the price of promotional materials and the training video.

If the program is designed to make a 25 percent **profit** (i.e., if expenses are equal to 75% of revenue), the registration fee could be set at $40 per person ($40 fee × 10 participants = $400 in revenue − $300 in expenses = $100 in profit ÷ $400 in revenue = 25% profit margin).

Pricing is also a function of the market. Before pricing a program or service, the manager should collect current information through market research about the pricing of similar programs or services in the area. Here are some questions to consider: How similar are the programs or services being compared? What price will the organization's constituency be willing to pay? What is the demand at this price?

BUDGET SUBMISSION AND APPROVAL

Once the budget is developed, it is submitted to the supervising authorities for approval. Budgets often need to be reviewed and approved at multiple levels before being finalized, often by the organization's governing board. The exact process and timeline vary by organization. Some require budgets to be submitted with supporting rationales and documentation; others require the manager to make a formal presentation and answer questions in defense of the budget. Some require the proposed budget to be submitted 3 months in advance, whereas others demand a full year. As with other aspects of the budgeting process, the manager must be aware of the organization's rules and expectations before embarking on the process.

BUDGET MANAGEMENT

Budget management consists of the third and fourth elements of the budget cycle: budget execution and budget review.

Budget Execution

Budget execution is the stage in the budget cycle when financial resources are directed toward achieving the organization's goals and objectives. To administer the budget, the manager must understand how to purchase items, how to decide whether to purchase or lease, how subcodes should be used, and how to make adjustments to the budget once it is already approved.

Purchasing and Procurement

An organization typically has multiple ways to purchase necessary items. It might use a preferred vendor for certain purchases (e.g., office supplies, catering) by means of a prearrangement for ordering from that vendor, who can then directly charge the department account. Large organizations also have a mechanism for making budget transfers from one department to another within the organization. It is also common for organizations to issue credit or purchasing cards for managers to use for individual transactions up to a certain dollar limit; additional limits on daily and monthly spending often vary depending on the manager's job responsibilities and authority (e.g., $2,500 transaction limit with a $5,000 daily limit and a $10,000 monthly limit for all but the senior administrators). Larger purchases (e.g., more than $2,500) often require a requisition and purchase order to be submitted and approved before the order can be placed; sometimes the organization also requires that a vendor be registered with the organization before any orders are placed. The competitive bidding process is normally reserved for sizable purchases (e.g., more than $25,000); it can be a complex and time-consuming process, since it requires the manager to thoroughly detail the intended purchase, formally put the requested purchase out for bid to multiple vendors, document all written quotes received, and provide justification for the final purchasing decision.

Beyond the method of purchase, the organization is likely to establish detailed rules governing what can be purchased (or reimbursed) and when. An organization may set a dollar limit on how much can be spent for meals during travel and require receipts for reimbursement; alternatively, it may issue travelers a preset per diem to cover meals. Some organizations allow a department to roll over extra funds from one fiscal year to the next, but others strictly limit funding access to the stated fiscal year. In addition, some organizations encourage units to spend only what is needed to accomplish stated goals, whereas others encourage units to spend all dollars allocated in the budget in order to protect the funding level in future years (which leads to spending sprees at the end of the fiscal year).

Buying or Leasing Equipment

Some larger capital purchases require the manager to decide whether to lease or purchase. Purchasing equipment is typically the more cost-effective method and is often the better choice if the agency can make the initial capital outlay, if having ownership of the asset is advantageous,

Photo courtesy of Virginia Tech.

With knowledge of basic budgeting principles, the manager can make decisions about buying or leasing equipment that balance the needs of facility users with the financial stability of the center.

or if the equipment promises to have a long useful life. Leasing might be a better option for organizations with limited capital, for expensive items that have a short useful life or will become obsolete quickly, for organizations that do not want responsibility for asset disposal, and for an organization that wants to budget a fixed cost for the equipment.

Comparing the cost-effectiveness of the options involves many considerations, including the following: amount of down payment, sales tax rate, investment rate of return, length of the lease or loan, lease fees, security deposit, depreciation percentage rate, interest rate on the lease or loan, and expected resale (or trade-in) value of the asset. Even so, it isn't always an overly complex computation. If the organization is tax-exempt (e.g., municipal recreation centers, university recreation departments), then the sales tax rate and tax incentives are not considerations. If the organization has the initial capital outlay available, then a loan and the associated interest and down payment are not considerations. If the decision is being made at the department level (instead of at the upper echelons of the organization), then little or no consideration may be required of depreciation or the investment rate of return. In large organizations, if the asset is purchased across the organization (e.g., computers), lease terms may be prearranged so that all deposits and fees are included in the stated monthly fee for the lease, further simplifying the computation and decision.

Let's consider an example involving a decision to lease or buy cardio equipment:

Purchase terms: $120,000

Lease terms: $41,556 per year for 3 years; $195 fee, with $1 buyout option

If the manager plans to, after 3 years, either (a) trade in the purchased equipment or (b) establish a new lease, the costs would compare as follows:

(a) Total purchase cost: $120,000 – $18,000 trade-in value = $102,000

(b) Total lease cost: $41,556 × 3 + $195 = $124,863

In this example, the total cost after 3 years is considerably less with the straight purchase option. Thus, if the manager has the initial $120,000 available, with no competing priorities and no worries about obsolescence or asset disposal, then purchasing may be the best option. If, however, the manager does not have the initial funds, or if he or she wants the consistency of a set monthly cost, then a lease should be considered.

Subcodes

Breaking down revenue and expenses into subcodes increases the level of detail available to a manager about how the business is operating. It is important for the manager to understand subcodes and follow the organization's expectations about them. Subcodes vary by agency, but here are some categories commonly used for recreation:

- **Revenue**—membership fees, rental fees, program and service fees, merchandise sales, taxes (for municipal recreation departments), student fees and state appropriations (for universities), donations, grants, and sponsorships
- **Expenses**—part-time wages, salaries, benefits, equipment, furniture, repairs and maintenance, subscriptions, computer software, advertising, postage, telecommunications, copying costs, entertainment, dues, supplies, educational materials, printing, seminars and conferences, travel, vehicle rental, insurance, meals and hospitality, and consultant services

The level of detail varies in subcode classification. For example, one agency might use a single subcode to cover all travel, whereas another uses separate subcodes for in-state travel, out-of-state travel, relocation expenses, and recruitment travel. Similarly, one agency might use a single subcode for equipment, whereas another uses separate subcodes for general equipment, furniture, computer equipment, vehicles, instructional equipment, custodial equipment, and maintenance equipment. The manager must become familiar with the agency's subcodes and descriptions in order to use them appropriately.

Adjustments

Budgets are often submitted and approved well before they are put into action, and they can be affected by various factors, such as a change in circumstances that leads to reduced revenue or increased expenses (e.g., a recession, new legislation, a spike in energy costs), a change in the institution's priorities, or a shift in timing for lower construction costs. Thus it is helpful for the manager to know what flexibility exists for operating outside of the officially approved parameters. For example, let's say that you face an unexpected need to fund an unfunded mandate, such as a state-mandated increase in the minimum wage. In dealing with the shortfall, will the institution allocate additional dollars? Can you make a permanent adjustment in the base budget? Can you pull from reserves? Can you overspend in the current budget, then increase the expense request (or decrease revenue expectations) for future years? Or do you need to offset the new expenses by curtailing spending in other areas?

As in other areas, the process of and rules for making adjustments in an existing budget vary by institution. Consider two agencies—agency A and agency B—with identical budgets in three subcodes ($250,000 in personnel, $35,000 in supplies, and $55,000 in equipment, for a total of $340,000) but very different spending rules.

Although agency A has allocated a certain amount of money to each subcode, its spending is not restricted by those amounts; in other words, the manager can spend as needed in each subcode as long as the total spending does not exceed the $340,000 total. Agency B, on the other hand, does not allow spending beyond the allocation in each subcode. Thus if the manager anticipates needing $40,000 in supplies and only $245,000 in personnel, he or she must fill out the appropriate budget change form to request a $5,000 transfer from personnel to supplies. These forms then need to be signed by both the supervising authority and the manager's supervisor before the funds can be transferred and used as desired.

Budget Review

Most U.S. organizations are currently required to adhere to **generally accepted accounting principles** (GAAP), which are established by the Financial Accounting Standards Board. GAAP is the accepted set of accounting rules and procedures used to prepare financial statements, and using GAAP helps ensure that the organization's presentation of financial information is consistent, relevant, reliable, and comparable. A majority of other countries now use the International Financial Reporting Standards (IFRS), and there has been some movement toward convergence of the two sets of standards and some discussion of adopting IFRS in the United States.

Cash Versus Accrual Accounting

GAAP recognizes two types of accounting systems: cash and accrual. In a **cash-based accounting system**, revenue is reported when collected and expenses are reported when paid. In an **accrual-based accounting system**, which is generally preferred by GAAP, revenue is reported when earned and expenses are reported when obligated to be paid. Here are three examples to illustrate how these two systems operate.

Example 1 An institution rents space to a 6-week summer camp that operates for 2 weeks in June and 4 weeks in July. The total rental payment of $60,000 is received in June. In a cash-based accounting system, the full $60,000 is recorded as June revenue. In an accrual-based accounting system, $20,000 (2 weeks of revenue) is recorded in June and $40,000 (4 weeks of revenue) is recorded in July.

Example 2 An agency makes one $600 payment for a 3-year membership (e.g., publication subscription, professional association dues, access to an online survey service). In a cash accounting system, the entire expense is recorded when paid. In an accrual accounting system, the expense is allocated over the 3 years of the membership.

Example 3 A patron pays $600 for a full year of facility membership. In a cash system, the revenue is recorded in the month in which it is paid; in an accrual system, the revenue is evenly distributed ($50 per month) over the 12 months of the membership.

Reviewing Financial Statements

It is important to periodically review financial statements in order to verify the veracity of the information they present and to monitor the unit's financial performance.

To verify the accuracy of information presented in a financial statement, compare actual performance to what is reported in the statement. For example, if the **point-of-sale** (POS) system shows $4,128 in merchandise sales for March, the financial statement should also show $4,128 in merchandise sales for March. Similarly, if POS rentals totaled $1,800 and departmental transfers totaled $525 for rentals in August, then the financial statement should record $2,325 in rental sales for August. If the department submitted documentation indicating $32,190 in part-time payroll expenses for October, that same amount should be reflected in the financial statement.

Unfortunately, mistakes happen in financial reporting. For example, a mistake in inputting an account number could send the recreation department's revenue to the parking department, or a number might be transposed, or an expense might be debited to the wrong subcode, after which a new clerk trying to fix the previous mistake might debit the wrong subcode again instead of crediting it. The best way to catch, and correct, mistakes is to frequently review the financial statements.

Some variations are expected, whereas others constitute mistakes. Table 4.5 presents 4 months of a P&L statement that includes the following examples:

- There is significant variation in the membership line, but membership revenue is expected to be highest in January because voluntary memberships at the university recreation center are more frequently purchased at the start of the academic term. In addition, in northern climates the coldest months are the busiest months for a recreation facility.
- The cable TV line is an example of an ongoing expense that doesn't change from month to month, so the manager is looking for consistency; it is easy to see here that the wrong account was debited in December and two numbers were transposed in February.
- The computer line is an example of a subcode that is used only periodically (often for one or two big purchases a year); as a result, it is neither unusual nor unexpected to see several months of inactivity followed by a large purchase.
- The part-time wages line is an example of an expense that varies from month to month, but the differences should be easy to explain. In this case, January shows a larger part-time payroll expense because of the increased facility usage (and therefore higher staffing levels) during the cold months, and although December usually has a lower part-time payroll expense at a university because it includes a substantial

Table 4.5 Four-Month Snapshot of a P&L Statement

	November	December	January	February
REVENUE				
Membership	112,695	143,781	206,136	154,198
Instructional classes	5,733	24,336	18,423	11,728
EXPENSES				
Cable TV	346	0	346	364
Contract services	0	346	0	0
Computers	0	0	0	3,300
Part-time wages	38,281	52,882	48,102	46,553

break period, the December expense is higher here because it includes three 2-week pay periods instead of the usual two.

Thus you can see that is much easier to understand and review financial statements if you are aware of the various factors that can influence revenue and expense lines.

Periodic review of financial statements is also an important tool for monitoring the unit's performance; in fact, financial performance should be reviewed at least quarterly and preferably monthly. Budget actuals should be compared with both the budgeted figures and the projected or expected performance. Because budgets are submitted up to a year before they take effect, circumstances often change in the interim, which means that performance expectations for the unit may vary substantially from what was approved for the budget.

When reviewing the budget, compare monthly revenue and expenditures with the budgeted amounts for that time period. Compare them also with the figures for previous months and with the same month in the previous year. Consider any changes in circumstances that would affect the unit's financial performance (e.g., increased local unemployment might explain a decrease in membership revenue). Also analyze the variations in the numbers: Are there reasonable explanations for any discrepancies?

Table 4.6 shows 4 months of earnings in three revenue subcodes for a university operation; in this example, one-third (33.3%) of the year has elapsed. Simply comparing the percentages of revenue collected is not overly helpful unless revenue is expected to be earned in a relatively uniform manner over the course of the fiscal year, which is not usually the case in a university recreation center, where generated revenues are often seasonal, or tied to the academic calendar, or both. More funds are typically earned when school is in session (August through May), and revenue from membership and programs is often highest in the winter months (January through March). In this light, we need not be concerned about the seemingly subpar performance (less than 33.3%) in the membership and programs categories. The high percentage in the rentals category is also expected, since rentals are generally highest in the summer months when more space is available due to academic break periods.

Table 4.6 Reviewing the Budget

	Budget	July	August	September	October	Total	Percentage
REVENUE							
Membership	825,000	49,224	56,726	70,142	62,448	238,540	28.9%
Rentals	45,000	13,250	3,225	150	4,100	20,725	46.1%
Programs	210,000	2,648	29,456	12,844	10,234	55,182	26.3%
Total revenue	1,080,000	65,122	89,407	83,136	76,782	314,447	29.1%

An **encumbrance** is a charge that is pending on a budget. If a purchase requisition has been submitted, but the item has not yet been received (and thus payment has not been made), then the amount owed is listed on the financial report as an encumbrance. Table 4.7 shows how an encumbrance may be shown on a financial report and illustrates the fact that, although the funds have yet to be paid, the encumbrance decreases the amount available for spending.

Table 4.7 Example of an Encumbrance

	Budget	YTD actuals	Encumbered	Remaining final budget
Equipment	85,000	24,311	11,980	48,709

Adjusting Performance Expectations

Reviewing monthly financial statements gives the manager a clearer understanding of the organization's overall performance. He or she can use that understanding to make year-end projections and any necessary adjustments in operations. It is advisable for the manager to start producing a projected year-end budget in the second half of the fiscal year.

If any revenues are projected to fall short of budgeted levels, the manager should make adjustments in the corresponding direct, variable expense categories. Here is a simple example: If private swim lessons were expected to earn $1,000 in revenue and spend $800 in direct, variable expenses but the year-end projected revenues were only $500 (thus 50% of the budgeted amount), then the direct, variable expenses for that area should be adjusted down to $400.Table 4.8 shows a more complex example.

In this example, we are 7 months (58.3%) into the fiscal year (7 months / 12 months = 58.3%). Projected year-end revenue from fitness services is expected to be just $131,000, which is $19,000 lower than the budgeted amount. In this example, fitness services are priced to produce a 25% profit ($150,000 revenue less $112,500 expenses equals $37,500 profit). Because in this example the direct expenses are variable (i.e., vary with output), the projected part-time wages for fitness services should be adjusted down to 75 percent of the projected year-end revenue. (i.e., instead of earning $150,000 and spending $112,500, you are expecting to earn $131,000 and thus only spend $98,250, which is $14,250 less than was budgeted). Making this adjustment in revenues and expenses lowers the variance from the fitness services area from $19,000 to $4,750 (the difference between the $14,250 of savings in part-time wages and the unrealized $19,000 revenues from fitness services).

Similarly, revenue from facility memberships is expected to come in under budget by $8,000. Because no direct costs are associated with membership in this example, there is no corresponding expense to decrease to partially offset the "lost" revenue. Thus, if the organization expects the bottom line net profit of $111,626 to be maintained, the manager must find an additional $9,876 of expenses to trim in the remaining 5 months of the fiscal year or find ways to generate more revenue.

It is important for the manager to clearly understand what flexibility exists for making adjustments in the budget once it is approved. If, for example, revenue generated in a fiscal year is clearly outpacing the budgeted number, does the manager have the authority to spend those additional dollars (excluding the additional expenditures required to generate the additional

Table 4.8 Projected Statement

	Budget	Actuals	Projected year-end	Variance (budget–projected)	Percentage (actual/budget)
REVENUE					
Membership	724,000	418,388	716,000	(8,000)	57.8%
Fitness services	150,000	73,724	131,000	(19,000)	49.1%
All other revenue	328,000	190,200	328,000	0	58.0%
Total revenue	1,202,000	682,312	1,175,000	(27,000)	56.8%
EXPENSES					
Part-time wages (fitness services)	112,500	56,229	98,250	14,250	50%
All other expenses	977,874	557,390	975,000	2,874	57%
Total expenses	1,090,374	613,619	1,073,250	17,124	56.3%
Net profit (loss)	111,626	68,693	101,750	9,876	

Statement date: January 31, 2011. Fiscal year: July 1, 2011, through June 30, 2012.

funds), or do all the extra funds go back to the university?

INTERNAL CONTROLS

Internal controls are measures enacted by an organization to ensure compliance with policies and regulations, to protect the organization and its assets by managing risk, and to help the organization achieve its business objectives efficiently and effectively.

Components of Internal Controls

Internal controls involve five elements: the control environment, risk assessment, control activities, communication and information, and monitoring.

- **Control environment**—Does the organization's culture encourage ethical behavior? Does the organization hire qualified and competent staff? Does it establish clear lines of authority and responsibility? Are the organization's policies comprehensive and clear?
- **Risk assessment**—Does the organization systematically analyze and identify risks and assemble a risk management plan? Are the costs of the control activities weighed against the risk of inaction? Does the organization consider what the highest-risk legal areas are and consider reputational risk?
- **Control activities**—Do the controls sufficiently mitigate risk? Are policies in place to help the organization reach its goals and objectives?
- **Communication and information**—Do staff members have the information they need in order to do their jobs? Does management have access to the information it needs in order to monitor the effectiveness of policies, systems, and staff? Is information made available in a timely manner?
- **Monitoring**—Are activities regularly assessed to ensure that the controls are adequate? Are internal and external audits performed periodically?

Types of Controls

There are two types of controls: preventive and detective. **Preventive controls** are intended to prevent theft or fraud from occurring. Examples in a recreation operation include alarming the doors, password-protecting documents, securing assets, requiring supervisory signatures on requisitions, and segregating duties. **Detective controls** are designed to detect theft or fraud after it has happened. Examples include reconciling POS reports with inventory counts, monitoring the budget for unexplained inconsistencies, and conducting audits. Some controls, such as surveillance cameras, serve both a preventive and a detective function.

Balancing Risk and Controls

Managing risk means effectively balancing risk and controls. The benefit of implementing a control should outweigh the cost of the control, in terms of both tangible and intangible factors. It is important to avoid being either too lenient (e.g., leaving the doors to the facility unlocked) or too excessive (e.g., requiring three forms of identification to enter the facility). Extreme leniency with controls could lead to losing assets, having staff make poor business decisions, or ruining the reputation of the organization. Excessive controls could lead to reduced productivity, low staff morale, noncompliance from staff, or poor customer service.

It is helpful to classify operational activities graphically by representing the range of high risk probability to low risk probability on one axis and the range of high negative outcome to low negative outcome on the other axis (see an example in figure 4.2). The activities that need immediate attention are those with high risk probability and high negative outcome (e.g., activities that are likely to happen and can have a devastating effect on the operation). The next most important quadrant addresses activities with high negative outcome but low risk probability (e.g., embezzlement, which could profoundly affect your bottom line and reputation but is less likely to happen than many other forms of theft). The third group to get attention should be those with low negative outcome but

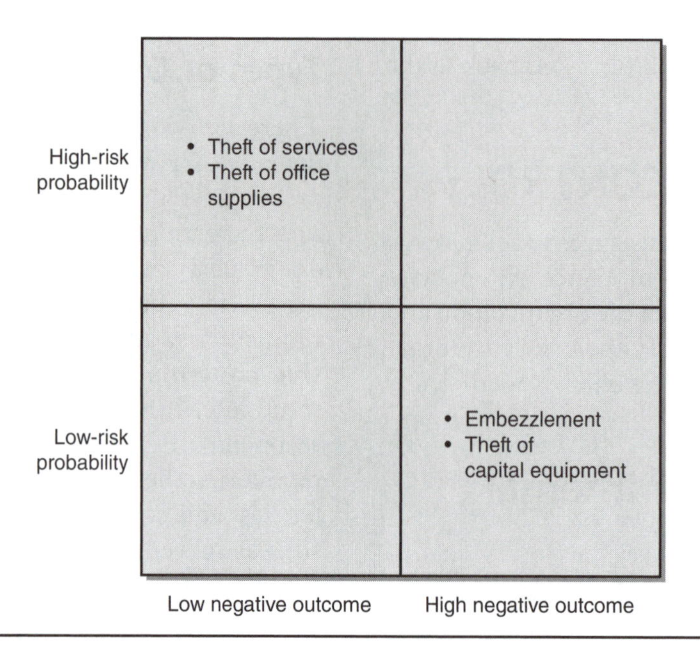

Figure 4.2 Matrix of risk vs. impact.

high risk probability (e.g., users sneaking into the facility without paying, which carries fairly low monetary and reputational risk but is not an uncommon occurrence). And of course the last activities to address are those with both low probability of occurrence and a low negative outcome.

Additional Concepts

Materiality is an auditing concept that addresses the relative significance of a discrepancy in the financial statements and supporting documentation; the key determinant is whether eliminating the discrepancy would change the judgment of the person relying on the information. No standard amount or percentage is used to determine materiality, which varies by industry and circumstances. Here is an example: If $1,200 is missing from revenue, the amount would be considered material if total revenue were $10,000 but likely immaterial if total revenue were $4,500,000.

Audit of financial statements refers to the process in which an organization's financial statements are reviewed by an independent party to determine whether the financial statements are accurate, complete, relevant, and fairly presented.

Collusion exists when two or more people conspire to commit an illegal act, such as fraud or theft.

Bonding insurance protects against loss caused by fraud, dishonesty, or incompetence. Bonding might be required for staff whose job responsibilities involve activities in which it is difficult to minimize risk (e.g., handling large amounts of cash, working independently in areas with little supervision).

Reviewing Your Internal Controls

Each area of the organization should be reviewed and analyzed to ensure that appropriate procedures are in place; areas to be evaluated include general controls, cash receipts, petty cash, inventory, equipment, information security, workstation security, and facility security. Here are three important concepts to incorporate into workplace policies:

- **Separation of duties**—Ensure that at least two different staff members are involved in the various steps of a transaction process (e.g., one person processes the sale, another person reconciles the accounts, another person makes the deposit, and another person reviews the records).
- **Access limitations**—Restrict access to assets and information to a small group of authorized employees.

- **Authorization policies**—Articulate and enforce policies that dictate how transactions are to be conducted.

Here is a sample checklist of key questions for cash-handling procedures:

- Are all cash transactions entered into a point-of-sale (or cash register) system, and are customers always given a receipt?
- Does the organization accept only those checks made payable to the organization, and are checks immediately stamped with a restrictive endorsement (e.g., for deposit only)?
- Are cash receipts compared daily to POS or cash register totals?
- Are duties segregated for cash receipt collection, reconciliation, deposit, and verification (i.e., are different staff members responsible for accepting cash and checks, reconciling the accounts, making the daily deposits, and reviewing the financial statements?) Collusion is less likely when different people are involved in different segments of the process.
- Are daily deposits accompanied by signed deposit forms?
- Is the staff member completing the daily inventory lists different from the person selling the merchandise?
- Are staff prohibited from using cash to give reimbursements or refunds? Are refunds required to be approved by management?
- Are cash-handling duties rotated periodically?
- Are cash receipts stored safely until deposit?
- Is access to cash receipts limited to the lowest possible number of staff?

A manager is also well advised to consider how security could be breached and how theft could occur in a variety of typical situations, then consider implementing processes and systems to reduce the identified risks. For example, if management is concerned about frontline staff stealing money, it might be wise to implement internal controls such as reconciling daily POS reports with merchandise inventory counts, segregating the cash-handling duties from the reconciliation duties (so that one person handles the cash transaction, and another person balances the register at the end of the shift), requiring that sales receipts be shown for entrance into the facility (e.g., staff member A sells a guest pass and gives the patron a receipt, which is collected by staff member B, thus making it less likely that staff member A pockets the money, since it has to be entered into the POS system to generate a receipt), or installing a surveillance camera focused on the POS system.

Although internal controls cannot completely eliminate mistakes or illegal behavior, they can significantly reduce risk and improve operational effectiveness and efficiency.

SUMMARY

Although a budget is typically a short-term plan of resource allocation, savvy managers also use budgets as tools to help position their organizations for long-term success. A well-constructed budget plan allows a department to operate successfully in the upcoming fiscal year and also to strengthen its financial health in the long run. A budget should include some latitude for future opportunities and managed risk so that the organization is well positioned to take advantage of, or cope with, a changing landscape.

Recreation professionals at every level of the organization are responsible for budgeting and internal controls, whether they are tracking student payroll, researching equipment purchases, determining program pricing levels, compiling a capital spending plan, or overseeing several multimillion-dollar budgets. Given the increasing complexity of recreation management, recreation professionals must be knowledgeable about and competent in working with the operation's financial elements.

Glossary

accrual-based accounting system—System, preferred according to generally accepted accounting principles, in which revenue is reported when earned and expenses are reported when obligated to be paid.

audit of financial statements—Review of an organization's financial statements by an independent party to determine whether they are accurate, complete, relevant, and fairly presented.

bonding insurance—Insurance against loss caused by fraud, dishonesty, or incompetence.

bottom-up budgeting—Process in which a recreation manager develops and submits a budget to be approved by supervising authorities.

break-even program—Program for which revenue generated equal expenses incurred.

budget—Plan of expected income and expenditures for an organization.

capital budget—Budget used to finance long-term assets or projects (e.g., property, plant, and equipment; furniture, fixtures, and equipment).

cash-based accounting system—System in which revenue is reported when collected and expenses are reported when paid.

cash inflow—Funds coming into the organization (e.g., earned interest, incoming loans, revenue).

cash outflow—Charge incurred by the organization from business operations; also called expenditure or expense.

centralized budget—Single budget used by the various units within an organization and controlled from the top.

collusion—Conspiring by two or more people to commit an illegal act (e.g., fraud, theft).

comparative statement—Financial statement that includes more than one fiscal period.

cost center—Unit that has expenditures but does not have control over revenue generation (e.g., human resources department).

decentralized budget—Practice in which separate budgets exist for units within an organization and budget control is delegated down to the lowest possible level.

detective controls—Internal controls designed to detect theft or fraud after it has happened.

direct cost—Expenses that can be attributed directly to a specific program or service (e.g., the cost of tents for an outdoor adventure program).

encumbrance—Charge that is pending but not yet charged on a budget.

expense—Another name for a cash outflow or expenditure.

fiscal year—Period of time for which a budget is developed.

fixed cost—Expense that does not vary with the level of output or participation. Fixed costs can be indirect (e.g., rent, depreciation) or direct (e.g., salary for program staff).

generally accepted accounting principles (GAAP)—The accepted set of accounting rules and procedures, established by the Financial Accounting Standards Board, used to prepare financial statements in the United States.

incremental budgeting—Method of budget development that starts with a previous budget and changes various line items incrementally based on anticipated changes in the operation.

indirect cost—Expense that cannot be attributed directly to a specific program or service (e.g., building depreciation, custodial costs).

internal controls—Measures enacted by an organization to ensure compliance with policies and regulations, to protect the organization and its assets by managing risk, and to help the organization achieve its business objectives efficiently and effectively.

materiality—Audit concept involving the relative significance of a discrepancy in the financial statements and supporting documentation (the key determinant is whether the elimination of the discrepancy would have changed the judgment of the person relying on the information).

operating budget—Detailed projection of estimated income and expenses during a defined, short-term fiscal period; does not include capital (long-term) outlays.

point-of-sale (POS)—Computerized system that facilitates the sales process (e.g., processing credit card payments, printing receipts, tracking inventory).

preventive controls—Internal controls intended to prevent theft or fraud.

profit—The surplus after total expenses are subtracted from total revenue.

profit and loss (P&L) statement—Financial statement showing budgeted and actual revenues and expenses over a defined period of time; also referred to as an income statement.

profit center—Unit that controls the generation of revenues and expenses.

pro forma statement—Financial statement based on assumptions different from the current reality.

projected statement—Financial statement that estimates revenues and expenses for a fiscal period based on expected outcomes.

revenue—Funds earned through business operations.

subsidized program—Program in which revenues generated are less than expenses incurred (thus the program must be subsidized by funds generated by other programs).

top-down budgeting—Process in which the supervising authority dictates a dollar figure for the budget and the budget administrator then creates a plan for making the operational elements fit within the stated financial parameters.

unrelated business income tax (UBIT)—Tax paid by tax-exempt organizations on revenue earned from activities considered to be unrelated business.

variable cost—Expense that varies with the level of output or participation. Variable costs can be indirect (e.g., electricity, telecommunication costs) or direct (e.g., personal training wages).

variance—The difference between the budgeted number and the actual number. The amount is favorable if the actual revenue number is higher than budgeted, or if the actual expense number is lower than budgeted.

zero-based budgeting—Method of budget development that requires building a budget from a base of zero (rather than starting with a past budget) and needing to justify all expenses.

CHAPTER

5

Marketing

Evelyn Kwan Green
University of Southern Mississippi

Aaron Hill
The New School, New York City

Bradley Hunt
University of Minnesota, Twin Cities

Marketing has been part of trade and commerce systems for centuries. Some scholars date the practice of marketing back to the ancient Greek philosophers Plato and Aristotle (Shaw & Jones, 2005). Today we mostly think of marketing as a highly evolved practice that fuels the corporate economy. Increasingly, however, the science of marketing is also being applied to nonprofit and cause-driven organizations, including those that provide campus recreational sports programs and services.

This chapter first presents the fundamentals of program promotion, then describes a pragmatic approach to constructing a marketing plan and seeking sponsorship funding. Finally, we introduce the five phases of branding an organization, which is a growing trend in the recreation industry.

PROGRAM PROMOTION

Promotion is a catchall term that has become popular as one of the four Ps of marketing. **Promotion** is "the persuasive flow of marketing communication," including advertising, sales and sales force, promotions, public relations, publicity, packaging, point-of-sale displays, and brand name or identity (Green, Miller, & Cook, 1999). Before the marketing concept was introduced to campus recreational sports, many professionals in the field equated promotion with marketing. In reality, marketing is the umbrella that covers promotion as well as place, price, and product. Together, these four variables make up the marketing mix, which is commonly referred to in terms of the four Ps (Borden, 1965). Alternatively, the marketing mix can be addressed in terms of the four Cs—communication, convenience, cost, and customer needs and wants (Lauterborn, 1990).

Campus recreational sports departments often develop a program, event, or activity first and then decide how to market or promote it. This is a product-oriented approach, in which advertising and promotions are used to stimulate "wanting" in the market (Green et al., 1999). Even though this approach is less effective and less efficient than we would like, most campus recreational sports departments depended on it prior to the acceptance and proliferation of campus recreational sports marketing. The introduction of marketing professionals into the field enabled campus recreational sports departments to evolve their promotional efforts from a product orientation to a market orientation. In the market-oriented approach, the department first determines its market's needs and wants and only then develops programs, events, and activities (Green et al., 1999).

Marketing Planning Cycle

In the market-oriented approach, a marketing professional implements a planning cycle to determine the market's needs and wants. The **marketing planning cycle** involves analysis, research, plan development, implementation, and evaluation (see figure 5.1).

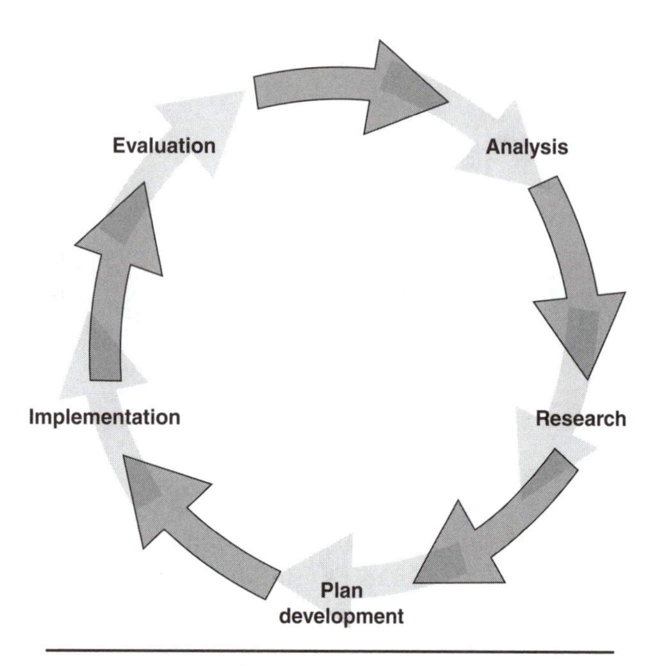

Figure 5.1 Marketing planning cycle.

Reprinted, by permission, from NIRSA, 2008, *Campus recreation: Essentials for the professional* (Champaign, IL: Human Kinetics), 227.

SWOT Analysis

Marketing analysis involves analyzing the department's strengths, weaknesses, opportunities, and threats (SWOT). Factors in a **SWOT analysis** could include student wages, office technology, and facility or equipment upgrades. The following scenario provides an example of how SWOT analysis can be used in a campus recreational sports setting. Let's imagine that a campus recreational sports department is thinking about creating its own social networking account to better connect with the student population on campus.

- **Strengths**—The Campus Recreational Sports Center (CRSC) is full of student employees who have social networking knowledge and experience.
- **Weaknesses**—Although the CRSC employs more than 100 students, none of them work a regular 40-hour week, and the department's marketing professional does not have time to manage a social networking site.
- **Opportunities**—The CRSC has more than 2,500 visitors every day, and 85 percent of these patrons are students. If the department committed to starting a social networking account, there could be significant interest if it were properly promoted.
- **Threats**—If the department were to dedicate more time to its Facebook account, other CRSC programs would receive less attention, which could ultimately lead to lower revenue and participation levels.

PEST Analysis

In addition to analyzing its internal environment, the campus recreational sports department must also perform a **PEST analysis**—a macroanalysis of external factors that can potentially affect the success of its operation. This macroanalysis includes political, economic, social, and technological factors (PEST). Let's return to the scenario used in the preceding SWOT analysis to see how PEST analysis can be used in a campus recreational sports setting.

- **Political factors**—Social networking in today's society is becoming increasingly complex. If the department introduced a social networking site, it would need to set strict parameters for managing all incoming and outgoing content.
- **Economic factors**—Membership prices will rise in 2 months due to an increase in state sales tax, which increases the department's need to determine how it could be affected economically if it were to dedicate more of its time to social networking rather than to promotion of certain programs and services.
- **Social factors**—The campus culture trends toward expertise on the topic of social networking. Therefore, if the CRSC supplies a social networking site to its patrons, the demand for real-time information will increase considerably. Thus the department

must be prepared to constantly update the site if it is to be embraced by the campus culture.

- **Technological factors**—Other campus departments regularly post videos and pictures of their recent events, but the CRSC does not own a high-quality video or digital camera. In addition, the department's shared drive does not have the space to begin housing large video or image files.

Target Audience

Before initiating promotion, the department needs to identify its **target audience**—that is, the market for whose needs and wants the program or service is to be developed. The identification process should also involve studying and considering other marketing variables (the four Ps) that can affect the success or failure of the program or service. For instance, belly dancing might be identified as a fitness activity that students (the customers) want, but the effectiveness of the belly dance class promotion (communication) could be diminished if the department fails to evaluate the feasibility of the class schedule (taking into account both place and convenience) or cost (e.g., of giving up a part-time job in order to take the class).

Current Audience

Marketing from the inside out means taking care of current customers before reaching out to prospective new customers (Green, 2000). If a campus recreational sports department is unable to meet the needs of its current customers, it is unlikely to find success in attracting new ones. Moreover, it makes economic sense to focus the department's efforts and resources on customers who are already sold on the programs and services. The goal here is to retain their patronage by continuing to meet their needs and wants—the higher the retention rate of current customers, the less pressure to attract new ones.

Program or Service Life Cycle

Every program or service has a life cycle, which begins with an introductory phase followed by growth. Once a program or service peaks, it has reached maturation, whereupon it can potentially plunge into a state of decline or be rejuvenated into a new program or service life cycle (Green et al., 1999). Tracking the life cycle of a program or service is a key role played by the marketing professional in campus recreational sports. The marketing professional needs to observe the cycle and use SWOT and PEST analyses to identify positioning or differentiation opportunities during the maturation phase in order to revitalize the program's or service's appeal to current and target customers.

Promotional Strategies for Campus Recreational Sports Programs and Services

The staple programs and services offered by a typical campus recreational sports department are intramural sports, sport clubs, fitness, wellness, outdoor adventure, aquatics, and special events. Each type of program or service calls for its own promotional strategies; the one-size-fits-all approach is not appropriate for promotional efforts. Here are some of the most common promotional strategies used by campus recreational sports departments.

Printed media, which include flyers, brochures, and calendars, can be expensive and wasteful. Developing printed media is also time consuming and requires computer skills and specialized knowledge.

Banners are relatively expensive because they include event dates and thus are seldom recyclable. Banners hung in strategic locations, however, are highly visible, which appeals to sponsors.

Before the Internet, electronic signage constituted the extent of technology in the campus recreational sports arena. Because of the high cost of such systems and the skills required to operate and maintain them, most electronic signs were brought onto campuses via sponsorships and were revered more as status symbols than as effective promotional tools.

Another promotional strategy involves vending machines. Soft drink, energy drink, and bottled water companies are often interested in exchanging sponsorship dollars for the right to place their vending machines in strategic locations in campus recreational sports facilities and across campus. This promotional strategy is often a win–win situation for both the department and the sponsor.

Press releases and publicity are two of the cheapest yet most credible forms of promotion. The marketing professional should possess the communication and public relations skills to consistently promote the department's programs and services to its target communities.

Advertising is the most costly form of promotion, and few campus recreational sports departments can afford it. Most advertisement derives from sponsorships solicited from the department, such as placing the campus recreational sports department logo on Greek life rush T-shirts.

Campus recreational sports is also a key consumer of promotional items, which range from intramural T-shirts to pens displaying the department's contact information. Such items serve as mobile forms of promotion since stakeholders wear or otherwise use them while out and about. Promotional items can be expensive, but most campus recreational sports departments budget for them.

Signs can be placed on department vehicles, such as golf carts and vans. Their mobility makes this promotional strategy a highly visible one.

In the 21st century, thanks to the ubiquity of the Internet, electronic media (e.g., websites, e-mail marketing, podcasting, online reservations) have become the most popular form of promotion for campus recreational sports departments. The medium itself is usually free, but technological skills and knowledge of web-based marketing are needed in order to develop and launch an effective website. For electronic promotional strategies to be effective, the department needs to ensure that the person or people given the responsibility possess both technical and marketing knowledge, as well as the skills to use this promotional avenue efficiently and effectively. Issues to address include the department website's loading speed and optimization of the site to appear high on the results lists generated by web search engines. For these reasons, it can be costly to simply rely on using graduate assistants who possess only rudimentary skills in handling electronic media promotion and who inevitably graduate, thus making it hard to attain consistency in communication and promotion efforts.

MARKETING PLAN

What is a **marketing plan**? And why do you need one? This section looks at the practical

Photo courtesy of University of Minnesota Recreational Sports.

Promotional items can provide mobile promotion of your program as stakeholders wear and carry them.

application of a proven marketing strategy to guide you through the process of developing a marketing plan.

Although marketing is commonly viewed as an "art"—with accoutrements such as creative posters, new media, and colorful communications—the practice of marketing is actually quite scientific and analytical. The process of creating a marketing plan allows an organization to flesh out its goals and objectives and examine how they relate to program issues of marketing concern, such as participation rates, revenue from fee-based opt-in programs, and the program's public image both on campus and in the wider community.

The process of creating a marketing plan is iterative and comprehensive. If done well, it should take about a year to complete, but don't be overwhelmed by this time frame—the outcome of all that work is extremely valuable. When broken down into manageable steps, the process should go smoothly and efficiently. Why does it take so long? Consensus building can take time, but it is absolutely necessary to the success of the marketing plan as a living document. The plan must be embraced by all staff—not just the marketing staff.

The marketing plan is created in seven steps:

1. Define your rationale.
2. Define your environment.
3. Perform a situational analysis and conduct research.
4. Identify your central goals and issues.
5. Develop tactics and strategies.
6. Write the plan.
7. Evaluate the plan.

Step 1: Define Your Rationale

This first step involves explaining the broad goals and major desired outcomes that your plan will help you achieve. Here are some common goals:

- **Increased participation in programs**: Would you like to increase program participation rates or the frequency of visits to the facility? By how much? By when?
- **Development of revenue-based programs**: Often, programs and facilities are included in a student fee paid as part of tuition. However, niche programs and services, or those provided outside the student base, are paid for by fees. What are your goals for these revenue-based services? What new revenue-based services are you considering?
- **Use of facilities**: How are usage rates? Could they be improved? Alternatively, are facilities stretched too thin? Do you need to evaluate the possibility of new facilities?
- **Enhancing the facility's image**: How are you viewed by students? The administration? Other departments? Are you merely a "program" or "facility," or does the university see you as integral to its mission—helping to fulfill other broad goals such as recruitment, retention, and student development?

Step 2: Define Your Environment

You can define your environment in three main ways:

- **Structure**: Take the time to define your situation thoroughly and exhaustively. How is your department structured internally? How is it structured within the university system? Who makes final decisions? How are those decisions reached?
- **Processes**: Create flow charts to represent common interactions with your customers (see figure 5.2 for an example). Doing so helps you illustrate these interactions and more easily identify improvements and possible collaborations as you develop the plan.
- **Institution direction**: What are the institution's priorities? Increased enrollment? Student safety? Define the priorities and begin to look for places where your programs might complement or enhance them.

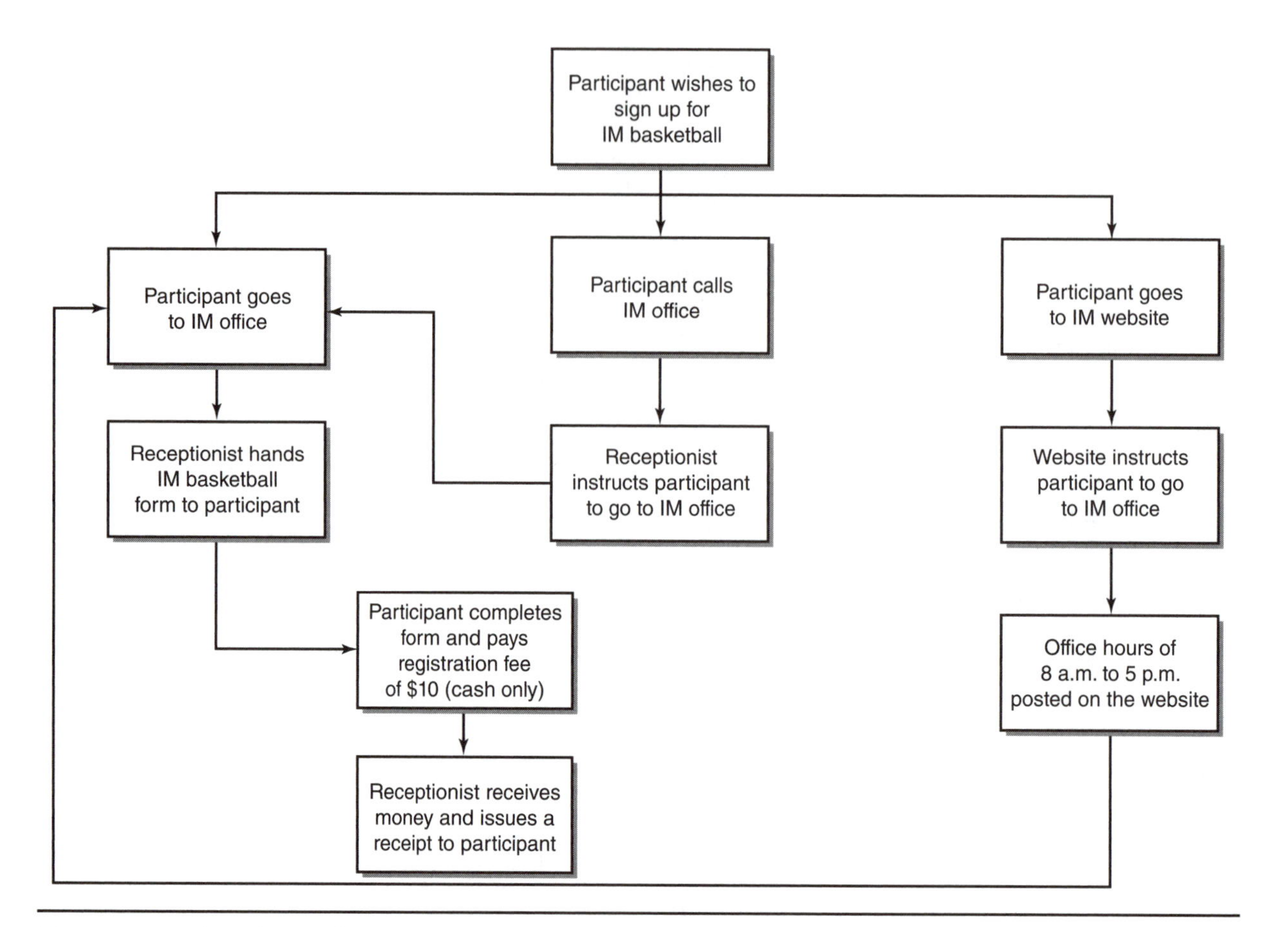

Figure 5.2 Flow charts of customer interactions help you visualize your processes.

Reprinted, by permission, from NIRSA, 2008, *Campus recreation: Essentials for the professional* (Champaign, IL: Human Kinetics), 231.

Step 3: Perform a Situational Analysis and Conduct Research

This step allows you to use the information gained in the previous step to expand your definition of your situation. Use qualitative analysis to map out specific parallels to similar departments within your institution, similar departments at other institutions, and overall trends in the field (i.e., NIRSA committees). This step involves doing a lot of benchmarking research—that is, capturing what others are doing and how that relates to what you want to do. Here are some tools for performing this step:

- SWOT analysis (strengths, weaknesses, opportunities, threats)
- PEST analysis (political, economic, social, technological)
- Table of key players
- Decision makers and allies
- Competitors and critics

Step 4: Identify Your Central Goals and Issues

During the previous three steps, prominent themes will have begun to emerge. In this consensus-building step, the senior staff of your department should work together, preferably during an off-site, day-long retreat for which the agenda is oriented strictly toward working together to narrowly define the marketing-related central goals and issues. These resulting statements should include the broad context as well as specific, measurable goals. Here are two examples:

- Participation in campus recreational sports programs is linked to greater satisfaction with the overall college experience. Satisfaction among students increases the university's retention rate, which is an institutional priority. Goal: Increase overall student participation in campus recreational sports programs from 66 to 75 percent by 2010.

- The department's mission includes enhancing the lifelong health of young people by educating them about exercise benefits and instilling in them practices that establish lifelong good habits. Goal: Reach every student with a strategic message of healthy living on campus and beyond.

Step 5: Develop Tactics and Strategies

The tactics and strategies developed in this step stem from the central goals and issues developed in step 4. It is also a consensus-building step. To reach consensus, the best approach is systematic. First, spend a half day transcribing *all* ideas by participants and taking care not to judge any of the ideas. Next, decide what criteria will be used in judging the ideas. Here are some suggestions:

- **Mission**: Complements the mission and agenda of the department and the institution.
- **Feasibility**: Could be reasonably implemented.
- **Cost**: Fits within the department's ability to pay or warrants pursuing additional funding.
- **Image**: Enhances the department's image in the eyes of participants and the administration and does not create political animosity.
- **Equality**: Reaches out to all populations.

Systemically compare all ideas against the criteria and desired project outcomes; this process is illustrated in table 5.1.

Step 6: Write the Plan

By now, you should have captured almost everything you need in order to create a single, cohesive document to serve as your final marketing plan. The structure should resemble the following outline:

1. Central goal or issue
   1.1. Strategy (and assessment measure)
      1.1.1. Tactic
         1.1.1.1. Plan for implementation

Table 5.1 Criteria

Ideas	Mission	Feasibility	Cost	Image	Equality
	+	+	–	+	+
Place full-page ads in newspaper for intramurals.	Intramural sports are an important part of the mission	Good relationship with newspaper	More than budgeted; takes away from other programs	Would enhance our brand	Reaches all students
	+	–	–	–	–
Build outdoor pool.	Great recreation	This is Michigan	No capital allocations	May seem extravagant	Benefits only summer students
	+	–	–	+	+
Offer free personal training session to all students.	Great for educating in good habits	Not nearly enough staff	Would be extremely costly	Great outreach	Great for those who can't afford to pay
	+	+	+	+	–
Have residence hall competitions.	Outreach	Good relationship with residence life	Could get grant from residence hall	Campus outreach	Misses off-campus students

Here is an example:

1. Our department mission includes enhancing the lifelong health of young people by educating them about exercise benefits and instilling in them practices that establish lifelong good habits.
   1.1. Reach every student with a strategic message of healthy living on campus and beyond. (Measure success by the total percentage of students who receive exposure to this message on an annual basis.)
      1.1.1. Integrate a campus recreational sports presentation into the new student orientation process.
         1.1.1.1. Meet with admissions staff (director, by 1/31/12).
         1.1.1.2. Create presentation (assistant director for marketing, by 2/28/12).
         1.1.1.3. Deliver presentations (alternating programming staff, summer 2012).
      1.1.2. Offer a free personal training session to all first-year students.
         1.1.2.1. Create a structure for free session (fitness director, by 4/30/12).
         1.1.2.2. Create signage for recreation facility (assistant director for marketing, by 5/31/12).
         1.1.2.3. Create a sign-up process (facilities manager, by 6/30/12).

Step 7: Evaluate the Plan

It is essential to evaluate every element of the marketing plan on an annual basis. The plan should be a living document, and changes in course should be easily decided on the basis of evaluation and assessment results.

In addition to assessment, the data you collect will be valuable for structuring your intelligence about how marketing strategies and tactics should evolve. Every interaction with a participant provides an opportunity to collect quantitative data about his or her experience; at the same time, avoid overassessment—there is a limit to participants' willingness to complete surveys.

Here are some sources for data collection:

- Evaluation survey (after the program or experience)
- Random sampling techniques to get broader data from fewer participants
- University databases

This process constitutes an undertaking for sure, but the result is tremendously valuable. A successful plan culminates from an analytic framework and involves the entire department staff and allies in its creation. Although the process can take a full year—or sometimes longer—it can be broken into manageable pieces. In measuring outcomes, it is helpful to quantify as much as possible (e.g., satisfaction is abstract but can be measured on a 10-point scale).

SPONSORSHIP SOLICITATION

Sponsorship involves cash or in-kind fees paid to an organization in return for access to the target audience of the program, event, or activity whose commercial potential appeals to the sponsoring organization (Green, Miller, & Cook, 2000). For example, at the University of Southern Mississippi's Payne Center fitness lounge, the Coca-Cola Bottling Company of Hattiesburg sponsored Club Natural High. In exchange for including campus recreational sports' Club Natural High logo on all Dasani vending machines across campus, the bottling company was allowed to place a machine in the fitness lounge, which is located outside the high-traffic fitness area. In this section, we first discuss why campus recreational sports departments need sponsorships, then explore the sponsorship development process.

Campus recreational sports departments, particularly those that are profit centers, often rely on income to defray the cost of putting together an event, program, or activity. Sponsorships—

A vending machine is a good example of a sponsorship.

Photo courtesy of Recreational Sport, The University of Southern Mississippi. Photographer Evelyn Kwan Green.

especially blue-chip sponsors such as Dasani and Nike—increase the visibility and credibility of an event, program, or activity. They also create relationship-building opportunities within the corporate community and sometimes create networking and placement opportunities for students. Sponsorship development requires careful market research, marketing planning, personal selling, negotiation, effective implementation, and follow-through to ensure success for both the sponsor and the department.

Weighing the Decision to Pursue Sponsors

Soliciting sponsors to supplement revenue is a strategic decision not to be taken lightly. Ultimately, in using sponsorships, the department is using the equity of a strong image to sell the right to directly market to its students and customers. First and foremost, then, a campus recreational sports department should participate only in sponsorships that support its mission, programs, and services. Equally important, any sponsors chosen should closely align with the department's mission and goals. Finally, students and customers should be considered. If they believe that programs and services have used invasive marketing techniques, they will likely resist, and you can avoid such a backlash by participating only in sponsorships that make sense for your department. Before embarking on any sponsorship partnership, administrators should ask the hard questions to ensure that it will add value for students and customers.

Market Research

Market research is critical to understanding the potential value of a sponsorship package to the sponsor (Green et al., 2000). To prepare a sponsorship package, the department must know the target audience for the event, program, or activity in terms of demographics, psychographics, and attendance levels. **Psychographics** describe the target audience's lifestyle, education, approximate income, type of career, preferred leisure activities, reading habits, and so on. Target audience data are important to the sponsor in estimating commercial potential and establishing a marketing database for future opportunities. Businesses are willing to pay for data that have strong commercial potential, but a target audience database, for example, is a campus recreational sports department's asset that should never be shared with sponsors. However, the department can give the sponsor statistics that summarize the demographics and characteristics of the target audience as a way of sharing valuable data without jeopardizing the integrity of the database and the trust of the audience. Therefore, it is critical for a campus recreational sports department to attain the expertise to carefully research and analyze its assets (e.g., target audience statistics) and their commercial value to potential sponsors.

Marketing Planning

This step leads to the tangible outcome of developing a sponsorship package. As mentioned earlier, the campus recreational sports department must first identify its assets and their commercial value to potential sponsors. Here are some examples of assets in campus recreational sports and their value to sponsors (Green et al., 2000):

- Marks and logos (promotional rights, official sponsor designation)
- Participating audience, spectators, staff (access for sales, sampling, surveying)
- Talent (athletes, staff, appearance, ID on uniform)
- Vehicles (ID and signage)
- Equipment, scoreboards, message boards, websites (ID, signage, or web banner)
- Venues or facilities (naming rights, signage, display, sampling, sales)
- Publications, collateral materials, websites (guaranteed exposure, impressions, visibility)
- Media buy (guaranteed impressions)
- Passes, event tickets, facility rentals (client, customer, employee entertainment)
- Mailing list (sales, promotional, marketing databases)
- Special events and programs (propriety platforms, sense of ownership)
- Cosponsors (cross promotions, business-to-business relationships)
- Participant or audience survey (market research)
- Merchandise (sales, ID, or promotional use)
- Broadcast and web package (advertising rights)
- Website (ID, banner ads or links, special programs)

Once the department has identified and valued its appropriate assets, it is time to identify potential sponsors. Potential sponsors should not be limited to the obvious (e.g., soliciting Powerade to sponsor an intramural event). The campus recreational sports marketing professional should use creative thinking to uncover unique or niche sponsors that might not ordinarily be considered.

Sponsorship Proposal Package

The department should package its assets into sponsorship opportunities and benefits that are customized to meet targeted sponsors' goals and priorities. A well-crafted proposal demonstrates professionalism and makes the solicitation process more efficient (Green, 2000). A sponsorship proposal should include at least the following components: cover letter, list of sponsor opportunities and benefits, event or

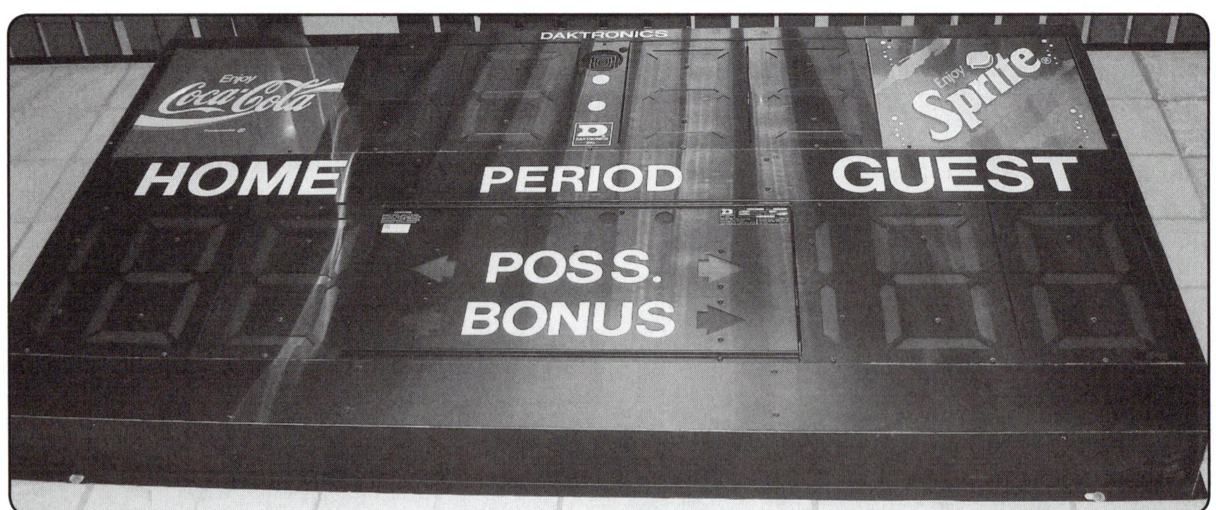

Photo courtesy of Recreational Sport, The University of Southern Mississippi. Photographer Evelyn Kwan Green.

Scoreboards are an asset of the campus recreational sports program that can be used to entice sponsors.

asset details, sponsorship contract, and any options for customization. The proposal can also include any additional information that helps illustrate its merits. Examples include a media buy schedule, press releases or coverage of a previous event, and photos of sponsorship exposure at previous events. The cover letter should state an invitation to participate and provide follow-up contact information. Sponsorship opportunities might include niche marketing, cross-promotion, market research, sales rights, exposure on signage and collateral materials, point-of-sale promotions, client entertainment, and employee benefits. Potential sponsors generally place a high priority on media exposure, increased visibility, positive image building, blue-chip cosponsors, and—most important—brand awareness building.

The sponsorship proposal package must include event details to allow potential sponsors to gauge the feasibility of sponsorship. One key to successful sponsorship solicitation is timing. Most corporations and organizations have their annual budgets planned and earmarked 3 to 4 months before the beginning of the fiscal year, and a good marketing professional stays abreast of potential sponsors' corporate fiscal year and solicits them during their budgeting period. It is best to offer potential sponsors some flexibility by presenting opportunities and benefits in terms of multi-level options. For instance, if a sponsor is not in a good position to commit at the level desired by the campus recreational sports department, the availability of other sponsorship levels can help avoid a total loss of sponsorship.

Personal Selling

Even a well-created sponsorship proposal is useless unless personal selling is involved to close the deal. Sponsorship solicitation often fails from lack of personal follow-through and failure to close the sale. The marketing professional in campus recreational sports must arrange for a face-to-face meeting to address any concerns a sponsor may have that could jeopardize the solicitation process. In the meeting, the marketing professional must convey the benefits to the sponsor and make sure that benefits exceed the cost of sponsorship. The face-to-face meeting also serves as an opportunity to close the sale by having the sponsor sign the contract. Commitments should be solicited while the excitement and enthusiasm are still fresh in the sponsor's mind.

Implementation of Contractual Terms

Once the sponsorship contract is signed, the marketing professional must execute the terms and conditions of the contract. Tangible outcomes must all be documented as proof that the department has delivered on the contract. Examples include press releases, advertisements, and photos of sponsor exposure at the event. Failure to deliver contractual items not only reflects negatively on the department but also could jeopardize future sponsorship opportunities.

Because most sponsored events, programs, and activities are handled by graduate assistants and students, the campus recreational sports marketing professional must pay close attention to details, including overseeing and supervising the implementation of all contractual items. For example, the professional must ensure that the sponsor is satisfied with the display of sponsor banners and mentions of the sponsor during speeches.

Follow-Through

Upon completing the event, program, or activity, the campus recreational sports marketing professional must compile all tangible outcomes of the sponsorship (e.g., media coverage, photos, T-shirts with the sponsor's name) and present them along with a letter of appreciation to the sponsor. In the same letter, the sponsor should also be asked to commit to the following year's event (if it is an annual event). By asking for a commitment immediately after a successful event, the department is more likely to get a recommitment from the sponsor, and the early commitment also allows the sponsor to set the needed money aside in its next budget.

E-MARKETING

The Internet offers opportunities to market to more customers than ever before through banner ads, sponsor logos, and so on. A campus recreational sports department can use the Internet as a communication tool, a registration tool, and a revenue-generating tool.

Wireless connections, laptop computers, and various mobile devices now give students access to the Internet wherever they go. As a result, accessibility and instant gratification are common expectations of the Net Generation. This trend toward constant connectivity bodes well for campus recreational sports departments because Internet promotion is relatively affordable as compared with printed media and other traditional forms of communication and advertisement. Departments can post various information online—for example, intramural calendars, fitness class schedules, and facilities' hours of operation—thus reducing phone traffic and thus labor cost. The convenience also strengthens patrons' perception that the department provides good customer service.

The department's website can also offer online registration, once again increasing convenience and making the registration process more attractive and user-friendly. In addition, the ease of updating or changing information on the web allows the department to be more responsive and up-to-date in its information sharing. For example, intramural results can be posted on the website shortly after the games have been played, and constant connectivity to programs and services encourages greater participation.

Most important, the department's website offers an attractive outlet for promotion and marketing for both the department and its sponsors. Advertising banners or tiles or sponsor logos can be sold or offered as part of a sponsorship package. The department can use data mining (careful analysis that gleans important facts from your data) to accumulate market research data that can be useful to the department in soliciting advertisers and sponsors.

BRANDING

Perhaps the easiest way to begin defining what a brand is would be to define what it is not. A brand is not a logotype, symbol, trademark, or graphic element. A brand is not a catchy tagline or an organizational mission statement. A brand

sonya etchison - Fotolia

Because the students who use your facility are rarely away from the Internet, e-marketing can be a very effective tool in reaching them.

is not the product that an organization sells to its consumer. By definition, **branding** is an advertising method that repetitively exposes the brand or logo of an organization in order to establish widespread recognition of the brand or logo and thus recognition of the organization it represents. Alternatively, when broken down into basic terms, branding has been defined as a person's gut feeling about a product, service, or company (Neumeier, 2006). Regardless of how branding is defined, the consumer—not the organization—ultimately determines what a brand is. Therefore, it is important to remember that there is more to branding than just creating a flashy logotype paired with a catchy phrase and a nice-looking website. The fate of a brand is determined by consumers' perceptions of a product or service.

Having a strong, consistent brand helps influence a consumer's perception of an organization. By presenting a homogeneous brand concept, an organization can further solidify its reputation, recognition, and credibility. For example, in the context of campus recreational sports, a strong brand can help fuel the decision-making process among prospective students and in turn influence recruitment and retention efforts for the college or university. Behind every strong organization is a strong brand, and behind every strong brand is a comprehensive set of guidelines that help an organization develop internal and external communications that accurately reflect and reinforce the brand.

The Brand Litmus Test

To define the strength of a current brand concept for an organization, it is helpful to break a brand down into several components. Doing so helps the organization develop a better idea of what it already knows about the existing brand.

Promise

What does an organization currently provide for its consumer? This part of the brand concept is self-explanatory and can be answered by taking a close look at factors such as the organization's sales figures, participation rates, course offerings, facility space, staffing structure, and organizational policies and procedures. The brand promise tells an organization where it is currently positioned—on paper.

Value

How does the consumer benefit from what is currently being delivered? This part of the brand concept can be based more on research and trends in the recreation industry. What are the outcomes that an organization is trying to accomplish through its programs and services? For example, many campus recreational sports programs are funded through student service fees and must provide reasons to university fees committees for continued financial support. Can campus recreation programs prove a correlation between the graduation rate among students involved in their programs and services versus that for students who choose not to participate? Answers to such questions help you define the brand value established within a recreational organization.

Personality

What kind of face does an organization present, and how well does the organization relate to its consumers? This part of the brand concept essentially involves assessing what consumers are saying about the recreational organization. What information has been compiled by the organization through mechanisms such as consumer surveys, formal or informal interviews, and focus groups?

If an organization answers the questions associated with these components of a brand concept, it will be well on its way to determining the brand's overall effectiveness.

When Is It Necessary to Brand?

The process of creating or re-creating a brand can be time consuming and expensive. Before committing to the project, determine whether it is in fact necessary. If the organization has already taken the brand litmus test, it should continue by asking the following questions:

- How strong is our brand awareness? When people see the organization's logotype or a commonly distributed communication piece, are they immediately able to identify it with the organization? Do their perceptions of and associations with the organization's brand align with the identity that the organization intended to present?
- Are there any trends within our organization or industry? Does the organization have its own identity, or is it required to reinforce the identity of similar organizations that make up a parent organization? How are benchmark organizations or potential competitors choosing to brand themselves?
- Is there a knowledge gap among members of our target audience? Is some aspect of the organization's message not getting through to the intended audience? If so, why does the gap exist, and what measures are being taken to bridge it?

The Five Phases of Branding

Organizations that decide to move forward with the branding process should ensure that several pieces are in place:

- **Gain approval from the higher governing body**. Consult the organization's media relations department early on to ensure that the plan complies with its standards.
- **Assemble a branding team**. The team should consist of individuals with a solid understanding of the organization, marketing and communication techniques, and graphic and website design. It is helpful if at least one member specializes in each area so that job responsibilities can be clearly defined.
- **Create a timeline**. Set deadlines for meeting certain project benchmarks in order to keep the process moving forward. It is reasonable to expect a timeline of about 4 months for the first three phases of branding and anywhere from 12 to 18 months for the final two phases.
- **Establish an internal approval process**. Keep everyone in the organization abreast of the process. Establish regular meetings to update organizational heads on the branding team's progress and gather feedback about any changes or revisions that should be made. Keep organizational decision makers informed—in the end, they will provide the authority for the branding process to proceed.

Once the groundwork has been laid, the organization can begin the branding process per se. Every recreation organization's branding process develops uniquely, and there are many different ways to complete the process. The following example illustrates the five phases of the branding process (Neumeier, 2006) as developed by the campus recreational sports department at a large, midwestern research university, but it effectively shows how to brand a recreation organization regardless of size.

Phase 1: Discover

This phase focuses on research and information gathering. It is a crucial phase that helps the organization become better informed and make the transition into the next four phases. Research should be well rounded and should explore the topic of branding from several angles: current trends in recreation, trends among similar organizations that make up a parent organization, history and tradition of the department itself, and general trends in graphic and website design. Conducting a thorough assessment of how a department is currently positioned allows the next several phases to develop more naturally. The following outline shows how this phase might begin for a campus recreational sports department.

- Trends in recreation
    - Campus recreational sports departments that currently have individual logotypes separate from their college or university
    - Campus recreational sports departments that currently use the college or university's colors schemes
    - Campus recreational sports departments that currently use a college or university's logotype in their branding concept
- Trends among other departmental units that make up a college or university
    - Partner organizations with identities closely tied to the college or university

  - Partner organizations with identities unique to the college or university
    - Different color schemes
    - Individual symbols or icons
    - Patterns, wordmarks, or other graphic elements
- The campus recreational sports department
  - Aggregate clientele and membership data
  - Review of current branding: Where are the strong areas? Areas for improvement?
  - Review of mission and vision statements: What does the organization stand for? Is its roadmap for the present and future still aligned with its mission and vision statements?
- Graphic design trends in the recreation industry
  - Clean and simple versus highly active and involved layouts
  - Different uses of logotype and graphic elements
  - Color palette choices
  - Typography: serif versus sans serif; font thicknesses

There is no perfect amount of time to spend in the research phase; rather, research should be thorough enough to inform and help but should not consume a large amount of time and resources. Once the organization is confident that it understands each of the areas just outlined, it should move on to the second phase of the branding process.

Phase 2: Define

This phase of branding focuses on clearly defining the characteristics of the organization's audience, as well as what the organization wants to accomplish. Using the organizational research gathered in the first phase, the branding team should proceed as follows.

Personification of the primary audience Creating a brand that effectively resonates with the target audience hinges on the organization's ability to understand its consumers' personality characteristics and how they interact with the organization. Using the clientele data gathered in phase 1, as well as any general observations from interactions with consumers, the organization can begin to create personas—detailed personality descriptions that reflect the types

Photo courtesy of University of Illinois Campus Recreation.

Knowing your clientele helps you define the general personality characteristics of your target audience.

of people who connect with the organization. To develop these descriptions, create a fictional (or semi-fictional) character to which you can assign the identified or presumed personality characteristics. The following examples were created for branding a campus recreational sports program at a large midwestern research university.

- **Proud Professor**—Representing the typical faculty patron, Proud Professor enjoys strong coffee, a good novel, and an early morning swim. This individual doesn't solely visit the recreation center to socialize but admittedly enjoys when students stop by to talk.
- **Sensible Staffer**—A characteristic staff patron, Sensible Staffer is a married spouse with three children and limited time for his/herself. This person escapes from life's daily demands in a low-impact workout performed over the lunch hour. Sensible Staffer would like someday to get more involved in group fitness classes, but for now the schedule allows only a 30-minute workout in the fitness center.
- **Gifted Grad**—A typical graduate student, Gifted Grad is in the second year of graduate school and also helps teach an undergraduate course. This individual is heavily involved with the recreation center's outdoor adventure program and enjoys playing intramural basketball and flag football with classmates during the early evening. Gifted Grad is quite mindful of what student service fees are paying for (including the recreation center) and therefore makes a point to take full advantage of the student-funded opportunities on campus.
- **Uplifted Undergrad**—Representing the recreation center's largest participant demographic, Uplifted Undergrad is a first-year undergraduate student looking for any opportunity to get involved. Time management isn't one of this individual's strongest suits at the moment, and student loans are hardly a topic of discussion. Uplifted Undergrad likes to stay up late talking with new roommates in the residence halls and wakes up five minutes before a 9:00 a.m. class. Participating in group fitness classes and intramural sports have helped this student stay in shape while meeting new friends.
- **Academic All-Star**—Representing a charismatic undergraduate patron of campus recreational sports, Academic All-Star is highly involved in Greek life and is currently interviewing with several large companies for jobs after graduation. This individual uses the recreational facilities for daily workouts, open recreational basketball, and intramural sports. However, Academic All-Star does not realize the department's full breadth of offerings due largely to the fact that there is a very small window in the day for recreational activity.

Once you have defined all of your personas, choose *one* to guide the direction of the graphic and website design and message development. If the organization tries to design its message for everyone, it will end up designing for no one. Thus the branding team in the preceding example has a decision to make—whether to direct its marketing message to the largest population (Uplifted Undergrad) or to select one of the other four personas. Selecting the persona that represents the largest population may help them develop the strongest, most effective brand, but ultimately it is up to each individual organization to choose the direction of its branding. Once an overarching brand strategy has been developed for a single persona, an organization may then choose to create subsidiary communication materials tailored specifically tailored to other representative personas.

A clear marketing message A clear marketing message can be seen as a tagline or short quip that effectively communicates what the organization stands for. The message should be created with the chosen persona in mind and should be clear and concise—something that the target audience can easily understand and remember.

Heath and Heath (2008) provide the following criteria for creating an effective and memorable marketing message:

- **Simple**—Strip the message down to its core. Be a master of exclusion. Find a way to construct a message that is both simple and profound. Have the branding team members list profound messages they have heard—it's likely that 9 out of 10 of the messages will be simple yet unforgettable.

• **Unexpected**—Get consumers' attention, then find a way to keep it by stimulating their curiosity. Use the message to systematically open up gaps in their minds, then strategically fill those gaps with other exciting information.

• **Concrete**—A penny saved is a penny ___________. Don't be ambiguous; ambiguous messages are meaningless. Create concrete mental images that naturally stick in the consumer's mind. Speaking concretely is the only way to ensure that an idea means the same thing to everyone in the audience. Have the branding team think of messages that are concrete and work to ensure that the organization's message is heading in that direction.

• **Credible**—Will the consumer believe the message? Building a message that is packed with hard numbers and statistics may not be the best way to establish credibility, especially if the message is to remain simple. Think of presidential slogans. Although presidential debates may address statistical and economic data, campaign slogans are much simpler—and, the candidate hopes, credible.

• **Emotional**—Whether it be fear, joy, excitement, or something else, the message must spur the consumer to feel something. When a message evokes emotion, it becomes more powerful and more likely to stick in the consumer's mind. Have the branding team determine what kinds of emotions would be most effective and memorable with your audience.

• **Storied**—Organizations are always looking for stories to back up their messages, and rightly so. Stories tie the whole message together and help prompt the consumer to act. Have the branding team think of stories that the organization's targeted consumers can relate to.

Phase 3: Design

Once the organization has chosen a direction for its brand, the design process can begin. Here are some key aspects to consider during this phase.

Typography To create a strong, consistent identity, select a typeface for the organization's logotype and establish typography standards for all print communication materials. Here are some things to consider when choosing a typeface for a logotype.

• **Serif versus sans serif fonts**—Which type better reflects the organization's identity? How do the consumers view the organization? As professional or playful? Relaxed or rigid? Competitive or informal? Exclusive or inclusive? These questions drive the process of deciding between serif and sans serif fonts. Websites such as myfonts.com or dafont.com are available to help you test various font choices prior to making a purchase.

• **Font thickness**—Does the organization put a specific emphasis on any given area? For example, a campus recreational sports department might be proud of its success in both recreational activities and competitive sports. In such a case, the branding team must decide whether to weight both phrases equally or treat them in contrasting fashion (see figure 5.3).

• **Font leading, tracking, and kerning**—The spacing of letters and words within the logotype can help tell the story of the organization's brand (see figure 5.4). Experiment with different font spacing settings such as **leading**

Figure 5.3 Font thickness can play an influential role in helping define an organization's brand.

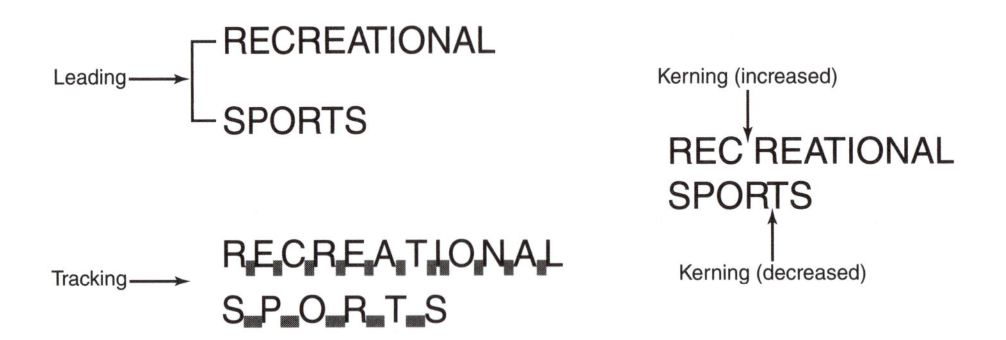

Figure 5.4 Variations of vertical and horizontal spacing between characters and words.

(vertical spacing between words), **tracking** (uniform spacing of all letters within a word), and **kerning** (unique spacing between letters within a word).

Graphic elements If you choose to build graphic elements into your organizational brand, consider these four basic design principles before moving forward:

- **Repetition**—Throughout the brand, repeat visual elements of the design such as color, shape, texture, spatial relationships, and line thicknesses in order to reinforce the brand in the consumer's mind. Repetition helps strengthen brand unity.
- **Alignment**—No graphic element should be incorporated into a brand arbitrarily. Every element should have some visual connection with another element of the brand. This practice establishes a clean, sophisticated appearance every time the brand is viewed.
- **Proximity**—Items relating to each other should be grouped together. When several items are placed close to each other, they become one visual unit rather than several separate units. This effect helps organize graphic elements and reduces clutter and confusion.
- **Contrast**—Determine which graphic elements should blend in with the logotype and which ones should stand out from it. Creating a strong contrast between a logotype and other graphic elements helps develop the brand's overall identity. Experiment with different colors and opacities.

Color palette Finding the right colors to represent the organization can be difficult, but it is important to do. One helpful resource for researching colors is the book *Color Index* by Jim Krause (2010). Here are some examples of elements to research:

- **Hues**—Different hues suggest different meanings. For example, a hue may be designed to evoke a sense of activity, progression, richness, quiet or calm, a certain culture or era, or nature. Have the branding team determine which hues resonate best with your organization.
- **CMYK versus RGB**—Computer monitors emit color as **RGB** (red, green, blue) light, whereas inked paper absorbs or reflects specific wavelengths in cyan, magenta, yellow, and black (**CMYK**) pigments. Consequently, art displayed on a computer monitor may not match the same art's rendering in a printed publication. Thus, when choosing a color palette, develop hues that appear relatively consistent in both formats. Parent organizations, such as a college's or university's media relations department, typically keep a list of design standards for their logotypes, and this material provides a good place to see the difference between CMYK and RGB colors.

Phase 4: Develop

Now comes the fun part—bringing the design to life! Phase 4 involves integrating the new design and any accompanying standards into all marketing and communication materials.

Print materials When developing print materials, give careful consideration to the treatment of internal communications (distributed within the organization's community) versus external communications (distributed to the outside community). The contrasting audiences might warrant a slightly different presentation of the organization's identity and other information.

For example, external communication materials might require a stronger affiliation with the parent organization or a more detailed explanation of what the organization represents. Your development of these materials should be guided by a strong understanding of the characteristics of each target audience and clearly identified communication goals.

Website If resources and time permit, the organization's website should be updated to align with the new branding identity. Today's culture is becoming increasingly web savvy, and the organization's website could very easily be a deciding factor when consumers are choosing whether to trust the brand presented to them. The more consistency you maintain across various types of media, the stronger your overall brand will be in the consumer's mind. Consult web analytics programs such as Google Analytics, Urchin, Clicky, and Crazy Egg to guide your development process and improve the usability and navigation of your site.

Phase 5: Deliver

Although framed as the final phase in the rebranding process, it is really an ongoing series of activities. This phase focuses on maintaining and preserving the integrity of the brand identity that the branding team has worked so hard to create. Here are some important final steps to ensure that you continue to present a consistent image of your brand:

Graphic standards Develop a set of graphic standards to provide clear guidelines for how to appropriately present the brand identity in communication materials. The standards should address the use of organizational logotypes, appropriate typography choices, use of graphic elements, and any other pertinent information regarding the visual representation of the brand.

Strong internal communications The brand will be effective only if it is embraced and reinforced by the entire organization. Organization staff must be mindful of the changes and of the importance of following the brand guidelines. Change is not always easy to embrace, and the branding team must devote time to creating a seamless transition. Meetings should be held early on with organizational program directors to clearly explain what changes are being made, how the new brand will benefit the organization, and how the staff can play a vital role in implementing the brand with consumers.

SUMMARY

In order to run successful programs, a campus recreational sports department must proactively market itself. A strategic marketing plan serves as a blueprint to guide the department in achieving its marketing goals and objectives. The marketing planning cycle involves conducting SWOT and PEST analyses and research and then developing, implementing, and evaluating the marketing plan. To efficiently manage its program, the department must also be aware of trends affecting the field of campus recreational sports, one of which is branding. The process of effectively branding a recreational organization is becoming increasingly important as institutions learn about the importance of campus recreational sports to recruitment and retention efforts.

Glossary

branding—Advertising method that repetitively exposes a brand or logo in order to establish widespread recognition of it and thus of the organization it represents.

CMYK—Color model used for the printing process that uses secondary colors (cyan, magenta, yellow, and black).

kerning—Unique spacing between letters within a word.

leading—Vertical spacing between words.

marketing plan—Detailed road map for planning and supervising all marketing activities for the following year; addresses the four basic questions in planning: (1) Where are we now? (2) Where do we want to go? (3) How do we get there? (4) Are we there yet?

marketing planning cycle—Continuously reoccurring cycle of planning that involves analysis, research, plan development, implementation, and evaluation.

market research—Data analysis pertaining to a target audience for the purpose of gleaning information that may be relevant for program planning, sponsorship sales, or assessment.

PEST analysis—Organizational analysis of political, economic, social, and technological factors.

promotion—"The persuasive flow of marketing communication," including advertising, sales and sales force, promotions, public relations, publicity, packaging, point-of-sale displays, and brand name or identity (Green et al., 1999).

psychographics—Statistics that describe a target audience in terms of factors such as lifestyle, education, approximate income, career, leisure activities, and reading habits.

RGB—Screen color model that uses primary colors (red, green, and blue) to emit color on monitors (e.g., of computers and televisions).

SWOT analysis—Organizational analysis of strengths, weaknesses, opportunities, and threats.

target audience—Market for whose needs and wants a program or service is developed.

tracking—Uniform spacing of all letters within a word.

Resources

NetMBA Business Knowledge Center

www.netmba.com/marketing

Content: Marketing concept, marketing mix, marketing definition, situation analysis, market segmentation, and target market selection

www.netmba.com/strategy

Content: The strategic planning process, SWOT and PEST analysis, and competitor analysis

U.S. Small Business Administration

www.sba.gov/gopher/Business-Development/Business-Initiatives-Education-Training/Marketing-Plan

Content: Marketing Your Business for Success Workbook

About.com

http://marketing.about.com

Content: Marketing topics, including Internet marketing and brand marketing

Jim Krause Design

www.jimkrausedesign.com

Content: Color, layout, and various design concepts

References

Borden, N.H. (1965). The concept of the marketing mix. In G. Schwartz (Ed.), *Science in marketing* (pp. 386–397). New York: Wiley.

Green, E. (2000). From the marketing perspective: Marketing from the inside-out. *REC Connections, 5*(2), 3.

Green, E., Miller, J., & Cook, J. (1999). *Marketing up close and personal: Learn to make cows fly.* Preconference workshop presented at the NIRSA Annual Conference, Milwaukee, Wisconsin.

Green, E., Miller, J., & Cook, J. (2000). *The price is right: How to create a successful sponsorship proposal.* Preconference workshop presented at the NIRSA Annual Conference, Providence, Rhode Island.

Heath, C., & Heath, D. (2008). *Made to stick: Why some ideas survive and others die.* New York: Random House.

Krause, J. (2010). *The color index* (rev. ed.). Cincinnati: HOW.

Lauterborn, B. (1990). New marketing litany: Four Ps passé: C-words take over. *Advertising Age, 61*(41), 26.

Neumeier, M. (2006). *The brand gap: How to bridge the distance between business strategy and design* (2nd ed.). Berkeley, CA: New Riders.

Shaw, E., & Jones, D.G. (2005). A history of schools of marketing thought. *Marketing Theory, 5*(3): 239–281.

Adapted, by permission, from NIRSA, 2008, *Campus recreation: Essentials for the professional* (Champaign, IL: Human Kinetics), 221-238.

CHAPTER

6

Assessment in Campus Recreational Sports

Jacqueline R. Hamilton
Texas A&M University–Corpus Christi

Campus recreational sports cannot operate in a vacuum; to the contrary, these services are enmeshed in the context of the institution and its organizational structure. In addition, certain commonalities have been established in the services that campus recreational sports should offer to its constituencies. At the same time, the department may be positioned differently across institutions, and each department must set its own mission, goals, and objectives. Once that is done, how can the department verify that services are being delivered effectively? The answer is assessment.

DEFINING TERMS

Assessment means "any effort to gather, analyze, and interpret evidence which describes institutional, departmental, divisional, or agency effectiveness" (Upcraft & Schuh, 1996, p. 18). Assessment is certainly not unique to campus recreation; in fact, it has evolved in recent years to permeate all areas and levels of higher education as a means of demonstrating **accountability**, **transparency**, and effectiveness. Two key factors in creating the climate for required assessment are accountability and economics. Stiffer competition for funding increases the need to justify the existence of campus recreational sports. We have to document the fact that what we do serves a defined purpose, that we are achieving or striving toward an acceptable level of competency and quality in doing so, and that we are acting as good stewards of resources. "Colleges and universities increasingly are being asked to demonstrate how they make a difference in the lives of students, how they contribute to the economic development of their communities and states, and how they contribute to the national welfare" (Schuh & Associates, 2009a, p. 2). In this culture of accountability, assessment is a must.

Furthermore, most decisions made in this context are data driven, and information gained through assessment contributes substantially to the decision making process. Such information can be used to justify decisions about budgeting, program expansion or reduction, and facility development. It can also validate the notion that campus recreational sports provides learning opportunities outside of the classroom that contribute to students' holistic development and to the wellness, recruitment, and retention of students, faculty, and staff. Assessment makes it possible to demonstrate cause and effect, or relationship, and thus to justify the use of resources to deliver the department's programs and services.

Research involves "studious inquiry or examination" using investigation or experimentation aimed at discovering and interpreting facts, revising accepted theories or laws in light of new facts, or making practical application of new or revised theories or laws (Merriam-Webster.com, 2010). Research with a properly narrowed focus can be applied to the practical task of assessment.

To demonstrate accountability, campus recreational sports departments must document outcomes and products across its program areas, as well as in facility and equipment use, personnel productivity, and student employment. In fact, programs should be developed and implemented with the intention of producing chosen learning and development outcomes (for more, see chapter 10 in this text).

Another important step in the process involves communicating the information gathered during research. This communication may be in the form of a publication or presentation for example so that others interested in the field or type of information may learn or benefit from such existing or previously conducted research. Transparency means making the information readily available to others, and the web enables you to make a large amount of information available to anyone who may be interested. If information is not made readily available, it may be requested through the open-records legal process, which may differ from state to state.

Once you have collected and analyzed the information, you can move on to evaluation, in which you make decisions geared toward improvement.

Evaluation means "any effort to use assessment evidence to improve institutional, departmental, divisional, or agency effectiveness" (Upcraft & Schuh, 1996, p. 19). This is crucial for campus recreational sports departments, which must continue to adapt in order to meet their stakeholders' changing needs and desires. Departments can continuously improve and advance by comparing their results with those set forth in accepted standards. Indeed, the goal of research, assessment, and evaluation in campus recreational sports is to ensure high-quality programs and services that support student learning.

Assessment is also used in the specific area of human resources, and certain parallels can be found with the department's overall assessment process. At the same time, some explicit laws and practices apply particularly to human resources. For specific discussion of managing and assessing personnel, see chapter 9 in this text.

THE PRACTICE OF ASSESSMENT—HOW AND WHY

Due to increased competition for public resources in the 1990s and early 21st century, the focus of accountability has shifted toward institutional productivity and student performance. Institutions are facing greater enrollment, higher costs for carrying out services, and a smaller percentage of budget funding from the states. As a result, students are paying more money out of pocket for their college education, and institutions are relying more on fundraising.

These stakeholder changes have contributed to the shift in the focus of accountability. Stakeholders' interests influence action, and it is now necessary for campus recreational sports to demonstrate how they are achieving desired outcomes and facilitating learning outside of the classroom. The process of assessing learning outcomes can be used to connect program and service outcomes to the mission, vision, and goals of both the institution and the department. In fact, "it is no longer enough for institutions to measure the effectiveness of what they do, including the outcomes their students achieve. They must now be purposeful, aligning departmental goals with institutional goals, and institutional goals with state and federal goals" (Mallory & Clement, 2009, p. 107).

The importance of firsthand experience outside of the classroom was recognized as complementary to academic work in a report by the Wingspread Group in 1993. The report emphasized that assessment and achievement are critical components of an improved edu-

The University of Texas at San Antonio, Department of Campus Recreation

Increased enrollments and costs have made accountability and documentation more important than ever.

cational system and that they go hand in hand. As a result, educators now seek documentation that goes beyond grades and test scores to represent genuine learning achievements across educational and training experiences. "In an institution focused on learning, assessment feedback becomes central to the institution's ability to improve its own performance, enhancing student learning in turn" (Wingspread, p. 22).

In 2004, a document titled *Learning Reconsidered* was published by the National Association of Student Personnel Administrators (NASPA) and the American College Personnel Association (ACPA). It called upon student affairs departments to serve as partners in the broader campus curriculum because the experiences generated through these departments affects student outcomes: "As important partners in the development and support of students' learning and learning environments, student affairs professionals have a unique opportunity and responsibility to lead and participate in the comprehensive, systematic, and consistent assessment and evaluation of student learning in all domains. Such assessment, when properly planned, implemented, and evaluated, can help institutions set priorities, allocate resources, and work to enhance student learning" (p. 26). Even societal expectations come into play: "Our society expects colleges and universities to graduate students who can get things done in the world and are prepared for effective and engaged citizenship. Both within the academy and among its observers and stakeholders, the need to identify the goals and effects of a college education has produced demands for, and commitments to, specific learning outcomes" (p. 3).

A follow-up document, *Learning Reconsidered 2*, was published in 2006 (ACPA et al.) to guide practitioners in developing and implementing student learning outcomes. It declared that, "as the emphasis on learning outcomes continues to grow, student affairs has a key role to play in the accreditation process" (Mallory & Clement, 2009, p. 111).

As the demand for assessment has escalated, so has the need for standards of comparison. As standard setters, **accreditation** agencies act as significant drivers of assessment. Six regional authorities accredit universities in the United States and some surrounding countries. The threat of losing accreditation and the associated funding motivates higher education institutions to demonstrate compliance with outcome statements for programs, services, and funding across the institution. For example, the mission of the Southern Association of Colleges and Schools Commission on Colleges (SACSCOC) focuses on "the enhancement of educational quality throughout the region" (SACSCOC, 2010). The group strives to "improve the effectiveness of institutions by ensuring that [they] . . . meet standards established by the higher education community [to] . . . address the needs of society and students. It [also] serves as the common denominator of shared values and practices among the diverse institutions" in its region (SACSCOC).

Another key organization, the Council for the Advancement of Standards in Higher Education (CAS), was formed in 1979 and published its first version of a professional standards book in 1986 (CAS, 2009). The standards cover 39 functional areas of the college campus outside of the classroom—including campus recreational sports. These standards, developed in conjunction with several professional organizations (e.g., NASPA, ACPA, and the National Intramural-Recreational Sports Association [NIRSA]), articulate best practices by which institutions can measure their effectiveness. The CAS standards and self-study process can be used as models in the accreditation process.

Standards are set through various processes, and best practices may have developed over time. Research projects may have inventoried items such as types of positions, categories of programs, demonstrated cause and effect, or verified other outcomes. Once standards have been established, they are extremely useful for entities interested in seeing how they measure up. According to Arminio (2009), standards provide a mechanism by means of which professionals can judge the quality of their work; provide the profession with a means of self-regulation; serve as a self-regulatory means for ensuring high-quality practice and continual improvement; and ensure public trust in professionals who meet established standards.

In addition to extensive programming, campus recreational sports departments hold responsibility for constructing and operating multimillion-dollar facilities and employ large numbers of full- and part-time personnel. The majority of campus recreational sports programs (72 percent) are positioned under the auspices of student affairs (Franklin, 2007), but some report to athletics, academics, business affairs, or other areas. In many public institutions, funding for campus recreational sports is handled through a separate fee, but regardless of funding method the department is expected to practice good stewardship in its use of fiscal, physical, and human resources. To ensure this optimum performance, assessment is necessary, and campus recreational sports professionals bear responsibility for generating research and assessment information.

In 2006, Haines and Farrell examined barriers to research in campus recreation. At that time, research was not commonly listed in job descriptions in the field. It is becoming more common, however, for responsibilities of assessment and research to be included in one or more job descriptions within a campus recreational sports department. "Research is an essential component of university recreational sports . . . because it is needed to scientifically test interventions, defend departmental existence, and . . . align for further departmental growth. Current data . . . [are] important documented criteria needed to substantiate an increased operating budget, to justify adding personnel, and to validate the need for additional facilities" (Haines & Farrell, p. 116).

CONTEMPORARY ISSUES IN ASSESSMENT

Learning Reconsidered and *Learning Reconsidered 2* spurred changes in how the field of campus recreational sports approached assessment. Chapter 10 in this text describes how to develop learning outcomes and identify measurable outcomes for programs. Student learning outcomes must be measurable in order to be assessed quantitatively, which calls for emphasis on research design and **methodology**. As connections grow between this work on outcomes and related efforts in institutional and departmental missions that address student learning, as well as CAS standards and accreditation, a group of best practices is emerging for assessment that sets the stage for further collaboration between curricular and cocurricular units.

Campus recreational sports departments should develop learning outcome statements for programs and for student employment, both of which contribute to holistic student development by giving students arenas in which they can develop and learn outside of the classroom. To close the loop, writing and defining learning outcomes connects to the departmental and institutional mission. Assessment is used to verify achievement of the learning outcomes and the degree or level to which they have been met. The assessment product can then be used to evaluate and to make decisions that ensure the department follows best practices and implements good stewardship. See table 6.1 for examples of measurable learning outcomes.

Economics

The state of the economy in the new millennium has contributed to the need for assessment. All areas of higher education have been affected by

Table 6.1 Examples of Measurable Student Learning Outcomes

Category	CAS domain	CAS dimension	Learning outcome statement	Item measured	Measurement description
Intramurals	Interpersonal competence	Meaningful relationships	Intramural team participants will establish mutually beneficial relationships with others and treat others with respect.	Good sporting behavior	A sportsmanship rating on a 5-point scale will be assigned for each team at each competition. The team rating reflects collective behaviors of team members.
Fitness and wellness	Practical competence	Maintaining health and wellness	Group exercise participants will engage in behaviors that promote health and reduce risk.	Cardiovascular endurance	3-minute step test administered at the beginning and end of the semester using beats per minute during recovery
Facility attendant	Knowledge acquisition, construction, integration, and application	Constructing knowledge	Facility attendants will make meaning from text, instruction, and experience to generate new problem-solving approaches.	Successful completion of required online training modules (institutional) and new employee orientation and shadow shifting (departmental)	Human resources transcript for completed courses, new employee test, and first-semester evaluation
Fitness and wellness	Interpersonal competence	Effective leadership	Group fitness instructors will demonstrate skill in guiding a group and communicating the purpose that encourages commitment and action in others.	Punctuality, attendance, class preparation with choreography and music	Semester evaluations, in-service presentations, attendance, patron survey

reductions in funding for public institutions and in fundraising in both public and private institutions. In addition, the use of fiscal resources is subject to heightened scrutiny. With resources shrinking, every dollar spent may be subject to justification, and the expression "doing more with less" has become part of our regular vernacular. In this climate, campus recreational sports departments must engage in effective evaluation and decision making, which, as discussed earlier, require the use of assessment and research information. By studying the value of programs and connecting them to the institution's mission, departments can make effective budgetary decisions about which programs to grow and expand, which ones to keep as is relative to funding, and which to reduce or cut.

Ethics

Ethics has been defined as "the study of how individuals ought to act in moral conflict situations where issues of right and good are at stake" (Dalton, Crosby, Valente, & Eberhardt, 2009, p. 168). In the context of assessment, ethics primarily relates to preventing harm in studying human participants. Higher education addresses this concern by routinely requiring that research be approved through a process involving an institutional review board to ensure that potential harm is minimized.

Ethics in higher education can also cover financial **stewardship** and professional behavior. In the sixth edition of the CAS standards (2006), the topic of ethics for professionals was included for the first time as a component of personnel assessment. In the Registry of Collegiate Recreational Sports Professionals (NIRSA, 2010b), personal and professional qualities (including ethical practices) make up one of the eight core knowledge areas.

Accountability

Accountability involves a focus on institutions of higher education from the outside looking in; it is about the role an institution plays in meeting general social, cultural, and economic needs (Wellman, 2006). Accountability is the assurance of a unit to its stakeholders that it provides education of good quality (Campbell & Rozsnyai, 2002). Stakeholders can range across internal and external entities to an institution. Institutional leaders want, of course, for the institution to receive favorable media attention and enjoy a respected reputation; in contrast, negative publicity can have very unpleasant implications. The National Commission on the Future of Higher Education (2006) emphasized the need for a robust culture of accountability and transparency in higher education. In that same year, "the commission of the Secretary of education (U.S. Department of Education, 2006) made it clear that assessment of student learning outcomes should be central to the accountability process" (Schuh & Associates, 2009b, p. 2).

Accountability has become more centralized within institutions (Mallory & Clement, 2009), and coordinated reporting of outcomes across an institution may be managed through one office with a title such as Planning and Institutional Effectiveness. Since the 1990s, the organization and distribution of information has also been affected by advances in computer technology in the form of electronic document management, the development of websites, and the proliferation of Internet communication. Proprietary software now exists to help institutions organize such data.

Accountability also involves legal compliance. Higher education institutions are governed by federal and state laws, as well as system and institutional rules, policies, and procedures. As a result, human resources training regularly covers topics such as sexual harassment, fiscal procedures, the Family Educational Rights and Privacy Act, risk management training, and preparation and proper certification of employees. Lack of accountability in any of these areas can result in various problems, including negative press for an institution. Stakeholders expect compliance with legal requirements.

Transparency

Transparency fits hand in hand with accountability. In 2006, the Secretary of Education's Commission on the Future of Higher Education recommended the creation of a consumer-friendly database for higher education. It would contain reliable information about institutions and would offer a search engine to enable students, parents, policy makers, and others to weigh and comparatively rank institutional performance. The Integrated Postsecondary Education Data System (IPEDS) is "the primary source for data on colleges, universities, and technical and vocational postsecondary institutions in the United States" (National Center for Education Statistics, 2011). Individual institutions continue to make information available electronically, but the sheer abundance of information can be daunting, and the host websites are not always intuitively navigable. Improving and maintaining transparency is an on-going process in making new information readily accessible to consumers.

Other ways in which institutions are meeting the demand for transparency include posting faculty and staff vitae and resumes, syllabi, and faculty intended course outcomes. Such postings provide opportunities for institutions to be proactive in transparency, and student affairs offices need to find ways to measure the effectiveness of their activities and share the results with a variety of stakeholders—students, parents, state and federal government officials, higher education coordinating agencies, and governing boards—in ways that are both easy to understand and readily accessible (Mallory & Clement, 2009).

When an institution fails to be transparent, interested parties may request documents through open records laws relating to the Freedom of Information Act. Every state has open-records and open-meetings laws that govern requests for information from public entities. Information requests made under such laws often come from the media and bring negative attention to the institution. In contrast, proactively practicing accountability and transparency enhances the institution's reputation.

STANDARDS OF COMPARISON

When assessing programs, services, and facilities, departments often use standards of comparison. The following sections explore what standards are used, who sets them, and where those groups get their authority.

Council for the Advancement of Standards in Higher Education

CAS is made up of 36 member associations whose primary purpose is to seek consensus on the fundamental principles of best practices (CAS, 2006). NIRSA collaborated with CAS to create the standards for campus recreation. The 7th edition of the CAS professional standards (2009) includes learning outcome domains that parallel the content of *Learning Reconsidered 2*. Campus recreational sports professionals should clearly understand the CAS standards and how they can be used to conduct a self-study to see how well programs stack up.

Regional Accrediting Authorities

Student affairs and, in turn, campus recreational sports departments now play a greater part in the accreditation process than ever before. Regional accrediting bodies set standards and guidelines by which institutions are assessed. As described by Schuh and associates (2009a), "the Southern Association of Colleges and Schools Commission on Colleges (2004) in its resource manual on principles of accreditation identifies relevant questions for student support programs, services, and activities that include providing evidence for the effectiveness and adequacy of support programs and services, and evidence that student support services and programs meet the needs of students of all types and promote student learning and development. Requirements such as these are unambiguous; assessment data are needed or the questions cannot be answered satisfactorily" (p. 6).

Maintaining accreditation is critical to an institution's long-term well-being. If an institution loses accreditation, it may lose considerable funding and suffer a reduction in applications and enrollment. Thus it behooves campus recreational sports departments to know what regional accrediting authority governs their state and what needs to be assessed in their area as part of the accreditation process for their institution.

Professional Organizations

Professional organizations operate to fulfill unique missions that vary by field; as a result, campus recreational sports employees may be members of multiple professional organizations to meet their needs. These organizations set standards and best practices for many situations. They also provide resources and networking to their constituents for continuous improvement in the field.

National Intramural-Recreational Sports Association

NIRSA is the most prominent professional organization serving the field of campus recreational sports; it also serves several program areas. Its mission is to provide for the education and development of professional and student members and to foster high-quality recreational programs, facilities, and services for diverse populations (NIRSA, 2010a). NIRSA collaborated with CAS to develop standards and, in *Learning Reconsidered 2*, with several professional organizations to address the development of learning outcomes. The NIRSA professional registry also sets professional standards for practitioners in the field.

Student Affairs Administrators in Higher Education (NASPA)

This group (formerly called the National Association of Student Personnel Administrators) provides professional development and advocacy for student affairs educators and administrators who share responsibility for a campuswide focus on the student experience (NASPA, 2010). One of NASPA's goals is to provide leadership for promoting, assessing, and supporting student learning and successful educational outcomes; accordingly, the group took the lead in coordinating and publishing *Learning Reconsidered* and *Learning Reconsidered 2*, which spurred change in how student affairs agencies participate in assessment and use learning outcomes.

Other Organizations

The needs of campus recreational sports professionals are served by numerous organizations. Examples include the Association of Outdoor Recreation and Education (AORE); the American Alliance for Health, Physical Education, Recreation and Dance (AAHPERD); and the National Recreation and Park Association (NRPA).

Recreation professionals can also attain certifications through a number of groups to meet industry standards. Here are some examples (not exhaustive in any given area). Lifeguards often hold certification through the American Red Cross. Personal trainers and group fitness instructors may hold certification through the American Council on Exercise, the American College of Sports Medicine, the Aerobics and Fitness Association of America, or the Les Mills company. Climbing wall staff may pursue certification through the American Mountain Guides Association.

The National Commission for Certifying Agencies (NCCA) is run through the Institute for Credentialing Excellence (ICE). Its mission is to "advance credentialing through education, standards, research and advocacy to ensure competence across professions and occupations" (ICE, 2010). Campus recreational sports departments may encounter the NCCA when our credits are pursued for certifications for positions such as personal trainers, group fitness instructors, athletic training, or professional registry.

Benchmarking

The United Nations Educational, Scientific and Cultural Organization defines **benchmarking** as "a standardized method for collecting and reporting critical operational data in a way that enables relevant comparisons among the performances of different organizations or programmes, usually with a view to establishing good practice, diagnosing problems in performance, and identifying areas of strength. Benchmarking gives the organization (or the programme) the external references and the best practices on which to base its evaluation and to design its working processes" (Quality Research International, 2011).

Within the context of campus recreation, data could be collected from multiple campuses to examine common practices in addressing a particular topic. For example, what certifications do campus recreational sports departments accept for group fitness instructors? If the researcher used a well-designed methodology for data collection and properly analyzed the data, the results might show that it is good and common practice for departments to accept certifications through agencies accredited by the National Commission for Certifying Agencies. This finding might then lead to a benchmark by which campus recreational sports departments measure themselves.

Institutional Mission

The responsibility for education lies with the state, and state agencies govern the educational process. For example, the Texas Higher Education Coordinating Board (THECB) oversees higher education in that state (THECB, 2010). The board ensures that public institutions of higher education in the state pursue unique institutional missions to serve the people. The institution itself must ensure that its overall mission is aligned with the various divisional and departmental missions. Departments may set their own specific goals and objectives, but they should operate within a context of agreement across the institution about desired learning outcomes—and all should ultimately support the common overarching institutional mission in order to establish a cohesive focus at all levels of the institution.

TYPES AND AREAS OF ASSESSMENT

Assessment can be approached in numerous ways, and the quality of results hinges on choosing the appropriate method for the item being assessed. Since assessment can be labor intensive, it may be necessary to set priorities. For program areas, critical areas might include learning outcomes with measurable results for each assessment item. For facility usage, statistical reporting may be adequate to serve the purpose of informing budgetary decisions, and valuable inventory data can be gathered by means of surveys. In other situations, it may be important to demonstrate cause and effect.

To assess identified items, an institution may use a standardized process or proprietary software. In any case, campus recreational sports professionals need to meet the requirements of their institution's process as they carry out their assessment responsibilities and demonstrate that they are meeting acceptable standards and predetermined outcomes.

Programs

Programs are the products delivered by campus recreational sports departments to the campus community and in some cases to the greater community. In delivering programs, departments must strive purposefully to meet or surpass standards, and they should develop measurable outcomes for each program area. Assessment allows the department to investigate the questions of who, what, when, where, why, and how. Who are the programs serving? What purpose do they serve? What are the learning outcomes? Are they being met? When is the best time of the semester to offer this program? Where is the best place to market this program? Why are these programs offered? How do they contribute to student learning? Do they support the departmental mission and in turn the institution's mission? Are they funded appropriately? Including these questions in the assessment process helps the department to maximize desirable outcomes.

Facilities

With the facility development movement that began in the 1980s, campus recreational sports departments became responsible for multimillion dollar facilities, more full-time and part-time employees, and related increases in budgetary responsibility. Facilities serve a support function for programming. Campus recreational sports managers can find out how facilities use patterns and perceptions compare to national standards by obtaining benchmarking data through surveys. Areas to investigate might include, for example, the impact of new facilities on participation levels, importance level of recreation facilities in selection of attending an institution, or perceptions of perceived health improvements through participation.

Although facilities assessment may not connect directly with student learning outcomes, it affects stewardship of resources and helps the department understand its ability to accommodate program activities and special events that do affect outcomes directly. Facility assessment information may also be used to justify new facilities or expansions and new equipment purchases. Other budgetary decisions that might be affected by facility assessment information include hiring additional staff (e.g., program coordinators or custodians) to address increased programming and traffic or determining adjustments to hours of operations.

Personnel

Assessment, or evaluation, of full-time personnel is covered in chapter 9 of this text. For student staff, assessment should be conducted based on learning outcomes. Campus recreational sports is among the highest-employing departments on most campuses, and student development through employment is often considered to be a type of programming. Learning outcomes connected to student employment might include, for example, acquiring and applying knowledge, exercising leadership, solving problems, and engaging in effective interpersonal relationships.

From a broader perspective, student employment serves a dual purpose. Campus departments depend on the student workforce to help deliver their programs; at the same time, departments invest considerable resources in training these students, which enhances their holistic development. These out-of-classroom learning experiences help students develop skill sets that are necessary to becoming a contributing member of society. In this light, each student position should include written learning outcomes that are specific to the position, and assessment should address the student's achievement of the stated outcomes.

darren wise

Assessment is crucial to justifying the need for new facilities.

Budgets

As with facilities, budgets have an indirect but important connection with the assessment of learning outcomes. The economic stress and funding reductions that have characterized recent years have increased the pressure to justify the mere existence of certain programs, facilities, and positions. Sometimes tough decisions must be made about cutting programs and positions, and the call for transparency means that departments must often disclose budgets to demonstrate their good stewardship of resources. "Institutions are being called upon to provide evidence of the success of their various operations, or they can expect more involvement of politicians and various governmental agencies and greater scrutiny of their operations" (Schuh & Associates, 2009a, p. 5). In addition, apart from learning outcomes, the department must assess the budget itself in order to identify how changes are affecting spending and determine whether funds are being used in alignment with departmental and institutional missions.

Departments or Divisions

As with missions, learning outcomes should be aligned throughout the institution's divisions and departments. *Learning Reconsidered* (NASPA & ACPA, 2004) recommended specifying intended student outcomes and committing resources to measuring, assessing, and documenting students' achievement of the desired outcomes. These efforts should be coordinated between academic affairs and student affairs offices.

METHODOLOGY AND RESEARCH DESIGN

It is critical to select and develop an appropriate methodology and research design for assessment, and extensive resources are available to help campus recreational sports staff members develop skills in these areas. In order to generate high-quality research, practitioners need to be able to critically evaluate existing research in the field and understand the concepts of replication, validity, and reliability. Research design can pose a challenge, especially since "some learning outcomes related to personal and social growth are difficult to measure" (NASPA & ACPA, 2004).

Experimental Research and Nonexperimental Research

Broadly speaking, there are two types of research—experimental and nonexperimental. In experimental research, the researcher administers or otherwise controls treatments, observes changes in behaviors or outcomes, and presents results in the form of statistics. True experimental research involves randomization, observation, treatments (including a comparison group), and post-treatment observation. It must meet a high standard and is not always accomplishable in applied research settings such as those encountered in studies of campus recreational sports participants and employees. One potential obstacle, for example, rests with the necessity of a comparison group, which means the researcher might be denying access and thus the benefits of recreation participation to the control group during the study. Doing so could constitute harm inflicted on members in the comparison group (recall the institutional review board process). Within experimental research, there are several different designs that can be used.

Quasi-experimental designs use intact groups, or a group that is already formed by earlier circumstances. In this design, individuals are not randomly assigned into treatment groups. However, the groups are randomly assigned to treatments. Within campus recreational sports, numerous opportunities exist for studying these pre-existing groups—for example, intramural teams, group fitness classes, or employees grouped by position—by administering a treatment to the group and observing the results.

In nonexperimental research, researchers make observations without administering experimental treatments (Patten, 2009). They can choose from several methodologies, such as surveys, case studies, causal-comparative research, and correlational research. Results of qualitative research are presented in discussions of trends or themes based on words (Patten).

Quantitative and Qualitative Research

Conceptually, **quantitative** and **qualitative** research are similar in that they both contribute to knowledge, use a systematic approach to data collection, and involve interpretation. However, quantitative research presents findings with numbers or statistics, whereas qualitative research communicates findings with words. Furthermore, quantitative research uses a deductive approach in which studies are formed through the use of existing literature to test concepts. Other characteristics include random sampling for quality assurance, high ability to replicate studies, and the design of all aspects in advance. Qualitative research, in contrast, uses an inductive approach in which a researcher may begin collecting data and use preliminary findings to guide the progress of the study. In this type of research, sampling is intentionally selective and small, the ability to replicate and generalize is low, and the design emerges as the study unfolds (Patten, 2009). Mixed-methods studies combine both qualitative and quantitative methodology in a synergistic manner.

Surveys

Surveys are commonly used to gather research data from sample participants and to make inferences, but they do have limitations. For example, surveys have often been used to gather information about student satisfaction with programs and services. However, *Learning Reconsidered* advises using assessment methods focused primarily on student learning rather than on student satisfaction because while satisfaction surveys do provide data about student fulfillment, the evidence they produce does not indicate how students learn or what they know (NASPA & ACPA, 2004).

Another limitation of surveys lies in the fact that the response rate tends to decline as students are bombarded with multiple requests to complete surveys. In addition, the usefulness and representativeness of survey data can be questioned when response rates are low and responses are voluntary. Offering incentives for completing a survey can also call into question the student's motivation for providing the information.

Developing survey instruments can also be challenging. Expressing questions with clarity is critical to obtaining the desired information; as a result, it is advisable whenever possible to use proven survey instruments to ensure high validity and reliability.

In the area of student affairs, two long-running national surveys are the National Survey of Student Engagement and the Noel-Levitz Student Satisfaction Inventory survey. These surveys investigate a plethora of issues across campuses, with only a few questions particular to campus recreation. In order to gather more extensive data specific to campus recreation, StudentVoice (now called Campus Labs) partnered with NIRSA to produce benchmarking surveys (for an example of analyzed survey data, see table 6.2). With each of these organizations, the institution or campus recreational sports department pays a fee in order to participate in the survey and receive the survey results and data analysis.

Focus Groups

Qualitative researchers generally use an inductive approach with a purposive sample to investigate a topic about which little is known or understood (Patten, 2009). They may direct the discussion by means of guiding questions. A focus group involves "a carefully planned discussion designed to obtain perceptions on a defined area of interest in a permissive, non-threatening environment" (Kruger, 2000, p.18). The group session allows interactions between participants to stimulate them to state feelings, perspectives, and beliefs that they might not have expressed if interviewed individually. This technique also reduces the interviewer's profile in the process (Gall, Gall, & Borg, 2007).

Data Collection

Data are collected as part of the research and assessment processes. The form of the data depends on the research design and methodol-

Table 6.2 Analyzed Survey Data From StudentVoice

Do you use any of the on-campus recreational sports facilities, programs, or services?			
	2010 national average (%)	**2009 national average (%)**	**2008 national average (%)**
Yes	73.44	83.68	80.80
No	26.56	16.32	19.20
Total Respondents	*33,028*	*22,181*	*24,779*
How often do you participate in intramural sports?			
	2010 national average (%)	**2009 national average (%)**	**2008 national average (%)**
5 or more times per week	1.20	1.09	1.36
3–4 times per week	3.87	3.48	3.64
1–2 times per week	15.42	15.19	14.94
1–2 times per month	7.95	6.90	7.75
1–2 times per semester/quarter	15.56	13.42	15.04
Never	56.00	59.92	57.11
Total Respondents	*21,325*	*17,208*	*19,524*

Reprinted, by permission, from K. Vanderlinden.

ogy selected and developed for a particular study. Quality control is needed in order to ensure that, where appropriate, data are kept confidential and secure. Data may also need to be transcribed or entered into software programs. Quantitative data takes the form of numbers and statistics, whereas qualitative data takes the form of words.

Data Analysis

Once the data are collected, they must be analyzed in order to be interpreted. The statistical procedures used to analyze quantitative data can be complex and go beyond the scope of this text. Statistical software is available to aid researchers in analyzing data. For qualitative data, software is also available to help researchers transcribe and develop themes. It may be necessary to use both on-campus and off-campus resources to assist with data analysis.

Documentation

In the production of scholarly work, such as research or information for publication, proper documentation is required. All sources must be properly cited and referenced. Journals in the field (e.g., *Recreational Sports Journal*) typically require that submitted articles follow the style guide presented in the *Publication Manual of the American Psychological Association* (APA, 2009).

DISSEMINATION OF INFORMATION

Publishing and disseminating research is a critical component of the process. Peer review helps ensure that the studies included in publications meet standards of rigor. Research presented in journal articles typically follows a consistent format that includes the following elements: introduction, methods, results, discussion, limitations, and recommendations for further research. Research may also be disseminated through forums other than publications such as conference presentations, dissertations, or white papers.

Sharing information with colleagues through professional publications helps promote the organization's research agenda; in addition, other professionals in the field can benefit from reading research. Research publication can be used to communicate trends, best practices, and the development of standards. Colleagues can also follow research and consider replicating studies in their own campus settings. According to Haines and Farrell (2006), reporting research outcomes allows others to apply the results to data-driven decision making and strategic planning, thus improving the efficiency and effectiveness of how campus recreational sports operates by helping professionals in the field test new interventions and evaluate new ways of doing business.

ASSESSMENT RESOURCES

Assessment is not a new concept in higher education, student affairs, or campus recreational sports, and resources exist both on and off of campus to aid in the process. Thus there is no need to reinvent the wheel.

Software

A number of proprietary software packages are available to institutions of higher education to help with the assessment process (specific names are not included here because this area changes rapidly). For example, some packages can help you manage the accreditation process by allowing you to attach supporting documentation to narratives in order to demonstrate compliance. Other programs can help you organize goals, measures, and objectives by department or functional area. Some companies conduct assessment projects for departments and institutions through outsourcing and provide products through web-based software. Cost varies according to the scope of service. The example shown in table 6.3 is a **rubric** from StudentVoice, and it is one of many rubric templates available to help clients in the assessment process.

Institutional Requirements

Campus recreational sports departments cannot operate entirely on their own; to the contrary, the department's mission and outcomes must align with the established overarching emphases of the institution. Similarly, whenever the institution requires use of a systematic method of assessment, the campus recreational sports department must meet that requirement. The process can be made more manageable at many levels if the department is aware of the available resources. The department can readily meet institutional requirements and use best practices in the field at the same time.

Opportunities for collaboration exist on campuses, and campus recreational sports departments may be able to use local resources by fostering good relationships with other areas on campus that regularly conduct research. Areas to consider approaching include the research office, the institutional effectiveness office, and faculty members overseeing graduate students who need to produce research. Student affairs may also include an assessment person who is able to serve as a resource to campus recreational sports.

Professional Organization Support

Campus recreational sports departments may also find research support through conferences, journals, and networking offered or facilitated by professional organizations. For example, by publishing results in a professional organization journal, the department can further its own research agenda while also helping ensure that the profession remains strong in the future. Replicating previous research is another helpful way to investigate outcomes on a particular campus or tailor existing research to a particular setting. To obtain larger sample sizes, consider collaboration across institutions. You are also well advised to attend and participate in conferences and workshops in order to share and learn more about research in campus recreational sports.

SUMMARY

Although assessment in higher education has been in existence for centuries, it continues to evolve to meet the needs of the industry. Recent changes that have affected campus recreational sports include the publication of *Learning Reconsidered* and the increasing demand for

Table 6.3 Rubric Template for Student Employee Learning Outcomes—Providing Customer Service

	1—Beginner	2—Developing	3—Accomplished	4—Advanced
Attitude	Frequently portrays a negative attitude in speech, behavior, or body language.	Occasionally portrays a negative attitude.	Consistently portrays a positive and pleasant attitude.	Consistently portrays a positive and pleasant attitude and encourages the same in others.
Response to customers	Does not greet or respond to customers in a timely manner.	Usually greets and responds to customer but could be more timely or attentive.	Greets and responds to customers in a timely manner with few exceptions.	Always greets and responds to customers in a timely manner.
Approachability	Does not appear approachable or welcome questions.	Is usually approachable but does not invite questions.	Is always approachable and sometimes invites customer interaction.	Is always approachable and proactively invites customer interaction.
Customer questions	Responds to customer questions inaccurately or incompletely.	Responds to customer questions accurately but may struggle with clarity or comprehensiveness of response.	Fully and clearly responds to customer questions.	Fully and clearly responds to customer questions and often anticipates questions.
Difficult customers	Is unable to handle difficult customers or crisis situations.	Struggles to handle difficult customers or crisis situations.	Addresses difficult customers and crisis situations but requires occasional assistance or correction.	Handles difficult customers with ease, responds quickly and appropriately to crisis situations, and proactively identifies and addresses problems.
Total				

Reprinted, by permission, from K. Vanderlinden.

accountability, which will only grow if budgets continue (as is generally expected) to be lean. "The drive for greater accountability in higher education remains a resounding imperative that will continue to be a focus for our institutions and the profession" (Mallory & Clement, 2009, p. 109). To put it more specifically, assessment in campus recreational sports is a resounding imperative for which professionals in the field need to prepare.

Glossary

accountability—Focus on institutions of higher education from the outside looking in; the role the institution plays in meeting general social, cultural, and economic needs (Wellman, 2006). The assurance of a unit to its stakeholders that it provides education of good quality (Campbell & Rozsnyai, 2002). Stakeholders can range across internal and external entities to an institution.

accreditation—In higher education, a type of quality assurance process in which services and operations of postsecondary educational institutions or programs are evaluated by an external body to determine whether applicable standards are met.

assessment—Any effort to gather, analyze, and interpret evidence that describes the effectiveness of an institution, department, division, or agency.

benchmarking—Standardized method for collecting and reporting critical operational data in a way that allows relevant comparisons between the performances of different organizations or programs.

evaluation—Any effort to use assessment evidence to improve the effectiveness of an institution, department, division, or agency.

methodology—Body of practices, procedures, and rules used by those who work in a discipline or engage in an inquiry; a set of working methods.

qualitative research—Research in which results are presented in the form of discussion of trends or themes (i.e., in words).

quantitative research—Research in which results are presented in the form of quantities or numbers (e.g., statistics).

research—"Studious inquiry or examination" using investigation or experimentation aimed at discovering and interpreting facts, revising accepted theories or laws in light of new facts, or making practical application of new or revised theories or laws (Merriam-Webster.com, 2010).

rubric—Guide that lists specific criteria for grading or scoring academic papers, projects, or tests.

stewardship—Careful and responsible management of something entrusted to one's care.

transparency—Opposite of privacy (an activity is transparent if all information about it is open and freely available).

References

American College Personnel Association (ACPA), Association of College and University Housing Officers–International, Association of College Unions–International, National Academic Advising Association, National Association for Campus Activities, National Association of Student Personnel Administrators, et al. (2006). *Learning Reconsidered 2*. Washington, DC: Author.

American Psychological Association (APA). (2009). Publication manual of the *American Psychological Association* (6th ed.). Washington, DC: Author.

Arminio, J. (2009). Applying professional standards. In G.S. McClellan, J. Stringer, & associates (Eds.), *The handbook of student affairs administration* (pp. 187–205). San Francisco: Jossey-Bass.

Campbell, C. & Rozsnyai, C. (2002). Quality Assurance and the Development of Course Programmes. Papers on Higher Education. Philadelphia: Carfax Publishing.

Council for the Advancement of Standards in Higher Education. (2006). *CAS professional standards for higher education* (6th ed.). Washington, DC: Author.

Council for the Advancement of Standards in Higher Education. (2009). *CAS professional standards for higher education* (7th ed.). Washington, DC: Author.

Dalton, J.C., Crosby, P.C., Valente, A., & Eberhardt, D. (2009). Maintaining and modeling everyday ethics in student affairs. In G.S. McClellan, J. Stringer, & associates (Eds.), *The handbook of student affairs administration* (pp. 166-186). San Francisco: Jossey-Bass.

Franklin, D.S. (2007). *Student development and learning in campus recreation: Assessing recreational sports directors' awareness, perceived importance, application of and satisfaction with CAS standards.* Ohio University.

Gall, M.D., Gall, J.P., & Borg, W.R. (2007). *Educational research* (8th ed.). Boston: Pearson.

Haines, D., & Farrell, A. (2006). The perceived barriers to research in college recreational sports. *Recreational Sports Journal, 30*, 116–125.

Institute for Credentialing Excellence. (2010). National Commission for Certifying Agencies accredited certification programs. www.credentialingexcellence.org/GeneralInformation/AboutUs/tabid/54/Default.aspx.

Kruger, R., & Casey, M. (2000). *Focus groups: A practical guide for applied research* (3rd ed.). Thousand Oaks, CA: Sage.

Lindner, J. (1998). Understanding employee motivation. *Journal of Extension 36*(3).

Mallory, S.L., & Clement, L.M. (2009). Accountability. In G.S. McClellan, J. Stringer, & associates (Eds.), *The handbook of student affairs administration*. pp. 107-111. San Francisco: Jossey-Bass.

National Association of Student Personnel Administrators (NASPA). (2010). About us. www.naspa.org/about/default.cfm.

National Association of Student Personnel Administrators (NASPA) & American College Personnel Association (ACPA). (2004). *Learning reconsidered*. Washington, DC: Author.

National Center for Education Statistics. (2011). Integrated postsecondary education data system. http://nces.ed.gov/ipeds/

National Intramural-Recreational Sports Association (NIRSA). (2010a). Mission statement. www.nirsa.org/Content/NavigationMenu/AboutUs/MissionVision/Mission_Vision.htm.

National Intramural-Recreational Sports Association (NIRSA). (2010b). The registry of collegiate recreational sports professionals. www.nirsa.org/Content/NavigationMenu/Education/Registryof-CollegiateRecreationalSportsProfessionals/professionalregistr.htm.

Patten, M.L. (2009). *Understanding research methods* (7th ed.). Glendale, CA: Pyrczak.

Quality Research International. (2011). *Analytic quality glossary*. www.qualityresearchinternational.com/glossary/benchmarking.htm.

Schuh, J., & Associates. (2009a). *Assessment methods for student affairs*. San Francisco, CA: Jossey-Bass.

Schuh, J. & Associates. (2009b). *Assessment Methods for Student Affairs*. San Francisco, CA: Jossey-Bass.

Secretary of Education's National Commission on the Future of Higher Education (2006). *A test of leadership: Charting the future of U.S. higher education*. www2.ed.gov/about/bdscomm/list/hiedfuture/reports/final-report.pdf.

Southern Association of Colleges and Schools Commission on Colleges (SACSCOC). (2010). [Mission statement]. http://sacscoc.org/.

Texas Higher Education Coordinating Board. (2010). Mission statement. www.thecb.state.tx.us/index.cfm?objectid=69CCD897-E595-39AA-828AADCA6DBD75D2.

Upcraft, M.L., & Schuh, J.H. (1996). *Assessment in student affairs: A guide for practitioners*. San Francisco: Jossey-Bass.

Wellman, J.V. (2006). Accountability for the public trust. In N.B. Shulock (Ed.), *Practitioners on making accountability work for the public*. New Directions for Higher Education, no. 135. San Francisco: Jossey-Bass.

Wingspread Group on Higher Education. (1993). *An American imperative: Higher expectations for higher education*. Racine, WI: Johnson Foundation.

CHAPTER

7

Risk Management

Jeff Sessine
Centers LLC

Campus recreational sports professionals need to demonstrate the ability to provide prudent care for patrons and, when needed, to defend employees' actions in programs offered inside the recreation facility as well as scheduled activities off site. The nature of the profession itself means that these professionals practice risk management on a daily basis, and that pressure is only growing. Campus recreational sports programs increasingly offer creative and value-added services to meet demands for innovation driven in part by the entitlement mentality common among today's college consumers. As recreation facilities expand to offer increased capacity and amenities, facility operators must be risk managers.

This heightened level of risk and responsibility has influenced the industry to hire full-time staff members who oversee risk management and to require varying degrees of risk management training for all staff. As a result, the lens of risk management is now used to vet the methodologies used for developing programs, renting space and equipment, offering services, and handling all business and operating practices. The burden of responsibility must be shared by all recreation professionals, which requires an intentional and thoughtful business-minded approach to minimize the risk of injury and liability while maximizing the recreational experience for all involved. This chapter identifies the primary risk factors associated with managing a campus recreational sports facility and explains best practices for minimizing those risks.

PRINCIPLES OF RISK MANAGEMENT

Though the basic principles of **risk management** are not complicated, it is important to understand the law as it applies to **negligence** liability. One of the first models, and still a generally accepted articulation of the rule, derives from the negligence calculus or Hand rule. This approach was put forth by Judge Learned Hand (United States v. Carroll Towing, 1947) to describe whether a legal duty has been breached or a party has been negligent. Based on Hand's ruling, a service provider's duty is a function of three variables:

- The probability of an accident's occurrence
- The gravity of loss if it should occur
- The burden imposed on the service provider to make adequate precautions

If only risk were in fact that easy to determine! In reality, there is often no specific calculus or rubric to follow. In most cases in the United States, a jury decides what particular acts or omissions constitute negligence. As a result, operators are well advised to exercise common sense rather than relying on a formulaic equation to ascertain what an ordinary, careful person would have done under the circumstances.

When using common sense as a guidepost in managing risk, the first step is to identify existing parameters or best practices that have already been established in order to standardize risk management protocol and risk mitigation. Standards—or recommendations, or best practices—are produced by a range of organizations, such as the National Intramural-Recreational Sports Association (NIRSA) and the American College of Sports Medicine (ACSM).

The next step is to establish a threshold of risk for providing services that meets these basic recommendations and is acceptable to all involved parties who are held accountable (e.g., operator and institution). First, one must ask why risk and risk management have become a major issue in campus recreational sports. In fact, the answer has nothing to do with the activities themselves—very little has changed about recreational activities in the past 30 years. Rather, the perception of risk has grown into the dominating factor in evaluating and controlling risk. Peter Sandman, an expert in risk communication, has developed a definition of **risk** that is independent of any legal reference. His definition of risk has more to do with public perception or, as he calls it, "the Outrage Model": "risk = hazard + outrage" (Covello & Sandman, 2004). In this model, the **hazard** is the objective factor (e.g., the playing surface or the nature of the activity), and outrage is the subjective factor, which is based on personal values and opinions and is often clouded by emotion. In an article written in SportRisk titled, "The Scariest Four Letter Word in Campus Recreation," Matt Campbell cited Sandman's outrage model by illustrating how the emotional response or outrage triggers litigious behavior by participants or parents of minors who participate in sports.

Campbell further asserts that the emotional response, or outrage, plays a large role in analyzing risk. To illustrate, the hazards of sliding into a base during a baseball game are well known and traditionally assumed to be a part of the game. So if the hazard has been recognized and controlled, the outrage, or emotional reaction, distorts the assessment of acceptable risk (Covello and Sandman, 2004).

When this model is applied to the campus recreation setting, it is apparent why risk management has become a pressing issue (Campbell, 2011).

The increase in outrage about perceived risk has necessitated risk assessment, **assumption of risk** clauses, releases from liability, **waivers**, and exculpatory clauses in an area that previously involved little formality and was based instead on common sense. Though recent developments in health and technology have reduced hazards in campus recreational sports, the growth of the outrage factor means that departments must enact additional and enhanced risk management strategies.

With all this in mind, facility operators must identify the acceptable threshold of risk when

Photo courtesy of Colorado State University.

Measuring risk includes more than assessing hazards associated with activities and equipment; it also must take into account the potential for highly subjective outrage.

developing and enforcing policies, designing programs, and offering services. These thresholds should be developed in concert with state law, the university's risk management office, and its general counsel. For example, facility operators must determine whether certain certifications should be required of staff in order to teach or supervise certain activities or spaces within the facility.

Since the majority of risks in campus recreational sports facilities fall under the legal doctrine of **tort**, managers must develop a basic understanding of this legal concept and include it in staff training. A tort complaint consists of four basic components:

1. **Duty to act** is an obligation imposed on an individual to adhere to a reasonable **standard of care** while performing any acts that foreseeably could harm others.
2. **Breach** is considered to occur when one's conduct falls short of the expected standard.
3. **Causation** refers to a reasonable connection between the breach of duty and the injury.
4. **Damages** are the monetary compensation sought or awarded in a lawsuit as a remedy for breach of contract. The basis for tort law is to compensate for an injury resulting from a wrongful act; if there is no injury, then there is no compensation (see Campbell, SportRisk, McGregor & Associates, 2011).

Each of the four elements is essential for a claim, and each builds on another. The first area to establish is duty, which exists in everyday life and controls social interactions. For example, when driving a car, I have a duty to obey traffic signals; when waiting for a train, people have a duty not to push and shove. One way to determine the appropriate standard of care is to apply the reasonably prudent person test, which is in fact the legal standard developed over years of case law in the United States. A reasonably prudent person is an individual who uses good judgment or common sense in handling practical matters. This standard is meant to be applied to industry-wide best practices such as determining supervision ratios, creating policies and procedures, developing programs, and offering services.

When someone believes that conduct has fallen short, or there is a perceived **breach** of duty, then he or she can file a **claim** citing the cause and seeking **damages**. In response, the principles of tort law raised most frequently by defense teams in recreation and sport injury cases are contributory negligence, assumption of risk, and waiver or consent (Campbell, SportRisk, McGregor & Associates, 2011). The **contributory negligence** principle weighs the plaintiff's conduct as a potential contributing party to the harm that he or she suffered. Therefore, it is imperative for campus recreational sports staff to document all information at the time that an accident or incident occurs, especially if the injured party may have contributed to his or her injury. A timely and descriptive incident report may help bar any claims against the employee or university.

Another approach to minimizing the risk of a claim is to require patrons to sign an informed consent, release from liability, and waiver. In order for a person to assume the risk factors outlined in this legal document, he or she must know and appreciate them, and state laws differ in whether or not they favor the use of these forms. Facility managers should research if the state for which they operate has laws that minimize the effectiveness or prohibit the use of these forms. Before a risk may be assumed, the person must understand that risk varies by program, facility, and activity. Some risks constitute an **inherent risk**—that is, one residing in the very nature of the activity or for which the connection between the risk and the activity is so significant that the risk cannot be removed without substantially changing the activity (e.g., pulling a muscle while lifting weights, twisting an ankle while playing volleyball, getting hit by an elbow while playing basketball).

Informed consent derives from a person's inherent right to control what happens to his or her body and from the caregiver's duty to help that person understand the risks inherent in the care. These two aspects undergird disclosure and consent, and both are required to establish informed consent. By this definition, of course, someone who is unconscious, confused, or seriously ill or injured may not be able to grant informed consent. In such cases, the law assumes **implied consent**—in other words, that the victim would give consent if he or she were able to do so. One can also assume implied consent in regard to a **minor** who needs emergency assistance when no parent or guardian is present.

Some institutions maintain that the student's consent is implied when he or she enrolls and thus that no additional consent is required to participate in programs or activities managed by the staff either inside or outside of the facility. However, all nonstudent members, including employees, should be required to sign a consent form. In general, courts uphold such agreements if it is unmistakably clear that the parties' intent was to shift the risk of loss. Thus waivers must be well drafted and signed by all legal participants prior to their participation in any campus recreational sports activity. Though facility managers should take into account relevant cases and common laws in shaping their approach to risk management, they should never assume that these legal **precedents** will permanently hold or that court cases in other jurisdictions will have no bearing on them (Fried, 2010). Precedents will continue to be defined and redefined as courts hear new and compelling arguments in this litigious era.

Should a facility operator ever limit the level of care provided in response to an injury or incident? It depends. For example, first responder protocols governed by the university may require the operator to manage risk in a certain way that supersedes specific facility or membership policy. Thus facility operators should take precautionary steps when establishing or revising policies to ensure that they comply with requirements set forth by all relevant governing bodies (e.g., state, local, institutional) for all membership classifications (e.g., alumni, employee, community) and unaffiliated user groups (e.g., **invitee**, minor, **recreational user**). Doing so may require developing multiple protocols for responding to the same injury or incident.

A facility manager may have greater latitude to intervene if the user is an alumnus or community member as opposed to a university student or employee as there are established university protocols and designated personnel who directly oversee certain situations (e.g., counseling services, dean of students, sexual harassment office, human resources). For example, even if a student using the facility appears to be overexercising and battling anorexia, the facility manager cannot directly intervene or prohibit use of the facility as the student paid fees through enrollment requirements and the facility manager is not authorized to intervene due to privacy mandates per the university protocols. The facility manager is limited to advising the student to speak with a counselor. The health and liability issues in this situation boil down to two litigious matters: manage to minimize the risk of a wrongful death suit or risk a discrimination suit. In other words, if the facility manager revokes her membership, the facility runs the risk of being sued for discrimination. On the other hand, if the facility is perceived to have done nothing and enabled the behavior, the facility could be sued for not acting. The university recreation environment is challenging to navigate, especially when servicing multiple users.

Also, some individuals may refuse care even if they appear to be injured. In such cases, the care provider should disclose the necessary information and request that the person at least allow someone more highly trained, such as EMS personnel, to make an evaluation. It should be made clear that the staff is neither refusing to care for nor abandoning the victim. Also, request that another person be present to witness the **refusal of care** and document it by requesting a signature from all parties involved. **Good Samaritan laws** may or may not provide protection, since state statutes vary, and they apply only as long as the party rendering care owes no duty to the injured person.

MANAGING RISK

A facility operator can implement certain measures to manage risk. At a minimum, the operator should designate one member of the staff to serve as the risk manager. That person should meet annually with the university's general counsel and risk management representatives to do the following:

- Discuss any changes or rulings in tort liability that may affect the program.
- Draft or review the waiver and consent form.
- Establish minimum certification standards for student employees.
- Establish an exact minimum threshold for incidents requiring documentation.

Depending on the overall perceived risk to the operation, department, and institution, the facility operator might also assemble a risk management team. The team can include key campus recreational sports staff (e.g., facility and program staff) and designated staff from other campus areas, such as campus safety, dean of students, and health services. The group might meet annually or every term or even on a case-by-case basis as determined by the risk manager. Operators should also secure the appropriate amount of general liability insurance coverage since there is no chance of eliminating risk—just becoming proficient in managing it in a high-risk environment.

The countless opportunities for injury and the potential legal ramifications of managing a high-risk facility can lead operators to fall into a trap of hindering the staff's innovation and creativity that bring life to these unique quality-of-life facilities. To avoid operational paralysis, facility operators should accept the current state of risk that is inherent in managing these types of facilities and focus on taking reasonable steps to keep patrons safe from potential dangers. Of course, facilities should be designed and built to reduce potential hazards, but the manager should also be proactive in identifying and assessing potential risks that do exist and choosing the appropriate way to address them (Cohen, 2010). As noted in figure 7.1, risk management can be viewed as a cycle of continuous improvement: preparation, response, assessment, further preparation, and so on.

One of the first steps in assessing risk is to consider the following key areas of an operation:

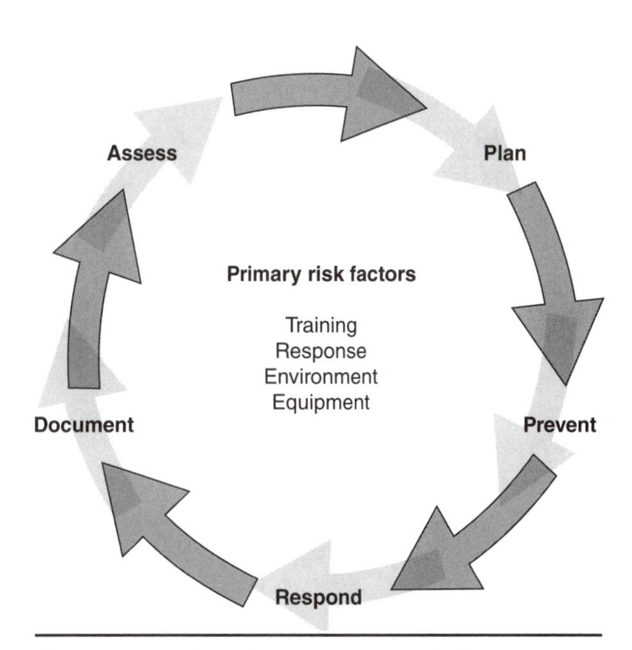

Figure 7.1 The risk management cycle.

training, response, environment, equipment, and documentation (McGregor, Risk Management Planning Resource). These areas are explored in detail throughout the remainder of this chapter.

TRAINING

A thorough risk management plan is a strategic road map for how an organization measures and responds to risk. It serves as an organization's standard for maintaining a safe environment and describes the methods by which all employees should care for the facility and equipment. When developing the plan, operators should do the following:

- Identify all safety training protocols needed for a specific program.
- Make sure all supervisors are trained and certified in appropriate emergency protocols (e.g., first aid, CPR, use of an automated external defibrillator [AED], blood pathogens, methicillin-resistant Staphylococcus aureus [**MRSA**]).
- Develop an emergency response plan in which all staff positions are given specific tasks to complete in an emergency (see table 7.1).

- Demonstrate the importance of documentation.
- Develop protocols to test staff members' understanding of procedures through interactive situational illustrations.
- Continually update and refresh employees in safety protocol.
- Communicate changes or issues to student staff.

The risk management plan should also identify the standard of practice for specific services. For example, what types of certification or training are necessary for lifeguards or personal trainers? Do they need to be credentialed by specific governing bodies? Standard of practice deals with developed paradigms published by professional organizations such as NIRSA, ACSM, the American Council on Exercise (ACE), and the American Alliance for Health, Physical Education, Recreation and Dance (AAHPERD). Taking the form of recommendations, guidelines, or position statements, these standards serve as benchmarks for desirable minimum safe practices for professionals in the field. They may also be referred to as best practices or industry standards. By any name, they support the reasonably prudent person test described earlier in this chapter.

Facility operators may choose to establish a higher safety standard than what is considered best practice. In these cases, the operator takes on greater responsibility and risk if protocols are not administered correctly. For example, best practice recommends that patrons wear safety goggles when playing racquetball, but if the wearing of goggles is *required* then the onus is placed on the facility operator to enforce the rule. One can argue that since risk is inherent in the very nature of an activity or facility space (e.g., a pool, climbing wall, or ropes course), it is incumbent upon the employee to provide the instruction and supervision necessary for a safe playing environment. Operators can minimize the risk of participant injury by requiring proper certification and conducting staff training on a scheduled basis. In addition, if an activity is supervised or designed for progressive skill development (e.g., advanced pilates, yoga, or dance), it is advisable for instructors to develop learning outcomes and activity plans. These

Table 7.1 Code Red: Fire

First responder	Pull the nearest fire alarm and call the code
Facility supervisor	Evacuate patrons from studios and track Stay in contact with all staff members Call the assistant director of facilities Call code green when and if the fire department gives the all clear Be the last one out of the facility
Front desk	Call 911 Evacuate the administrative offices and the lobby Evacuate the basketball courts, cardio corridor, game room, racquetball courts, and outdoor pursuits
Equipment issue	Shut down the computer Evacuate members from the women's locker room
Weight room	Evacuate patrons from the weight room and cardio area
Intramurals	Evacuate patrons through the nearest exit
Aquatics	Evacuate patrons from the men's and family locker rooms
Fitness instructors	Evacuate patrons through the nearest exit Radio to the facility supervisor after each area is clear
Adventure or climbing wall	Evacuate patrons through the nearest exit Radio to the facility supervisor after each area is clear

documents provide facility managers with a better understanding of the activity, enabling them to forecast potential risks associated with it, and documentation of the content the instructor will provide.

All job responsibilities (for full- and part-time employees) should include orientation and in-service training held periodically to maintain employees' requisite skills and knowledge. Detailed job descriptions and manuals for all employment positions should be well documented, and all procedures should be outlined in the risk management plan.

RESPONSE

Facility managers should develop specific protocols to govern employees' responses to injuries, incidents, and accidents. Such protocols provide clear parameters for what first responders should and should not do. For example, they should include requirements for both acute and chronic injuries (see table 7.2 for an example).

In the event of a life-threatening accident or injury, contact the appropriate emergency personnel immediately. According to the American Red Cross (ARC; 2011), sudden cardiac arrest is the leading cause of death in the United States; each year, cardiac arrest strikes more than 300,000 victims, of whom only 5 percent survive. The ARC recommends following four critical steps called the cardiac chain of survival:

1. Early access to care
2. Early cardiopulmonary resuscitation (CPR)
3. Early defibrillation
4. Early institution of advanced life support

Before emergency personnel arrive, employees should prudently follow these steps to maximize the opportunity to save lives. Toward this end, all staff should earn and maintain certifications in CPRAED. In addition to directly following the ARC chain of survival, follow these guidelines when caring for a victim:

- Give only the first aid you are capable and qualified to provide.
- Stop profuse bleeding with direct pressure over the wound.
- Always use personal protective equipment when handling an accident or injury involving blood or other bodily fluid.
- Keep airways unobstructed (nose and mouth uncovered and clear).
- Keep victim calm, still, warm, and lying down. Keep bystanders away.
- Supervisor is responsible for obtaining proper assistance.

The decision to require staff to maintain certifications in first aid is a choice that each department or institution should make with guidance from the general counsel's office and the institution's risk manager. If first aid is part of the institution's standard of care, then all staff should be certified and provided with training on a scheduled basis. Supervisory staff should also wear first aid waist packs or have access to inventoried and well stocked first aid kits adjacent to all primary activity spaces.

There is a real danger in brushing off accidents that are not severe or life threatening. Investigate thoroughly and collect all information pertaining to the accident for documentation, filing, and follow-up purposes. Prior to giving any care, be certain to obtain consent. After care is given, ask the injured person to sign the accident form agreeing to what has been documented.

Operations that serve non-university patrons may use different protocols. For example, university policy might require that you contact the campus security office for immediate assistance if the victim is a student or faculty member but contact the local police department when an alumnus or community member needs immediate assistance. Ultimately, training aids such as these response protocols should minimize the risk of negligence and produce consistent customer service.

The practical application of the risk management plan takes the form of an **emergency response plan (ERP)**, which serves as the essential training tool for all employees. It provides a systematic, visual outline that identifies all possible emergency situations. An ERP should address (among others) the following emergencies: fire, medical emergency, chemical

Table 7.2 Injury Response Protocol

General first aid	Chronic injury (ice)	Acute injury	Severe or fatal injury
If certified: 1. Check, call, care. 2. Contact FM (facility manager). a. Explain injury. b. Give location. c. Describe nature of emergency. 3. Care for victim. 4. Wait for FM to arrive. 5. File accident report. 6. File follow-up report (48 hours). **Locations of first aid kits:** 1st floor: equipment issue 1st floor: pool office 1st floor: outdoor office 2nd floor: welcome desk 2nd floor: fitness specialist desk All studios: personal CPR packs Intramurals: IM supervisor	**Defer to FM:** 1. Contact FM (facility manager). 2. Communicate request. 3. Direct patron to equipment issue. 4. Dispense ice bag. 5. Sign accident report. **Do not offer:** • Tape for ankle wraps • Ace bandages • Instant ice or heat packs	**If certified:** 1. Check, call, care. 2. Radio-contact FM (facility manager). a. Explain injury. b. Give location. c. Describe nature of emergency. d. Dial 911 and campus police. 3. Care for victim. a. Use protective gear (blood, fluids). b. Stop bleeding with direct pressure. c. Keep airway unobstructed. d. Treat for shock. 4. Wait for FM and EMS to arrive. 5. Designate staff to wait for and direct EMS. 6. Fill out accident report. 7. Contact director if necessary. 8. File follow-up report (48 hours).	**If certified:** 1. Check, call, care. 2. Retrieve AED and bring to victim. 3. Radio-contact FM (facility manager). a. Explain injury and give location. b. Dial 911 and campus police. 4. Inform full-time staff (if available). 5. Care for victim (check vital signs). a. Use protective gear (blood, fluids). b. Stop bleeding with direct pressure. 6. If pulse and breathing: a. Keep airway unobstructed. b. Treat for shock. 7. If pulse but not breathing, perform rescue breathing. 8. If no pulse and not breathing, perform CPR and use AED. 9. Continue until FM and EMS arrive. 10. Designate staff to wait for EMS. 11. Contact director ASAP. 12. Fill out accident report.
If not certified: 1. Check, call, care. 2. Contact FM (facility manager). a. Explain injury. b. Give location. 3. Stay with victim. 4. Wait for FM to arrive.		**If not certified:** 1. Check, call, care. 2. Contact FM (facility manager). a. Explain injury. b. Give location. c. Describe nature of emergency. d. Call 911 and public safety office. 3. Defer to someone who is certified. 4. Wait for FM and EMS to arrive.	**If not certified:** 1. Check, call, care. 2. Retrieve AED and bring to victim. 3. Contact FM (facility manager). a. Explain injury and give location. b. Describe nature of emergency. c. Dial 911 and campus police. 4. Defer to someone who is certified. 5. Wait for FM and EMS to arrive.

emergency, power loss, natural disaster, bomb threat, active shooter, and abduction or missing person. It should not be created in a vacuum; rather, many campus stakeholders should actively participate in the development process (see figure 7.2).

Here are four keys to developing an effective ERP:

1. Establish supervised, direct routes for every area and floor.
2. List staff responsibilities, including positioning, instructions, and equipment.
3. Give directions for where groups should proceed.
4. Describe route and final destination.

Facility operators should develop multisensory training techniques to accommodate all learning preferences and to limit attention deficit or boredom. Consider active learning training (e.g., mock drills, role play) to keep staff engaged.

The ERP lists procedural duties for several potential emergency situations. The following examples provide abbreviated but detailed procedure summaries for some emergencies that should be included in an ERP.

Employee Emergency Procedures

All staff should be prepared to execute a predetermined emergency procedure for every accident, injury, and blood-borne pathogen, as well as evacuation procedures in case of a bomb threat, natural disaster, or fire. A designated staff member should serve as the point person for communication during such occasions, and every staff position should have precise responsibilities for each type of emergency situation.

The point person for communication is responsible for contacting emergency personnel and initiating the appropriate emergency protocol. Most contemporary recreation centers employ a dynamic student development model in which graduate or undergraduate student employees serve as point persons for communication and coordinate these emergency procedures. However, when such emergencies

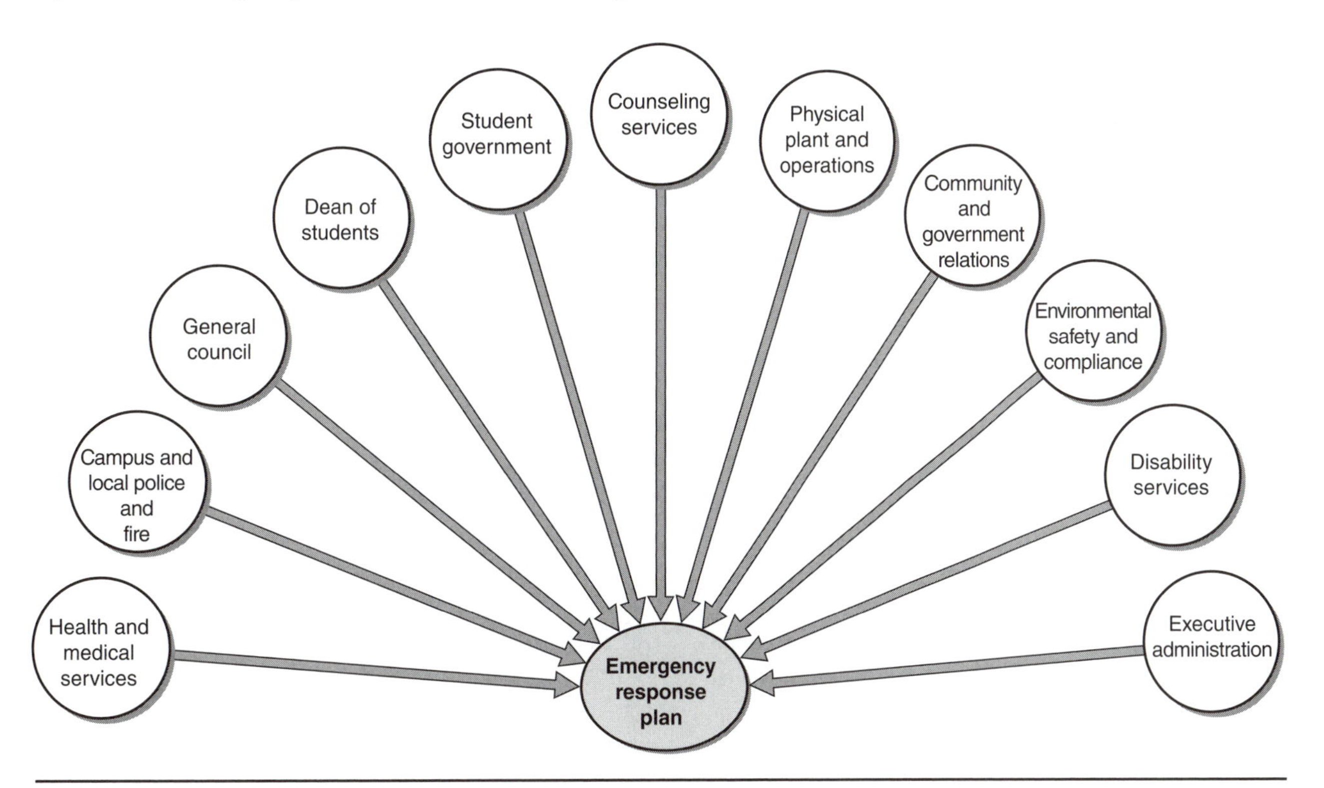

Figure 7.2 The development of an emergency response plan is a collaborative effort that should involve many campus stakeholders.

occur, the student staff should contact the director of the department or facility manager to inform or seek advisement.. Here is an example of a general emergency protocol coordinated by the first responder:

- Survey the scene and determine whether the victim is conscious.
- Contact the control desk or supervisor.
- Explain that there is an emergency and identify the location and the nature of the injury or condition.
- Wait for assistance from other staff personnel. Request an AED.
- Administer appropriate care for the victim.
  - Check vital signs (airway, breathing, circulation).
  - As needed, administer rescue breathing and CPR.
  - Control severe bleeding.
  - Treat for shock.
  - Stay with the victim.
- Assist the emergency transport personnel as needed.
- Stay at the site of the emergency and clear the area.
- Notify supervisor and make certain that reports are thoroughly completed by all involved staff or assistants.

General communication protocols in such situations include using handheld two-way radios between staff members unless radio silence is required (e.g., in a bomb threat) and a facility paging system. To enhance communication between department personnel, some institutions invest in a central repeater to centralize emergency communications on campus. Other forms of emergency communication include networked text messaging, designated emergency phones, and duress alarms.

Proper use of a facility-wide intercom system allows you to efficiently control the environment and provide direction that may be critical for survival. Staff should be trained to use the system and provided access to it. The system should be capable of overriding all other musical or paging zones throughout the building to ensure that announcements can be readily heard. Prepare specific scripted announcements for use in the most common emergency situations. This advance preparation allows for your staff to better respond and reduces human communication errors from elevated stress and anxiety.

Natural Disaster Emergency Procedure

Severe weather can occur without notice and require swift decision making to minimize risk of injury or death. Best practices for coordinating emergency procedures with staff involve clear communication, attention to detail, and preparation. Craft specific emergency procedures for common natural disturbances in your geographic region (e.g., tornado, flash flood, blizzard, intense heat, hurricane). In general, when the facility staff is informed of a severe weather alert near the facility, all persons in the facility should take shelter. The facility manager should immediately direct people to the ground level of the facility while maintaining radio contact with other employees. A staff designee should retrieve a battery-operated flash light to monitor conditions until it is safe to return to the activity areas. Entry control personnel should help people outside the facility come inside and provide them with directions to the sheltered area. Though it is unlawful to detain people against their will, you are strongly advised to communicate to them the dangers involved and then, if necessary, permit them to vacate the premises under their own initiative.

Fire Emergency Plan

The first few minutes of a fire are critical. What you do during these minutes can make the difference between a small blaze and a disaster. Facility operators must understand that fire and police authorities are in charge at the scene of the fire. The facility staff's job is to respond immediately, provide for safe evacuation of all patrons, and execute established emergency procedures until the firefighting crew arrives.

All employees should know the locations of all alarm pull stations throughout the facility—typically near exits and stairways. Alarm pull stations are activated by completely pulling down a lever located at the lower half of the alarm station cover. Note that some alarm stations may have pre-alarm covers, in which case the alarm that sounds is not the fire alarm but a warning alarm (it does not sound like a typical fire alarm). This alarm is intended to deter malicious activation and protect against accidental activation from bumping.

Some buildings are equipped with a central electronic display indicating the location of every pull station and identifying a particular pull station that has been activated. Thus if a fire alarm is pulled, this central display can indicate the location of the fire. The operator should immediately call the appropriate campus authorities and give the location and description of the fire. All facility personnel should assist in the evacuation process until it is no longer safe to remain in the building or they are told to leave by police, fire officials, or university authorities.

Some fire alarm systems can be activated automatically by means of smoke or heat detectors. When activated, the system causes an alarm to sound continuously throughout the building.

Active Shooter or Terrorist Attack

An attack can be initiated within a facility in several ways. As a result, this plan cannot begin to address every possible attack, and it should be used as a guideline in the event of a violent attack resulting in mass casualties. In these instances, prevention is the only way to ensure safety, and employees should report suspicious behavior from anyone who displays tendencies in the following directions:

- Threatens harm or talks about killing other students, faculty, or staff.
- Constantly starts or participates in fights.
- Easily loses temper and self-control.
- Swears or uses vulgar language most of the time.
- Possesses or draws artwork depicting graphic images of death or violence.
- Possesses weapons or is preoccupied with them.
- Becomes frustrated easily and converts frustration into physical violence.

Report only if you are in a safe area by following these protocols:

1. Call 911 and give your name, the location of the incident, and the following information (be as specific as possible):
    - Number of attackers
    - Identification or description of attacker(s)
    - Number of persons involved
    - Any known injuries
    - Individuals not immediately affected by the situation should take protective cover and stay away from windows and doors until notified otherwise. Depending on the specific threat, assist members in seeking shelter or evacuating the building.
2. If unable to evacuate, follow these best practice guidelines:
    - Individuals should lock themselves in the room they already occupy; secure and barricade doors and windows.
    - Call 911.
    - Do *not* stay in an open hall!
    - Do *not* sound the fire alarm! This could lead to an evacuation, thus putting others in harm's way.
    - Turn off all lights and audio equipment.
    - Try to stay calm and quiet.
3. If caught in an open area (e.g., hallway or lounge), decide quickly which of the following actions to take:
    - Try to hide, but make sure it is a well-hidden space.
    - Attempt to run out of the building only if there is a high probability of success.

- If you are unable to run or hide, remain still and motionless until the attacker leaves the area.
- Fighting back is dangerous and should be your last resort.
- If you are caught and decide not to fight back, follow the intruder's directions; do not look him or her in the eye.

Missing Person (Code Adam)

Created and named in memory of 6-year-old Adam Walsh, Code Adam is a widely recognized and effective procedure that should be immediately implemented when a child is reported missing or possibly abducted. Facility staff should be trained to take the following steps when a Code Adam is activated:

1. Obtain a detailed description of the child and what he or she is wearing.
2. Go to the nearest in-house telephone and page Code Adam, describing the child's physical features and clothing. Designated employees immediately stop working and look for the child. Designated employees monitor all entrances to ensure that the child does not leave the premises.
3. If the child is not found within 10 minutes, call law enforcement.
4. If the child is found and appears to have been lost and unharmed, reunite the child with the searching family member.
5. If the child is found accompanied by someone other than a parent or legal guardian, make reasonable efforts to delay their departure without putting the child, staff, or visitors at risk. Immediately notify law enforcement and give details about the person accompanying the child.
6. Cancel the Code Adam page after the child is found or law enforcement arrives.

As one can infer from these examples, the possibility of natural disaster, life-threatening injury, or an act of terrorism should not be taken lightly. This review provides only a sample of the various emergencies for which operators should plan, prepare, and practice. You should consider every possible emergency and thoroughly understand your environment, since some emergencies are more likely to occur in certain geographic locations.

During an emergency, communication systems are vital because they enable you to call first responders, direct traffic out of the facility or to safe zones within it, and coordinate with emergency personnel. Visual and audio communication devices provide essential tools commonly used by staff to control the environ-

Photo courtesy of Stephen F. Austin State University Campus Recreation.

Reliable communication devices are vital in responding to an emergency situation.

ment and provide awareness. Two of the more common devices are two-way radios and cell phones. When using these devices to communicate, use voice command protocols or designated call numbers for every position (e.g., Rec 1, this is Rec 2, over) to enable efficient and professional use, which is imperative in emergency situations. Developing symbols or codes for use in particular emergencies gives staff members an efficient way to describe certain situations and alert all facility personnel to initiate certain emergency procedures (e.g., code blue = aquatic emergency, code red = fire). Two more recent approaches—text messaging and web posting via social media outlets—have also provided very effective ways to communicate and maintain a controlled environment in an emergency.

ENVIRONMENT

Controlling facility access and supervising high-risk areas are both essential to mitigating risk, as we saw in 2009, when a gunman walked into a fitness club aerobics room, opened fire, killed three women, and wounded nine others before killing himself. Perhaps this tragedy could not have been prevented, but it served as an eye-opener for many fitness facilities and spurred them to reevaluate their safety measures with regard to facility access. It is advisable to limit access points in order to better control eligible patrons and users as they enter and exit the facility; it may also reduce personnel costs. You should also choose an easily identifiable access area as the central hub for communication and security to help you exchange information quickly and resolve problems efficiently. As a central hub, this primary location can be used to display or control the following building systems:

- Surveillance
- Emergency door, duress, and fire alarms
- Communication and emergency paging
- Building lighting
- Building HVAC
- Facility and member management software platform

In some facility designs, not all of these systems are centrally located, but full centralization should be considered when designing new facilities or added as a control feature for existing operations. It is essential to equip your operations staff with as much information as possible so that communication flows quickly to all designated responders and operational adjustments can be made as needed to maintain a safe, enjoyable environment.

Determining Access

Facility operators must determine how restrictive their access policy will be. While technological advances provide operators with several options for entry control and membership management software (e.g., digital photo, keyless entry, biometric identification, fingerprint scan), university policy may dictate the level of restriction and the degree of enforcement (e.g., all students must carry student identification on their person when on campus property). The challenge often lies in enforcing policy consistently.

The primary reason for controlling access is to provide a safe and enjoyable environment for those who have acknowledged the associated risks and are permitted to use the facility. Unauthorized use can jeopardize this environment, cause equipment damage, and threaten the safety of the unauthorized user or others. During life-threatening emergencies, facility operators should be able to swiftly secure the environment and account for all users, which means that it is essential to maintain a clean and accurate record of usage. Several facility software applications can provide real-time usage records, as well as options to use historical data for reporting trends, peak usage, and user frequency. Some examples of vendors providing this type of software include CSI, Rectrack and Fushion; some universities build customized applications through their IT departments.

Develop Facility Policies

Developing facility policies involves collaboration with the operating staff and university representatives to ensure that all proper measures are taken to minimize risk. Membership

eligibility and the broad menu of services should also be consistent with university policy and should not be violate other university-related agreements, financial or otherwise. For example, the funding source for the facility's construction may have been tax-exempt bonds, which limit the amount of taxable income that can be generated from nonaffiliated groups who purchase membership or services. Another example that requires careful consideration involves the university's definition of, and benefits provided to, employees, alumni, and their families. The facility's policies should be consistent with those of the home institution.

Operators must also ask whether all policies are realistic and can be enforced. To determine a policy's legitimacy, test it by answering the following three questions:

1. Is adequate staffing available to enforce the policy at all times?
2. Can you provide a substantial rationale for enforcing the policy?
3. Is the policy consistent with the mission of the department and the university?

If the response is yes to all three questions, then the policy is enforceable, substantial, and supportive of the operation's mission. In general, if the policy makes common sense and enhances the safety of others, it should be easy to enforce and should gain the support of users and staff alike.

When developing policies, one common pitfall is to use the word "require." Consider using "recommend" unless staff can enforce the policy at all times. For example, by recommending that patrons wear safety equipment before participating in an activity, the onus is placed on the participant to act on the recommendation. If it is requirement, however, the onus is placed on the operator to ensure that patrons follow the requirement, which could result in increased liability for the operator.

Security

Safety is a paramount concern for facility operators and a key component of risk mitigation. One primary step is to develop a risk management plan, which includes establishing protocols for authority and response and determining the balance of responsibility between operating staff, campus police, and local authorities. Your risk management plan should include a security plan, which entails developing a surveillance system inside and outside the facility, as well as protocols for defusing conflict and responding to emergency situations. Surveillance systems offer several features (e.g., zoom, motion activation, high-definition color), but the key is to locate cameras in high-traffic areas and position them to provide overlapping coverage. Some facilities relay the camera feed to a main source on campus (e.g., campus police), and it is advisable to purchase a web-based application with video recording capability. These features allow facility operators to view the system at remote locations and copy and save footage in order to document incidents. If used properly, these cameras can deter theft and be used as a training aid. For example, when conducting in-service or post-incident training, facility operators can play back footage and break down the entire incident to review with staff as a way to improve customer service and create better ways to diffuse a confrontation.

Patrons may react in various ways to surveillance. Some may view it as providing a desirably heightened level of security, whereas others see it as an invasion of privacy. You can minimize this negative—and incorrect—perception by means of proper signage, verbal communication, education, and careful placement of the cameras. Being transparent and positive are important practices in managing this perception well. For example, showcase all camera views on a flat screen monitor at the front entrance so users see what is being recorded.

More generally, signage that is easy to read and understand can be used to direct patrons to their destination in the facility, give them useful information (e.g., operational hours, scheduled activities, and room reservations), and educate them about the rules of the building. Signage falls into three basic categories: directional, procedural, and safety or compliance-related. Place signage strategically to aid the flow of traffic. Pay close attention to open sight lines in order to get the greatest potential exposure. Avoid making signage that accentuates a negative or prohibitive statement, which can set a negative tone and give the impression that the facility is unwelcoming. For example, instead of stating members may not bring more than three guests per visit, frame the policy positively by stating that members may bring three guests per visit. Although signage can be used to educate and give direction to patrons, operators should not feel obligated to post all policies and procedures in the facility. Advances in smartphone technology and social media offer you a creative means of communicating; you can also post information on the department's website. And remember that the best approach to minimizing risk of injury often lies in daily face-to-face interaction and supervision.

EQUIPMENT

Inspect and inventory all furniture, fixtures, and equipment and document the performance of scheduled preventive maintenance service and any repairs. Proper documentation allows operators to conform with governing regulations, proactively mitigate risks relating to damaged or faulty equipment, account for assets, manage asset disposal or trade per projected life expectancies, and demonstrate proper duty of care in cases where a third party may file a claim against the operation. Clearly designate which staff members are responsible for conducting inspections (and the frequency of inspections) of all playing facilities and program equipment. Most furniture and fixtures are cleaned and inspected on a static schedule and require less maintenance and care than fitness equipment, which is heavily used and should be cared for and inspected daily. It is worth your time to develop a systematic approach to cleaning and inspecting fitness equipment. One popular approach is to display an enlarged floor plan or diagram of the equipment layout and mark off the equipment as it is cleaned multiple times per day. Cleaning and inspection can be tracked electronically or on paper; either way, documentation of the work should be saved for future reference.

Routine inspections of the facility and surrounding outdoor playing areas should be conducted and documented on a daily basis. However, specific high-use areas (i.e., entries, hallways, playing surfaces, locker rooms) should be inspected multiple times a day and always prior to large-scale events (Nohr, 2009). See figure 7.3 for an illustration of a facility checklist. After inspections are recorded, immediately report any hazards, defects, or other concerns and take action to remedy the situation. When necessary, physical spaces should be temporarily closed with clearly marked signage.

Asset Management

Proactively caring for all facility equipment is essential to minimizing the risk of injury and prolonging the life of these assets. In general, the basic level of preventive maintenance entails following the manufacturer's guidelines found in the owner's manual. By following these guidelines and documenting the performance of scheduled service, you establish that you are following the industry standard of care in regard to maintaining equipment. You should develop an organized tracking system or database to tag and inventory all equipment. Give considerable thought to the frequency of inspections and inventory counts and to where you will store these documents either electronically or physically. Several asset management software platforms are available, and it is advisable to collaborate with the university overall to decide which system is most appropriate, especially if it needs to be compatible or interface with another system.

By creating this database, you can follow each machine or piece of equipment by collecting data to track its usage, repair, and replacement. An equipment database should collect the following information:

- Floor number (unique number that differentiates each piece of equipment)
- Manufacturer
- Model
- Equipment type
- Serial number

COURT INSPECTION CHECKLIST

Considerations	Yes or no (check one)	Notes for follow-up
If a hazard cannot be corrected before play, has it been determined whether the area is safe for play or whether to cancel the practice or game?	☐ Yes ☐ No	
If the area is safe for play but a hazard exists, have clear and adequate warnings been provided to all players and other persons who will use the area (e.g., officials and coaches)?	☐ Yes ☐ No	
Are extra balls removed during play?	☐ Yes ☐ No	
Are all protruding wall fixtures and switches padded or painted a bright color so as to warn players?	☐ Yes ☐ No	
If the area of play is inside and ventilation is insufficient on a hot and humid day, have you relocated or canceled the game or practice in order to prevent heat-related illness?	☐ Yes ☐ No	
Are there other considerations particular to preparing the court, gymnasium, or field for play?	☐ Yes ☐ No	

Figure 7.3 Sample equipment inspection checklist.

Reprinted, by permission, from K. M. Nohr, 2009, *Managing risk in sport and recreation: The essential guide for loss prevention* (Champaign, IL: Human Kinetics), 89.

- Audio and video display or serial number
- Floor locations (if equipment is rotated to extend life expectancy or for layout adjustments)
- Arrival date
- Retirement date
- Cost

This database should also provide a work history, including all repairs, service, usage, cleaning, and inspections; such records can be a vital tool for determining the most appropriate time to replace equipment. One of the bigger challenges that operators face is training staff members to clean consistently and to document each and every time that a machine or piece of equipment is cleaned. Operators must be able to demonstrate that all equipment is properly maintained and that the staff is working to prevent transmission of pathogens (e.g., MRSA) and to address mechanical problems in a timely fashion through daily routine safety inspections.

Replacement Plan

Consider also creating a prescribed life expectancy and replacement plan for each unit. Generally, the industry standard is to replace cardio equipment every 3 to 5 years and weight equipment every 8 to 10 years. Costly repairs performed on equipment that is out of warranty provide diminishing returns and increase the risk of liability. Once the warranty runs out on equipment, the onus is placed on the operator to properly maintain the equipment which places greater risk of liability on the operator if an injury occurs resulting from the use of this equipment. Consider all of these factors collectively in determining when to replace equipment.

Hazardous Material Management

Many facility operators store and require personnel to handle **hazardous material** (e.g., laundry detergent, pool chemicals, and cleaning supplies). Since these materials can be harmful to employees and patrons, their mere presence creates risk. As a result, facility operators should collaborate with appropriate university personnel to develop or adopt a hazardous material management policy in order to ensure that the institution is in compliance with all federal, state, and local regulations regarding hazardous material; to minimize any harmful effects to persons and the environment through exposure to hazardous materials; and to clarify areas of responsibility for all facility employees. For example, this policy should identify all facility spaces in which hazardous material is handled, stored, or used; and each space should be equipped with enough absorbent material to mitigate a spill from the largest container in the space.

In general, an institution should maintain an inventory of all chemicals used on its property. The inventory should be kept up to date by tracking purchases, sites of storage, use, and disposal records as provided by the various campus departments. Specific chemicals should be listed for all employees using a common area. These notices can be provided in the form of material safety data sheets, provided by the vendor at the time of purchase, to disclose the substance's physical properties, its toxicity, disposal requirements, safety hazards, and first aid information. These sheets should be copied and held in the departmental and university occupational safety offices and made available upon request.

In addition, all hazardous chemicals stored inside a fitness facility should be properly labeled according to the standards set by the Occupational Safety and Health Administration (OSHA). Proper labeling includes the name of the chemical, its hazard classification, the purchaser's name, and either the building address or the phone number. Refer periodically to the occupational safety office or related office for updated policy requirements.

All facility staff should exercise universal precautions in any situation involving exposure to blood or another bodily fluid. Bodily fluids that staff may encounter inside a facility include saliva, semen, sweat, and vomit. The chance of infection from saliva and sweat is negligible. Hepatitis- or HIV-positive blood can infect another person, especially if it comes into contact with skin that is cracked, lacerated, punctured, or affected by dermatitis or if it is transmitted through body openings during sexual contact. As a precaution, personal protective equipment should be provided in designated areas throughout the facility and replaced when equipment becomes contaminated. All infectious waste should be discarded according to federal, state, and local regulations.

- Latex gloves must be worn in all situations in which the employee may have contact with blood or other potentially infectious material.
- Personal protective equipment (e.g., gloves, apron, face mask) must be worn during transportation and handling of biohazardous material.
- All biohazardous material collected must be secured in a biohazard bag and placed in a properly marked container.
- Arrange for biohazardous waste disposal within 30 days of the material's placement into the properly marked container.
- All other equipment and work surfaces that have been contaminated with blood or other potentially infectious material shall be cleaned and decontaminated immediately with an appropriate disinfectant.

If case of exposure, a standard set of protocols should be strictly enforced and consistently followed. It is advisable to create or purchase exposure incident packets and store them in designated locations such as inside all first aid kits located throughout the building. This packet should contain an exposure incident checklist, exposure incident report, exposed employee medical release form, and source medical release form for the exposed victim.

DOCUMENTATION

Facility operators need to be able to provide documentation that personnel are trained appropriately and that the operation is managed safely according to industry best practice. In case of a claim filed against the operation, operators could be subpoenaed to provide such documentation or information that could be used to support a complaint (e.g., faulty equipment). The following list highlights common documentation requirements:

- Keep copies of all employees' certifications, credentials, training tests, and receipts in human resources and employee files.
- Check state law and university requirements for the length of time you are required to hold all files.
- Ensure that facilities and equipment are monitored daily through the use of daily safety checklists.
- Keep a general log of daily activities regardless of any incidents and of participant count to gauge usage.
- Complete the appropriate forms when an accident or incident occurs; professional staff should review, follow up on, and file all forms.

Ultimately, the most important tool at an operator's disposal is the persistence to rigorously document all activities in the pursuit of operating a safe, high-quality facility. Minutely detailed documentation of all hazards found, all repairs undertaken, all procedures followed in an emergency, and all medical care given can make all the difference in the event of a lawsuit (Cohen, 2010).

One way to assess the safety of an operation is to perform an audit, either internally or by hiring a third party. Reputable companies, such as McGregor & Associates, offer on-site consultation and online audits that provide a great deal of detail and benchmark data. An audit can expose existing risk factors and operational vulnerabilities that need to be addressed in programming, staff training, or general administration. More important, an audit can help you improve the safety of your operation by addressing the areas in need of attention. If, on the other hand, needed improvements are identified but not addressed, the operation is exposed to greater risk of liability, since the audit upped the ante on the operator's standard of care.

SUMMARY

Regardless of the recreation or leisure activity, it involves some inherent risk. Some pose greater risk (e.g., rock climbing, swimming), whereas some don't seem particularly risky but still involve the chance of injury (e.g., running on a treadmill, playing intramural basketball). Facility operators need to use the various options now available (e.g., website, print publications, facility signage, and staff interaction) to inform patrons that, ultimately, they are responsible for their safety and to help them realize that no place is 100 percent safe. Accidents and injuries happen, and you cannot completely stop them; nor are you necessarily liable for them.

Managing risk comes down to these essential points:

- Rigorously train staff to understand safety and be accountable for it.
- Be vigilant in enforcing current safety policies and review them often for improvement.
- Keep patrons safe from potential physical danger and supervise activities.
- Educate patrons about personal responsibility and the inherent risk associated with participating in recreational and fitness-related activities.
- Put an emergency action plan in place to deal with external forces.
- The best defense against risk is to be proactive.

Job responsibilities for full- and part-time employees should include proper orientation, as well as ongoing in-service training held periodically to maintain requisite skills and knowledge. Specific certifications and scheduled inspections should be maintained for specialized programs and to support high-risk facility features. The facilities and services you provide should be inspected and audited on a scheduled basis. More important, operators must constantly refine their decision making by staying current with the latest case law even as they remain innovative to continue inspiring the costumers they serve.

In closing, it is important to note that the new realities of managing recreation facilities go well beyond the physical nature and inherent risk associated with playing sports and exercising. While the majority of this chapter outlines the risks associated with injury, employee training, and proper care of facilities and equipment, the understanding of risk mitigation delves much deeper for campus recreation professionals who are also responsible for managing financial, contractual and reputational risks associated with the department for which they manage. The landscape has certainly changed while the potential exposure to liability has become harder to control. However, it has also created a unique opportunity for employees in this field to become relevant stakeholders on their respective campuses by serving in leadership roles to proactively affect change in the way risk is perceived and managed collectively.

Glossary

assumption of risk—Legal doctrine relieving the defendant of any duty he or she may have otherwise owed the plaintiff; bars the plaintiff from recovering for any injury received. In order for assumption of risk to apply, an injured party must have known, understood, and appreciated the potential risk involved in an activity and still voluntarily consented to participate in it.

breach—Failure to perform as promised under a contract. Depending on the type of breach committed and the subject matter of the contract, the aggrieved party may have several remedies, including a financial damages award and fulfillment of the contract terms.

causation—An act or failure to act that causes injury or damages. This is an important element in negligence and criminal cases; the conduct does not have to be the sole cause of the injury but should be a substantial factor.

contributory negligence—Principle of tort law that bars the plaintiff from recovering a damage award under negligence if the plaintiff contributed in any way, regardless of the extent, to the injury. Due to the harsh impact of contributory negligence, a number of states have adopted a form of comparative negligence.

damages—Monetary compensation sought or awarded in a lawsuit as a remedy for breach of contract. Typically, damages are awarded to compensate the victim for his or her economic losses, physical pain, and suffering.

eligibility—Qualifications necessary for an individual to participate in an activity. Courts examine eligibility requirements of state or governmental organizations but typically do not challenge the eligibility standards of voluntary athletic associations unless they are applied in an arbitrary and unreasonable way.

Good Samaritan laws—State statutes enacted to protect individuals who stop and render aid to persons injured in an accident or other emergency situation. The majority of statutes apply only as long as the person rendering aid owes no duty to the injured person, does not charge a fee for the service, and is not grossly negligent.

hazard—A chance of being injured or a possible source of danger.

hazardous material—Material or substance that if improperly handled can damage the health and well-being of humans and their environment. The primary tools used to determine whether a material is hazardous and how it shall be handled are the material safety data sheet, the container label, and shipping invoices.

implied consent—Assumption by the law, when surrounding circumstances exist which would lead a reasonable person to believe that consent would be given, that someone who is unconscious, confused, or seriously ill or injured and thus cannot grant consent would consent if he or she were able to do so. Also, when a parent or guardian is not present, one can assume implied consent for minors who need emergency assistance.

informed consent—Agreement to do something or to allow something to happen only after all the relevant information has been provided or facts known.

inherent risks—Risks that are a normal, integral part of an activity (i.e., that cannot normally be eliminated without changing the nature of the activity itself).

invitee—Individual who is on another's property by invitation, either expressed or implied, for the economic or mutual benefit of both parties. Property owners owe invitees a legal obligation to provide a safe environment and to use reasonable care in protecting them from unreasonable dangers.

minor—Person who has not yet reached the age of majority. In most states, a person reaches majority and acquires all of the rights and responsibilities of adulthood when he or she turns 18 years old.

MRSA—Methicillin-resistant Staphylococcus aureus is a type of staph infections that is more resistant to the more commonly prescribed antibiotics

negligence—Conduct that falls below the standard of care required of a reasonable and prudent person under similar circumstances and that injures an individual's person, property, or reputation. The four elements necessary to prove negligence are duty, breach of duty, proximate cause, and damage or harm.

precedent—Prior case or decision based on similar facts or issues of law as the case under consideration.

recreational user—Individual who is on another's property specifically for recreational purposes. The user must not have paid or been charged a fee for entering the property and, for liability purposes, must be directly involved in a recreational activity at the time of the injury. Generally, the property owner must refrain from any intentional conduct that would injure a user.

refusal of care—Refusal by an ill or injured person to receive emergency care. Some ill or injured persons refuse offered care; even if a person seems injured, one must honor this refusal of care. Request that the person at least allow someone more highly trained, such as EMS personnel, to evaluate the situation. Be clear that the staff is not refusing to care for the victim or abandoning the victim. Request that another person be present to witness the person's refusal and document it on an accident form.

risk—Probability that a hazard will cause injury or damage. Many hazards are inherent to the workplace or process or piece of equipment used to accomplish our mission, but risk can be reduced by deciding on ways to change or control the hazard (e.g., controlling the equipment, using safer materials, doing the process in a safer manner) and still accomplish the facility's mission.

risk management—Process by which an organization attempts to maintain greater control over financial and legal uncertainties by identifying and determining the best method for reducing the organization's exposure to danger, harm, or hazards that may negatively affect the organization.

standard of care—Degree of care that a reasonably prudent person would exercise in the same or similar circumstances. In a negligence lawsuit, if an individual's conduct falls below the required standard of care, he or she may be liable for injuries or damages resulting from such conduct.

tort—Private or civil wrong, such as assault, battery, negligence, or reckless misconduct, for which the court provides a remedy by awarding damages.

waiver—Agreement or contract in which an individual intentionally and voluntarily relinquishes his or her legal rights. A properly constructed waiver can protect an organization or service provider from the ordinary negligence of his or her employees in at least 45 states.

References

American Red Cross (ARC). (2011). AED frequently asked questions (external audiences). www.redcross.org/www-files/Documents/pdf/Preparedness/AED_FAQs.pdf.

Campbell, M. (2011, July 19). The scariest four letter word in campus recreation (parts I & II). *SportRisk*. www.sportrisk.com/2011/07/19/the-scariest-four-letter-word-in-campus-recreation/ and www.sportrisk.com/2011/07/19/the-scariest-four-letter-word-in-campus-recreation-part-ii/.

Cohen, A. (2010, July). How to recognize dangers in your facility. *Athletic Business*. http://athleticbusiness.com/articles/article.aspx?articleid=3582&zoneid=28.

Covello, V., & Sandman, P.M. (2004). Risk communication: Evolution and revolution. In A. Wolbarst (Ed.), *Solutions to an environment in peril* (pp. 164-178). Baltimore: John Hopkins University Press.

Fried, G. (2010). *Managing sport facilities, second edition*. Champaign, IL: Human Kinetics.

Nohr, K.M. (2009). *Managing risk in sport and recreation: The essential guide for loss prevention*. Champaign, IL: Human Kinetics.

United States v. Carroll Towing Co. 159 F. (2d Cir.1947).

CHAPTER

8

Technology for the Recreation Practitioner

Robert L. Frye
Florida International University

José H. Gonzalez
Plymouth State University

Modern technology exercises tremendous influence on the daily life of the recreation practitioner. During a walk from the parking lot to the office, the practitioner can answer a cell phone call, retrieve voice mail, read e-mail, have his or her photo ID or fingerprint scanned at the front desk, and set off the office's motion-sensitive fluorescent lights—all before sitting down to a day's work. From his or her desk, the practitioner might retrieve yesterday's facility usage counts, monitor the building's temperature flux throughout the day, check the number of memberships sold this month, and electronically sign off on the department's payroll. Then, after catching an online video clip of the previous night's flag football championship, the professional might check the head referee's blog to see if there were any problems with sporting behavior. Next, he or she might use web-based video feeds to observe current use of the basketball courts and fitness areas before editing the preventive maintenance contract attached to an e-mail message retrieved moments ago and forward the revision to legal counsel and to the vice president for their comments. All this in the first hour of the day!

In keeping with this scene, key words in today's business and recreation environments include information, mobility, speed, capacity, efficiency, and features. The modern recreation practitioner needs to know not only how technology can improve facility operations, programs, marketing, and staff development but also how to decide which technology to use. Toward that end, this chapter discusses the selection process and reviews some technologies for you to consider.

MAKING THE RIGHT SELECTION

Whether selecting management software, fitness equipment, or online marketing methods—or deciding whether to use videos for staff training—decision makers must consider a variety of issues in order to ensure that they make the best choice for their organization.

Determining Need

The most obvious reason to purchase, adapt, or incorporate new technology is the fact that someone has decided there is a need for it. Deciding, however, is different from determining. Deciding a need is usually based on personal preference, perhaps as an effort to keep up with the competition or to take advantage of a special situation or opportunity. For example, the department head can decide that, due to a recent rash of thefts in the facility, a new video surveillance system is needed.

In contrast, determining a need involves setting objectives, doing research, making comparisons, and visualizing long-term effects on the organization. In the surveillance system example, the decision maker might couple research into the history of thefts in the facility with data about other events happening on campus or in the community. If there is no significant history of theft, is the investment necessary? If participation in the facility is "at one's own risk," is there a duty to provide surveillance? If surveillance is set up, where will it be placed? Who will monitor and maintain the system? What are the costs? How clear must visual acuity be to positively identify a perpetrator? Are patrons' personal rights affected? All these questions must be answered within the boundaries of the organization's goals and objectives in order to determine actual need.

Establishing Objectives

Setting objectives is a common practice for most organizations because objectives provide direction in pursuing a primary goal. The same is true for determining technology needs. What objectives will be attained by adding new technology? Is the objective to perform a task or function more easily or efficiently? Does it need to be done more cheaply? How would the new technology fit into the current operation? Will it benefit patrons and participants?

Influential Factors

When exploring a possible purchase of new technology, consider the following factors: functionality, user-friendliness, technology requirements (compatibility with existing infrastructure), upgrade specifications, maintenance agreements, warranty offers, implementation timeframes, and cost (Nunziato, 2003). Frazier and Bailey (2004) looked at what a technology coordinator should consider when itemizing the cost of incorporating new technology into an operation. They found that the two largest components were hardware (35% of total cost) and staff training (20%). Another way to think of key considerations is to divide them into the following more-encompassing categories: price, compatibility, personnel, maintenance, and risk.

Price

The cost of new technology systems, materials, and services often acts as the deciding factor in decision makers' minds. Technology is not inexpensive, and when budgets are tight the department must get the best "bang for the buck." To estimate true cost, recreation administrators need to thoroughly analyze the entire technology package—and not always settle for face value. Consider these price-related questions:

- Is there a single source or provider, or must several vendors be used in order to meet all needs?
- Can competitive bidding or government-rated pricing be used?
- What are the package's components (e.g., software, hardware, networking, licensing, preventive maintenance)?
- Some software solutions are sold in modules that allow the buyer to purchase one, several, or all according to individual need. Can you purchase just those modules you need at the time?
- Do existing systems or equipment need to be surplused, or do they have trade-in value toward the cost of the new purchase?
- Can business arrangements be made wherein the organization becomes a "featured user" or "demonstration site" for the technology in exchange for discounted pricing, additional features at low or no cost, or other special terms?

Compatibility

Decision makers must also examine the ease of transitioning from old systems and equipment to new ones. You can do this by researching spec sheets and technical drawings and by developing your knowledge of available features to ensure that everything will work together. Here are some questions to ask:

- How does the software interface (or not) with existing applications on both departmental and institutional levels?
- Will current or archival data transfer easily to the new system? If not, how will transfer be accomplished?
- Does existing hardware need to be updated? Will it interface with new printers, networks, and other computer platforms that may be added?
- Does the facility infrastructure (e.g., electrical wiring, phone and data lines, temperature control) need to be updated in order to support the new technology?

Personnel

Decision makers must also consider what personnel will be required to make new technology work. New technology can present new challenges and costs for in-house support staff such as IT technicians, equipment maintenance specialists, and front desk managers who conduct training. Questions to ask include the following:

- How quickly will the new technology be implemented? Do existing systems or equipment need to be "down" when the transition is made?
- How fast will staff get up to speed on the new technology? Will you need a lengthy training period, or can they learn on the fly? Does the vendor provide initial training, or is staff given a manual from which to learn?
- Do new staff members need to be hired to operate or manage new technology? Does new office or physical space need to be added or allocated to house the new technology?
- Does the vendor provide ongoing training as part of the purchase? If so, is it part of the purchase cost and warranty?

Maintenance

No matter what the sales representative may say, new technology is not perfect. With this reality in mind, research the cost of short- and long-term maintenance, as well as the cost of new versions, upgrades, and updates for software, hardware, and other equipment. Key questions:

- Are the costs of maintenance, updates, and upgrades built in, or must an additional preventive maintenance plan be purchased?
- How accessible are service representatives (e.g., by phone, online, and at various time of day)? Are service personnel local, or do they come from the home office?
- Can in-house staff perform software updates and upgrades, or must they be done by the vendor?
- What is the availability of parts, and who can install them? How much downtime is expected during maintenance?

Risk

Administrative decision makers must also understand that risks are involved in purchasing, implementing, and maintaining any new software application or piece of equipment. Ask the following questions:

- How is the security of data protected? Where is it housed, and who has access besides the department? How are software back-ups performed?
- Are redundancies built into the system (in case of data loss, electrical failure, or the like)?
- Does the vendor have a long track record in the business, or is it new to the industry? What is the likelihood of the vendor being bought out by another company?
- Is the technology so new that it has outpaced its supply possibilities?
- Is the technology based on an industry fad, or will it be around for a long time?

Making the Choice

When trying to make an educated decision about purchasing technology, it can be very helpful to seek input from other sources. The best recommendations often come from departments that already use the technology, and most vendors are happy to give you contact information for other customers when you show interest in their product. They may even place testimonials or examples on their website. The most productive testimonials usually come from the customers' own mouths. Don't just ask cursory satisfaction-oriented questions (e.g., "Are you happy with the software?" or "What don't you like about that piece of equipment?"). Instead, ask specific questions about pricing options they received, the breadth of their preventive maintenance contract, how long it took for their staff to be fully trained, who *they* talked to before buying, and so on.

Another way to get information is to attend trade shows, which can serve as an excellent and economical way to talk with many vendors in a short time. It also gives you a good opportunity to see the product in action—for example, fitness equipment, software applications, facility maintenance electronics, and other tech items. Vendors are in top sales mode at these shows, so it pays to prepare good questions. Listen to their answers to questions from other potential customers as well. You can also gather valuable information about products by subscribing to trade magazines or e-zines (electronic magazines) and exploring other online media.

After establishing your objectives for the new technology, exploring all factors that could influence the purchase, and listening to vendors and colleagues praise (or decry) particular products, you can make an educated choice. It should be a sound one as long as your process has been comprehensive, unbiased, and based upon well-defined objectives. Be prepared, however, to start the whole process again—though technology may get cheaper over time, newer and improved products arrive every day.

The following sections look at ways in which new technology is affecting recreation facility management, equipment, marketing, and staff development.

NEW TECHNOLOGY IN FACILITY MANAGEMENT

The greatest technological change in the field over the past decade has probably occurred in facility management. What used to be performed on paper is now handled via the Internet. Notebooks full of forms, checklists, and headcounts

Photo courtesy of José H. Gonzalez. Plymouth State University.

Using an ID card reader system.

have been replaced by spreadsheets and databases housed on desktop and laptop computers or on servers. Recreation facility managers now enjoy many options for increasing the department's operational and financial efficiency, marshaling the vast array of facility data needed to make educated predictions and decisions, and using their staff more productively. The form of technology most likely to be used by today's recreation facility manager is a management software system.

Management Software Systems

Management software performs single, multiple, or system-wide management functions for a recreation department. These functions can include checking IDs at the facility entrance, producing reports that show facility usage patterns, managing memberships and registrations, tracking financial transactions, and facilitating staff scheduling. Depending on the department's goals, these systems can be either narrowly focused to perform one task (this is called single application software) or used in a broad array of functions and tasks across the entire department (this is called an **enterprise system**).

Single Application Software

Single application software is developed to address one management function—for example, locker or membership management, staff scheduling, or equipment checkout. This type of software is often developed by smaller companies who either do not offer many products or have been able to adapt a successful product from another management field (e.g., business or human resources) to the recreation environment. Single application software is characterized by lower-cost, in-depth functionality in its specific area of focus, along with good product support from the developer. The risk is that, without strong product sales to keep the developer in business, software support could evaporate—meaning no upgrades, new versions or customer support. On the other hand, the product could become so successful that it attracts a competitor, gets bought out, and ends up either incorporated into the buyer's own product or simply terminated.

Enterprise Software

Many departments are moving in the direction of enterprise software for facility management. The driving factors include the array of functions, the ability to purchase parts of the system without committing to the whole package, reliable customer support, Internet capability, and interconnectivity with existing institutional systems.

Unlike single application software, enterprise packages can perform many different functions thanks to the use of modules, which may address locker management, membership management, facility scheduling, accounting, staff scheduling, equipment checkout, and even intramural sports scheduling and fitness management—each with the ability to interface with other modules. The membership and locker management modules work together, for example, to allow the membership staff to register a new member and at the same time issue him or her a locker with a lock combination. In another example, the facility scheduler who takes a reservation can have an invoice automatically generated and e-mailed to the individual making the reservation. And, with the ability to accept EFTs (electronic funds transfers), online credit card payment can produce immediate revenue for the department.

Because the total cost of most enterprise systems is high, departments often look to purchase only those modules that meet their specific needs. For example, a university recreation department might purchase an accounting module to better manage its financial operation but skip the EFT payment component if such payments are prohibited by campus policy. Similarly, if a facility already handles user ID card access by means of custom-made single application software, it could omit that module from its enterprise purchase. If you consider buying only some modules from a total package, look at the future of your operations to see if adding a module now might be more cost-effective than adding it later.

With any new software—single application or enterprise—your staff must be trained to use it. Typically, due to its more complex nature, enterprise software involves a larger learning curve, which makes customer support a crucial factor to consider. Good companies provide on-site orientation to their software, training, follow-up help after installation, and possibly free upgrades and free or low-cost new versions. It is also helpful to have dedicated technology staff in the department itself to maintain regular contact with the company.

While some single application software gives users the ability to access functions via the Internet, this capability is the norm for enterprise systems. Internet access is imperative if the department manages multiple facilities, if management wants to access data from anywhere (e.g., from home or a mobile device), if other entities need to access or provide data, or if you simply want to give patrons the ability to access online functions. In addition, Internet capability can help departments that operate in a mixed computer platform environment (PC, Mac, Linux) as long as the enterprise software is written to conform to standard web specifications.

Finally, an enterprise system's ability to connect with existing campus, agency, or company computer systems is important for both practical and financial reasons. Interconnectivity facilitates the flow of data to areas that need it. For example, a college recreation center using an enterprise system to check IDs at the door needs current information from the registrar's office to validate a student's entry; to do so, the enterprise system must either be able to download a current database each evening or have direct access to the registrar's database for quick, accurate confirmation or denial.

Many of the current enterprise software companies started out doing business as single application companies, then grew by expanding their product base or buying out competitors and solidified their place in the management software field. As more recreation facilities move to using enterprise management software, providers will offer more functional modules, better customer support, improved interconnectivity with existing systems, and lower costs.

Business Functions

Business functions can be handled by some single application software products, but they are a standard component in enterprise systems, where they carry labels such as Accounting, Financials, **POS** (point-of-sale), Membership Management, or even Business Office. Business-oriented modules can also handle donor management, accounts payable, purchase orders, and more. The two basic modules found in most enterprise systems are Financials and Membership Management.

Financials encompass a variety of business functions, and most enterprise systems typically include the basic business functions of accounting, billing, and budgeting. Business modules are able to collect all financial transactions performed in any of the other enterprise modules and centralize data where financial staff can work with them to produce expense and revenue reports, generate invoices, track purchase orders, manage inventory, produce payroll, pay bills, and meet other requirements. Most also offer POS abilities that can handle retail sales through cash registers at a front desk, pro shop, or membership office. When a patron pays for a group fitness class at the register, the software not only generates a transaction that shows up in an end-of-day sales report but also automatically adds the patron's name to the class roster by which the instructor can take roll, add the class name to the patron's personal training database, and generate an e-mail indicating when the next class of that type is being offered.

The other business module found in most enterprise systems is membership management, which is especially important for private college and commercial recreation facilities who rely heavily on membership revenue. A membership management module not only increases the efficiency with which staff can track registrations and renewals but also improves marketing and other communication with members, helps track participation to enable management to make better programming decisions, and facilitates follow-up with prospective members. From the time when potential members first walk in the front door of the facility until the day they decide

Photo courtesy of Robert Frye, Florida International University.

Enterprise systems can make the processes of running a class fit together seamlessly.

to cancel, membership management software helps keep them satisfied, informed of events, in tune with their health, and up-to-date on their membership payments. In fact, it can serve as the department's best salesperson.

Operations

Technology exerts a major influence on the physical operation of recreation facilities. Whether progress is made through mechanical, environmental, electronic, or structural advances, new technology outpaces the ability for most facility managers to keep up. The three areas of operation most likely to improve due to new technology are security and access control, scheduling, and facility maintenance.

Security and Access Control

Recreation facility managers place great importance on controlling access to their facilities and ensuring that users and staff are kept safe and secure. New technologies have improved how managers allow access, keep track of what is happening, and communicate with staff in the facility.

Most indoor recreation facilities require the user's identity to be verified electronically in order to qualify him or her for entry. This type of access control technology is typically divided into two categories: data card readers and biometrics. The data card process involves swiping an ID card through a card reader that is connected to a master database by either enterprise or in-house software; in a university setting, the student's status is checked against the registrar's database. The card reader system offers the advantages of relatively low cost and usually instantaneous verification. Databases are typically updated automatically overnight, and all data rests behind protective institutional computer firewalls. One drawback is that users without their ID (i.e., whose ID has been forgotten, lost, or stolen) are unable to get their eligibility verified quickly, if at all. In addition, the opportunity to customize the information displayed by either an enterprise or in-house system can be restricted in a university setting as a result of the Family Educational Rights and Privacy Act (FERPA), which protects students' personal data.

A biometric process uses a fingerprint, handprint, or even optical scan to verify eligibility for access to the facility. As with the card reader, the scan is verified against an existing database, but in this case a potential user must enter an initial scan into the system for comparison (usually during an initial registration process, since it is not normally collected in the institution's administrative process). Biometric systems offer the advantage of being more than 99 percent accurate, and the administrative software in usually controlled within the recreation department because of the need to enter initial scans. Disadvantages of a biometrics system include the need to store an extremely large amount of data (fingerprints, handprints, and optical scans for each individual fill up hard drives quickly), as well as the possibility of long lines at turnstiles and entrances since some scanners can take up to 30 seconds for verification if the database is large.

Another important technology in security and access control is the security camera. These cameras are gaining in popularity at areas of access and egress, at cash-handling locations, outside locker rooms, and on building exteriors as a way to increase safety, theft protection, and simple activity monitoring. Important considerations in purchasing a security camera system include the number of cameras needed for complete coverage, the degree of facial recognition needed, who monitors the cameras, and how long the video is retained.

The number of cameras used depends on the purpose for using them. For example, fewer cameras are needed for simple observation and activity monitoring than for safety and theft prevention. The same is true for the level of facial recognition—the need to identify perpetrators requires a high-resolution security camera, whereas normal activity monitoring does not. Will cameras be monitored continuously, occasionally, or only when deemed necessary? Will footage be deleted or recorded over after a certain period of time or retained for possible future reference? The answers to such questions can determine the need for additional staff or law enforcement involvement, as well as the capacity of video storage devices. Legal determination may be needed to address concern about risk and liability regarding video content or lack thereof (e.g., whether putting up fake or dummy cameras does or does not create a false sense of security).

Technology is also affecting facility security and access control in the area of communication. Walkie-talkies have long been the communication standard in both indoor and outdoor locations, but the ease or difficulty of using them depends on interference from or with other departments' frequencies (e.g., facilities management, campus police), antenna and repeater locations, and FCC regulations. Today's radios are more powerful, with longer-lasting rechargeable batteries, and the expansion of the number of useable frequencies has reduced the problem of interference from or with other users. More important, though, cell phones have proliferated. Cell phones, and especially **smartphones**, offer not only voice capability but also texting, instant messaging, photography, web access, and GPS (Global Positioning System) functionality. Cell phones do have some issues, such as dropped calls and "dead zones," but they are quickly becoming the "radio" of choice.

Scheduling

Many recreation facilities are multipurpose, which means that managers must be able to identify current usage, available spaces, and equipment needs in order to make scheduling decisions efficiently and effectively. They must also be able to manage financial transactions (e.g., rental charges, personnel costs) related to scheduling. The most efficient way for recreation facility managers to schedule nowadays is to use either an enterprise system scheduling module or a stand-alone scheduling or calendaring software solution.

A scheduling component in an enterprise system module gives the manager a way to schedule multiple facilities easily and to interface with business functions such as billing and equipment rental. Using a scheduling module can increase efficiency by enabling you to use facility categories (e.g., indoor or outdoor; rental or nonrental), to set specific parameters for different types of events or activities per venue, and to be web-accessible. The only real drawbacks are the time necessary to input facility parameters in the initial setup and to educate department staff. In addition, if the module was not part of the original system purchase, integrating it may require vendor support.

Stand-alone scheduling or calendaring software solutions are not as popular as they once were, but their strength has been the depth and breadth of doing a single task well. These solutions are made viable, especially in low-budget scenarios, by their ease of setup, capability for customization, full range of reporting methods, and multiplicity of calendar formats. Most lack integration with business functions on a larger scale, but some do provide for basic invoice creation and user notification.

Photo courtesy of Robert Frye, Florida International University.

Double-paned glass with custom "frits" and tinting reduces heat transfer and UV rays.

Facility Maintenance

Maintaining the facility can be a daunting task for the recreation manager, but it must be done for the sake of safety, customer service, environmental concerns, and cost savings. New technologies can make the facility manager's job easier, improve the facility's environmental footprint, reduce costs and staff time, and enable facility users to have a safer and more enjoyable experience.

Enterprise system software can help managers improve efficiency by tracking work requests, keeping a parts inventory, managing repair and replacement schedules, and monitoring utility costs. It can also enable the manager to integrate these functions with the institution's facilities management operation, thus allowing even more comprehensive supervision of mechanical, electrical, maintenance, and plant operations while keeping costs at a minimum.

Making smarter buildings is another way in which technology helps recreation managers handle operations and maintenance. It also requires the manager to be knowledgeable about new technologies in areas such as improved construction materials, HVAC controls, utility monitoring systems, window (glazing) materials, security and emergency systems, plumbing and lighting fixtures, solar power, and energy-efficient program equipment. New technologies are being considered not only for recreation centers but also for swimming pools, ice rinks, and even playing fields. Developing technology promises to allow building systems the ability to capture energy created by activity inside and convert it to power the venue itself (for example, floor systems capture the dynamic energy of a group fitness class and convert it into energy to power the lights within the room) (Oberlander et al, 2005). Investing in some of these technologies may be initially expensive, but in the long run it can reduce operational costs and improve the way in which facility managers do their job.

Thus technology is exerting, and will continue to exert, a major effect on both new and old facilities. As a result, the recreation facility manager must be fluent in many areas—hardware and software systems, electronic and mechanical innovations, sustainability and energy management, and other areas not yet conceived—in order to deliver top-quality operations and facilities.

NEW TECHNOLOGY IN SPORTS AND FITNESS EQUIPMENT

New technologies are created daily that affect the products being manufactured for both institutional and personal use in sports and fitness markets. As with recreation facility managers, the professionals who select, purchase, and incorporate equipment into programs and facilities need to be aware not only of the "latest and greatest" but also of what might be coming in the future. One way to keep up is to review online and printed trade media, which provide an enormous amount of information about equipment vendors, their product lines, their newest technology, and even what may be on the drawing board. In addition, trade shows and show-room demonstrations allow you to examine or even try out models of possible interest for your programs or facilities. Good recreation consumers do their homework prior to purchase and do not rely solely on the word of the salesperson or representative.

Exercise and Fitness Equipment

Recreation centers are not only adding flat-screen and high-definition televisions to entertain users in fitness areas; they are also changing their exercise equipment itself. Recreation professionals now face a wide array of possibilities for cardio and strength equipment, and each brand continually updates and adds features to its product line as the market becomes increasingly competitive. Improvements include new materials, better production methods, updated looks, and new features. Several longtime companies have closed, but newer ones have claimed their spots on institutions' rosters of eligible vendors.

In this environment, equipment users are targeted by frequent new product announcements, traditional and online media reviews, and either word-of-mouth or personal experience with a variety of brands. This intensity has led to an increasingly shorter "state-of-the-art" appeal than in the past, and replacement schedules that were traditionally based on 5 to 10 years of use are now being cut by 50 percent or more. At the same time, although manufacturing costs have dropped in certain areas (e.g., electronic components and materials), the overall price of new technology has risen due to inflation, increased labor costs, and the increased cost of raw materials such as steel for frames.

Cardio Equipment

As manufacturers compete to attract users, new cardio equipment increasingly offers features that call for web access and compatibility with personal MP3 players. The traditional static exercise bike, rowing machine, elliptical machine, and treadmill have been upgraded to allow users to experience more than sweating, elevated heart rate, and development of muscle strength. Network access gives users access to television shows, Internet surfing, and music playlists; it also fosters interactivity through competition with other users across the room or even across the country. To accommodate the increasing demand for this technology, architects and planners must now make sure to include adequate power and data infrastructure when building or renovating facilities.

Moving forward, new equipment will also improve the efficient use of energy—even the energy generated by the very people using the equipment. For example, energy collected from exercise bikes, treadmills, and other specially designed equipment can be either reused by the machine itself or channeled back into the facility's power grid. This type of equipment will be seen in more and more recreation centers as more facilities seek to become LEED certified (i.e., certified as exercising Leadership in Energy and Environmental Design) and generally greener.

New cardio technology also allows users to monitor their fitness levels and take advantage of both machine-based and web-based fitness assessment software. Users who log onto the software while using the machine can access training programs, receive feedback and benchmark data, and monitor their vitals as they work out. Some new machines even remember

Photo courtesy of Robert Frye, Florida International University.

Synthetic turf enhances the multipurpose aspect of outdoor playing fields.

personal settings for each user. In addition, exercisers can get tips for improving their workout, explore nutritional information about what is best to eat or drink before or after an exercise session, and log their daily results for record keeping and analysis of short- and long-term fitness.

Other cardio-related innovations are affecting how recreation professionals program and equip their spaces beyond typical exercise equipment. For example, the combination of exercise and entertainment (i.e., exergaming) brings mass-market computer and video games into the exercise arena to engage users in nontraditional methods of exercise. Whether the theme is dance, sports, fitness, or role playing, these games enable users to participate physically in active and interactive play against a computer or other players. Recreation programmers schedule competitions by providing game access in a building's public or social space. The variety of game types and platforms will continue to grow as hardware and software companies increase their research and development in this area.

Strength Equipment

The improvement of product materials has allowed strength equipment manufacturers to fabricate longer-lasting dumbbells, weights, bars, and accessories. Improvement in the composition of polyurethane weight plates and dumbbells has extended their life span and reduced the wear and tear they exact on the facility. All-metal weight equipment is now built with composite materials that give a better grip and reduce the chance of loosening up on the user. Purchasing options now also include new color schemes, coatings, and upholstery materials.

The design of strength equipment is also influenced by the home user market. Dumbbells no longer have to come in a single weight; users now have several weight options for changing the weight by taking off or adding components to reach the desired amount. In addition, equipment designed for light home use (e.g., back-of-the-door pulley system or space-saving treadmill) is being modified to handle the heavier usage that is typical in recreation centers.

Sports Equipment

Though new technology has touched personal sports equipment only lightly, it has exerted greater effect on sports fields and gymnasiums, and synthetic surfaces are becoming the standard in campus recreational sports. Trade journals report that the construction of synthetic field surfaces is the most common item on a recreation department's list of planned additions, and this technology will remain in high demand due to the variety of fabrication methods and installation techniques, coupled with need for all-weather capability. For indoor spaces, both poured surfaces and wood flooring have become longer lasting and easier to maintain, but they are also increasing in both purchase and installation cost. Price will be the driving force behind selection as manufacturers see demand increase and production costs decrease.

Other Recreation Equipment

New equipment technologies are also influencing other areas of recreation practice. In aquatics, drowning detection devices help lifeguards identify swimmers in distress in both large and small pools, and lightning detectors help pool operators and recreation field supervisors keep participants safe by identifying imminent strikes earlier. Outdoor recreation trip leaders use GPS devices to track location and thus minimize the chance of lost participants or leaders. In distance running programs, participants use specialized body suits and smart clothing (called humionics) to monitor distance and body functions, to communicate, and to listen to music. Personal trainers use computer programs, **tablet computers**, and assessment devices to allow body imaging for their clients and even to enable clients themselves to interact with a virtual coach or trainer.

New innovations and inventions will continue to improve and increase the variety of equipment technology. Everyone wants to have the latest equipment and a state-of-the-art facility in order to attract and retain participants and users. But today's recreation professional is continually challenged just to keep up with the curve of changing technology, much less stay ahead of it. Technology now affects not only how facilities are designed, equipped, and operated, but also how professionals communicate with participants and train their staff.

USING MARKETING TECHNOLOGY

New marketing technology enables recreation programs not only to better reach their populations but also to build a more interactive community. To do this successfully, the organization must set clear objectives for the technology to be used. For example, if the department decides that it is better strategy to market a newsletter to patrons via **smartphone** than on paper, then using a weekly podcast for program updates might be a good option. When setting goals, consider the following questions:

- What is my population's preference for consuming information, news, and updates?
- Who can update my website?
- Who can provide interaction via social media?
- What is a reasonable expectation of content, frequency, and media format for patrons consuming the information?
- What kind of technology do my patrons own (e.g., web access, cell phones)?

It is also important to measure the effects of using a specific technology in order to maximize the organization's use of resources and deliver the best possible service. For example, if the organization uses a text message blast to inform participants about upcoming events, leagues, game cancellations, league standings, and schedule changes, then it should measure the effectiveness of this strategy as compared with other strategies (e.g., social network update page).

Available Technology

In 2009, 80 percent of American teens carried a wireless device, about 75 percent of North Americans were Internet users, and about 55 percent of American adults connected to the Internet wirelessly (Lejnieks, 2010). In addition, electronic message boards are replacing traditional bulletin boards on college campuses across the nation. Each of these modes of communication—personal electronic devices, the Internet, and electronic message boards—can be used for marketing purposes. Here are a few examples:

- Uses for personal electronic devices include text message updates, podcasts about how to use equipment, and sharing of intramural sports results or standings.

- The Internet makes it possible to use web pages, blogs, microblogs, and **social networking**. These tools are great for building community, presenting users with calendars and last-minute changes, sharing pictures and videos, and exchanging ideas about programs.
- An electronic message board can be set up by using a flat-screen television. This is a sustainable approach that eliminates the paper waste of bulletin boards and allows easy and timely updates of information and news through user input via internet access either directly or through a vendor.

Benefits and Limitations of Technology in Marketing

Using technology to market recreation programs has advantages and disadvantages. As shown in table 8.1, benefits include cost-effectiveness, sustainability, and better results-tracking capability. Limitations include the staff learning curve, patron preference of how to receive marketing, and access to newer and faster technology.

Making an Online Presence

If you are thinking about creating an online presence, consider these three factors:

- Departmental goal (i.e., to create a community)
- Content (e.g., information, questions, polls, calendar)
- Time allocated for the endeavor

Establishing a website or blog that offers current, high-quality content enhances the organization's image of professionalism. At the same time, increasing traffic on the organization's website means more individuals are helping create a community. In this light, **Web 2.0** comes at a great time for recreation programs because it allows interaction before, during, and after program sessions and regular facility hours of operation. The term Web 2.0 refers to the second generation of the web, which focuses mainly on human collaboration. Examples include blogs, **wikis**, **RSS**, social networking, and social bookmarks. Social networking sites give the organization the opportunity to create an online community, provide high-quality content, and track participants. Here are some Web 2.0 applications and possible uses for recreation programs:

- **Blog**—Platform best used for posting information and news from events (e.g., photos and videos) that allows patrons to interact, post their own photos, and make comments, all of which helps build community (e.g., WordPress, Blogger).
- **Microblogging**—Writing platform subject to character limits and thus best used for quick updates (e.g., Twitter).
- **Web-based digital photography or video portal**—Platform best used to post program photos or videos (e.g., Flickr, YouTube).
- **Social network**—Platform offering some features of previously mentioned platforms that also allows users to create profiles from which to share information (e.g., Facebook, LinkedIn).
- **Podcast**—Platform that allows subscriber-based broadcasting of audio, audio with

Table 8.1 Benefits and Limitations of Using Technology in Marketing

Benefits	Limitations
Green and cost-effective Timely Local and global in reach Easy-to-track results	Audience must use newer technology. Audience must have Internet access (preferably high-speed). Audience must prefer receiving marketing via technological sources (vs. more traditional ways). Staff needs to know how to use the technology.

pictures, videos, and PDF delivered by RSS feed via the Internet and that can be played on a computer or in a digital player (e.g., Apple's iTunes).

If you decide to use Web 2.0 marketing, consider the following five tips:

- Claim your space online in every possible platform (e.g., website, blog, video sharing, photo sharing).
- Create high-quality content.
- Spend at least 30 minutes every day having "live" interactions with your patrons.
- Think about marketing before, during, and after an event.
- Designate a person to oversee your Web 2.0 marketing.

All of these tools can enhance a recreation department's marketing efforts and help it build community. At the same time, the recreation professional must be selective and intentional in choosing the right tools to meet the organization's goals.

USING TECHNOLOGY IN STAFF DEVELOPMENT

The growing emphasis on providing users with excellent customer service and high-quality products means that it is critical to properly train program staff. New technology can help you achieve this goal; indeed, incorporating technology into training and development constitutes a logical extension of employees' daily use of technology on the job.

Creating a Strategy for Incorporating Technology

Using technology in training and development can motivate your employees. Noe (2004) has defined motivation to learn as the trainee's desire to learn the content of the training program (p. 85) so employees who are comfortable with technology are more expectant of, and receptive to, being trained to use it. It is important to find out what drives people before introducing any new initiative (Martinelli, 2007). Therefore, when incorporating technology, the first step for staff development is to select the right vehicle. Here are some questions to be addressed:

- What type of technology support is available from the organization or institution?
- What platform is used for the academic program or other programs?
- What software and hardware are needed, and are they already available?
- What devices do the end users have?

Benefits and Limitations of Using Technology for Staff Development

When considering benefits and limitations of using technology for staff training, keep in mind that today's young adults have grown up using the Internet and communicating instantly via text messages. They've been exposed early and often to computer games, videos, and chat rooms. As a result, they may perceive these technologies as a source of fun or something they do in their leisure time rather than as elements in a process of teaching and learning. Nevertheless, many employees are eager to learn a skill through a video game, an online chat, or a video explanation rather than sitting through a traditional lecture. Online training can also be very useful for recreation staff members who are absent when on-site training is conducted.

It is difficult at this point to determine whether online training will replace face-to-face interaction, but the combination of online and traditional face-to-face training can be extremely powerful. At the same time, trainers must balance the amount of staff time spent training in front of the computer with time spent actually performing job responsibilities.

You must also decide how to handle content for staff training and development. Creating your own content provides the benefit of ownership and the ability to customize it to your programs' particular needs. You can then modify and upload the content as needed. On the other hand, content takes time to develop, produce, and upload to a **learning management system**—that is, a software package or platform that lets you deliver and manage training content. Another possible limitation is the cost of hiring an expert who possesses the technical skills to create and deliver the content.

Off-the-shelf training packages offer systematic and validated approaches for developing staff in specific jobs. Off-the-shelf online training is available to address first aid and CPR, personal trainer certification, group exercise instructor certification, sport official certification, and leadership training; this type of training is discussed in more detail later in this chapter.

Developing Online Modules

Online learning can be cost-effective, flexible, and useful in simultaneously engaging staff members in different locations. Online modules can be used as part of new-hire training in order to systematize traditional staff training. To determine which training components can be brought to an online format, break them down. Putting some modules online (this is called hybrid or blended training) can be a time-saver as compared with in-person training. Complete online training can also be helpful in training staff members at midyear or helping them review daily processes with which they are struggling.

Staff trainers can ensure effective online training by including the following components: solid design, useful content, the right tools, and cutting-edge technology (Dublin, 2007). Successful training also depends on the trainer's ability to engage learners, motivate managers, and energize the organization. Dublin presents a three-phase process for successful online training:

- During the installation phase, ensure that everything works as intended.
- In the implementation phase, ensure that participants know what training solutions are available and how to use them.
- In the integration phase, ensure that the new online modality is absorbed and well received in all layers of the organization.

Ultimately, the success of an online learning program relies more on the trainer's ability to engage and motivate people than on great

Photo courtesy of José H. Gonzalez. Plymouth State University.

Using a tablet computer in evaluating proper weight-training form.

content or design. Consider the following ways to engage online learners:

- Use a chat room (**synchronous communication**).
- Use a blog or a personal space (**asynchronous communication**).
- Use customized videos.
- Use customized video games.
- Have participants create content about the topic.

Chat Rooms, Videos, and Blogs

One way to engage employees in online learning is to provide a synchronous space in which they can exchange ideas and knowledge. Synchronous platforms are best used for getting acquainted with the material and for discussing less complex topics. Because a quick response is expected, learners are committed and motivated. Two examples of synchronous spaces are the chat room and the videoconference (Hrastinski, 2008). Chat rooms and instant messaging can be combined online through the Meebo platform. Two platforms that allow videoconferencing are Skype and Polycom.

Asynchronous platforms give the learner more flexibility because no immediate response is expected and they can learn in their own time and at their own pace. For these reasons, many online learners prefer this type of platform. For Hrastinski (2008), this platform is best used for discussing complex topics. Examples of asynchronous communication include e-mail, discussion boards, and blogs. Websites offering this option include Google, Yahoo, and WordPress.

Videos offer you an effective way to give learners access to real-life footage of job skills in action (Halls, 2010). This approach is, of course, suited to delivering content that can be learned by watching—for example, how to repair a broken treadmill or fix a flat bicycle tire. With hundreds of videos uploaded to the web every day, chances are that you can find a video on your topic of choice at any of the major video websites (e.g., YouTube, Vimeo, iTunes). You can also create educational videos and upload them to these sites.

Video Gaming

Some organizations also use video games for staff training, and Gartner Research predicted that by the year 2011 video games would be a critical component in a majority of corporate learning solutions (Clark, 2006). According to John Beck (2007), half of Americans play some form of video game, and the characteristic traits of game players are often welcome in the workplace: sociability, the desire to feel connected with peers, desire to win, competitiveness, loyalty to one's team, and strong analytical skills. Beck goes on to say that what complicates matters is that the game player's learning style is also one that ignores formal instruction, relies almost entirely on trial and error, incorporates learning from peers rather than authority figures, and operates through the absorption of knowledge in very small increments. Effective training via video games must recognize both the positive and negative traits.

Why do video games make powerful learning tools? The chief operating officer of Caspian Learning proposed the following reasons (Beck, 2007):

- Games are motivational and keep the employee engaged in the learning experience.
- Games are immersive and physically involving.
- Games provide a safe space for failure.
- Games can create a personalized training environment.
- Games provide instantaneous feedback.

Another, similar learning solution can be found in the form of minigames—immersive learning simulations that are easy to access, are typically based on Adobe Flash, and last from 5 to 20 minutes (Aldrich, 2007, p. 1). Aldrich feels confident that minigames are going to explode onto the learning scene because they are easy to consume, offer engaging content, motivate learners, and are cost effective. Both video games and minigames can serve as great training tools because they have proven to be engaging, fun, and successful as learning vehicles.

Web-Based, Off-the Shelf Training and Assessment

One advantage of using technology for staff development is the possibility of finding already-developed courses or certification programs in a virtual classroom that can both satisfy your training need and fulfill job requirements. These courses and trainings are usually put together by well-established and accredited organizations. They are geared toward (among others) personal trainers and group exercise instructors; campus recreational sports officials; those needing first aid, CPR, and AED certification; and people seeking personality profiles or leadership style assessments.

- **Personal trainer and group fitness instructor certifications**—Employees can use several online modules to obtain the knowledge needed for personal trainer or group fitness instructor certification. The final examination is administered online or at a national testing center. Organizations offering this service include the Aerobics and Fitness Association of America (AFAA) and the American Council on Exercise (ACE).
- **Campus recreational sports official training**—The National Federation of State High School Associations (NFHSA) offers an online project that integrates video, animation, and interactive forms to educate officials in several sports (e.g., basketball, ice hockey, soccer, football, and softball).
- **First aid, CPR, and AED certification**—Employees can participate in online courses to obtain the knowledge and skills necessary to perform first aid, CPR, and AED. Some organizations that offer this type of online course also allow participants to test their own skills at the end of the course, whereas other organizations require a face-to-face assessment.
- **Personality profiles and leadership style assessments**—Personality and leadership style inventories can be completed through online tools that provide excellent assessments to help you understand your organization's staff and cater to their needs. Two examples available online are the Myers-Briggs Type Indicator and the DISC Profile personality test.

Overall, technology can enhance an organization's training program by motivating and engaging its employees. The key to doing so successfully is to determine what's best for your particular organization.

SUMMARY

Recreation practitioners must be prepared to keep up with advancing technology lest their facilities, programs, and services fall behind the times. It important to know not only what technologies are available but also what new technologies are needed. Tradition has its place in many things that recreation professionals do, but technology is one area where sticking to tradition for tradition's sake can negatively affect not only how things operate but also how a facility, program, or service is perceived by administrators, management, and, more important, patrons. Then, as IT specialist Frank Connolly (2005) suggests, "To determine the effectiveness of a new technology implementation on campus, [you must] measure the difference it makes to your constituencies."

Glossary

asynchronous communication—Online process in which individuals exchange ideas at different times.

enterprise system—Management software that includes modules for business, facility management, program scheduling, human resource management, communication, and network access functions.

learning management system—Software that allows delivery and management of training content.

podcast—Method of broadcasting audio, audio with pictures, videos, or PDF delivered by RSS feed to subscribers via the Internet for use on a computer or digital player.

POS (point-of-sale)—Label for software that allows management of sales, inventory, and financial reporting by means of a cash register.

RSS (Really Simple Syndication or Rich Site Summary)—Web feed that provides users with content updates; commonly used in blogs, news websites, and other websites heavy with audio, video, and pictures.

smartphone—Cell phone typically equipped with voice, data, texting, imaging, and web access capabilities.

social networking—Online interaction between people who share a common interest.

synchronous communication—Online process in which individuals exchange ideas at the same time.

tablet computer—Newest generation of computers, which possess many of the capabilities of laptops but at a fraction of the size.

Web 2.0—Second generation of the web, which focuses mainly on human collaboration.

wiki—Website (e.g., Wikipedia) where users create and edit the content.

References

Aldrich, C. (2007). Engaging mini-games find niche in training. *Learning Circuits: ASTD's Source for E-Learning.* www.astd.org/LC/2007/0707_aldrich.htm.

Beck, J. (2007). How employees can "play" to win at learning. *HR Focus, 84*(7), 5–6.

Clark, D. (2006). Games and evidence. Caspian Learning. www.caspianlearning.co.uk/games_and_evidence.doc.

Connolly, F. (2005). It's not the change, it's the difference: Evaluating technology on campus. *Educause Quarterly, 28*(4). www.educause.edu/EDUCAUSE+Quarterly/EDUCAUSEQuarterlyMagazineVolum/ItsNottheChangeItstheDifference/157365.

Dublin, L. (2007). Success with e-learning. *Learning Circuits: ASTD's Source for E-Learning.* www.astd.org/LC/2007/0507_dublin.htm.

Frazier, M., & Bailey, G. (2004). *The technology coordinator's handbook.* Eugene, OR: International Society for Technology in Education.

Halls, J. (2010). Shooting Web video for training. *Learning Circuits: ASTD's Source for E-Learning.* www.astd.org/LC/2010/0610_halls.htm.

Hrastinski, S. (2008). Asynchronous and synchronous e-learning. *Educause Quarterly, 31*(4), 51–55. http://net.educause.edu/ir/library/pdf/EQM0848.pdf.

Lejnieks, C. (2010). *A generation unplugged.* CITA. www.files.ctia.org/pdf/HI_Teen-MobilityStudy_ResearchReport.pdf.

Martinelli, A. (2007, July). People power . . . brings power to the business. *Credit Management,* 30–31.

Noe, R. (2004). *Employee training and development* (3rd ed.). New York: McGraw-Hill.

Nunziato, T. (2003). Choosing the right recreation software.*California Parks and Recreation,59*(2), 26. www.cprs.org/membersonly/Spr03_RecSoftware.htm.

Oberlander, A., Patton, J., Stubbs, K., & Klein, P. (2005, August). Facility futures. *Athletic Business.* http://rdgusa.com/news/2005/08/facility-futures.php.

CHAPTER 9

Human Resources

Stephen Kampf
Bowling Green State University

The basic objective of a recreation program (or any program) is to perform work that helps fulfill the organization's mission statement. To carry out the services it offers, of course, the organization relies on employees to do the necessary work; thus staff members are positioned at the core of any recreation program's success. U.S. president Ronald Reagan once stated, "Surround yourself with the best people you can find, delegate authority, and don't interfere as long as the policy you've decided upon is being carried out." This is advice that everyone who manages people should follow.

Indeed, few things are more important to an organization than hiring the right people. Without them, no amount of resources can make the organization successful. More specifically, recreation programs offer users a variety of services and facilities (e.g., pool or gym), and each one uses a variety of trained and certified employees. This chapter addresses the various types of employees found in recreation, as well as the processes of recruiting, hiring, evaluating, and rewarding employees.

TYPES OF RECREATION EMPLOYEES

Depending on the size of their programs, campus recreational sports departments can be staffed by just one employee or by many employees; furthermore, these employees may possess various levels of experience and education as required by each staff position. This section of the chapter identifies types of employees found in campus recreational sports organizations and briefly describes their roles.

Full-Time Professional Staff

Full-time professional staff receive benefits and are required to work between 37.5 and 40 hours per week. This group includes **salaried employees** paid a yearly salary and **hourly employees** paid for their actual hours of work each week.

Under the federal Fair Labor Standards Act (FLSA), salaried employees are not entitled to overtime, but employees paid on an hourly basis are entitled to it. Typically, however, salaried employees who work more hours than required can accumulate **compensatory time**, which is an accepted form of compensation for employees subject to overtime provisions. Compensatory time is generally awarded to eligible employees for all hours worked beyond 40 in a single work week. Currently, compensatory arrangements are illegal in the private sector but are legal and widely practiced in the public sector. Hourly employees receive cash compensation for hours worked in excess of 40 in a single work week. According to the FLSA, the current overtime pay rate for eligible employees is one and one-half (1.5) times their regular rate of pay. This rate is referred to as "time and a half" by most people in the workforce.

Part-Time Professional Staff

The **part-time professional** staff refers to individuals who work fewer hours a week than full-time professional staff. Typically, part-time staff members are not afforded benefits (e.g., health insurance), and they receive less total pay when compared with full-time professional staff.

Administrators need to pay special attention to part-time employees (Stier, 1999). Many jobs in the recreation field are staffed by part-time employees who provide an outstanding service. At the same time, since they work fewer hours and are paid less, questions may arise regarding their commitment to the organization and their role in the decision-making process. Therefore, administrators need to define the role of the part-timer at the initial stages of his or her employment. This can be accomplished in an initial meeting with the employee to find out his or her goals for the employment period.

Student Employees

College recreation programs typically employ numerous students to help provide services and programs to their constituents; in fact, on most campuses, the recreation program is a leading employer of students. For example, the University of Maryland, College Park, enrolls more than 32,000 students and employs more than 1,000 (www.crs.umd.edu/cms/Employment.aspx), Bowling Green State University enrolls more than 19,000 students and employs between 200 and 300 student employees annually (www.bgsu.edu/offices/sa/recwell/page32437.html), and Slippery Rock University enrolls 7,800 students and employs more than 130 (www.sru.edu/studentlife/campusrec/Pages/Home%20Page%20Student%20Employment.aspx).

The role of the student employee can range from collecting student identification cards in a weight room to opening and closing a recreation facility. Professionals working in the field need to be aware of the student employee's motivation for employment. Most student employees view the campus job as a monetary contribution to their finances; some, however, use it as a mechanism for entering the profession of recreation and facility management.

Professionals who work with students generally describe a positive environment that improves their morale and keeps them current with contemporary culture. Even so, employing student staff can involve some drawbacks, such as working with an unseasoned employee who may lack responsibility and respect, and some students take the job less seriously than their professional counterparts. In addition, students tend to bring their personal lives into the working environment and seek out other employees for counseling advice. Professionals also need to be aware that students are motivated by incentives such as resume building, monetary raises, advancement, recognition, and positive feedback. Supervisors are well advised to set up a working and learning atmosphere that helps student staff grow as employees.

Astin (1987) found a strong correlation between students' involvement on campus and their successful completion of their course of study. Campus involvement leads to greater academic success and happiness with the institution. One key source of involvement is the part-time campus job, which gives student staff members the chance to forge friendships and a sense of belonging with fellow student employees.

Graduate Assistants

Graduate assistants are enrolled graduate students who hold a position within the organization and normally work 20 hours per week. Along with their employment duties, they face many responsibilities associated with taking 6 to 12 academic credits per semester. Graduate assistants are generally more mature than undergraduate student employees but less mature than full-time professional staff. They are provided with a stipend and tuition credits, and some institutions also provide housing and meals. Most graduate assistantships last for 2 years or however long it typically takes for an individual to obtain a master's degree.

The University of Texas at San Antonio, Department of Campus Recreation.

Working on campus is a great way for students to get involved in campus life.

The graduate assistant position is sometimes referred to as the stepping stone into a full-time professional position. Most entry-level job descriptions in campus recreational sports require at least 2 years of experience and a master's degree. Thus the graduate assistantship makes an optimal choice for undergraduates looking for a future in college recreation.

Graduate assistantships are offered by many college recreation programs. To explore opportunities, see the *Recreational Sports Directory*, published annually by the National Intramural-Recreational Sports Association (NIRSA), which provides information about graduate assistantships available within the group's membership.

Interns

Working with **student interns** in a recreation setting creates a win-win situation. Students benefit by gaining hands-on work experience in a profession they have learned about in academic courses; in some cases, they are even offered a full- or part-time position at the conclusion of the internship. The internship provider benefits by gaining an employee who is full of new ideas and a willingness and commitment to provide meaningful and productive work.

College academic programs routinely require an intern to meet specific objectives and perform certain tasks in order to gain academic credit for the experience. Requirements might include a daily work schedule typically set by the student in consultation with their supervisor, student goals and objectives, activity reports, and the keeping of a journal that outlines daily work accomplishments. The intern must also complete paperwork prior to, during, and at the conclusion of the internship. Paperwork may include a preliminary acceptance contract, evaluation forms (e.g., weekly, midway, or post-internship), certification of hours, and a final grading report.

Each intern should be assigned a professional supervisor who can play the vital role of educating the intern in all aspects of the operations so that he or she understands both the job and the profession. The supervisor needs to feel comfortable that the intern is capable of accomplishing a variety of tasks associated with the job. Since the intern is learning the ins and outs of projects and daily operations for the first time, it is helpful for him or her to meet with the supervisor on a daily basis. The supervisor should provide the intern with a detailed listing of facility operations and a tour to observe the operations. Interns also need to be educated about the process of planning and scheduling; here again, a daily meeting can ensure that the intern is aware of what to expect.

Volunteer Staff

A **volunteer staff member** offers his or her services freely without the expectation of receiving compensation for the work. Volunteers are essential in conducting large special events, and the event organizer must provide them with a satisfying experience if he or she wants to use them again in the future. Most volunteers' primary motivation is to help make the event successful (Farrell, Johnston, & Twynam, 1998).

Other keys to volunteer satisfaction are communication and recognition (Farrell et al., 1998). Event coordinators need to establish clear and concise modes of communication throughout an event. Recognition can take various forms—for example, public acknowledgement, a personal letter, or mention in a document covering the event. One unique aspect of using volunteer staff is that they can quit at any moment if they feel their presence is not needed or appreciated (Stier, 1999). As a result, they need to be treated differently than full- and part-time paid employees. It is essential for the event coordinator to formally and informally recognize volunteers for their time and effort. Formal acknowledgement might take the form of a certificate of participation or a personal note; informal acknowledgement might involve recognizing the volunteer's work in person or through a public announcement.

HIRING

Jack Welch, former CEO of General Electric, recognized the value of employees and the hiring process. He once said, "If you pick the right people and give them the opportunity to spread their wings—and put compensation as a carrier behind it—you almost don't have to manage them." Hiring and retaining the right people improves employee productivity and saves the organization money in the long run. This section of the chapter discusses how to develop a job description, how to fill a job vacancy, and what to look for in a candidate interview.

Job Descriptions

The starting point for recruiting and hiring new employees is to write **employee job descriptions**. These descriptions serve as a vital tool in recruitment, compensation, performance evaluation, training, and legal compliance, but they offer little value if they don't truly reflect what an employee actually does.

A well-written job description accurately describes, in words, the current functions that an individual performs in his or her job throughout the year. Most job descriptions include the employee's title, the immediate supervisor's name, a general description, a list of position responsibilities, and a list of minimum qualifications. The document serves as a one- or two-page synopsis of what the individual does while working. It should not list every single routine task or specify how to perform the job.

Content of Job Descriptions

Most well-written job descriptions include the following components:

Job title—Very brief general characterization of the job (e.g., assistant director for facilities, staff assistant, office assistant).

Immediate supervisor—The position's direct supervisor, who evaluates the employee and makes appropriate recommendations for renewal, dismissal, and salary adjustments.

General description—Brief summary of the job's main purposes and functions.

Position responsibilities—List of the job's duties, usually given in order of importance.

Minimum qualifications—List of the education, training, experience, and skill requirements considered essential to satisfactorily perform the job.

Job Description Purposes and Uses

Job descriptions can be used for a variety of purposes, including the following:

Recruitment: A concise, well-written job description serves as the initial step in attracting high-quality candidates for open positions; it can also deter potential candidates who don't meet the minimum qualifications.

Compensation: An accurate job description serves as a guide for classifying an employee within the organization's compensation system.

Performance evaluation: Appraisal of employee work performance is a constant process, and all employees are subject to performance evaluation under guidelines set forth by the organization. The job description serves as the written document on which to base the performance evaluation.

Training: Your employee orientation program should use the job description as a road map for giving the employee the information he or she needs in order to be productive in the job. Training of current employees should also reflect the current job description, which delineates the major tasks associated with the position.

Legal compliance: Job descriptions can be a factor in determining compliance with governmental regulations. Examples of regulations could include FSLA, ADA, OSHA, and others. They can also be used to address employment discrepancies—for example, in cases where an employee believes he or she is being required to perform work not associated with the position. Conversely, the employer can refer to the job description when employees are not performing the entire scope of their job. Remember that job descriptions are valid only to the extent to which they accurately reflect job content; in other words, an out-of-date job description may not be valid. Thus employees and employers should ensure validity by reviewing job descriptions on an annual basis.

A sample job description is shown in figure 9.1.

Organizational Chart

An **organizational chart** outlines the organization's structure. It identifies all staff positions and defines the reporting relationships between positions. Graphical representation of these relationships makes it easier to visualize how information, decisions, and policy discussions are developed, transmitted, and shared within an organization. A sample chart is shown in figure 9.2.

Recruitment

Recruitment involves attracting and examining potential employees, selecting new employees, and placing them into the workforce. The process also involves advising management in identifying, attracting, and retaining a high-quality and diverse workforce that is capable of accomplishing the organization's mission.

Gorter and Van Ommeren (1999) suggest two common recruitment strategies for hiring new employees: advertisement and informal search. Advertisement involves placing job announcements in various media (e.g., newspapers, trade magazines, relevant websites) and waiting for the résumés to be submitted. Candidate résumés will arrive in bunches, and the screening and review process will culminate shortly (2 to 4 weeks) after the announcements are placed. This process allows you to screen all applicants simultaneously, thus minimizing the use of a search-and-screen committee time.

The informal process canvasses current employees, colleagues at other organizations, and colleagues in professional organizations to see if they or someone they might know might be interested in the open position. Informal recruiting reduces cost by avoiding advertising expenses, finder's fees, and other search-related expenses. Gorter and Van Ommeren (1999) conclude that informal search methods are potentially more efficient than advertisement. However, if the informal search turns out to be unsuccessful, employers should switch to other recruitment channels, such as advertisements.

JOB TITLE

Assistant director for intramural and club sports

Immediate Supervisor

Director of recreational sports

General Description

The assistant director is responsible for intramurals and sport clubs, student development, youth and family programming, and the overall and day-to-day management of intramurals, sport clubs, and facility programming, with primary emphasis in the intramural and sport club areas. The assistant director should also promote and carry out the mission of recreational sports in spirit and action.

Position Responsibilities

- Facilitate and manage the daily operations of the intramural and sport club programs, which include scheduling of facilities, programs, and staff; budgeting and payroll; and discipline and policy implementation.
- Select, schedule, manage, and evaluate student employees—namely intramural attendants, intramural advisory board members, managers, and student supervisors.
- Directly supervise two graduate assistants and two student supervisors and indirectly supervise the administrative assistant for intramurals, the field house, and outdoor programming.
- Oversee publicity for entry deadlines utilizing intramural software system.
- Secure indoor and outdoor intramural and sport club sites and load all events into the facility and event management software.
- Facilitate selection, purchase, inventory management, and maintenance of equipment for the intramural and sport club programs.
- Serve as advisor of the Intramural Sports Advisory Board, the Extramural Sports Organization, and the Sport Club Advisory Board.
- Serve on committees and volunteer for campus service opportunities.
- Perform other duties as assigned.

Minimum Qualifications

- Master's degree in recreation, physical education, sports administration, or a related field
- Organizational and communications skills
- Experience in training officials in a variety of sports
- Knowledge of fiscal management
- Knowledge of student leadership development
- Knowledge of specific intramural and sport club activities and events, rules and regulations, and safety practices
- Knowledge of computer software, preferably software for managing recreational sports programs and events
- First aid and CPR certification

Figure 9.1 Sample job description, assistant director for intramural and club sports.

Courtesy of Bowling Green State University, Division of Student Affairs.

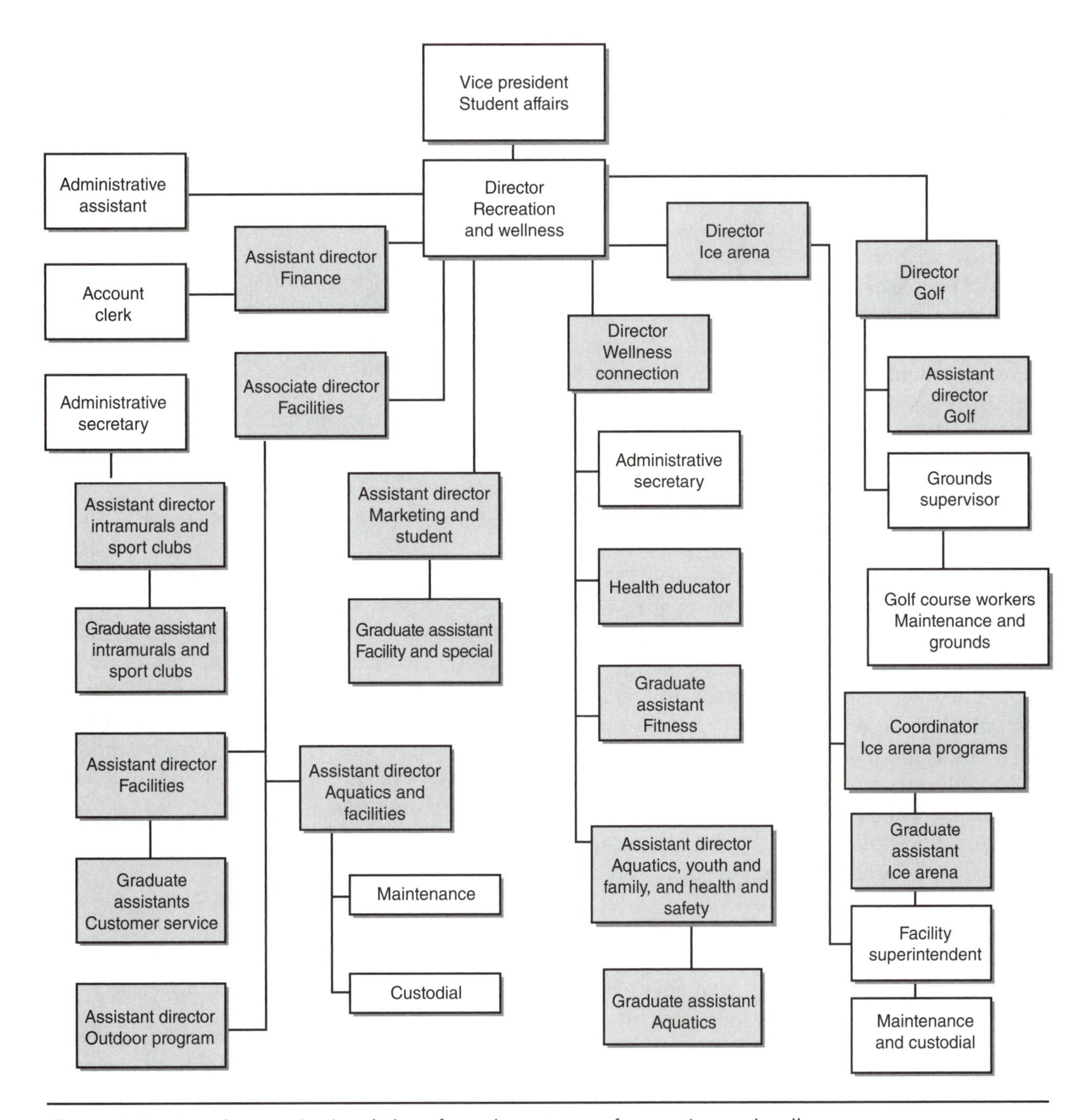

Figure 9.2 Sample organizational chart for a department of recreation and wellness.
Courtesy of Bowling Green State University, Division of Student Affairs.

Résumé Review

When reviewing résumés of job applicants, look for questionable areas that might be problematic. The résumé and cover letter should, of course, be written with proper sentence structure and without error; the document should be presented in a clean, concise, and well-structured manner. Reviewers of résumés should question any suggestion of a gap in the applicant's employment history. Other red flags include overlap of jobs, frequent job changes, and anything that might be confusing.

References

Checking references can provide useful information about a candidate's past performance or accomplishments; this process corroborates, clarifies, or adds to information that has already been gathered. Reference checks are used for two purposes: to evaluate the reliability and security of an applicant's qualifications and to evaluate the candidate's abilities, skills, personal suitability, and other qualifications.

Contacting a candidate's references can result in either positive or negative reactions. As Stier (1999) describes, search committees can not only call people listed on a candidate's reference sheet but also communicate with individuals whose names were not supplied. Committee members might, for example, call upon any of their own past colleagues who have knowledge of the candidate's ability to perform work tasks.

Interviewing

When interviewing candidates, members of the search committee should come prepared. They should review résumés prior to the face-to-face interview in order to make efficient use of interview time. Personal bias should be left at the door. The interviewer should dress professionally and smile in order to help the interviewee feel comfortable and relaxed.

The interview process should be structured, standardized, and focused. Questions should be asked to force applicants to display the required knowledge or the ability to execute behaviors on the spot. The interviewee should do most of the talking. More specifically, interviewers should follow the 80/20 rule—that is, 20 percent questions and 80 percent listening. The interviewer should be willing to adjust his or her technique and approach when interviewing applicants who are difficult (e.g., nervous, defensive, angry, shy, or overly talkative).

The face-to-face interview provides a search committee with approximately 1 to 2 hours to evaluate a candidate. Members will have an initial reaction with their first introduction to the candidate: How is the interviewee dressed? Is his or her appearance professional? A 2006 survey of NIRSA recreation directors identified the most sought after qualifications in individuals applying for a professional position as follows (Schneider, Stier, Kampf, Wilding, & Haines, 2006):

1. Excellent oral communication
2. Prior experience in campus recreational sports
3. Neat overall appearance
4. Excellent written communication
5. A graduate degree

Conversely, they found that the following qualifications were the least sought after in individuals applying for a professional position (Schneider et al., 2006):

1. GPA of 3.0 or higher
2. Membership in a professional organization (e.g., NIRSA)
3. Recreational sports specialist certification

Interviewers should pay close attention to the interviewee's words, responses, and actions. Are his or her answers passive, aggressive, demeaning, too relaxed, too opinionated? Does the interviewee say whatever he or she thinks the interviewer wants to hear, or is he or she sincere? Does the interviewee come off as too confident or cocky? What is his or her body language? Pay close attention to the interviewee's eye contact, level of comfort, and any fidgeting.

Interview Questions

Here are some examples of questions typically used during an interview:

Frequently asked questions: What are your long-term goals? Why did you apply for this position? What kind of supervisor do you prefer? What are your strengths? What are your shortcomings and what are you doing to improve on them?

Decision making or problem solving: Describe a time when you had to be quick in coming to a decision.

Leadership: What is the toughest group that you ever had to get cooperation from? Have you ever had difficulty getting others to accept your ideas? What was your approach? Did it work?

Motivation: Describe a time when you went above and beyond the call of duty. Describe a situation when you had a positive influence on the actions of yourself and others.

Communication: Tell me about a situation when you had to speak up (be assertive) in order to get across a point that was important to you. Have you ever had to "sell" an idea to your co-workers or group? How did you do it? Did they "buy" it?

Interpersonal skills: What have you done to contribute to an environment of teamwork? Describe a recent unpopular decision you made. What were the results?

Planning and organization: How do you decide what gets top priority when scheduling your time? What do you do when your schedule is suddenly interrupted? Give an example.

Other: Describe a time when you conformed to a policy with which you did not agree. Describe an instance when you had to think on your feet to extricate yourself from a difficult situation. Give an example of an important goal you set in the past and tell me about your success in reaching it.

EMPLOYEE TRAINING

Training both new and current employees is essential to an organization's success. Training should involve all employees, including students, professionals, and paraprofessionals. New employees need to go through an orientation process, and it is critical that you establish a standard orientation program to ensure that each employee is trained in a similar and succinct manner. Current employees also need to be trained in areas that call for review of policies and procedures and for the purpose of facilitating employees' development and growth.

Communication

Effective communication is essential to workplace productivity. Sometimes managers get so caught up in outside meetings and other concerns that they forget to communicate important information to their own employees. Successful communication requires the free exchange of information. The ways in which people choose to transmit information can make a difference in staff morale, prevent rumors from arising, and make for an efficient workplace.

E-mail has become a useful mode of communication but is not ideal for every situation. Employees need to be reminded that e-mail is a written form of communication and that we are generally more accountable for written words than for spoken ones since writing provides physical evidence of what was communicated. Therefore, employees who use e-mail need to refrain from slang, foul language, and any other words that might be viewed as inappropriate. Take care, as well, when using sarcasm or humor in e-mail; without face-to-face contact, a joke may be viewed as a criticism. It is also unprofessional to send an e-mail message full of spelling or grammar errors. With all of this in mind, employees should review their e-mail messages before sending them.

Staff meetings can serve as another great means of communication—if they are run effectively. Meetings provide a face-to-face opportunity to get feedback immediately. Meetings should be planned well in advanced so that participants can prepare, and the convener should distribute an agenda outlining the important points to be discussed. Managers also need to be aware that some people may not speak up during meetings, whereas others may speak too much. For those employees who speak too much, it could be beneficial for the meeting organizer to establish guidelines prior to a meeting as to how much discussion will be needed on certain subjects. Another suggestion would be to have the meeting organizer talk to the excessive talker and explain to them their suggestions are appreciated, but more input is needed from others in the group. Conversely, the meeting organizer might need to set ground rules prior to the start of the meeting encouraging all participants to voice their views while remaining cognizant of others. A meeting's length can also influence its usefulness; in general, shorter meetings are more

Photo courtesy of Robert Frye, Florida International University.

Interacting with staff in their work spaces gives the manager authentic feedback about employees' performance and satisfaction, as well as other personnel issues.

effective than longer ones. Meetings that last longer than an hour tend to bore participants, who then lose their focus. Productive meetings are well organized and focused on the main points. Indeed, Judge and Miller (1991) found that management decisions made and implemented quickly were of higher quality than decisions made more slowly.

Another effective way to communicate with staff members is to visit them at their worksite. In this approach, referred to as **management by walking around**, the manager literally walks to each employee's work area and converses with him or her there. Doing so gives the manager a great opportunity to observe "moments of truth" in which employees interact with clients. This is a great opportunity to take in everything. Listen to the employee's words and tone as they speak to you and to each other. Walk around armed with information about recent successes or positive initiatives. This is also a chance to lighten up, joke, and show your softer side without being disrespectful. Try to catch employees in the act of doing something right, look for victories rather than failures, and when you find one applaud it.

Improving your communication with employees can help you build stronger and more productive relationships. Keeping employees informed and showing concern helps create a productive work environment.

Sexual Harassment

Unfortunately, **sexual harassment** has become more prevalent in the workplace. Contrary to popular belief, it is rarely based upon physical attraction; rather, it is usually about power. There are two basic types of sexual harassment: quid pro quo and hostile environment. Quid pro quo means "this for that" or "something for something." Quid pro quo sexual harassment occurs when submission to sexual advances is required for job advancement, ending a relationship will result in demotion or termination, or rejecting sexual advancement will result in some sort of punishment.

A hostile environment arises when behavior creates an intimidating, uncomfortable, or nonproductive work or study environment. Here are some ways to determine whether actions, words, or the environment constitute sexual harassment:

- Are the parties involved initiating an equal level of behavior?
- Would I do this to a person who is not of a gender to which I am attracted?
- Is power equal between the parties?
- Would I want this behavior to be made completely public?
- Would I behave this way if my partner or spouse were standing next to me?
- Would I want someone to do this to my child, sister, brother, or other loved one?

Emergency Procedures

Emergency situations that require immediate attention are going to occur, particularly in a fitness or sport atmosphere. To be prepared, you need a well-written crisis management and emergency action plan so that workers know what to do in an urgent situation. Cotton and Wolohan (2003) suggest addressing the following issues in a crisis management and emergency action plan:

- Personal injury of participants, spectators, staff, or visitors
- Fire
- Bomb or terrorism threat
- Civil disturbance
- Medical emergencies (care for the injured)
- Weather (e.g., tornado, hurricane, lightning)
- Earthquake
- Hazardous material spill
- Evacuation procedures
- Dealing with participants, family members of victims, lawyers, and the media

The crisis management and emergency plan be reviewed regularly. Personnel should be well trained in following the plan and should hold proper certifications (e.g., first aid, CPR, automated external defibrillator [AED]). They should also practice implementing the procedures listed in the plan. All of this training should be documented for legal reasons.

Customer Service

Walmart founder Sam Walton said, "There is only one boss. The customer, and he can fire everybody in the company from the chairman on down, simply by spending his money somewhere else" (Entrepreneur.com, 2008). It has also been said that every customer who receives poor service will tell 10 (or more) other people about their negative experience. This reality makes plain the need to train and educate employees to deliver proper customer service.

More specifically, employees should be trained to handle situations in which they are confronted by angry or hostile customers. A good customer training program educates employees to understand why the customer is angry, which usually comes down to cold, insensitive, and unsupportive surroundings. Angry customers need to vent their frustrations, and they typically do so to the frontline employee. It is crucial to speak to the customer in a friendly manner that is receptive to his or her problem. Listen carefully to the customer's words and try to reflect his or her statements to show interest and concern. Avoid using such phrases as "This is our policy" and "I only work here—I don't make the rules."

Professional Development

Professional development is the process of learning and keeping current in an area of expertise. It includes developing knowledge and skills through study, research, travel, workshops, retreats, and interaction with a mentor.

Professional development offers employees many benefits. It gives them opportunities to sharpen old skills and develop new ideas. It can be used as a mechanism to network with others who work in similar jobs in order to share new ideas and learn about what they do in their workplace. Networking can be an energizing and renewing experience. Sometimes employees simply need a break from their routine, or an opportunity to create balance in their lives, and professional development can provide this break even as it helps improve your programs—for example, through new ideas brought back from conferences.

EVALUATION

Employee evaluation can be one of the most important aspects of management. An evaluation system provides a process for assessing employee competence in order to assure quality. The evaluation process functions as a tool for improving employees' skills and knowledge by identifying strengths and weaknesses. Evaluations also provide specific information that can be used as the basis for employment decisions. Four main types of employee evaluation are used in today's workplace: top-down, peer-to-peer, 360-degree, and self-assessment.

Top-down evaluation is conducted by the employee's immediate supervisor. It can be problematic for the employee because it produces a rating generated by only one individual, though supervisors often ask peers of the employee being evaluated informally to rate an individual to help with this type of evaluation. Figure 9.3 shows a sample rubric for an evaluation. Using a rubric can allow the evaluator to assess an employee's level of competency based on predetermined skill levels and defined outcomes. The rubric can be beneficial if an evaluator is able to meet with the employee throughout the year to track progress.

Peer-to-peer evaluation requires employees at the same level to review each other. This approach is based on the theory that nobody knows a worker's ability better than his or her co-workers. However, organizations tend to resist peer evaluation because peers are thought to be uncomfortable with serving in the role of rater when material consequences are at stake.

In 360-degree evaluation, many people are consulted about the employee's performance, perhaps including customers, suppliers, peers, and direct reports. In the case of a manager, employees are often asked to give "upward feedback" about how well they are being managed. DeNisi and Kluger (2000) offer recommendations for improving the 360-degree process. They suggest informing the employee of the extent to which the 360-degree evaluation will affect important decisions (e.g., promotion, termination). Because the process involves many people, it may produce conflicting reactions from the individuals providing feedback, and a supervisor should help the employee being evaluated understand the data generated by the evaluation. Avoid having raters evaluate the employee in every area of his or her job; some individuals may not even know enough about the employee to provide a valid rating. If you use the 360-degree approach, conducted evaluation regularly—the results are effective only if they can be used to help improve the employee's performance. Continuous evaluation also helps you measure any improvement.

In self-assessment, of course, employees rate themselves, often using the same form that a manager might use to review them. Inderrieden, Allen, and Keaveny (2004) found that self-ratings have a positive effect on the evaluation process since the employee participates actively in the entire process. In addition, employees are usually harder on themselves than their supervisors would be, and they generally give themselves lower ratings. As a result, having employees do self-assessment performance reviews prior to a manager's review can set a positive tone for the meeting, since the manager often has better things to say than the employee has said about him- or herself.

MOTIVATION

Motivation is an internal state or condition that activates behavior and gives it direction. It can be a desire or want that energizes and directs goal-oriented behavior. Motivation can be external or internal. External motivation comes from outside the employee and typically takes the form of a tangible reward. Internal motivation involves the employee's personal goals or achievements.

Demotivators, in contrast, exert a negative impact on staff morale. Here are some examples:

- Failure to get the most out of your people
- Emotional and behavioral problems
- Stressful work environment
- Lack of perceived fairness in compensation
- Interpersonal motivation killers
- Inflexible work rules
- Lack of advancement opportunities and lack of perceived fairness regarding advancement issues
- Discrimination, harassment, and abuse
- Aiming too low when hiring
- Lack of autonomy

SAMPLE EMPLOYEE EVALUATION RUBRIC

Read the following definitions and provide a numerical rating in the space provided that most clearly describes the staff member's performance for each required performance element.

Performance element	Below standards (1)	(2)	Meets standards (3)	(4)	Greatly exceeds standards (5)
Quality of work: Standard of work; value of end product	Needs excessive supervision. Product frequently needs rework. Quantity of work completed is insufficient. Does not use or understand quality standards. Does not apply knowledge to improve process. Fails to accomplish assigned tasks.		Demonstrates competence in required job skills and knowledge. Shows accuracy, clarity, and thoroughness in work. Follows through and follows up on task completion. Upholds quality standards. Connects knowledge gained in day-to-day work. Works independently, is reliable, and requires little supervision.		Always produces exceptional work. Demonstrates thorough understanding of processes, methods, systems, and procedures. Refines as needed and provides feedback for continuous improvement. Exceeds relevant quality standards. Permits complete trust in successfully completing any task assigned.
Numerical rating:	**Comments:**				
Professional knowledge: Technical knowledge, proficiency, and practical application	Lacks basic professional knowledge to perform effectively. Cannot apply basic skills. Fails to develop professionally or achieve timely qualifications.		Understands job requirements; has thorough professional knowledge relevant to position. Competently performs both routine and new tasks. Steadily improves skills and achieves timely qualifications. Participates in training and development activities provided by unit, division, university, or industry associations.		Is a recognized expert, sought after to solve difficult problems. Develops project alternatives and presents recommendations. Develops and implements innovative ideas and improved systems. Develops and leads training and development programs for others.
Numerical rating:	**Comments:**				
Teamwork: Contributions to team building and results	Creates conflict, is unwilling to work with others, and puts self above team. Becomes self-focused as opposed to goal-focused. Fails to understand team goals or teamwork techniques. Does not take direction well. Fails to develop and maintain effective working relationships with supervisors, staff, co-workers, and others.		Reinforces others' efforts and meets personal commitments to team. Understands team goals and employs good teamwork techniques. Attends to and meets needs of the customer to achieve optimal results. Actively and constructively participates in university and external committees and councils. Networks with campus colleagues, external community, and industry leaders.		Is a team builder and leader who inspires cooperation and progress. Is a talented mentor who focuses goals and techniques for the team. Is the best at accepting and offering team direction. Gets involved and goes beyond assigned role. Presents a positive impression of self and university while participating in university and non-university service activities.
Numerical rating:	**Comments:**				

Figure 9.3 Sample employee evaluation rubric. *(continued)*

Courtesy of Bowling Green State University, Division of Student Affairs.

Figure 9.3 *(continued)*

Performance element	Below standards (1)	(2)	Meets standards (3)	(4)	Greatly exceeds standards (5)
Leadership: Organizing, motivating, and developing others to accomplish goals	Neglects growth, development, or welfare of subordinates. Fails to organize and creates problems for subordinates. Does not set or achieve goals relevant to the university, department, or mission. Lacks ability to cope with or tolerate stress. Operates in a reactionary mode, responding to issues only after they have fully developed into problems. Fails to properly assign tasks or monitor and redirect progress toward successful completion.		Stimulates growth and development in subordinates. Sets and achieves useful, realistic goals that support the university mission. Properly aligns responsibility, accountability, and authority. Instills pride in performance, service, innovation, and quality. Anticipates need and does not wait to be told to take appropriate action. Delegates work appropriately, providing direction and support to individuals and teams to improve their effectiveness.		Is an inspiring motivator and trainer whose subordinates reach the highest level of growth and development. Is a superb organizer with great foresight who develops process improvements and efficiencies. Leadership achievements dramatically further the university mission and vision. Initiates long-range plan development. Perseveres through the toughest of challenges and inspires others.
Numerical rating:	**Comments:**				
Communication and professionalism: Effectively exchanging relevant information with others	Is an inadequate communicator who fails to accept constructive criticism. Fails to consistently exhibit a courteous, conscientious, and generally businesslike manner in the workplace. Does not identify and effectively bring together the right stakeholders for decision making. Is unable to maintain professional confidentiality.		Is a clear, timely communicator. Is cooperative, considerate, and tactful in dealing with managers, subordinates, peers, faculty, students, and others. Demonstrates effectiveness of expression in individual and group situations. Challenges status quo processes in appropriate ways. Effectively assembles right stakeholders for decision making. Values and promotes equity and diversity in the workplace. Prepares written documentation and administrative or system procedure manuals.		Sets the standard for adapting to changes in job, methods, and surroundings. Anticipates need and does not wait to be told. Is an exceptional communicator. Uses holistic perspective to link insightful assessment of external business landscape with keen awareness of profit to execute strategy and deliver desired results. Demonstrates superior application of interpersonal communication skills.
Numerical rating:	**Comments:**				

Performance element	Below standards (1)	(2)	Meets standards (3)	(4)	Greatly exceeds standards (5)
Resource management: Using available financial and personnel resources to meet commitments, minimize risk, and promote safety	Wastes resources. Fails to use available resources to achieve desired results. Is unable to plan or prioritize. Makes flawed decisions and is disconnected from performance results. Does not require, enforce, or follow safety work practices; ignores safety hazards and concerns.		Uses available resources to meet productivity standards. Manages time and prioritizes to achieve desired results. Develops short-term goals and alternatives for accomplishing tasks. Measures business decisions with clients and stakeholders in mind. Monitors financial status of unit, area, and projects against budget. Understands, follows, and communicates safety practices for the organizational unit; encourages others to report and resolve workplace hazards.		Seeks out and implements appropriate cost-saving measures. Consistently exceeds expectations through foresight and innovation. Prepares, analyzes, and interprets performance results and statistics and benchmarks against industry data and standards. Demonstrates leadership in identifying and resolving workplace risks; consistently attains an exemplary safety and risk management record; actively participates in safety discussions or committees.
Numerical rating:	**Comments:**				

Employees can be motivated by intrinsic and extrinsic factors, or both. **Extrinsic motivation** occurs when employees are motivated by external rewards (Gagne and Deci, 2005). One example of how to externally motivate employees is to reward them for outstanding performance above and beyond their job requirements and expectations. An employee incentive program formally recognizes extraordinary job performance (see figure 9.4). Recognition can take the form of written documentation of extraordinary behavior witnessed by co-workers, patrons, or supervisors—for example, subbing for others, providing outstanding customer service, helping in an emergency, or resolving a difficult situation. Each employee might receive a star for every positive submission written about him or her. At the end of each month, the employee with the most stars could be recognized with a reward such as a special parking spot for the employee of the month, a gift certificate to a local restaurant, or a special recognition plaque.

Intrinsic motivation occurs when employees perform a task that is felt to be interesting and that they find rewarding and enjoyable (Gagne and Deci, 2005). For example, a personal trainer who gets great satisfaction from seeing the progress of a client is being motivated by intrinsic factors.

CERTIFICATION

Certifications are required for certain job duties in the campus recreational sports department. At the very least, most positions require certification in first aid and CPR, and specific areas such as aquatics and group exercise require more specialized certification. Campus recreational sports professionals must require employees to possess the certifications needed for each job title.

General Certifications

Various specialty certifications are needed for various jobs. Certification programs offered by professional organizations ensure that individuals who receive certification possess the

STUDENT EMPLOYEE INCENTIVE PROGRAM

The Bowling Green State University "Rec Buck" is an example of a student employee incentive program designed to recognize student employees who go above and beyond their job description to help improve the recreation and wellness department. In the 2009–2010 academic year, more than 280 recognition dollars were redeemed for prizes.

Rec Buck Award Criteria

Nine categories were created for employee recognition:

1. Training and Orientation Expected duties (examples): Attendance at all training meetings Active participation in training sessions Completion of all online trainings Rec Buck–worthy actions (examples): Planning a training session Leading a training session Training new employees	**5. Shift Coverage** Expected duties (examples): Covering a single shift with advance notice Rec Buck–worthy actions (examples): Picking up a last-minute shift Staying late or coming in early to cover a shift Picking up multiple shifts
2. Customer Service Expected duties (examples): Interacting with patrons on your shift Resolving a conflict correctly and calmly Organizing and cleaning areas Rec Buck–worthy actions (examples): Receiving a written compliment from a patron Going above the expected interaction with patrons Going out of your way to assist a student	**6. Crisis Management** Expected duties (examples): Participation in emergency exercises Following the emergency action plan correctly Remaining calm and controlled Rec Buck–worthy actions (examples): Organizing and leading emergency exercises Taking proactive action to ease a crisis Performing superbly in emergency exercises or a crisis
3. Meetings Expected duties (examples): Attendance at all meetings Active participation at meetings Keeping up to date with RecWell information Rec Buck–worthy actions (examples): Leading and planning a staff meeting Giving outstanding input or ideas during meeting Bringing up new or unknown concerns to be addressed and offering solutions	**7. Leadership** Expected duties (examples): Arriving on time for shifts and completing required duties Handling issues as they arise Providing answers to questions from other staff Rec Buck–worthy actions (examples): Taking initiative to address an issue without supervisor prompting Giving outstanding effort in helping new staff and patrons
4. Special Events Expected duties (examples): Special event set-up and teardown Decorating for special events Cleaning up after a special event Rec Buck–worthy actions (examples): Working an overnight event Going above and beyond in set-up and cleaning Picking up multiple shifts to cover a special event	**8. Marketing** Promoting programs and events for students and patrons Handling assigned promotional tasks (e.g., flyers, Facebook) Keeping up to date with RecWell information Rec Buck–worthy actions (examples): Creating a new marketing technique Going above and beyond expected promotional efforts Creating new program ideas

Figure 9.4 Sample employee incentive program.

Reprinted, by permission, from Bowling Green State University, Department of Recreation and Wellness.

9. Volunteer Service
Volunteer opportunities exist within each area of the department. Rec Bucks will be awarded on an individual basis by supervisors for volunteer time within respective areas.

Rec Buck Tracker System

When awarding a Rec Buck, supervisors must record the award in the system tracker (i.e., an Excel spreadsheet) and indicate the relevant Rec Buck category (e.g., number 1) and a brief reason for the award. The tracker enables us to determine eligibility for prizes and awards.

Sample Prize Structure

$15

- Graduate assistant or professional staff work a student's paid 3-hour shift.
- Free group exercise semester pass
- Free climbing wall semester pass

$10

- Free 18 holes of golf with cart
- Large bucket of golf balls for driving range

$5

- Free 9 holes of golf with cart
- Small bucket of golf balls for driving range

Employee Quote

Student employee Liz Jennings stated, "The Rec Buck program has helped me as a supervisor to provide my employees with incentives that let them know they are doing a great job and to keep up the good work."

---

necessary skills and knowledge to competently plan and administer programs. Here are the most common certifications found in recreation facilities:

- **CPR** certification teaches participants how to respond in emergency situations that involve choking, heart attack, or other nonbreathing victims. Participants learn what to do when confronted with an emergency situation and how to implement actions that could to save a victim's life. For more information, contact the American Red Cross (www.redcross.org) or the American Heart Association (www.americanheart.org).
- **First aid** certification teaches the skills needed to respond to emergency situations at work or home. Participants learn how to render first aid to help save lives, prevent casualties, and help injured persons recover. For more information, contact the American Red Cross (www.redcross.org) or the American Heart Association (www.americanheart.org).
- **AED** certification qualifies participants to use an automated external defibrillator to provide assistance in cases of sudden cardiac arrest. Participants learn how to set up and how to use an AED. All 50 states have adopted laws or regulations regarding AEDs (Florida was first, in 1997, and Maine was last, in 2001). Facility management professionals should check their state laws regarding AEDs because some states have updated their laws by enacting more stricter guidelines and specify business types that are now required to have an AED.

Aquatics-Related Certifications

Certifications specific to aquatics include the following:

- **Lifeguard** certification provides training in lifeguarding, rescue skills, and first aid. Those who receive certification are qualified to work as lifeguards at many swimming pools, water parks, and waterfront swimming areas. For more information, contact the American Red Cross (www.redcross.org).
- **Water safety instructor** certification aids in developing the skills needed to instruct and plan courses in aquatics training. It covers the following training areas: learning to swim, infant and preschool programs, and water safety. For more information, contact the American Red Cross (www.redcross.org).
- **Certified pool operator** training serves pool operators or anyone associated with the operation of swimming pools. It provides instruction regarding current pool codes, regulations, water chemistry, filter operations, flow meters, monitoring equipment, aquatic administration, common operational errors, and safety concerns. For more information, contact the National Swimming Pool Foundation (www.nspf.com).

Group Exercise and Fitness Certifications

Teacher certification is available through workshops for all the common group fitness classes, including step, kickboxing, senior, and aquatics. The best-known certifying organizations for group fitness are the Aerobics and Fitness Association of America (AFAA) and the American Council on Exercise (ACE). For more information contact AFAA (www.afaa.com) or ACE (www.acefitness.com).

Personal Training

Personal training certification instructs participants about safety and proper methods of exercise. These programs address physical fitness and performance, teach participants how to write appropriate exercise recommendations, demonstrate proper exercise techniques, and explore motivation techniques. Personal training certification is offered by many organizations and companies. The most widely accepted ones are AFAA, ACE, and the American College of Sport Medicine (www.acsm.org).

SUMMARY

Campus recreational sports departments employ workers in a variety of classifications and with various degrees of experience and job responsibility. Each employee plays a vital role in helping the department succeed. Supervisors must understand the various employee types in order to appreciate and cultivate each employee's role and value within the organization.

Hiring an employee may be the most important decision a supervisor makes. The supervisor begins the process by creating a job description that accurately describes the work to be performed. The description is then used to create a job announcement and recruit potential employees. Next, the department sifts applicants through a review of résumés and reference checks, then conducts interviews to evaluate which candidate best fits the job opening. Interviewers ask questions that prompt candidates to reveal their knowledge, oral communication skills, and other qualifications. The process culminates, of course, in the selection of a new employee, who then requires training throughout the year to become acclimated to his or her new job environment.

Communication with employees is essential in order to ensure productivity, and it allows supervisors to gain knowledge of workplace issues and employee accomplishments. Employee communication takes various forms. Professional development, for example, allows employees to learn and keep current in their job areas, and supervisors should consider it annually as a way for employees to constantly improve. End-of-year evaluation serves numerous purposes—none greater than providing feedback for improvement. Supervisors can motivate employees through an employee incentive program. Possible incentives should be explored to find out what employees would appreciate as a way to motivate and recognize exceptional performance.

Supervisors must understand the various certifications needed in campus recreational sports programs. They should also be engaged with certifying groups in order to be stay abreast of changes in the industry standard for certifications.

Glossary

compensatory time—Form of compensation for employees subject to overtime provisions.

employee evaluation—Process to assess employee competence in order to assure quality.

employee job description—Verbal description of the functions that an individual performs in his or her job.

extrinsic motivation—Occurs when employees are motivated by external rewards.

graduate assistant—Enrolled graduate student who holds a position within the organization (typically required to work 20 hours weekly).

hourly employee—Employee who is paid for his or her actual hours of work and who receives overtime pay for time worked beyond 40 hours per week.

intrinsic motivation—Occurs when employees perform a task that is felt to be interesting and they find the activity to be rewarding and enjoyable.

management by walking around—Practice in which the manager walks to each employee's work area and discusses his or her job in person.

organizational chart—Document outlining an organization's structure.

part-time professional—Employee who works fewer hours per week than full-time professional staff and typically is not afforded benefits.

professional development—Process of learning and keeping current in an area of expertise.

salaried employee—Employee who typically works between 37.5 and 40 hours per week and accumulates compensatory time when working more than 40 hours per week.

sexual harassment—Imposition of a hostile environment or quid pro quo requirement of submission to sexual advances in order to retain or progress in one's job.

student intern—Student who works in a professional setting to gain experience and academic credit.

volunteer staff member—Person who offers his or her services freely without expectation of compensation.

References

Astin, A.W. (1987, September/October). Competition or cooperation? *Change*, 12–19.

Cotton, D.J., & Wolohan, J.T. (Eds.). (2003). *Law for recreation and sport managers*. Dubuque, IA: Kendall/Hunt.

DeNisi, & Kluger. (2000). Feedback effectiveness: Can 360-degree appraisals be improved? *Academy of Management Executive*, 14(1): pp. 129-139.

Entrepreneur.com. (2008). Sam Walton: Bargain Basement Billionaire. Retrieved from http://www.entrepreneur.com/article/197560

Farrell, J.M., Johnston, M.E., & Twynam, D.G. (1998). Volunteer motivation, satisfaction, and management at an elite sporting competition. *Journal of Sport Management, 12*(4), 288–301.

Gagne, M. & Deci, E. L. (2005). Self-determination theory and work motivation. *Journal of Organizational Behavior*, 26, 331-362.

Gorter, C., & Van Ommeren, J. (1999). Sequencing, timing and filling rates of recruitment channels. *Applied Economics, 31*(10), 1149–1160.

Inderrieden, E.J., Allen, R.E., & Keaveny, T.J. (2004). Managerial discretion in the use of self-ratings in an appraisal system: The antecedents and consequences. *Journal of Managerial Issues, 16*(4), 460–482.

Judge, & Miller. (1991). Antecedents and outcomes of decision speed in different environmental contexts. *Academy of Management Journal*, 34: 449–463.

Schneider, R.C , Stier, W.F, Kampf, S., Wilding, G.E., & Haines, S.G. (2006). Characteristics, attributes, and competencies sought in new hires by campus recreation directors. *Recreational Sports Journal, 30*, 142–153.

Stier, W.F. (1999). *Managing sport, fitness, and recreation programs.* Needham Heights, MA: Allyn & Bacon.

CHAPTER

10

Program Planning Using a Student Learning Approach

Julia Wallace Carr
James Madison University

Every recreational building, whether multi-use or strictly recreational, is only a structure until someone begins to program it for people. Then it becomes a vibrant scene of action, excitement, competition, and exploration. It becomes a magnet to attract thousands of members of the campus community to be part of the phenomenon called campus recreation (Jones, 1999, pp. 89).

This chapter discusses the nuts and bolts of programming in order to help administrators make good decisions in creating activities and services in campus recreational sports. When effective, programs offered by a campus recreational sports facility keep alive the "wow factor" that participants feel during their recruitment tour or their first visit as part of student orientation. The following discussion provides campus recreational sports professionals with the tools and concepts necessary to incorporate **college student development** theory and practice into their day-to-day activities. The chapter discusses the process of **mapping the environment** (Borrego, 2006) by examining institutional and departmental priorities, such as the impact of mission and CAS standards on the program's focus, the concept of intentionality, the use of **learning outcomes** in program planning, types of programming, and staffing.

The discussion employs the Harper Wallace Hardin planning model (HWHPM), which was developed by using the cycle of intentionality (COI) (Ward & Mitchell, 1997) as the foundational piece to inform the planning process. Intentionality is a key concept for programmers to embrace. It can be defined as creating conditions that motivate, inspire, and help participants to acquire and make sense of knowledge, skills, and behaviors. This concept of intentionality forms the basis of both the COI and the HWHPM. It requires the professional to think beyond the day-to-day—the way we have always done something—and to consider the end vision for a given experience (Ward & Mitchell). The COI was expanded to incorporate steps for learning outcome development into program planning. Figure 10.1 provides a graphic depiction of the model.

The HWHPM is cyclical. If a campus recreational sports professional is thinking about developing a new recreation program (e.g., a new unit within the department or an individual program), he or she would enter into the process at the "determining priorities" phase. Otherwise, he or she can enter into the process with existing programs wherever he or she thinks makes the

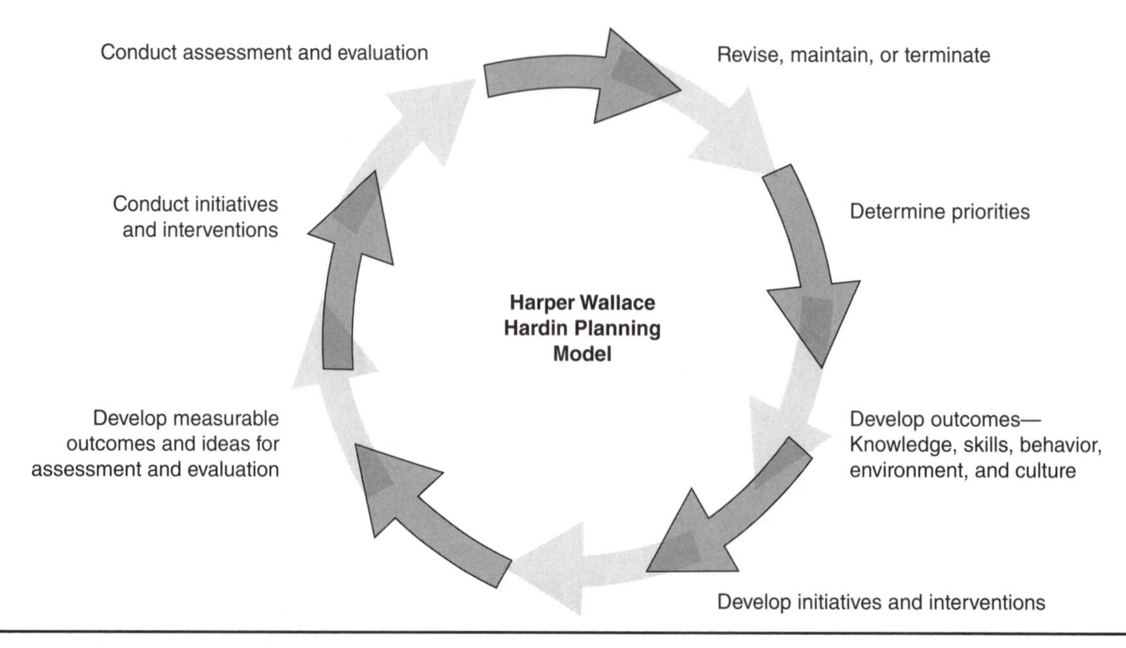

Figure 10.1 Harper Wallace Hardin planning model.

most sense for the planning cycle. In this chapter, we discuss the model in terms of numerical steps as we walk you through the HWHPM and give you practical examples of how it can be used in program planning in a campus recreational sports center.

STEP 1: DETERMINE PRIORITIES

When developing a program plan, campus recreational sports professionals must understand the priorities of their institution, division, and department. Programs often fail because the professionals who created the experience failed to do the foundational work of understanding why prospective participants would want the opportunity or service (Ward & Mitchell, 1997). Determining priorities, then, is step 1 of the HWHPM.

The data for exploring priorities come in the form of mission statements, bottom-line goals and objectives, and general philosophical foundations and educational experiences of the recreation staff. You can also use information gleaned from needs assessments and other areas that create priorities for the department (e.g., budget implications). This approach can be used to develop the program plan for an entire recreation department or to determine the needs for an individual programming unit (e.g., fitness, intramurals, informal recreation, group fitness, aquatics, adventure, instructional programs, sport clubs). Priorities are also driven by the administrative unit in which the department is housed on the institution's organizational chart.

Mission, Focus, Purpose

You should explore three major issues related to the department's mission, focus, and purpose (Franklin & Hardin, 2008, p. 5):

- The mission and scope of the institution
- The department's placement within the university structure
- The disciplines in which administrative professionals in the department have received their foundation and training

The outcome of this exploration is a key to developing a program plan for the organization.

Mission

Mission statements—whether of the university or the department—provide stability, direction, and clarity of purpose (Warner, 1995).

This purpose then helps you determine the focus of program development. Many campus recreational sports directors view their mission as supporting the overall educational mission, either by helping participants develop lifetime activity skills and wellness habits or by providing cocurricular opportunities to support the curricular educational mission (Frankin & Hardin, 2008). Institutional and departmental missions can be driven by the following orientations:

- Educational (student learning and student development)
- Service (customer needs and wants and community involvement)
- Business (revenue generation)

The key question is whether the mission espoused by the director matches the program plan set up by the recreational practitioner (Argyris, 1991). Administrators should periodically map or survey their campus environment to ensure consistency between the mission and the program plan and to determine the learning opportunities and activities available for students.

Mapping a learning environment means recognizing, identifying, and documenting the sites for learning activities on campus; it provides a framework within which student affairs educators can link their programs and activities to learning opportunities (Borrego, 2006, p. 11). The following questions address how a professional working in an education-focused institution might map his or her environment in order to determine what priorities have been established by the mission and the campus learning objectives. Borrego suggests that it is important to map the learning environment of the institution and to explore opportunities for growth and development in curricular and cocurricular environments. The process assumes that the entire campus is a learning environment; it could be adapted, however, to map the environment of any administrative structure by adapting Borrego's questions to the institution's bottom line focus—for example, student learning and development, revenue generation, or community involvement.

Here are some questions to drive the process of mapping the learning environment (Borrego, 2006, p. 12):

- What is the mission of the campus?
- What are the campus learning objectives or outcomes?
- How does the work of student affairs support those outcomes?
- What new opportunities might arise when one asks first, "What is the intended outcome?" and then, "What programs or services can be organized to support that outcome?"
- How can one create interventions with the understanding that learning happens in multiple dimensions across the campus environment?

Organizational Position

Programming can also be driven by the placement of the campus recreational sports department within the university's organizational structure; specifically, programming can be affected as much by the division's bottom-line goals and objectives as it is by the departmental or institutional mission. Campus recreational sports programs can be found in a variety of administrative structures, including athletic departments, physical education programs, and business units (Dean, 2009, p. 330). Nearly three-quarters, however, are housed in student affairs and therefore share its focus on student development and learning (Franklin, 2007); in contrast, a unit located in business operations or in administration and finance may focus more on a business model and on revenue generation.

Disciplines

Administrators' academic disciplines can influence the department's focus and ultimately the programming options it offers (Franklin & Hardin, 2008). Table 10.1 shows how education can affect the focus of the programming staff; the table also lists foundational theories for those who want to delve further into these areas of influence.

Table 10.1 Educational Influences on Program Development

Academic discipline	Programming emphasis	Theoretical foundations
Sport and recreation management	Sport and competitive activity Recreational activity Informal or drop-in play	Experiential learning (Kolb, 1984) Flow (Csikszentmihalyi, 1997) Adventure experience paradigm (Martin & Priest, 1986) Neulinger's paradigm (Neulinger, 1976)
Exercise science and health education	Fitness-related activity Wellness education Behavioral change	Transtheoretical model of change (Prochaska, Norcross, & DiClemente, 1994) Health belief model (Simons-Morton, Green, & Gottlieb, 1995) Theory of planned behavior (Simons-Morton et al.)
College student personnel	Student development	Chickering's seven vectors (Chickering & Reisser, 1993) Student learning theory of involvement (Astin, 1999) Epistemological reflection model (Baxter Magolda, 1992)

Data from Franklin and Hardin 2008.

Philosophical Foundations: College Student Development Theory

Mable (1980) stated that the emphasis of student development practice is "to prepare students to work on complex, dynamic, and unpredictable future problems" (p. vii). Rodgers (1990) recommended that student affairs professionals examine their practice through the lens of formal theory. College student development theory is a specific application of human development theory (Newton & Ender, 1980) that focuses on the phases applicable to college students. Professionals who work in organizations focused on student development must develop a strong understanding of college student development theory and be able to put it into practice.

Student development theories can be assigned to the following categories: **cognitive-structural theory**, **psychosocial theory**, **typology theory**, and **person–environment theory**. This chapter examines psychosocial theories, especially **Chickering's seven vectors** (1993), because of their particular relevance to the typical day-to-day interactions between campus recreational sports professionals and student participants and student employees. This body of work lends itself nicely to many focal areas of program planning in a campus recreational sports center, especially those that are student focused and learning centered.

Psychosocial Theory

Psychosocial theory examines the content of development (Evans, Forney, Guido, Patton, & Renn, 2010). It is based on the premise that individuals go through developmental stages defined by a biological and social timetable (Rodgers 1990). This type of theory focuses on the issues that people face as they move through life—their identity, their relationships, and what they will do with their life. These theories posit that development occurs in a sequence of age-linked stages over the course of a life span (Evans et al., 2010). The psychosocial theories typically used to examine college students' day-to-day activities and interactions include Erikson's theory of psychosocial development, Havighurst's proposed developmental tasks, Gould's transformations, Hudson's decade orientations in the lifecycle, and Chickering and Reisser's seven vectors. The seven vectors theory lends itself nicely to the development of student learning outcomes and is commonly used by departments housed in the student affairs division.

Seven Vectors

In 1969, Chickering authored the first edition of *Education and Identity*. Like many others, Chickering built on the works of Erikson—specifically, stages five and six (identity and intimacy). He examined the developmental issues of college students and later included in his research the environmental conditions that influence development. He considered identity to be the core developmental issue for college students and proposed that once a sense of identity is established the student can address other issues in the developmental process (Evans et al., 2010).

Chickering (1969) identified seven vectors of development that contribute to identity formation. Students move through each vector at different rates and sometimes regress to a previously completed vector to reexamine issues. The vectors build on one another but are not rigidly sequential; rather, they serve as "major highways for journeying toward individuation—the discovery and refinement of one's unique being—and also toward communion with other individuals and groups, including the larger national and global society" (Chickering & Reisser, 1993, p. 35).

Building on Chickering's original work, Chickering and Reisser modified the seven vectors to produce the following group (Chickering & Reisser, 1993; Evans et al., 2010; Newton & Ender, 1980):

- Developing competence
- Managing emotions
- Moving through autonomy toward interdependence
- Developing mature interpersonal relationships
- Establishing identity
- Developing purpose
- Developing integrity

Chickering and Reisser (1993) viewed educational environments as powerful influencers on student development. They identified seven key factors:

- Institutional objectives
- Institutional size
- Student–faculty relationships
- Curriculum
- Teaching
- Friendships and student communities
- Student development programs and services

These factors, in turn, rest on a foundation made up of three key principles (Chickering & Reisser, 1993):

- Recognition and respect for individual differences
- Acknowledgment of the cyclical nature of learning and development
- Integration of work and learning

Many of these concepts can be incorporated into learning outcomes for educational program planning.

Standards

When developing a program plan—whether for the department or an individual programming unit—the planner should review the CAS standards (Dean, 2009) for campus recreational sports programs that were developed by a NIRSA committee through the merger of previous CAS documents and the NIRSA *General and Specialty Standards for Collegiate Recreational Sports* (1996). The resulting CAS standards dictate that the mission of a campus recreational sports program "must be to enhance the mind, body, and spirit of students and other eligible individuals by providing programs, services, and facilities that are responsive to the physical, social, recreational, and lifelong educational needs of the campus community as they relate to health, fitness, and learning" (Dean, p. 332).

The CAS standards mention formal education, student learning and development, and preparation for a satisfying and productive life following graduation. They focus programmers on using theory, being intentional in their planning, creating learning outcomes, assessing their effectiveness, and being sensitive to their participants' needs. These focuses require practitioners to look at their offerings through the lenses of service, developmental stages, learning, and equal opportunity. "The formal education of students, consisting of curriculum and the co-curriculum, must promote student learning and development outcomes that are purposeful and holistic and that prepare students for satisfying and productive lifestyles, work, and civic participation" (Dean, 2009, pp. 332).

The following standards are also set for campus recreational sports programs (Dean, 2009, p. 332):

- Explore possibilities for collaboration with faculty members and other colleagues.
- Be integrated into the life of the institution.
- Be intentional and coherent.
- Be guided by theories and knowledge of learning and development.
- Reflect developmental and demographic profiles of the student population.
- Respond to needs of individuals, diverse and special populations, and relevant constituencies.
- Reflect the needs and interests of students and other eligible users.

Two sections relate to program planning and program operational planning. Program planning and implementation processes must be inclusive and should include the following elements (Dean, 2009, p. 333):

- Equitable participation for men and women, with opportunities to participate at various levels of ability and disability
- Interpretation of institutional policies and procedures
- A variety of opportunities that reflect and address cultural diversity
- Participant involvement in shaping program content and procedures
- Co-recreational activity with opportunities to participate at various levels of ability
- Disability

Program operational planning and implementation processes must address the following elements (Dean, 2009, p. 333):

- Participant safety through rules, regulations, and facility management
- Effective risk management policies, procedures, and practices
- Supervision of campus recreational sports activities and facilities
- Facility coordination and scheduling
- Consultation with groups and organizations for sport and fitness programming
- Training of office and field staff
- Conflict resolution management protocols
- Procedures for the inventory, maintenance, use, and security of equipment
- Recognition for participants, employees, and volunteers
- Publicity, promotion, and media relations
- Volunteerism in service delivery and leadership
- Customer service practices
- Promotion of socially responsible behaviors

Finally, here are some other items to consider when determining priorities:

- Needs assessment data
  - Participants' wants and needs
  - Professional staff members' perceptions of participant needs
- Budget
- Staffing requirements
- Campus priorities or goals
- Special project areas of emphasis for the year such as alcohol use, sustainability, community service
- Overall outcome—providing the greatest good for the greatest number of people

As you can see, many areas need to be considered before jumping into the actual development of a program. Determining priorities serves as foundational work that needs to be completed before creating the program itself in the following steps. Clear priorities help you develop a successful implementation plan.

STEP 2: DEVELOP OUTCOMES

The next stage of the HWHPM for programming—developing outcomes—follows the requirements of CAS and incorporates the premise of being intentional and focusing on the outcomes of the experience. Learning outcomes focus practitioners and help them create a vision for what they want the participant to gain from his or her engagement in the activity. The CAS standards articulate several considerations when developing learning outcomes:

- Knowledge acquisition and application
- Cognitive complexity
- Intrapersonal development
- Interpersonal competence
- Humanitarianism and civic engagement
- Practical competence

Table 10.2 provides further detail about each of the student learning and development outcome domains and their related dimensions.

Recreational programs focus largely on the domains of knowledge acquisition, interpersonal competence, and practical competence. Mager (1997) describes learning outcomes as blueprints—guides to teaching what is intended to be taught. They are all about participant performance, about the end rather than the means. They describe what a participant will be able to do in displaying competency. Silberman (1998) suggests that learning outcomes are "the pillars of your program, not straitjackets" (p. 37), and they drive the design of each **intervention**. An intervention is any opportunity for learning—whether **passive learning** (e.g., bulletin board, newsletter article, podcast) or **active learning** (e.g., meeting, educational session, staff training, game). Komives and Schoper (2006) identify three keys to determining student learning outcomes for a programming unit, an individual program, or the campus as a whole: mission, philosophy, and assessment. They encourage practitioners to ask the following questions (pp. 21, 26):

- What is the mission of the department, division, college, or university?
- What do you want students to learn that will move them closer to achieving the mission?
- How do the philosophy and values of the institution shape the outcomes valued in the environment?
- How do you plan to measure your learning outcomes, or what are the opportunities for demonstrating learning?

Table 10.2 CAS Student Learning and Development Outcome Domains and Dimensions

Domains	Dimensions
Knowledge acquisition, integration, construction, and application	Understanding knowledge from a range of disciplines; connecting knowledge to other knowledge, ideas, and experiences; constructing knowledge; relating knowledge to daily life
Cognitive complexity	Critical thinking, reflective thinking, effective reasoning, and creativity
Intrapersonal development	Realistic self-appraisal, self-understanding, and self-respect; identity development; commitment to ethics and integrity; and spiritual awareness
Interpersonal competence	Meaningful relationships, interdependence, collaboration, and effective leadership
Humanitarianism and civic engagement	Understanding and appreciation of cultural and human differences; social responsibility; global perspective; and sense of civic responsibility
Practical competence	Pursuing goals; communicating effectively; technical competence; managing personal affairs; managing career development; demonstrating professionalism; maintaining health and wellness; and living a purposeful and satisfying life

Reprinted, by permission from L.A. Dean, ed., 2009, *CAS standards and guidelines for higher education,* 7th ed. (Washington, DC: Council for the Advancement of Standards in Higher Education), 332.

Creating Learning Outcomes

Learning outcomes can be created by means of two approaches: **outcome-to-practice** and **practice-to-outcome** (Komives & Schoper, 2006). Outcome-to-practice is often the best approach, particularly if your goal is to determine the end product of the experience before creating an intervention. In this approach, the recreation professional uses data gathered in step 1 (determining priorities) to create the desired learning outcome, then develops an intervention or learning opportunity to enable participants to achieve the outcome. This approach satisfies the concept of intentionality, or beginning with the end in mind.

For an example of the outcome-to-practice approach, imagine that in reviewing information from a needs assessment on nutrition, the fitness and nutrition coordinator sees that only 25 percent of the surveyed first-year students can identify the right number of servings from the various food groups to create a healthy diet. In response, the coordinator determines what he wants students to be able to articulate about eating right, then develops a learning opportunity to help them do so.

The practice-to-outcome approach, on the other hand, is best used by people who are new to outcome writing. In this approach, the professional examines an existing program to determine what outcome it can allow, or is allowing, participants to achieve. For an example of the practice-to-outcome approach, suppose that the adventure coordinator is running a very successful overnight canoe trip. In talking with a park ranger, she realizes that there is a need for Leave No Trace training. In this case, the learning opportunity—the canoe trip—is already in place, and the coordinator develops the related learning outcome of understanding and practicing the Leave No Trace philosophy.

The ABCD Method

Mager (1997) formulated the components of a learning outcome as follows: (a) "do what," (b) "with what," and (c) "how well" (p. 75). Jordan, DeGraaf, and DeGraaf (2005) adapted these components into a unique approach called the ABCD method. Wallace Carr and Hardin (2010) have likened this method to the act of diagramming sentences in English class. Each letter of the ABCD method relates to a specific part of the learning outcome:

- **A**udience—the person(s) responding to the intervention and performing the specific action
- **B**ehavior—the action that the audience performs
- **C**ondition—the key circumstances under which the performance occurs (i.e., when and with what)
- **D**egree—how well the behavior must be accomplished

Table 10.3 presents each letter, its basic definition as formulated by Jordon et al. (2005, p. 134), and examples of language for each part of the outcome.

Silberman (1998) cautions outcome writers to avoid using commonly misinterpreted words and fuzzy verbs (Wallace Carr & Hardin, 2010) when formulating the behaviors to be performed by a participant. Table 10.4 provides a list of acceptable action verbs for each specific learning level in Bloom's Taxonomy (1956), as well as a list of fuzzy words to avoid.

The following examples of learning outcomes were created by practitioners in the field at James Madison University for many of the program areas commonly seen in campus recreational sports.

Adventure

At the completion of the backpacking trip, participants will describe Leave No Trace (LNT) using the UREC Adventure definition with 90 percent accuracy.

At the completion of the backpacking trip, participants will provide two specific examples of recommended LNT practices for the area in which the trip takes place according to the guidelines presented at http://LNT.org.

Aquatics

At the completion of the lifeguard instructor course, participants will complete the written exam with 80 percent accuracy.

Table 10.3 Components of the ABCD Method

Component	Definition	Language examples
A	**A**udience (who)—the person(s) responding to the intervention and performing the specific action	The participant will, the student employee will, the camp participant will
B	**B**ehavior (what)—the action that the audience performs	Demonstrate, articulate, describe, diagram, solve, calculate
C	**C**ondition (when and with what)—the key circumstances under which the performance occurs	At the end of the training session, when asked by a customer, following a staff meeting
D	**D**egree (how well)—how well the behavior must be accomplished	With no prompts from a supervisor, with 100 percent accuracy, 8 out of 10 times

Data from Jordan, DeGraaf, and DeGraaf 2005; Mager 1997; Silberman 1998; Wallace Carr and Hardin 2010.

Table 10.4 Action Verbs versus Fuzzy Terms

Skill	Action verbs	Fuzzy or easy-to-misinterpret terms
Knowledge Remembers content learning in another session or setting.	Label, define, repeat, name, list, arrange, memorize, recall	Know, learn
Comprehension Understands facts from previous lessons.	Restate, discuss, describe, explain, review, locate, defend, paraphrase	Understand, appreciate
Application Uses knowledge in other situations to solve problems and complete tasks.	Demonstrate, operate, illustrate, use, schedule, interpret	Show, apply a thorough knowledge of
Analysis Breaks down information into smaller parts and uses it as evidence to support arguments in other assumptions, hypotheses, or questions.	Differentiate, diagram, compare, contrast, experiment, operate	Analyze
Synthesis Proposes new ways to use major ideas	Compose, propose, plan, design, manage, create, invent	Establish creativity
Evaluation Uses particular criteria to judge information	Evaluate, rate, select, judge	Show good judgment

Data from Silberman 1998; Wallace Carr and Hardin 2010.

Following the first session of the Breaststroke 101 swimming clinic, participants will demonstrate the breathe, kick, and glide technique in 6 out of 10 strokes.

Fitness

At the completion of the fitness instructor training program, participants will define the acronym FITT according to guidelines put forth by the American College of Sports Medicine.

At the completion of the Fitness Assessment Program, participants will identify three barriers to achieving their desired outcomes.

Group Fitness

Following the completion of Cycle 101, participants will demonstrate a bike setup with 100 percent accuracy.

After taking Outdoor Yoga for three consecutive classes, participants will execute the forward fold, sunflower, spinal balance, downward dog, warrior 2, tree, and knees to chest poses with 90 percent accuracy according to YogaFit standards.

IM Sports

At the end of the flag football captains meeting, team captains will identify the four components of the rating system for good sporting behavior with 100 percent accuracy.

Following the completion of the basketball officials training, student officials will demonstrate the mechanics of reporting a foul to the scorer's table with 85 percent accuracy.

Sport Clubs

After reading the sport club manual, club presidents will list the three steps for reserving a campus recreational sports facility with 100 percent accuracy.

After attending a new presidents workshop, participants will list the disciplinary procedures regarding team travel conduct as defined in the sport club operation manual with 100 percent accuracy.

When using the ABCD method to write outcomes, recreation professionals should pay close attention to the various elements outlined in table 10.3. If even one element is missing from an outcome statement, the practitioner will find it very difficult to assess the effectiveness of the intervention. Wallace Carr and Hardin (2010) provide two examples of learning outcomes for a training session for student employees about the organization's emergency action plan. One fails to fully incorporate all four ABCD components, whereas the other contains them all.

- After completing training, each student staff member will know the emergency action plan. In this example, A = "each student staff member," B = "will know" (fuzzy), C = "After completing training," and D = (?).
- In response to four scenarios, each student staff member will articulate the steps of the emergency action plan procedures as outlined in the student staff manual. In this case, A = "each student staff member," B = "articulate," C = "in response to four stated scenarios," and D = "the steps of the emergency action plan procedures as outlined in the student staff manual."

As you can see, the second learning outcome is presented more fully and in more specific terms. Full inclusion of all four ABCD elements makes it is easier to determine how to assess the activity. In this example, a checklist approach would be very appropriate to test participants' retention of the information provided.

STEP 3: DEVELOP INITIATIVES AND INTERVENTIONS

Borrego (2006) urges practitioners "to remember that the potential for learning is limited only by our imagination" (p. 11), and this is certainly the case in developing programming options for campus recreational sports. Initiatives and interventions are any opportunity that presents itself where learning can occur. Silberman (1998) discussed three types of learning that can help you structure the learning opportunities in your department: **affective learning**, **behavioral learning**, and **cognitive learning**. Affective learning focuses on attitudes, feelings, and preferences. Behavioral learning develops competence in skills, techniques, procedures, and methods. Cognitive learning relates to course content. What concepts and information do you want to help your participants develop? When developing learning outcomes, look at the audience (A) and behavior (B) to determine whether the activity fits into the affective, behavioral, or cognitive type of learning and *then* create your initiative.

Consider also whether your outcome requires a formal or informal learning environment and whether it is best presented in an active or passive way. **Formal learning** is typically considered as traditional classroom learning—that is, lecture style or a way of presenting the information that is highly structured (Wallace Carr, 2005; Marsick & Watkins 1990, 2001). Fried (2006) refers to this approach as the teaching/learning model, in which the main form of teaching is lecture. She also presents this format of gaining information from the participant's perspective as "informative learning which changes what we know" (p. 5). In training student employees in campus recreational sports, much of what we do is conveyed in a formal learning environment.

Information can also be conveyed in an **informal learning** environment—one that is less structured and, typically, highly experiential—or in ways that combine formal and informal learning environments. One good example of a combination approach is lifeguard training, in which the American Red Cross rules and standards are often conveyed in some form of lecture (i.e., a formal learning environment) but basic skill sets are taught in a practical session in the pool (i.e., an informal learning environment).

Informal learning can take place on a ropes course, on the playing field, in a pool, in a meeting, or on the job—just to name a few areas. In addition, technology has assisted us greatly in creating informal learning environments or passive education opportunities in the form of webcasts, online newsletters, chat rooms, and discussion boards. Other opportunities include bulletin boards, handouts, fairs, and tours. In fact, in developing appropriate interventions, the sky is the limit, especially when using the outcome-to-practice approach, in which the learning opportunity is created by looking first at the practitioner's end vision for the participant.

Many student affairs professionals believe that students are best able to learn and demonstrate knowledge, skill acquisition, or behavior change when they are engaged in the learning rather than simply being fed the information. This viewpoint is expressed in the following quotation from Russell Edgerton (Ward & Mitchell, 1997, p. 63):

> *Students learn about things by listening.*
>
> *They learn how to do things by doing them.*
>
> *They learn understanding and judgment through immersion and intense encounters, being in the play rather than just reading it.*

Table 10.5 provides several examples of initiatives and interventions, or opportunities for learning, as well as various ways in which participants can receive or engage with the content.

Table 10.5 Opportunities for Learning: Initiatives and Interventions

Opportunities for learning: initiatives and interventions	Delivery methods
Student employee training	Classroom instruction
Group fitness class	Clinic
Weight training clinic	Group or individual lesson
Certification class	Personal training session
Mind-body session	Video
Adventure trip	Panel discussion
Climbing wall activity	Staff meeting
Youth camp	Bulletin board
Skills clinic	Podcast
Nutrition seminar	Handout
Cooking demo	Health fair
Intramural game	Guest speaker presentation
Sport club presidents meeting	Master trainer workshop
Sport club activity	
Informal recreation	
Racquetball tournament	
Swimming lesson	

From Belk, Highstreet and Rapp 1995; Wallace 1998, Wallace Carr 2005; Marsick and Watkins 1990, 2001; Wallace Carr and Hardin 2010.

STEP 4: DEVELOP MEASURABLE OUTCOMES

At this point in the program planning process, the recreation professional develops the measureable part of the outcome. This element helps the professional determine the success of the outcome and guides the assessment plan. How are you going to measure the degree to which an outcome was completed? In this chapter, this question was answered in step 2 (developing learning outcomes). If the programmer did in fact create the D component (degree in measureable terms) in step 2, then he or she should now review the developed outcomes and begin to develop ideas for assessment. The development of assessment tools is not discussed here because assessment is covered in detail in chapter 6 of this book.

Wallace Carr and Hardin (2010, p. 143) have stressed the value of assessment: "The practice of defining and assessing the outcomes of programs and other interventions allows practitioners to support statements that have been made for years and determine the profession's contribution to student learning and growth." As a professional, you want your participants to really be able to demonstrate their competence, but how do you know they can? This is the value of creating a solid assessment plan to determine the effectiveness of the interventions and initiatives you developed in step 3. Here are some assessment options to consider:

Document analysis
Focus groups
Intercept interviews
Journaling
Observation
Policy analysis
Portfolios
Pre- and post-tests
Quizzes
Skills checklist
Standardized instruments

From Hardin and Wallace Carr 2005; Cissik 2009; Shuh et.al. 2001; Upcraft and Shuh 1996; Haines and Davis 2008.

Administrators need to be aware of the language that is used on their campus to talk about assessment. Some institutions draw a distinction between *assessment* and *evaluation*—thus the use of this terminology here. **Assessment** in this case means measuring effectiveness: Can participants do what you said they were going to do in your learning outcome? **Evaluation** means measuring efficiency and satisfaction. Examples include participant satisfaction, participation numbers, facilitator effectiveness, satisfaction with the facility, and satisfaction with the content delivered. Assessment is crucial to your program planning cycle because it helps you "target the interventions that are most effective for student learning and growth . . . [and facilitates your] ongoing efforts to strategically develop other successful methods for increasing the value of current programs" (Wallace Carr & Hardin, 2010, p. 143).

STEP 5: CONDUCT INITIATIVES AND INTERVENTIONS

Now is the time to conduct your initiative or intervention. It may be implemented by the programmer responsible for the specific area or by a student employee, a contracted employee, or an outside vendor. Staffing should be determined by departmental philosophy and resources.

If a department is focused on student learning and development, then it might choose to train a student to play the role of instructor or facilitator. If generating resources is a priority and a big name is available in the area to draw a large crowd, then the department might bring in an outside contractor. This happens frequently, for example, in master classes offered in the group fitness and wellness areas. An outside facilitator might also be used if resources (e.g., time, money, personnel) are tight and the expertise to train a student or another staff member is not available. We see this frequently in adventure programming—for example, using a whitewater rafting company to lead a trip.

The key is to make sure that whoever staffs the intervention or initiative can handle the activity's risk management requirements, understands the learning outcomes chosen for the experience, and possesses the skills and abilities to facilitate participants' achievement of the outcomes. Here are some considerations in determining staffing for an initiative or intervention:

- Skills or certification
- Level of responsibility
- Type(s) of participant with whom the individual will work
- Basic job description and performance expectations
- Designated learning outcomes and what is required of the individual to help participants achieve them

STEPS 6 AND 7: CONDUCT ASSESSMENT AND EVALUATION AND THEN REVISE, MAINTAIN, OR TERMINATE

Following the initiative or intervention, implement step 6 by conducting an assessment and evaluation to help you determine the effectiveness and efficiency of the activity or learning opportunity. Then move on to step 7 by using the data to determine whether the initiative or intervention should be revised, maintained as is, or terminated. Many professionals fear assessment because they worry that negative results might negatively affect their performance evaluation. Administrators must recognize this fear and convey to their staff members that the purpose of assessment is to improve our use of resources. A negative result may simply mean that an event has had its moment in the sun but no longer meets the needs of the current generation of college students.

SUMMARY

In 1940, Ester Lloyd-Jones (Dungy, 2006) stated that our role as professionals is to assist students with their campus experience by helping them learn both practical and theoretical information and acquire life skills that will serve them well for years after they leave our institutions. That role has not changed. What has changed is the way in which we go about planning and delivering content, and this chapter presents one practical method for planning programs in a campus recreational sports facility. The point is not to say that this is the one and only way to plan but to emphasize that the recreation professional must develop a system that is intentional and that incorporates some form of accountability for the resources used on a daily basis in our programs.

Glossary

active learning—Participation in a meeting, educational session, staff training, or game.

affective learning—Educational experience focusing on attitudes, feelings, and preferences (Silberman, 1998).

assessment—Measuring the participant's ability to demonstrate competency following engagement in an educational initiative or intervention (Wallace Carr & Hardin, 2010).

behavioral learning—Educational experience focused on developing competence in skills, techniques, procedures, and methods (Silberman, 1998).

Chickering's seven vectors—"Vectors of development that contribute to the formation of identity" (Evans et al., 2010, p. 66).

cognitive complexity—"Critical thinking; reflective thinking; effective reasoning; and creativity" (Dean, 2009, p. 332).

cognitive learning—Educational experience related directly to course content (Silberman, 1998).

cognitive-structural theory—Theory that examines "the process of intellectual development during the college years" (Evans et al., 2010, p. 43).

college student development—Ways in which "a student grows, progresses, or increases his or her developmental capabilities as a result of enrollment in an institution of higher education" (Rodgers, 1990, p. 27).

evaluation—Measuring the participant's satisfaction with a program or service or participation rates.

formal learning—Learning typically considered as traditional classroom learning; lecture style or a way of presenting the information that is highly structured (Wallace Carr, 2005; Marsick & Watkins, 1990, 2001).

humanitarianism and civic engagement—"Understanding and appreciation of cultural and human differences; social responsibility; global perspective; and sense of civic responsibility" (Dean, 2009, p. 332).

informal learning—Educational experience that is less structured than formal learning and is typically highly experiential.

interpersonal competence—Ability to engage in "meaningful relationships; interdependence; collaboration; and effective leadership" (Dean, 2009, p. 332).

intervention—The activity or experience a student engages in to enhance their knowledge, increase their skills or change behaviors.

intrapersonal development—"Realistic self-appraisal, self-understanding, and self-respect; identity development; commitment to ethics and integrity; and spiritual awareness" (Dean, 2009, p. 332).

knowledge acquisition and application—"Understanding knowledge from a range of disciplines; connecting knowledge to other knowledge, ideas, and experiences; constructing knowledge; and relating knowledge to daily life" (Dean, 2009, p. 332).

learning outcomes—"Measureable statements of intent" (Mager, 1997, p. 74).

mapping the environment—"Process of recognizing, identifying, and documenting the sites for learning activities on campus; . . . provides the framework within which student affairs educators can link their programs and activities to learning opportunities" (Borrego, 2006, p. 11).

outcome-to-practice approach—Approach in which the goal is to determine the end product of the experience before creating an intervention (Komives & Schoper, 2006).

passive learning—Approach to learning in which the participant is relatively inactive (e.g., reading from a bulletin board or newsletter article or watching a video or podcast).

person–environment theory—"Exploration of satisfaction, achievement, persistence and degree of fit between persons and the environments in which they find themselves" (Evans et al., 2010, p. 33).

practical competence—Ability to engage in "pursuing goals; communicating effectively; [developing] technical competence; managing personal affairs; managing career development; demonstrating professionalism; maintaining health and wellness; and living a purposeful and satisfying life" (Dean, 2009, p. 332).

practice-to-outcome approach—Approach in which the professional determines the outcome(s) to be achieved by engaging in an existing program (Komives & Schoper, 2006).

psychosocial theory—Theory "examin[ing] the content of development or important issues people face as their lives develop" (Evans et al., 2010, p. 43).

typology theory—Theory that examines differences between unique individuals, such as personality, interests, and interaction styles (Evans et al., 2010).

References

Argyris, C. (1991). Teaching smart people how to learn. *Harvard Business Review, 69*(3), 99–110.

Astin, A.W. (1999). Student involvement: A developmental theory for higher education. *Journal of College Student Development, 40*(5), 518–528.

Baxter Magolda, M. (1992). *Knowing and reasoning in college: Gender-related patterns in students' intellectual development.* San Francisco: Jossey-Bass.

Belz, D., Highstreet, V., & Rapp, N. (1995). *Instructional programs: A resource manual.* Corvallis, OR: National Intramural-Recreational Sports Association.

Bloom B.S. (1956). *Taxonomy of educational objectives, handbook 1: The cognitive domain.* New York: McKay.

Borrego, S.E. (2006). Mapping the learning environment. In American College Personnel Association et al., *Learning reconsidered 2: A practical guide to implementing a campus-wide focus on the student experience.* pp. 11-16. Washington, DC: Authors.

Brown, S.C., & Schoonmaker, L. (1999). *Managing the collegiate recreational facility.* Corvallis, OR: National Intramural-Recreational Sports Association.

Chickering, A.W. (1969). *Education and identity.* San Francisco: Jossey-Bass.

Chickering, A., & Reisser, L. (1993). *Education and identity* (2nd ed.). San Francisco: Jossey-Bass.

Cissik, J.M. (2009). Assessment and the recreational sports program. *Recreational Sports Journal 33*(1), 2–11.

Csikszentmihalyi, M. (1997). *Finding flow. The psychology of engagement with everyday life.* New York: Harper Collins.

Dean, L.A. (Ed.). (2009). *CAS standards and guidelines for higher education* (7th ed.). Washington, DC: Council for the Advancement of Standards in Higher Education.

Dungy, G.J. (2006). Learning reconsidered: Where have we come? Where are we going? In American College Personnel Association et al., *Learning reconsidered 2: A practical guide to implementing a campus-wide focus on the student experience.* pp. 1-2. Washington, DC: Authors.

Evans, N.J., Forney, D.S., Guido, F.M., Patton, L.D., & Renn, K.A. (2010). *Student development in college: Theory, research and practice.* San Francisco: Jossey-Bass.

Franklin, D.S. (2007). Student development and learning in campus recreation: Assessing recreational sports directors' awareness, perceived importance, application and satisfaction with CAS standards. *Dissertation Abstracts International.* (UMI no. 3269236), 209 pages; AAT 3269236.

Franklin, D.S., & Hardin, S.E. (2008). Philosophical and theoretical foundations of campus recreation: Crossroads of theory. In NIRSA (2008), *Campus recreation: Essentials for the professional.* Champaign, IL: Human Kinetics, pp. 3-20.

Fried, J. (2006). *Rethinking learning.* In American College Personnel Association et al., *Learning reconsidered 2: A practical guide to implementing a campus-wide focus on the student experience.* pp. 3-9. Washington, DC: Authors.

Haines, D.J, & Davis, E.A. *The art of assessment.* In NIRSA (2008). *Campus recreation: Essentials for the professional.* Champaign: Human Kinetics, pp. 253-266.

Hardin, S. & Wallace Carr, J. (2005). *Assessment, Oh the places you'll go.* National School of Sport Recreation Management, Hilton Head, SC.

Jones, T.R. (1999). Programming facilities. In S.C. Brown & L. Schoonmaker (Eds.), *Managing the collegiate recreational facility.* Corvallis, OR: NIRSA, p. 89.

Jordan, D., DeGraaf, D., & DeGraaf, K. (2005). *Programming for parks, recreation, and leisure services: A servant leadership approach* (2nd ed.). State College, PA: Venture.

Kolb, D.A. (1984). *Experiential learning.* Englewood Cliffs, NJ: Prentice Hall.

Komives, S.R., & Schoper, S. (2006). Developing learning outcomes. In American College Personnel Association et al., *Learning reconsidered 2: A practical guide to implementing a campus-wide focus on the student experience.* pp. 17-43. Washington, DC: Authors.

Mable, P. (1980). Foreword. In F.B. Newton & K.L. Ender (Eds.), *Student development practices: Strategies for making a difference.* Springfield, IL: Charles C. Thomas.

Mager, R.F. (1997). *Making instruction work.* Atlanta: Center for Effective Performance.

Marsick, V.J., & Watkins, K.E. (1990). *Informal and incidental learning in the workplace.* London: Routledge.

Marsick, V.J., & Watkins, K.E. (2001). Informal and incidental learning. In L.M. Baumgartner (Ed.), *New directions for adult and continuing education* (Vol. 89). San Francisco: Jossey-Bass. pp. 25-34.

Martin, P., & Priest, S. (1986). Understanding the adventure experience. *Journal of Adventure Education, 3*(1), 18–21.

National Intramural-Recreational Sports Association (1996). *General and specialty standards for collegiate recreational sports.* Champaign, IL Human Kinetics.

Newton, F.B., & Ender, K.L. (1980). *Student development practices.* Springfield, IL: Charles C Thomas.

Neulinger, J. (1976). The need for and the implications of a psychological conception of leisure. *The Ontario Psychologist, 8*, 15.

Prochaska, J.O., Norcross, J.C., & DiClemente, C.C. (1994). *Changing for good: the revolutionary program that explains the six stages of change and teaches you how to free yourself from bad habits.* New York: Morrow.

Rodgers, R.F. (1990). Recent theories and research underlying student development. In D.G. Creamer & associates, *College student development: Theory and practice for the 1990s* (pp. 27–79). Alexandria, VA: American College Personnel Association.

Schuh, J.H., Upcraft, M.L., & associates. (2001). *Assessment practice in student affairs: An applications manual.* San Francisco: Jossey-Bass.

Silberman, M. (1998). *Active training: A handbook of techniques, designs, case examples and tips.* San Francisco: Jossey Bass.

Simons-Morton, B.G., Greene, W.H., & Gottlieb, N.H. (1995). *Introduction to health education and health promotion.* Long Grove, IL: Waveland Press.

Upcraft, M.L., & Schuh, J.H. (1996). *Assessment in student affairs: A guide for practitioners.* San Francisco: Jossey-Bass.

Wallace, J.E. (1998). The why's, what's and how's of instructional programming. *NIRSA Journal,* Winter.

Wallace Carr, J.E. (2005). An explanation of how learning and development emerge for student employees during the on-campus work experience. *Dissertation Abstracts International.* (UMI no.3161580). DAI 304998049, p. 230.

Wallace Carr, J.E., & Hardin, S. (2010). The key to effective assessment: Writing measurable student learning outcomes. *Recreational Sports Journal, 34*(2), 138–144.

Ward, W.L., & Mitchell, R.I. (1997). Being in the play: Student employment and learning. In A. Devaney (Ed.), *Developing leadership through student employment.* Bloomington, IN: Association of College Unions, pp. 63-84.

Warner, M. (1995). Health center 2000: The mission statement development challenge. *The Journal of American College Health, 44,* 141.

CHAPTER 11

Facilities

Gordon M. Nesbitt
Millersville University

Facility management is a core component in the administration of any campus recreational sports program, whether the department controls its own facility or shares it with other departments. Facility management skills require working knowledge of a number of subjects: facility types, standards, and design; requirements of the Americans with Disabilities Act (ADA); future trends; staffing and scheduling; and facility maintenance.

FACILITY TYPES

Recreation and athletic facilities come in many types and include both indoor and outdoor options. These various facility types involve different maintenance needs and in some cases different managerial skills.

Indoor Facilities

The National Intramural-Recreational Sports Association (NIRSA, 2009a) has identified the following types of indoor facility: strength and conditioning units, multipurpose rooms, **natatoriums**, gymnasiums, multipurpose activity courts, indoor tracks, rock climbing walls, racquetball courts, handball courts, squash courts, and locker rooms (pp. 106–112). The gymnasium space can include basketball, volleyball, badminton, and **pickleball** courts. Other indoor spaces may include but are not limited to dance studios, martial arts rooms, wrestling rooms, indoor soccer courts, and in-line skating rinks.

Basketball, volleyball, and badminton courts are often combined into multi-use courts since these sports can all be played on the same type of surface—traditionally, a hardwood floor, though synthetic surfaces are becoming commonplace as their quality improves. When combining facilities, one must ensure that the courts do not get so cluttered with lines for different sports that it becomes difficult to tell where the court for each sport ends. Thus, combining areas into multi-use courts helps keep costs down but increases the need for effective scheduling.

Racquetball, squash, and handball courts take up considerable space for sports in which few players can compete at the same time since most games are one-on-one (though doubles games can also be played). Even though racquetball and squash are similar, their courts require different dimensions and therefore different spaces. Handball can be adequately played on a racquetball court even though the official dimensions of the courts differ slightly. Some courts allow you to run both racquetball and squash by using moveable walls, but for purists these areas need to be separate. Racquetball enjoyed a surge in popularity in the 1980s and early 1990s, but the number of players has fallen in recent years. Squash and handball are less popular, but their followers are dedicated.

For aerobics classes and dance teams, special arrangements need to be incorporated into the facility to ensure proper shock absorption and sound control. Because some aerobics activities and dance classes require a great deal of jumping and stepping, the floor needs to be specially designed with shock absorption in mind to minimize damage to the feet, legs, knees, and back. In addition, these rooms need to have sound dampening features so that they don't disrupt adjacent activities. Storage is also critical in these areas since the classes often require equipment ranging from steps to balls to stationary bicycles.

Martial arts and wrestling rooms also need to be designed for special uses. They require soundproofing since the activities can be very loud and special mats that can be moved around and easily removed from the room since different arts require different types of mat or mat arrangement. Maintenance and cleaning of these facilities is very important in light of the communicable diseases that can be transmitted through blood and sweat on the mats.

Indoor soccer and in-line skating facilities are becoming increasingly popular, especially in northern states where soccer players and in-line skaters want to play year round. Indoor soccer facilities can be designed with either a hard floor, a carpet with a short pile, or a synthetic turf surface. Each of these surfaces creates an almost completely different game since the ball travels much faster on the hard or short-pile carpet surface then it does on synthetic turf surface. In-line rinks need a hard surface, and a synthetic surface seems to be much more effective than hardwood as the hardwood floor can be slippery. Both indoor soccer facilities and in-line rinks are generally smaller than their traditional counterparts (outdoor soccer fields and ice rinks) due to cost of building an indoor facility or need for less space.

Outdoor Facilities

Outdoor facilities for campus recreational sports typically include fields for baseball, softball, soccer, football, field hockey, lacrosse, rugby, and ultimate, as well as ropes or adventure courses. Some campuses also have equestrian areas, polo fields, and cricket fields; since these areas are not as popular and are mainly isolated, they are not addressed here.

Ball State University Office of Recreation Services and University Marketing & Communications.

The type of surface used for an indoor soccer facility affects game play.

NIRSA (2009a) has identified the following activities that may take place at an outdoor facility: beach volleyball, tennis, softball, flag football, ladder toss, croquet, bocce, home run derby, disc golf, kickball, soccer, free throws, hot shots, basketball, baseball, pickleball, dodgeball, floor hockey, water polo, swim meets, ultimate, volleyball, Wiffle ball, archery, badminton, golf, broomball, biking, bike hike, hiking, biathlon, triathlon, field hockey, horseshoes, scavenger hunt, tug-of-war (p. 115).

Baseball and softball fields must meet certain requirements for each sport, and they also increase in size as the participants grow in size and strength. In addition, fast-pitch softball fields differ from slow-pitch fields. Because men participate in slow-pitch softball more often than in fast-pitch softball, and because a softball is easier than a baseball to hit, a regulation slow-pitch softball field is generally larger than a regulation fast-pitch softball field. To ensure safety and genuineness of play, baseball and softball fields should have skinned infields that inhibit their use for other sports requiring a turf field throughout.

Sometimes the same type of field can be used for multiple sports, as is often the case with soccer, football (and flag football), lacrosse, rugby, field hockey, and ultimate. The main constraint is the size of the field. Soccer requires a larger space than football for adequate play. Field hockey requires a flat, well maintained field so that the ball does not take unexpected bounces that could cause severe injury. Other sports don't necessarily require as much attention to the flatness and maintenance as field hockey as small irregularities in the field don't have as much impact on safety. The biggest question regarding this type of fields is whether to use natural grass or a synthetic surface. The multi-use nature of the fields is leading many programs to switch to a synthetic surface that, though initially more expensive, can stand up to more use than grass fields and that does not need special accommodations in wet weather.

Disc golf courses are also increasing in popularity and can be very easy to set up. Many disc golf players create their own "holes" by using natural obstacles, and fabricated holes can be purchased commercially and installed in any area that offers sufficient space. Disc golf courses tend to attract a wide variety of players and can be somewhat uncontrollable in terms of the duration of play. Once the course is installed, participants need only a disc in order to play whenever they have time. Typical courses are similar to golf courses with either 9 or 18 holes.

The ropes course or adventure challenge program has also grown in popularity. There are two main types: low (team-building) and high (adventure). The low elements or activities are generally done between 1 and 10 feet (0.3–3 m) off the ground and usually require a team of people to overcome a physical challenge. After the activity, a skilled facilitator processes or discusses what happened in order to help the group with team-building. By exploring problems that arose in communication, trust, support, or other areas, the facilitator can work with the group to identify ways in which the members can overcome these problems back on the job or in whatever type of work the group regularly conducts. The high activities range from 20 to 40 feet (6.1–12.2 m) off the ground and are generally used more for overcoming personal challenges. These activities usually involve one participant and a facilitator who actively belays, or anchors, the participant on the ground so that if the participant slips off of the element he or she does not fall. Sometimes other participants in the group act as anchors for the belayer, and they can also be involved in supporting and encouraging the participant who is currently off the ground.

Ice Rinks

Ice rink facilities can be used for activities including hockey, figure skating, speed skating, curling, broomball, and recreational skating. Some of these activities—hockey, figure skating, broomball, and recreational skating—use similarly sized rinks which they can share, whereas curling and speed skating require different types of facilities, and even within speed skating the short- and long-track varieties require different facilities as well. In northern regions, you may see outdoor rinks, but most of the sports listed here have moved to indoor facilities to eliminate the hazards posed by weather.

Ice rink facilities require special planning due to the ice surface itself. Obviously, the temperature must be controlled once the ice surface is in place, and humidity also poses a big challenge. Sawyer (2009b, p. 293) indicates that "airborne moisture in an ice rink will also deposit on cold surfaces, and of course the coldest spot is very likely the ice surface itself. When this happens, the ice will cloud over, losing its desired sheen, and will start to become sluggish to skate on." Scheduling can also be problematic for ice rinks. You must schedule time between and during events for the ice resurfacing machine (commonly known by the brand name Zamboni) to treat the ice. Ice rinks generally open very early in the morning for figure skating clubs and stay open until well after midnight for hockey leagues and practices. Rental rates for ice rinks are generally higher than for other facilities due to higher demand and smaller size. Thus the staff of an ice rink must be ready to arrive early in the morning and leave late in the night.

Ice rink managers must also constantly monitor indoor air quality. Fried (2005) reported that "in a study of 19 rinks, those with propane and gas-powered resurfacers showed a much greater likelihood of having a dangerous level of nitrogen dioxide" (p. 133). Zambonis play an essential role in operating an ice rink, and special areas must be designed into the facility to store the Zamboni between resurfacing and disposal of the ice that the machine picks up during resurfacing. Because of the need for these machines, ice rink facilities must also be designed with good air flow to ensure that nitrogen dioxide from the exhaust does not become a problem.

Aquatic Facilities

Aquatic facilities also feature dimensions and requirements that vary depending on the activity. Hunsaker and Cook (2009, pp.134–135) reported that "college leisure pools typically do not include water slides or other 'kiddie' features found in water parks and community aquatic centers; instead, students are more interested in fitness and socializing. Because fitness swimming remains one of the most popular forms of exercise among students and faculty, lap lanes are popular." Even so, some collegiate aquatic facilities do include water slides, which can be very attractive for social gatherings and are always a hit for summer instructional camps.

Overall, however, colleges—especially smaller institutions where facilities are shared—are more concerned with lap and competitive swimming. Hunsaker and Cook (2009, p. 135) indicate that "at minimum, a competition pool must be 25 yd by six lanes (45 ft or 13.7 m) for short-course events and 50 m by eight lanes (25 yd or m) for long-course competitions. Many current standards require a minimum depth of over 5 ft (1.5 m) for starting block dives and a minimum of 4 ft (1.2 m) for flip turns." Recreational lap swimmers can use a competition-sized pool for their exercise routines, but varsity athletes may not be able to use pools that do not meet the minimum dimensions of their governing body. Due to injury concerns, diving tanks require a minimum depth that depends on the height of the dive. Divers also appreciate a warmer pool than competitive swimmers and a hot tub located nearby to keep their muscles warm between dives.

Water polo can be played with modified rules in pools with shallow ends, but regulation games require enough depth throughout the pool to ensure that players cannot stand on the bottom during the game. Synchronized swimmers also require a pool with adequate depth, as well as an underwater sound system that lets them hear the music even when they are completely submerged. In contrast, pools used for giving lessons to younger swimmers require a shallower depth so that participants *can* stand on the bottom and still have their head above water.

Water slides and water parks require varying levels of water depending upon the type of activity. Wave pools generally start at zero depth and grow deeper until they reach about 7 to 10 feet (2.1–3 m) deep. Water slides generally dispense the rider into a pool that is 2 to 3 feet (0.6–0.9 m) deep, depending on the length of the ride and the speed at which the participant can travel. Some aquatic centers are even large enough to host sailing regattas or offer indoor water skiing. All pool facilities require specific maintenance to ensure that the water is safe and does not transmit disease.

Other Facilities

Some campuses offer other facilities that are not typical and thus are not discussed in this chapter. These may include snow skiing facilities, outdoor aquatic facilities (e.g., boat launches), lakes and oceans, picnic areas, campgrounds, whitewater rafting facilities, and skate parks.

STANDARDS AND GUIDELINES

When working with any sports facility, the manager must be aware of the various standards that affect design, construction, and administration. This section describes some of the standards that should be reviewed in the planning stages and during operation of a facility.

The American National Standards Institute (ANSI, 2011) "oversees the creation, promulgation and use of thousands of norms and guidelines that directly impact businesses in nearly every sector. . . . ANSI is also actively engaged in accrediting programs that assess conformance to standards." When building a facility or purchasing new equipment, risk management strategy calls for the manager to find out whether the equipment you are installing or purchasing meets ANSI standards. Reputable dealers should be able to tell you that their equipment meets ANSI standards; you can also go to the ANSI website and purchase the applicable publication.

The American Society of Testing and Materials International (ASTM, 2011) "is one of the largest voluntary standards development organizations in the world—a trusted source for technical standards for material, products, systems, and services. Known for their high technical quality and market relevancy, ASTM International standards have an important role in the information infrastructure that guides design, manufacturing and trade in the global economy." When participating in major construction projects, the project manager should know the standards for the materials being used. The ASTM website contains standards for all materials and can be consulted when concern arises about the quality of construction materials.

"With the Occupational Safety and Health Act of 1920, Congress created the Occupational Safety and Health Administration (OSHA) to ensure safe and healthful working conditions for working men and women by setting and enforcing standards and by providing training, outreach, education and assistance" (OSHA, 2011). It is important for employee safety that all programs adhere to OSHA standards. Areas like ropes courses require stronger adherence to the guidelines due to the risk factor involved in the activity.

The history of the American College of Sports Medicine (ACSM) indicates that, "ACSM was founded in 1954 by a group of physical educators and clinician/scientists who recognized that health problems were associated with certain lifestyle choices, such as poor nutrition and lack of exercise. Since then, ACSM members from all professional backgrounds have applied their knowledge, training and dedication in sports medicine and exercise science to promote healthier lifestyles for people around the globe" (ACSM, 2012a). The *ACSM's Health/Fitness Facility Standards and Guidelines* "presents the current standards and guidelines that help health and fitness establishments provide high-quality service and program offerings within a safe and appropriate environment" (ACSM, 2012b). Adherence to ACSM guidelines is very important for fitness related activities. Fitness directors should strongly consider membership with ACSM to keep informed about advances in fitness activities.

The NIRSA publication *Space Planning Guidelines for Campus Recreational Sport Facilities* (2009b) "offers valuable information that can be used very early in the facility planning process to answer basic questions regarding approximately how much facility space is needed to adequately meet the recreation needs of a campus community. It provides easy-to-use guidelines for matching the size of a recreation facility with the needs of the institution. It also provides detailed instructions for applying the space guidelines, including a list of factors to consider when applying the guidelines to individual colleges or universities" (Brown & Haines, 2009, p. 8). Nothing is worse than building a facility that is too small for the population it serves on the day that it opens!

Design

The development and construction of a facility involves six general phases:

1. Preliminary planning
2. Development of design
3. Contract or construction documents
4. Bidding
5. Construction administration
6. Management and training

The preliminary planning phase starts with the development of a planning committee. The planning process should include everyone who will have an interest in or play a critical role in the operation of the new facility. Thus, from the outset, you should determine who will use the facility and include someone from that constituency (e.g., varsity athletics) to represent its needs on the planning committee. Students and possibly some faculty and staff members should also have a place on the committee. Surveys and questionnaires can help you gather important information about possible facility needs for this committee to use in developing the program plan.

Once the committee has been developed, the first planning stage is to conduct a program analysis. The committee should begin by establishing the need for the facility, which requires thorough analysis of the programs that would be offered in it. Information for this analysis can be gathered from usage or attendance records, program and event schedules, maintenance reports, and equipment ledgers. Current trends and future developments also need to be considered so that the facility does not become obsolete shortly after its opening ceremony. With all of this information in hand, the committee can begin to plan a facility that meets the needs of the constituents who will use it.

Photo courtesy of Colorado State University.

Follow space planning guidelines to ensure that you plan a large enough space to comfortably accommodate facility users.

Once the committee has a working plan for what will be included in the facility, an architect should be hired to turn the plan into a facility design. The architect should not be brought on board either too early or too late in the process. If the architect is hired too early, the facility may end up suiting the tastes of the architect rather than the needs of the future users. If the architect is hired too late, he or she may have to change much of what has already been completed. Hiring an architect is similar to hiring any other type of contractor. You must be confident in his or her ability to design a facility that meets your needs. You should check recommendations and see some of the buildings that the architect has designed in order to make an informed decision. Here are some things to look for:

- **Is the architect professional and easy to work with?** This can be established through conversations and interviews with architect candidates. You should also contact references and ask previous customers about the manner in which the architect interacted with them. Was he or she open to suggestions and changes?
- **Does the architect have the credentials (training) for the job?** Ask for information about certification and education. You need to know that the architect has achieved certification and graduated from a reputable institution.
- **What is the architect's philosophy for and approach to designing facilities?** Does his or her philosophy meet your needs? Is the architect more interested in designing a beautiful building than one that meets your needs? Architects sometimes want to build monuments, but these monuments sometimes result in a great deal of wasted space. On the other hand, you do want a facility that is attractive and pleasing to the eye so that participants want to come to it.
- **What is the architect's experience, especially with athletic facilities similar to the one you are designing?** There is a big difference between designing an educational building and designing a recreation facility. Recreation facilities have special needs, especially aquatic centers and ice rinks, and the architect must understand these needs in order to design an appropriate facility.

Asking these and other substantive questions that you come up with can help you make an informed decision and hire the right architect for the job.

The next step is to develop a comprehensive or master plan for the facility. The master plan accumulates all of the information needed to develop the project. It is a formal, comprehensive building scheme that identifies the organization's facility needs and establishes the order in which new construction or renovation will be accomplished. This scheme collects data from the various feasibility studies, assesses the needs and demands for the new facility, examines budgetary plans, observes trends, and analyzes the organization's purpose and objectives, including both short- and long-term projections. Generating the master plan is a complex process, and it should not be rushed. Spending the time to create a sound master plan saves you time and money later in the development process. The master plan provides the structure from which to work and keeps the planning team focused on the main direction of the project. Throughout the composition of the master plan, consider the following points:

- The primary focus throughout the development of the master plan is on the purpose for which the facility is being built.
- Develop the facility to accommodate programs rather than adapting programs to fit the facility.
- Plan for the best building your organization can afford, which should be determined through a thorough investigation of financial resources.
- Avoid biased and restrictive viewpoints. Be open to new and different ideas and approaches. Conduct research regarding innovations and new technology in design.
- Do not compromise with the architect or give up essential aspects of the design that are important to the program.
- Include complete building accessibility in the plan. Conduct research regarding the requirements of current legislation and the Americans with Disabilities Act.

- Avoid costly errors and omissions by planning thoroughly. Include feasibility studies in all related areas: legal, site, potential uses for the facility, design, financial, and administrative.
- Identify the needed spaces and map out how they interface. **Bubble designs** may be useful in ascertaining the types of programs desired. The connecting bubbles represent the major areas in the facility.
- Consider how the facility will be controlled and managed. Build management and control features into the design itself.
- Visit similar facilities and inquire about the best and worst features of the design and use.
- Examine current trends and plan for the future. Project 20 years ahead in the plan for the building.
- Pay close attention to the project's environmental impact on the community and the surrounding area.

The last step in the preliminary phase is to write a report that may be called a program plan or program statement. This report, prepared primarily for the architect, summarizes the major components of the master plan. Allow for the following categories:

- Program objectives
- Basic assumptions
- Trends that affect planning
- Current and proposed programs
- Preliminary data design specifications and space allocation
- Space needs and relationships
- Activity, auxiliary, and service facilities
- Facility usage
- Equipment and furniture list
- Environmental necessities
- Any other important considerations

Once the program plan is in place, the facility can be constructed with the knowledge that everything that should have been done to plan the facility has in fact been done.

Americans With Disabilities Act

The Americans with Disabilities Act requires facilities to accommodate individuals who may not be able to access or use facilities without accommodation. These accommodations can take various forms, such as wheelchair access, emergency lighting for those who are hearing impaired, and handrails for sloped entries into swimming pools. The *ADA Accessibility Guidelines for Recreation Facilities* state, "The Americans with Disabilities Act recognizes and protects the civil rights of people with disabilities. Titles II and III of the ADA require, among other things, that newly constructed and altered state and local government facilities, places of public accommodation, and commercial facilities be readily accessible to and usable by individuals with disabilities. Recreation facilities are among the types of facilities covered by titles II and III of the ADA" (United States Access Board, 2002, p. 2).

The essence of the ADA was summed up by then President George W. Bush as follows (United States Access Board, 2003, p. 4):

> *Whenever a door is closed to anyone because of a disability, we must work to open it. . . . Whenever any barrier stands between you and the full rights and dignity of citizenship, we must work to remove it, in the name of simple decency and justice. The promise of the ADA . . . has enabled people with disabilities to enjoy much greater access to a wide range of affordable travel, recreational opportunities and life-enriching services.*

As programmers, we need to be vigilant to ensure that all of our facilities are accessible to anyone who might want to participate in our programs. As Sharp, Moorman, and Claussen (2007) put it, "managers should ensure that individuals with disabilities are generally able to access the sports facility and that they have access to and use of the various amenities or elements offered within the facility" (p. 449).

Photo courtesy of University of Cincinnati Campus Recreation.

Handrails and sloped entries make swimming pools accessible to users with disabilities.

Unfortunately, recreation programs use facilities constructed before the ADA requirements became law, and many of these facilities include areas that are not fully accessible to everyone. When programs use facilities that are in some way inaccessible, accommodations may need to be made for persons who would otherwise be unable to access the facilities in order to participate. These accommodations may mean moving the program to an accessible space or, if possible, renovating the facility to make the area accessible. Renovation construction can be quite expensive but may be necessary in order to allow everyone to participate. The ADA guidelines "apply to newly designed or newly constructed buildings and facilities and to existing facilities when they are altered" (United States Access Board, 2002, p. 2). Existing facilities do not have to be renovated for accessibility unless they are being altered, but a proactive manager tries to incorporate renovation for accessibility into the master plan. All new construction must include accessibility in the plan.

Future Trends

Seidler and Miller (2009) outline the following future trends in stadiums and arenas:

- Luxury suites
- Personal seat licenses
- Multi-use designs
- Retractable-roof stadiums
- New breed of synthetic turf
- Removable natural grass
- Fabric structures
- Tension structures
- Air-supported structures
- Wooden domes

Several of these trends (luxury suites, personal seat licenses, and retractable-roof stadiums) will probably not affect campus recreational sports programs unless they share space with varsity athletic programs that are taking part in these trends. The other trends may or may not affect your campus recreational sports facilities, but it is important to be aware of them.

For a campus recreational sports professional, multi-use design may mean different things. Will the facility's design allow it to be used for a wide variety of recreational activities? Can multiple activities be held in the space at the same time, or can the facility host only one type of activity at a time? How long does it take to break down one activity and set up another? Gymnasium space must definitely be planned for multiple uses in order to benefit a campus recreational sports program. Can you play basketball, volleyball, badminton, and pickleball games in the same space with room for lines for every activity? In the winter months, can rugby, lacrosse, or ultimate teams use the space for practices? How will these activities affect the floor? Some facilities are also constructed for use in hosting concerts and graduation ceremonies, which makes acoustical treatment very important.

Fabric and air-supported structures may have a place in a campus recreational sports facility, since they are less expensive to build than regular brick-and-mortar facilities. Seidler and Miller (2009) discuss "three basic types of fabric structures in use: (1) tension structures, (2) air-supported structures, and (3) cable domes. Tension structures are made by stretching the fabric between rigid supports and/or steel cables. Air structures are sealed buildings that, through the use of fans, maintain a positive internal air pressure that supports the roof. . . . The cable dome is actually a modified tension structure that uses a complex network of cables and supports to suspend and hold up the fabric roof" (p. 400). Due to their lower initial expense, these structures may be feasible for programs that cannot afford the complete cost of a typical structure but need a place to host indoor activities.

SCHEDULING

With more and more activities occurring in limited space, it is essential to schedule facilities effectively in order to ensure that all users have sufficient time and space in the campus recreational sports facilities. Baletka (1999) defines facility scheduling "as the process of attempting to achieve maximum use of facility space within the resources and staff capabilities of the department" (p. 23). Developing schedules that achieve this maximum use of facility space requires careful planning and documentation. There is nothing worse for a building supervisor than having double-booked space. Accurate documentation of facility use requests helps alleviate the problem of scheduling more than one group in an area at the same time.

Sawyer (2009a) posits that scheduling involves at least four distinct patterns: "(1) seasons; (2) block periods, such as two-, three-, four-, or eight- to 10-week periods; (3) monthly or weekly; and (4) daily time frame, such as sessions held during the early morning (6 to 9 a.m.), morning (9 a.m. to 12 noon), early afternoon (12 to 3), late afternoon (3 to 6 p.m.), early evening (6 to 9 p.m.) and late evening (9 to 11 p.m.)" (p. 69). The individual in charge of scheduling the facility must decide whether to use one of these patterns or multiple patterns. Depending on your facility's size and demand, it may also be worth your time to investigate the numerous facility scheduling software packages now on the market.

Once you have decided your pattern of scheduling, it is time to develop a priority schedule that outlines which group or organization has priority in the facility during the season, block period, month or week, and during the daily time frame. Priority schedules are especially important for facilities shared by several departments. For example, if academic classes, varsity athletics, club sports, and intramurals share the same facility, all of these groups must know when each has priority in the facility. The priority schedule depends heavily on the philosophy of the institution. In general, academic classes may have priority in a shared facility between 8 a.m. and 3 p.m. (typical class time), whereas varsity athletics may have priority before 8 a.m. and between 3 p.m. and 9 p.m. and club sports and intramurals may have priority after 9 pm. All organizations involved should meet and discuss the priority schedule, and members of upper administration may need to be present.

When working with a group that intends to reserve a facility or space, it is essential to obtain the following information:

- Name of the organization
- Name and contact information of the individual in charge of the event
- For student organizations, the name and contact information of the group's advisor
- The exact facility they want to reserve
- The time and date for which they want to reserve the facility (including setup and clean-up time)
- The exact nature of the intended activity (essential to know since some groups might try to use the facility in ways that could damage it)
- Payment procedures if a rental fee is involved
- Arrangements for any needed security
- How the group intends to publicize the activity
- Confirmation that the group understands its responsibility for any damage done to the facility or equipment by the group or its guests
- Waiver information approved by the appropriate university legal counsel
- Any other information deemed necessary by the institution

You must also decide whether outside organizations are allowed to reserve the facility. If so, you need to determine a rental rate (most collegiate facilities that allow outside groups to reserve their facilities do charge some type of fee). Fees should be determined based on rental rates for similar facilities and on the facility's location; a facility located in New York City, for example, can charge more than one in West Lafayette, Indiana. **Benchmarking** with other colleges and universities can help you develop appropriate rental rates. You must also establish fees for maintenance staff, supervisory staff, and other essential personnel (e.g., police or security), and it is important to work with the university contracts office and legal counsel to develop appropriate contracts for outside groups.

STAFFING

Another important aspect of operating a recreational facility is the staffing. Any program that uses facility space needs to plan the appropriate supervision of that space. Sharp et al. (2007) report that "many liability concerns relating to participant injuries occur because of a failure of supervision. Proper supervision of participants means that the person(s) entrusted with this responsibility are competent to oversee the participants (quality of supervision) and that there are sufficient supervisors to fulfill the duty of care (quantity of supervision)" (p. 480). It is crucial to assign the appropriate number of staff members to supervise a facility. Different facilities need different amounts of supervision and possibly different levels of supervision depending on the time of day. For example, a gymnasium space with three basketball courts requires minimal supervision in the morning hours when the number of participants is low; during the evening, however, when participation is highest, the gym may require additional staff to provide adequate supervision.

Quality of supervision refers to the training and competence of the individuals supervising the facility. Are they properly trained to meet the supervision requirements for that specific area? Fitness center supervisors, for example, require different types and amounts of training than do gymnasium supervisors. Supervisors of an entire facility cannot focus on just knowing how to supervise one area but instead must possess working knowledge of all areas. Sharp et al. (2007, p. 481) offer these strategies:

- Make sure that all employees who have supervisory responsibilities are competent to identify unsafe behaviors within the activity or sport they are supervising.
- Develop supervisory plans that have an appropriate ratio of supervisors to participants, considering such factors as the nature of the activity, the age and maturity of the participants, the skill level of the participants, and any limitations posed by the type of activity area or facility.

- Develop supervisory plans that designate certain areas of the activity area for each supervisor. You may have a reasonable number of supervisors, but if they all congregate together, you will not have proper coverage.
- Ensure that all supervisors are trained to identify and stop rowdy behavior.

Every program must also identify the type of supervisor to be employed in each area. Does the facility require a full-time professional staff member on duty at all times when the facility is open? Or can graduate assistants adequately supervise the facility without assistance from full-time professional staff? Should a full-time professional staff member be on call while the facility is being supervised by a graduate assistant? Can undergraduate employees adequately provide the required supervision? Each campus is different and will answer these questions in different ways, but in any case you should develop a rationale for why the facility is being supervised by certain staff so that you will be able to justify the decision if needed. One of the most essential components is the amount of training that the supervisor receives before being given responsibility for supervising the facility. Make sure that you have a well thought out training program that covers all areas that might come up during a shift.

Photo courtesy of Colorado State University.

Employee training and competence are essential to ensure participants' safety.

MAINTENANCE

Sports facilities are very expensive to build, so it makes sense to keep a new facility in the best possible shape for as long as possible. Most surfaces and areas require regular maintenance to ensure that the product lasts for the expected lifespan. Hardwood floors can last for as long as the facility is standing if regularly maintained. Synthetic flooring can last anywhere from 15 to 30 years with regular maintenance. Artificial turf has a lifespan of 10 to 15 years if properly maintained. You should develop a regular maintenance plan for all facilities to make sure that they remain worthy of being used. Cotts and Lee (1992) identify the following six categories for scheduling maintenance:

- Inspection and repair (only when absolutely necessary)
- Cyclical repairs (e.g., replacing the roof every 20 years)
- Preventive or routine maintenance, which means maintaining the equipment or facility according to established standards (e.g., oiling motors every 100 hours of use) to prevent problems
- Breakdown maintenance (e.g., burnt-out light bulb or stopped machine)
- Repair projects, ranging from a broken window to major repairs
- General housekeeping and janitorial services (In Fried, 2005, pp. 172–174)

All of these maintenance categories carry associated costs that should be included in either a regular or a reserve budget. Follow manufacturers' recommendations for maintenance of equipment and most surfaces. Two areas, however, require special attention: flooring and locker rooms.

Flooring

The Maple Flooring Manufacturers Association (MFMA; 2011) proposes the following six steps for proper daily maintenance of a hardwood floor:

- Sweep the floor daily.
- Wipe up spills and any moisture on the floor surface.
- Make sure the heating, ventilating, and air conditioning system is functioning properly.
- Remove heel marks with an approved floor cleaner.
- Inspect the floor for tightening or shrinkage.
- Always protect the floor when moving heavy portable equipment.

The MFMA (2011) also gives the following information about wood flooring: "Wood is naturally porous and can absorb and release moisture. If the humidity in your facility rises, your wood floor will absorb the moisture, causing it to expand. If the humidity falls, your wood floor will release moisture, causing it to shrink." The important thing to remember is that water is the enemy of a hardwood floor. Spills or leakages should be cleaned up immediately to prevent floor boards from warping or expanding, which can cause serious damage. Overflowing water fountains or rainwater coming in through the roof can cause considerable damage to a hardwood floor.

Mahana (2008) addresses long-term floor care: "Yearly maintenance for hardwood and synthetic gym floors consists of scrubbing or stripping and recoating the floor surface. In reality, the term 'yearly' can mean several times a year or once every two or three years, depending on the amount of finish wear." Hardwood floors should be recoated or refurbished annually, and the entire surface should be stripped down and resealed every few years. An older floor may need to be stripped and sanded down and repainted before being sealed again. Regular daily, monthly, and yearly maintenance reduces the frequency with which complete sanding is needed and thus saves you money over the years.

For synthetic floors, Abacus Sports Installations (2011) recommends dust mopping once or twice a day, depending on use, and damp mopping on a weekly basis to keep the floor looking new. Regular maintenance also extends the life of the finish on a synthetic floor. Automatic scrubbers help reduce the time and effort required to scrub a floor. It is also important to ensure that staff are careful when chairs, tables, and stages are being set up on a synthetic floor to reduce the chance of damage to the floor.

Recreation Management magazine (Ahrweiler, 2004) outlined the following maintenance requirements:

Maintenance Musts

Even the best floors and surfaces are only as good as the proper attention and care they're given. Designers, manufacturers, and facility managers alike recommend constant, vigilant maintenance to keep both wood and synthetic floors at their best. Below are tips on wood and synthetic care.

Wood Floors

Daily

- Use floor mats at entrances to gym to keep dirt and grit away and vacuum mats daily.
- Pick up any garbage.
- Remove chewing gum.
- Dust-mop floor with a clean, treated mop.
- Wipe floor with bare hand to test if dust remains on the floor. If dust remains, mop again.
- To remove soil, use a waterless cleaner designed for wood surfaces.

(continued)

(continued)

Monthly

- Remove rubber burns and floor marks with a solvent-dampened cloth.
- Tack or damp-mop floor with a solvent-based cleaner.
- Keep people off floor until dry.

Yearly

- For lightly worn floors, a light "screening" may be required and one coat of floor finish.
- For badly worn or damaged floors, consider heavy screening or sanding.

In General

- Encourage users to only wear gym shoes to avoid scuffing.
- Keep a constant indoor environment, ideally between 35 percent and 50 percent humidity.
- Never use a floor scrubber.
- Don't let water or other liquids remain on floor.

Synthetics

Daily

- Dust-mop as needed to remove dry dirt and debris using an untreated mop head.
- Wet-mop any spills and remove any large amounts of dirt or dust.
- Damp-mop daily, using a white cotton (damp with water, but not too wet with water) towel. Rinse the towel every few passes. For dirtier surfaces use a neutral floor cleaner.

Occasionally

- A low-speed floor scrubber may be used with a neutral or citrus-based cleaner diluted according to the manufacturer.
- Remove scuff marks with a clean towel dampened with a ready-to-use citrus- or butyl-based cleaner. Rinse the floor with clean water after removing scuff marks.

In General

- Do not allow patrons to wear spikes.
- Do not use abrasive brushes, pads, or steel wool.
- Do not use high-speed floor equipment.
- Do not use floor wax.

Other Handy Tips

- To remove those pesky scuff marks from black-soled shoes on both wood and synthetic floors, attach a tennis ball on the end of a stick and rub. TMP architect Dave Larson promises it works.
- Make sure your maintenance team understands care instructions. The Maple Floor Manufacturers Association offers floor-care posters and training videos in English and Spanish.

Reprinted, by permission, from M. Ahrweiler, 2004, "Special supplement: Recreation management's complete guide to sports surfaces and flooring," *Recreation Management* pg. 20.

The most important aspect of floor or any other maintenance is to make sure you are following the guidelines set forth by the company that installed your floor.

Locker Rooms

Locker room maintenance is important both for customer service and for reducing the transmission of diseases and fungi. Two types of flooring are common in locker rooms—tile and carpet, each of which has its own issues. Michael Swain reports that "slip-and-fall accidents are the most common hazards associated with locker room wet areas" (Scanlin, 2009). To reduce the hazard of slipping on a wet tiled floor, custodial staff must be observant and quickly clean up wetness as soon as possible. Adding a rough surface can reduce the risk of slipping on wet floors.

At the same time, Scanlin (2009) indicates the following problems with using carpet in a locker room: "It is difficult to keep clean and to disinfect, and powder, lotions and other personal care products can get into the carpet fibers. Vacuuming alone won't cut it for cleaning." Scanlin also reports that newer types of carpeting are more resistant to moisture build-up and bacteria and can be cleaned by soap and water.

Thus the facility manager must decide which surface the staff will be able to keep cleaner. Carpets can be vacuumed, but doing so may not remove the bacteria and fungi that can grow in locker rooms. Whichever surface is chosen, a strict maintenance scheduled must be maintained.

Brown (2007) reports that "fungal infections, like athlete's foot, have long been associated with humid locker rooms. Now the bacterium methicillin-resistant staphylococcus aureus, or MRSA, which was once thought confined to hospitals and prisons, has been making its way into some athletic facilities." In order to combat MRSA and other bugs, Brown suggests that, "most fitness clubs will have staff dedicated strictly to the locker room—picking up towels, removing trash and wiping down sinks, vanities, and countertops with disinfectant spray." Thus it is crucial that you develop a plan of action for keeping all surfaces clean—both for sanitary reasons and to make the locker room hospitable to users.

SUMMARY

Facility design, construction, and management can be daunting tasks, but using good processes makes them easier. For example, a building designed with one focal entry point makes it relatively easy to monitor who is coming into the facility. When facilities are designed to be accessible to anyone who wants to participate, programs become accessible to all. And you can keep your facility current for many years by considering future trends and planning for uses that don't exist at the time of planning. Proper scheduling policies and procedures can make the facility available at the right time for the right people. Appropriate and well-trained staff help reduce the risk of injury to participants and ensure that when accidents do occur emergency care is on site as quickly as possible. And, lastly, proper maintenance keeps the facility looking good for many years.

Glossary

benchmarking—Process of getting information from other managers about facilities or events to help you develop your own facility or program.

bubble designs—A facility and event planning technique which identifies different important aspects of the facility or event, placing them in "bubbles" or circles on the page, and then drawing lines to show the connections between bubbles.

natatorium—Indoor swimming pool.

pickleball—Racket sport that uses a Wiffle ball and wooden paddles and is played on a badminton court with the net touching the ground like a tennis net.

References

Abacus Sports Installations. (2011). The simple maintenance steps to keep your floor looking like new for years. www.abacus-sports.com/maintenance.htm.

Ahrweiler, M. (2004). Special supplement: Recreation management's complete guide to sports surfaces and flooring. *Recreation Management*. http://recmanagement.com/features.php?fid=200407fe00&ch=5.

American College of Sports Medicine (ACSM). (2012a). History. www.acsm.org/about-acsm/who-we-are/history.

American College of Sports Medicine (ACSM). (2012b). *ACSM's health/fitness facility standards and guidelines,* 4th ed. Champaign, IL: Human Kinetics. www.humankinetics.com/products/all-products/ACSMs-HealthFitness-Facility-Standards-and-Guidelines-4th-Edition.

American National Standards Institute (ANSI). (2011). About ANSI overview. www.ansi.org/about_ansi/overview/overview.aspx?menuid=1.

American Society of Testing and Materials (ASTM). (2011). About ASTM International. www.astm.org/TRAIN/IMAGES/petroleumcourses.pdf.

Baletka, M. (1999). In S.C. Brown & L. Schoonmaker (Eds.), *Managing the collegiate recreational facility.* Corvallis, OR: National Intramural-Recreational Sports Association, pp. 23-35.

Brown, N. (2007, July). Maintenance and repair: Fitness pros take a closer look at locker room cleanliness. http://athleticbusiness.com/articles/article.aspx?articleid=1577&zoneid=17.

Brown, T. & Haines, D. (2009). *Space planning guidelines for campus recreational sport facilities.* Champaign, IL: Human Kinetics.

Cotts, D. & Lee, M. (1992). *The facility management handbook.* New York: American Management Association.

Fried, G. (2005). *Managing sport facilities.* Champaign IL: Human Kinetics.

Hunsaker, D.S., & Cook, D. (2009). Aquatic facilities. In National Intramural-Recreational Sports Association, *Campus recreational sports facilities: Planning, design, and construction guidelines* (pp. 133-156). Champaign, IL: Human Kinetics.

Mahana, D. (2008, November). Maintenance and repair: Maintenance program keeps gym floors looking their best. *Athletic Business,* www.athleticbusiness.com/articles/article.aspx?articleid=1906&zoneid=17.

Maple Flooring Manufacturers Association (MFMA). (2011). Taking care of your MFMA maple sports floor. www.maplefloor.org/literature/wall_chart.htm.

National Intramural-Recreational Sports Association (NIRSA). (2009a). *Campus recreational sports facilities.* Champaign, IL: Human Kinetics.

National Intramural-Recreational Sports Association (NIRSA). (2009b). *Space planning guidelines for campus recreational sport facilities.* Champaign, IL: Human Kinetics.

Occupational Safety & Health Administration (OSHA). (2011). About OSHA. www.osha.gov/about.html.

Sawyer, T.H. (2009a). *Facility management for physical activity and sport.* Champaign IL: Sagamore.

Sawyer, T.H. (Ed.). (2009b). *Facility design for health, fitness, physical activity, recreation, and sports facility development.* Champaign, IL: Sagamore.

Scanlin, A. (2009, January). Signage, supervision are keys to keeping locker rooms safe. http://athleticbusiness.com/articles/article.aspx?articleid=3484&zoneid=25.

Seidler & Miller. (2009). Design trends in stadiums and arenas. In T.H. Sawyer (Ed.), *Facility design for health, fitness, physical activity, recreation, and sports facility development* (pp. 389–405). Champaign, IL: Sagamore.

Sharp, L.A., Moorman, A.M., & Claussen, C.L. (2007). *Sport law: A managerial approach.* Scottsdale, AZ: Holcomb Hathaway.

United States Access Board. (2002). *ADA Accessibility Guidelines for Recreation Facilities.* www.access-board.gov/recreation/final.htm.

United States Access Board. (2003). *Accessible Sports Facilities.* www.access-board.gov/recreation/guides/sports.htm.

CHAPTER

12

Services

William F. Canning
University of Michigan and Centers LLC

Jennifer R. de-Vries
Oregon State University

Historically, the first responsibilities of campus recreational sports departments were traditional student programs (i.e., intramurals and sport clubs). Access to shared facilities was a given for students, faculty, and staff, and many services (e.g., lockers, towels, equipment checkout) were either free or carried only a nominal cost. Many campuses also provided workout clothing and laundry service on an exchange basis. Activity classes were part of the academic requirements for physical education. In those days, contemporary ideas such as day care, food offerings, membership, personal training, and wellness services were not even germinating in the setting of campus recreational sports.

This changed dramatically in the 1970s due to three major factors:

- Physical education academic hours were dropped from graduation requirements. In response, many physical education departments directed their focus toward research areas in kinesiology and movement studies or teacher education rather than campus-wide activity instructional classes.
- The passing of Title IX opened many doors for women. Girls at high schools across the country were now competing in the same number of interscholastic sports that their male counterparts had enjoyed for decades. In addition, for the first time, women and men were attending colleges and universities in equal number.
- Campus recreational sports facilities were built with support from dedicated student fees that covered capital costs for construction, debt retirement, operations, and programming. These fees were not optional for full-time enrolled students. Traditional programs for students were still the first priority, but campus recreational sports now also took on new responsibilities, such as facility management, business operations, membership sales, student employment, and noncredit instructional programs.

This chapter lays out the structure of campus recreational sports services to help professionals effectively plan recreation centers in this modern era. We provide information you need in order to make informed decisions about what goes into a facility, what gets left out, and how to handle complicated decisions. The chapter helps you understand your options in deciding what services to provide in a recreational facility and what those services entail.

MEMBERSHIP

Membership is now a fundamental service provided by campus recreational sports departments; it is also a primary source of revenue. Once student fees were instituted, it followed logically that others (i.e., faculty and staff members) should also pay an access fee. At most institutions, this fee is equal to or higher than

> **Caution**
>
> The recreation center's location may cause it to infringe on the business of other recreation centers in the area. On the other hand, the facility may be the only one of its kind in the area.

the dedicated fee paid by students. Membership can include a wide variety of populations, and professionals must consider many factors when determining the nature of membership for a facility. Here are some initial questions to answer:

- Who can use the facility?
- How much should membership cost?
- What kinds of membership should be offered?

Most public institutions cannot sell to individuals who are unaffiliated with the university, since the public institution enjoys an unfair business advantage due to the fact that it does not pay property taxes. In fact, private sport clubs pay taxes that support the institution. Private universities have some leeway to offer this type of membership sales. All university policies should be well vetted by the institution's legal and public relations departments.

Identifying Users

In establishing a campus recreational sports facility, you must determine who can use the facility. Start by assessing targeted communities, or determining the **target audience**, which can help you establish a starting point for both marketing and eligibility protocols. The choice of target audience is affected by the facility's location and by any affiliation with outside groups, athletic programs, or educational institutions (e.g., university alumni associations).

The primary audience, however, should always be the students of the home institution. Here are some factors to consider regarding the student population. Should the same fee be paid by all full- and part-time students? By graduate and undergraduate students? By distance learning students? The standard practice is generally to keep it simple and treat all students equally; in other words, if a student is enrolled, he or she should pay a set fee and be granted access. Across-the-board fees can be assessed upon enrollment for the first credit hour or a portion of each credit hour fee. A larger number of "taxed" students means a larger amount of predictable revenue. Some institutions use a reduced tax for part-time or graduate students, who then have the option of paying the difference. This scenario causes trouble at the membership desk and leads to student confusion and frustration as the membership desk employees need to profile students into these exceptions and special groups. In an attempt to be financially fair, the institution has singled out groups and divided the student population.

The next-largest targets for membership are the institution's faculty and staff (e.g., professors, instructors, lab assistants, staff members). These groups can be the primary portion of membership sales as their fees are typically higher and their accounts are serviced within the recreational sports database and membership program. Additional groups include the families of the students, faculty, and staff, as well as retirees, alumni, and in some cases unaffiliated persons.

Membership Categories

Because universities involve many constituencies, membership categories must be established deliberately. For example, will graduate and undergraduate students be treated equally? Should faculty be treated differently than other employees? Is the facility designed for children? This section explores various types of membership.

Student Membership

Typically, all full-time undergraduate and graduate students pay a membership fee as part of their educational cost (i.e., general tuition and fees). To enter the facility, they must show valid student identification. Self-sponsored single-entry passes are available to part-time students and non-enrolled "**continuing students**" for

> **Recommendation**
>
> When planning the business model for a facility, it is better to require the membership fee of a larger number of student categories.

> **Caution**
>
> When defining family or spouse, consider the variety of relationships within our campus communities.

a daily fee; valid identification is required of them as well.

Institutions use varying definitions of full-time, and campus recreational sports has no input into these definitions. It is a fallacy that undergraduates have greater opportunity to use recreational facilities than do graduate or part-time students. In fact, graduate and older part-time students tend to understand their need for physical activity and have established individual workout patterns. Their time management skills are also much better developed. Thus here again it makes sense to establish an across-the-board, first-credit-hour fee for all enrolled students.

Families of students can often purchase a term membership at an established rate. Campuses typically establish definitions through the human resource department, and membership definitions should reflect these institutional definitions. Membership sales staff should not be placed in situations to judge a potential member's lifestyle. Procedures and definitions must be well defined, understandable, and in line with the institution's culture. Here are two sample liberal definitions:

- Family member must meet two of the following three criteria: same last name, same address, or financial dependency (e.g., both names on a shared checking account).
- Every current affiliated member can sponsor one adult of his or her choice.

Students not enrolled for the current term can purchase a "continuing student" membership at the voluntary student rate with proof

Louisiana State University - University Recreation.

The benefits of student membership can be extended to students' family members.

of enrollment for the previous or upcoming quarter. The majority of these memberships are sold during the summer months, but a sound continuing student policy also allows access to the facility for students who take a semester off.

Faculty/Staff Membership

The faculty/staff rate is available to current university employees, retirees, and subcontracted employees. As with students, valid identification is required. Payment options include cash, credit card, monthly credit card deduction, check, monthly checking account deduction, and payroll deduction.

Membership management software programs allow for wide variation in real-time sales. Membership options should include annual, multiple-month (e.g., 3- or 4-month), and monthly. An annual pass sold on October 15 expires on October 14 of the following year. Pricing strategies are discussed later in this section. Nonstudent membership should not be tied to the university calendar. Real-time membership is an annual or shorter-length pass that can be sold on any day for the prescribed length of time. Real-time sales eliminate all mid-term discounting of the pricing structure and the prorating of any refunds. All of these options can be processed by most membership software packages, many of which also generate renewal messages.

An additional membership strategy is to sell an annual **perpetual membership**, which sets up a contractual arrangement between the individual and the department by means of which the membership is automatically renewed on its anniversary date. Contractually, the individual must give a month's notice in order to cancel the membership, and the department must give a 90-day notice of any fee increase. Both real-time and perpetual memberships offer the advantage of reducing the long lines that can form at the time of academic term renewals.

Department financial managers need to accurately predict monthly revenue in order to correctly reflect the department's status at year end. Departments will also have deferred income at year end for services sold but not yet rendered.

For faculty and staff who do not want to buy a long-term membership, you can sell self-sponsored, single-entry passes for a daily fee; valid identification, of course, must be presented.

Families of faculty and staff can purchase memberships at established rates. Such memberships follow the same policies delineated for students earlier in this section.

> **Caution**
>
> The collection of monthly fees for real-time memberships will cross year-end budget reporting periods.

Alumni Membership

Alumni are typically considered affiliates. Universities want to remain affiliated with alumni, and allowing alumni memberships helps establish good alumni relations and adds to the department's financial bottom line. Departments should, however, make sure that they have facility capacity to accommodate such memberships.

Different universities may define alumni differently, and campus recreational sports departments should follow the established campus protocol. Alumni associations may define membership differently than the university does; most alumni associations include not only matriculated graduates but also friends, parents, and other donors. Alumni memberships should be sold for time frames similar to those made available to faculty and staff. Families of alumni may purchase memberships at established rates, following the campus recreational sports guidelines.

Dependents and Children

Dependents are young adults of any membership category other than actual students, faculty, and staff. The age parameters may vary according to university policy; they typically range from 16 to 25 years. Dependents can have their own membership card and can use the facilities without a parent or guardian in attendance. Their membership rate is usually the same as the rate for their parents.

Caution

Facilities that allow dependents and children should be prepared to deal with parents who enter the facility with their children and then leave, thus in effect dropping off their children to be supervised by the facility staff.

Children of any membership category range from infant to 18 years. Children should be able to use the facility only with a parent or guardian in attendance; they should not have their own membership card. The cost of adding children to a parent's membership may vary by the number of children or be a set rate regardless of number.

Policies should be clear, logical, and enforced. Many campus recreational sports facilities, or venues within a facility, are not designed for children. The decision of whether to offer such membership options should be handled during the facility design process rather than as an afterthought.

Community Membership

At some facilities, any adult (18 years or older) who is unaffiliated with the university can be eligible for a community rate. The time periods for community membership are similar to those for other nonstudent categories. Most institutions charge an additional initiation fee that is due in full at the time of joining. The availability of community memberships may be limited by a maximum number established in the department's business plan. The maximum number is set to ensure that the facility's capacity for student usage is not in jeopardy.

Caution

The typical financing vehicle for campus recreational sports facilities is the tax-exempt bond. These bonds include strict requirements designating a percentage of facility usage to be non-university in nature. Exceeding the percentage can put the tax-exempt bonds in jeopardy of defaulting.

Guest Passes

One privilege of membership is the option of sponsoring single-entry guests. Passes are available for purchase by students, faculty, staff, alumni, and community members for a set daily fee. The limit is typically three guests per member per day.

Pricing Strategy

Membership prices should be determined based on the campus fee tolerance and the local market. You should complete a full analysis of the off-campus market, then have the membership pricing strategy reviewed and approved by the university.

You also need to address the proximity of the campus recreational sports center to any nearby community or private facilities. The center may be the only one of its type in the local area or even the region. If other centers are located close by, consider arranging competition clauses when determining your target audiences so as to avoid potential lawsuits.

Depending on the type of recreation facility, membership can entail many different benefits—for example, the option of sponsoring a guest; access to weight and cardio equipment, swimming pools, and sports equipment; and organized activities such as structured leagues and other wellness options. In many facilities, the membership fee makes the user eligible for a basic level of group fitness classes; other specialized instructional classes may require an additional fee. The basic fee may or may not cover locker and towel services.

Not all members come to your building to do the same thing, and if the facility design allows, or if multiple facilities exist, membership can be set up to offer access only to certain spaces or programs. For example, a membership might grant access to fitness classes but not to the aquatic center, or it might grant daily access only to the climbing wall. Membership classifications must be determined by the facility staff since opportunities within a recreation facility differ from one facility to the next. In any case, be aware that these separable memberships should be priced so as not to erode the all-access membership fees.

Another pricing strategy can be used to encourage use of the facility during times when it tends to operate under capacity: **limited access** membership for a discounted rate. Typically, limited-access members are allowed to enter the facility between 8:00 a.m. and 4:00 p.m. on weekdays and at any time during operating hours on Saturday and Sunday. During the summer, a limited-access member may be allowed to use the facility during all building hours. The hours of use must be established by entry statistics, which means that limited access memberships can make sense once a facility has gathered at least 2 years of operational statistics.

The initial pricing of all memberships should stem from the dedicated mandatory fee that students are charged—no membership should be sold at a lower rate than the annual cost for students. If no fee exists, then divide the amount of total university financial support for the center by the number of students in order to set a reasonable starting point. You should also factor local competition and the local economy into your rate decisions.

Typically, a long-term **business pro forma** provides goals for the speculative income portion of the annual budget, and the largest portion of **speculative income** for campus recreational sports comes from membership sales. If the term student fee is $100 and the academic year includes two terms plus a summer session, then the annual cost for the least expensive basic membership should be between $250 and $300. Faculty/staff and retiree memberships are usually the lowest-cost memberships sold, and alumni and community rates are incrementally higher. Family and dependent memberships are typically priced at the sponsor's rate.

> **Caution**
>
> The pricing strategy for a limited-access membership should not undermine the full membership revenue goals by category.

In terms of membership duration, annual or perpetual memberships carry the best rates. Multiple-month memberships should be significantly higher; for example, a 4-month membership should cost more than the annual rate divided by three; in turn, a 1- month membership should cost more than the 4- month fee divided by four. The goal of a pricing strategy should be to encourage the most possible long-term memberships. If the institution does not offer community memberships, then the alumni price should be set at the higher rate. Table 12.1 shows a sample membership table.

Some campuses use service pricing strategies that vary by income level; for example, parking passes may cost less for lower-paid employees. Investigate whether your institution follows such a practice before setting membership rates for campus recreational sports.

Summary

Membership can account for the largest portion of a recreation center's speculative income; therefore, both the number and the satisfaction of members are essential to the center's operation. To sustain the operation of any facility, it is crucial that you implement a competitive membership structure. In determining the nature of membership for your facility, consider numerous factors. Determine a target audience from which to capture the bulk of your membership and extend that membership to include eligible members of the immediate community: faculty, staff, graduates, affiliates, and, when

> **Caution**
>
> Current tax regulations bar employees of an institution from receiving a discount of more than 20 percent on any items available to the public unless the amount above the 20 percent is treated as taxable income. According to current interpretation, these regulations apply to services, tickets, membership, parking, and so on.

Table 12.1 Sample Membership Pricing

	Annual	4-month	1-month
Faculty/staff	$300	$150	$75
Faculty/staff family	$300	$150	$75
Alumni	$330	$165	$82.50
Alumni family	$330	$165	$82.50
Community	$360	$180	$90 (+ $100 initiation fee)

Student fee per term = $100 × three full terms per year = $300 total.

applicable, the general public. The typical private fitness club experiences a 50 percent turnover rate in membership each year, whereas for campus recreational sports facilities the nature of the members' affiliations with the university keeps most annual turnover rates below 20 percent. This does not, however, mean that you can ignore the question of member retention policy. In fact, strong member affiliation also means high expectations of customer service. Remember also that many services offered by a recreation center (e.g., opportunities to stay fit, classes, certifications, programs promoting wellness) would simply cease to exist without eager members to take part in them.

EQUIPMENT CHECKOUT AND RENTALS

A visible, centrally located equipment area can be essential to the successful operation of a campus recreational sports facility. Many facility designs incorporate the equipment checkout area into a hub that also handles facility access, general information, guest pass sales, towel and locker services, and pro shop retail operations. Such an area serves as the facility's nerve center. If properly designed, it may be staffed by as few as two people during low-use times and as many as four or five during peak hours. For many participants, the employees at this hub serve as the facility's public face, which means that customer service training is essential for these employees. This portion of the chapter covers equipment checkout, equipment rental, retail sales, and locker and towel service.

Equipment Checkout

Many activities within a facility require equipment, and the facility should provide users with abundant, high-quality equipment. The need for equipment varies greatly and depends primarily on how many members use the recreation center on a daily basis. Maintaining steady usage of various areas depends on offering the right types of equipment within the facility. The facility's philosophy helps determine what equipment to provide for the users and what products to offer for sale to enhance the user's experience. For example, racquetball rackets could be a no-cost checkout item, an hourly rental, or a sales item. Management must decide what level of services will be provided for their participants.

Table 12.2 presents some types of equipment that might be required for a given space within a facility; the information is based on the setup used at Oregon State University.

Managing Equipment

Making sure that equipment is managed properly can save a facility a great deal of cost in terms of maintaining equipment and replacing broken or stolen equipment. A facilities operation needs to make enough equipment available in workout areas—for example, stability balls, yoga mats, small dumbbells, cleaning supplies, kickboards, and pull buoys. Campus culture helps dictate the amount and quality of self-service items you make available. At the University of Virginia, the student code of conduct is so well ingrained that racks of high-quality basketballs and volleyballs are located in each gymnasium. Virginia does not have a theft problem.

Table 12.2 Sample Equipment List

Gym floors (courts)	Weight room	Cardio areas	Locker rooms	Pool(s) or spa	Tennis or racquetball courts	Miscellaneous
Basketballs	Weight straps	Reading racks	Locks	Fins	Rackets	Goggles
Volleyballs	Weight belts	Ear buds	Hair dryers	Aqua joggers	Balls	Jump ropes
Nets	Dip belts	Water bottles	Towels	Hydro cuffs	Stringing service	Towels
Paddles	Ankle straps	Rags	Swimsuit dryer	Hand paddles	Strings	Table tennis paddles
Other balls	Rags		Hair bands	Goggles	Goggles	Table tennis balls
Birdies	Resistance bands					Medicine balls
Rackets						Yoga mats

To maintain a healthy equipment inventory, it is critical to effectively check equipment out to participants and check it back into your inventory. The best way to check out equipment is through a software program that enables attendants to swipe the membership or student ID card and thus account electronically for the specific piece of borrowed equipment. Most of today's identification cards can record stored value for campus meal plans or debit amounts for various campus services or products; however, it is not advisable to exchange the card as collateral unless the recreation department wishes to take on the liability of the card's value. Here are some things to consider when determining which tracking software will work best for your recreation facility:

- Ease and speed of each transaction
- Compatibility with existing membership and student software
- Capacity to control hundreds of items
- Direct connection to an inventory control system

The equipment checkout process is also important to the customer's overall recreation experience.

Damaged and Abused Equipment

One of the major problems facing a recreation center is the need to maintain the quality of checkout items. You must keep sufficient inventory to retire worn, damaged, or broken equipment. The fact of the matter is that equipment breaks, cracks, or becomes worn through normal use; this is all part of the life span of a piece of equipment. Normal wear and tear is fairly easy to observe. On the other hand, when good equipment is checked out, it is also very easy to tell when it has been abused by the user. Proper protocols need to be followed in order to ensure that the broken piece of equipment is paid for by the individual at fault. To do this, you must develop firm actions and clear policies regarding damaged and abused equipment.

The standard protocol for dealing with abused equipment is to hold the guilty party financially responsible. Many pieces of checkout equipment are expensive. Equipment budgets vary, but in all cases good management of inventory and consistent enforcement of misuse policies can help you make good use of the center's equipment assets. The first step in this process is to document all equipment and make note of worn, broken, and abused items. For reasons of both efficiency and cost, strong documentation is needed when tracking equipment inventories and purchasing equipment. Conduct frequent audits that address equipment cost, frequency of damage, administrative fees, and replacement costs to help you budget appropriately for equipment needs.

Equipment Rental

Not all checkout equipment is free. Many items (e.g., racquetball, squash, and badminton rackets) can be rented for a nominal fee that helps cover replacement costs. Other typical rental items include bowling shoes, climbing shoes, and day-use lockers (with towel service). These financial transactions must adhere to the established departmental cash handling plan, and **point-of-sale systems** must be coordinated with the equipment checkout software.

Retail Sales

Many users like to purchase their own equipment, clothing, or other personal workout items, and you can provide convenience for them by adding a retail sales operation. By no means, however, should a campus recreational sports center go into the sporting goods business; to the contrary, most retail operations are viewed more as a customer service than a profit center. Many popular items (e.g., logoed t-shirts, shorts, or socks) can be used to promote the center. Other popular items include batteries, shoelaces, tennis balls, racquetballs, and shuttlecocks. You can keep the inventory small to avoid tying up departmental resources. The retail operation can also be fully incorporated into the equipment issue operation, where the software system already has point-of-sale capability and controls inventory and where no additional staff members are needed. Table 12.3 shows a sample of retail items offered for sale at DePaul University.

Table 12.3 Sample List of Retail Items for Sale

Retail item	Price
Boxing hand wraps—multicolored Mexican style	$6.00
Earbuds	$5.00
Hat with campus recreational sports logo	$10.00
Headphones	$4.00
Heart rate monitor (Polar Beat)	$55.00
Nalgene water bottles	$7.25
Racquetball (blue Ektelon)	$3.25
Racquetball (green Ektelon)	$4.00
Racquetball eye guard (Phoenix Leader)	$16.50
Racquetball eye guard (Wilson Omni)	$8.50
Racquetball gloves	$7.50
Shorts with campus recreational sports logo	$21.00
Shuttlecock	$1.75
Socks	$3.00
Swim cap	$3.00
Swim diaper	$5.00
Swim goggles (adult Michigan Leader)	$4.50
Swim goggles (adult Speedo Pro)	$10.00
Swim goggles (adult TYR Technoflex)	$11.50
Swim goggles (children's)	$6.25
Swim goggles (Speedo Hydrospex Jr.)	$11.25
T-shirt with campus recreational sports logo	$15.00
Weight belt	$35.00
Weightlifting gloves	$6.00
Weightlifting wrist straps	$5.00
Wind shirt with campus recreational sports logo	$26.00

Lockers and Towels

All campus recreational sports facilities should have locker rooms and lock-use policies. Lockers fall into one of two categories—permanent storage and daily use—both of which can either be offered free of charge or carry an associated rental fee. Locker rooms must be carefully planned and thoughtfully designed; in fact, locker rooms with showers, bathrooms, grooming areas, saunas, and whirlpools entail the second-highest square-foot cost to construct and then maintain (swimming pools and other wet areas are the most expensive). Ancillary laundry rooms are typically located nearby. Many institutions incorporate locker room and towel services into the basic membership fee, thus making this service seem free to users. Some institutions cannot permanently rent storage lockers because either the number of lockers or the size of locker rooms is too small; these facilities allow only daily use. If you have enough lockers, it is best to offer a mixture of storage and daily use, since annual locker leases can be an attractive service, especially for nonstudent users, who, along with swimmers, constitute the majority of locker users in today's recreation facilities.

Locker room configuration is a function of activity areas, climate, and geographical location. Many warm-weather universities can limit the size of storage lockers to half-size, thus potentially doubling the number available for use. Many cold-climate schools configure six lockers of one-third size surrounding a full-size changing locker that can accommodate heavy boots and coats; the full-sized locker is shared. The possible combinations and configurations are endless.

Some institutions require patrons to bring their own locks, others sell locks, and still others use permanently installed key-controlled combination locks. If an institution rents storage lockers, the common practice is for that institution to provide secure space with a combination or keyed lock. In these cases, the membership software program should be able to list, control, and provide security to hundreds of combinations. Rental storage lockers most likely include a towel service on a per-use basis.

Caution

When numbering lockers in a locker room, make sure that there is no possibility of mixing up the women's and men's lockers. Do not start each room at the number 1. For example, even if you have only 200 lockers in each room, begin the women's lockers at 1,000 and the men's at 2,000.

Recommendation

Even if children are not allowed in the facility, provide at least one family or gender-neutral changing facility. These areas should be handicap-accessible and unlockable from the inside. Such rooms accommodate transgendered individuals, families with small children, and partners who may be assisting a person of a different gender with special needs.

Lockers designated for daily use are typically controlled through the equipment issue desk and are handled like any other piece of borrowed equipment. Towel service typically carries a nominal daily fee.

Locker rentals provide a good revenue source. The University of Michigan, for example, generates $200,000 each year from annual and daily locker rentals.

When placing daily use lockers, spread them throughout the locker room rather than all in the same row. They are used more often and can create crowded, uncomfortable changing situations that are easily avoided with proper spacing.

Towels

Recently, many managers of new facilities have decided not to provide towels but instead to require individuals to bring towels to the center as part of their normal routine. Reasons include lack of space, lack of aquatics, and limited locker room facilities. Still, facility-provided towels add a level of service that your patrons may expect, especially if storage lockers are provided and the facility caters to swimmers. Towels can be purchased annually or handled as an expense if provided by an outside laundry service. Both of these options have their benefits and problems:

- **Self-provided service**—Newer facilities are currently designing laundry facilities with properly sized rooms for equipment, folding, and storage. Many also have an outdoor rental center that may rent items such as tents and sleeping bags that require laundering for health concerns or safety requirements. Advantages of this approach include the fact that the facility controls the variety and quality of towels offered and that employees can be used effectively during slow periods if the laundry room is contiguous to the check-in equipment area. Disadvantages include towel inventory costs, initial facility and equipment costs, and storage issues. The life cycle of towels or linen goods is greatly extended if they are allowed to recover after each washing; for this reason, the standard in the restaurant business is to use linens every third day. Thus the number of towels in the inventory should be three times the number used each day, and storage shelving is needed to accommodate that number.
- **Laundry service**—Traditionally, many institutions provide laundry services through athletic departments or hospital operations, and recreation centers can contract with these on-campus providers. Benefits of this approach include fixed contract costs, lack of inventory and replacement costs (the laundry provider includes these costs in its contracted expense), freedom from laundry and dryer purchases and repair, lower utility expenses, and increased storage space. Problems include timely delivery, delivery paths through the facility, storage of clean and soiled towels, and towel quality.

Many facilities also provide workout towels that each weight room participant uses to wipe down equipment after each use. These towels are always available at no charge since they keep the facilities' equipment sanitized and create a better experience for all.

Towels are typically included in the rental cost of storage and daily lockers. In fact, locker rental fees are directly associated with the costs of laundry services.

If the facility has a laundry, it can also periodically clean other types of program items, such as game jerseys, team pinnies, and even floor mops.

Summary

Equipment makes up the bulk of the individual items that the recreation center provides for its participants. Many activities require some sort of equipment, and providing ample equipment is crucial to participant satisfaction. Keeping up with inventories can be difficult, and the facility must accurately replace equipment that comes back broken or abused.

Whether to provide lockers and towels is an important service decision that needs to be made during the design phase of a new facility. Lockers can be combined and configured in many ways. Adding a towel service adds to the combinations. These questions should not be answered by recreation personnel or even architects or planners. The best approach is to first determine the quality and level of service that is preferred on campus, then visit other facilities.

The final four services discussed in this chapter—childcare and babysitting, food service, athletic training, and massage—have a significantly different focus than the preceding two (membership and equipment checkout and rental). All four of these services require specially designed areas and are subject to local or state requirements. Each area also has needs unlike any other venue in the campus recreational sports center—for example, requires specific plumbing, enhanced electrical service, and, in two cases (training and massage), privacy. Each area is unique and is not multifunctional.

With all of this in mind, facility managers must make careful, informed decisions during the facility planning process about whether to include these services. Initial questions might include the following: Does this service already exist on campus? Would adding this service enhance or compete with other campus entities? Do these services add to the desired campus recreational sports experience? Who will bear responsibility for the operations? In many instances, these services should be the responsibility not of campus recreational sports professionals but of professionals trained in the particular field relevant to the service. These are campus decisions and need proper vetting before the architects begin the facility design. If your center is competing for memberships and needs to serve as a consistent revenue source, these services may be needed in order to enhance your ability to retain members, who may expect that the services will be offered. Experience has shown that if you do offer them, your facility should partner with other campus or local providers rather than trying to operate these services by itself as there is typically no need to duplicate services.

CHILD CARE AND BABYSITTING

Child care can be an important service for a recreation facility to offer. For one thing, lack of child care can inhibit individuals who cannot work out or join a facility unless they have accommodations for their young children. Even so, most campus recreational sports facilities do not offer full child care; they do, however, provide limited hours of babysitting. Opening a licensed child care center involves complicated local and state requirements that vary by area. However, child care facilities should exist on our campuses, and in planning a new recreation center or addition, the campus might decide to include a campuswide child care facility adjoining the recreation center. This kind of partnering makes sense. The child care center can make use of the recreation facilities during low-use hours and provide babysitting services for parents during the parents' workout time. A fully operational child care center also provides the campus recreational sports department with clients for children's programming, such as swim lessons, camps, and birthday party rentals. Thus this arrangement can be a win-win for the campus community.

One of the many considerations in determining whether to offer child care is cost. Since it is often difficult to operate a child care center

Photo courtesy of Stephen F. Austin State University Campus Recreation.

There are many benefits to offering child care services to clients.

on a traditional child care model, especially in a collegiate environment, it must be expected that most child care facilities will operate at a loss. Therefore, the university must determine whether or not the organization has the financial resources to support child care. Second, you should conduct a needs assessment in the community that the campus is supporting in order to determine the feasibility of locating a child care facility near the recreation center; as part of this assessment, look at other options in the surrounding community.

Legal considerations are also important and can vary from state to state. You should research state laws, as well as certifications dictated by state regulations. The National Coalition for Campus Children's Centers can also help you determine the needs for a given facility.

When designing the facility, consider the space required for a child care center. Child care centers associated with recreation facilities typically commit 40 to 50 square feet (about 12 to 15 sq m) per child. When determining the makeup of the facility, consider first the number of children expected to be housed in it at any given time. Regulations also dictate that bathrooms, specifically for the child care facility, must be included in the design; this requirement includes toilets conducive to use by children. Child care facilities must also be located on the ground level in order to ensure appropriate access to the facility.

Another major cost associated with child care is the need for adequate staff, who must also carry the appropriate certifications, which are determined on a state-by-state basis. Maintenance cost is also a factor. Facilities must be cleaned according to state regulations on a daily basis.

Finally, you must consider the operating policies and procedures needed for a child care facility. You can do a needs assessment to determine hours of operation, cost, and maximum occupancy. There is also the question of how to operate the facility—for example, how to check children in and out; how to separate children of different age groups; and how to meet needs for bed space, play areas, and food service.

Babysitting service can be managed by the campus recreational sports staff. It usually operates on a limited schedule and in a limited space (many centers use classroom space). If you decide to offer babysitting, local regulations will dictate your operation. These regulations are not as stringent as those governing child care. When does babysitting become child care? The key is the duration of care, and the regulations will set a time period beyond which child care is considered to begin (e.g., if a child is with a caregiver for more than 2 hours, then state child care rules are in effect). As with other services, then, the decision about whether to offer babysitting must be made deliberately during the planning process. If babysitting is offered on a fee-for-service basis, then cash-handling procedures and accountability need to be consistent with other services. Babysitting employees should be well screened and subject to background checks. As with child care, a check-in and checkout procedure is essential for safety and liability purposes.

FOOD SERVICE

The recreation center provides services that push the body and challenge the mind. When these two entities are drained by vigorous activity—whether in yoga class or on the treadmill—they need replenishment in order to grow, develop, and maintain health. Thus a healthy lifestyle involves consuming nutrients shortly after strenuous activity. The question the recreation center must assess is this: Should we offer a food service within our facility? A needs assessment is an effective tool for answering this question.

Here are some considerations in determining whether food service is practical for your facility. After determining the need or demand for food service, clarify expectations with prospective vendors regarding menus, food options, and space. Issues of space should also be conveyed to the architectural team. Other aspects to clarify include power, water, storage, signage, counter space, and point-of-sale options. You must also consider the type of service, which could be a small retail food and smoothie bar, a front desk that serves prepackaged foods, or a full-service restaurant.

The campus recreational sports department should not attempt to manage food operations.

One proven option for a successful operation is an **in-house contract** or agreement between the recreation center and the organization that handles dining services on campus. This might be a university dining services office, a vendor who already has an arrangement with the student union, or an organization currently affiliated with a university department that provides food service or concessions. The other option is to create an **external contract**. Independent food providers typically build the space to their own specifications, have a multi-year contract, and pay rent or a percentage of gross sales to the recreation facility.

The choice between an in-house contract and a private contract should be made by the recreation center's management after performing a cost-benefit analysis of both options. All profitability in food service relies on customer traffic, minimization of waste, speed of service, and payment options. Thus two very important considerations for the recreation center are location and payment options. The location should be in public space that is open to all, not just to the recreation center's students and membership. One key to financial success and customer satisfaction is the ability to purchase products by using the university student debit card or, even better, being part of the student meal plan.

Menus

Most food retailers in a recreation center provide a light menu. These dietary choices include wraps, sandwiches, bars, fruit, vegetables, and light entrées such as burritos and quesadillas, all of which is complemented by shakes and smoothies. Food establishments are definitely not all the same, but within a recreational facility the trend is to strive for healthy options and light entrées that are filling. Consider the effect that the menu will have on members of the facility, as well as employees, and the facility itself (e.g., do you want the facility to smell of popcorn or freshly baked cookies?).

Another aspect of the menu to consider is the life of the food purchased and sold by the food service provider. The period for which a food can stay on a shelf or in an ice case is referred to as the **product life cycle**. Foods and ingredients that can last ease budgetary demands; going a step further, foods that possess nutritional value that will also last well on the shelf save costs and helps maintain a steady inventory. Some examples of such foods are protein bars, granola, and juice; in contrast, meat, produce, and dairy products have a rather short product life cycle. Such considerations illustrate why the recreational professional should not handle food service. Such decisions need to be left to the food provider.

Pricing

Setting food prices can be an extensive process for a recreation center. On one hand, the food service provider needs to make a profit in order to cover its operating cost, maintain food inventory, and recoup the cost of supplies and certifications. At the same time, prices need to be low enough to attract student customers; this pressure can be eased a bit by enabling students

Caution

Allowing students to use meal plan credits to buy food at a recreation center takes money away from the traditional dining meal plan provider. Even so, if you establish a good relationship with dining services during the facility planning phase, you may be able to create new or enhanced options that are profitable for both departments. Food service operations depend on high concentrations of potential customers. Student traffic in a recreation facility is a high concentration of students on campus, thus it may be a good satellite operation.

to use debit cards or meal plan credits purchased through the school's dining or housing office.

ATHLETIC TRAINING

Athletic training makes up a small portion of what a recreation center can facilitate, but it can be a very important service. Many campus recreational sports programs require certified athletic trainers to be present at all sport club practices and events. Others are expanding athletic training to include intramural sports or drop-in clinic hours.

Athletic training is a very specialized profession and should be assigned only to trained individuals. Athletic trainers can be mobile and provide on-site services or can have a home base that provides dedicated space within a facility. The dedicated space is similar in its requirements to the food service planning. Training rooms need specialty items, access to water, ice machines, drains, electrical power (both 110 and 220 volt), storage, towel service, and, in most cases, access to private changing facilities or privacy screens.

Athletic Trainers for Sport Club Programs

In deciding whether to offer athletic training in the recreation center, one key concern is staffing. Who will provide the athletic training? Will they be full-time or part-time campus recreational sports staff? If not, will they come from an affiliated department (e.g., athletics)? Or will these services be outsourced to a local hospital? These are serious questions to consider when deciding the nature of athletic training and safety in the facility.

The staffing question is critical, and the answer must be aligned with programmatic needs. A typical evening of sport club practices may involve four to ten venues operating at the same time or multiple teams using an outdoor field complex. In such a situation, a one- or two-person training staff cannot cover all areas adequately. In fact, the university may be at greater risk for liability issues in having too little coverage than in having none at all. Most campus recreational sports departments now hire outside service providers that schedule multiple part-time trainers. Another option is to employ a single master trainer who can oversee trainers required to have numerous hours of practical experience before receiving their certification. A number of institutions offer academic athletic training tracks in their physical education or kinesiology program. This option can be less expensive, but there are limitations and specified rules as to the extent to which a master trainer can provide such supervision. Again, this is a good reason to hire the professional providers who know the rules.

Additional Program Services

As campus recreational sports departments expand training options and coverage to intramural sports, the predictable hours of scheduling may expand to the point that a full-time cohort of trainers can be justified. In addition, if, say, a priority decision has been made to offer taping or icing services to any participant during clinic hours, this approach also lends justification to the notion of hiring full-time staff. Such operations can also supervise many training students and thus serve as a positive addition to academic programs.

If athletic training is provided by a staff based in the recreation facility, they can assume additional duties. For example, coordinators in program areas and building supervisors all have safety responsibilities and can be trained or supervised by a training staff; other candidates include personal trainers and floor staff in the weight room. The training and safety staff should also be firmly connected to other program areas to support various activities provided by the recreation center.

The safety staff should also conduct staff audits to verify that staff members across different program areas have their current certifications and can perform the certified actions in a simulated emergency. Monitoring performance in this way makes for a well-prepared staff and helps them negotiate the learning curve of retaining information related to first aid.

MASSAGE

Many campus recreational sports centers now offer massage as a service. Members and students are looking for personal attention and are willing to pay for additional services. Once again, the campus recreational sports manager needs to explore this option in the facility planning phase. Massage rooms are unique and typically do not serve any other purpose; as a result, massage is a nice service to offer but rarely pays back the expense of constructing the space, though it can exert a positive influence as members decide whether to continue their membership. Massage rooms must be private and must provide towel service, ambient lighting, and sufficient warmth and quiet. Typically, the staff is provided by an outside organization that has a financial arrangement with the recreation center. Masseuses are certified, and it is crucial for the recreation center's management to regularly check credentials and insurance.

SUMMARY

Recent decades have brought dramatic changes for campus recreational sports professionals. Thirty or forty years ago, the profession was geared toward programmers of sport clubs and intramural teams and officials. Today, campus recreational sport professionals are directors of membership and marketing, facility managers, business managers, trainers, student development coordinators—and the list goes on. When campus recreational sports professionals took on the management of facilities built with student fees, they took on the responsibility to fiscally account for the students' and university's investment. It became their fiduciary obligation to provide reasonably priced services and expanded programs. The lessons learned in the intervening years always boil down to good planning; there is no need to end up retrofitting a new facility after construction to provide a desired service.

Glossary

business pro forma—Plan or road map that predicts business revenues and expenses over a period of years (typically 10 or more).

continuing student—Student who has been enrolled for a previous semester but is not currently enrolled.

external contract—Formal legal arrangement with a business to provide a service that is not part of the institution's operation.

in-house contract—Formal arrangement with a unit to provide a service that is part of the institution's operation.

limited access—Characteristic of memberships sold at reduced rates and subject to limitations on hours of entry.

perpetual membership—Membership that is automatically renewed each year.

point-of-sale system—Automated cash and credit system (i.e., multiple location cash registers) that allows an employee to transact business.

product life cycle—Time period for which a particular item, typically food, can be sold and still be safe for the consumer.

speculative income—Nonguaranteed income derived from sales of memberships and services.

target audience—Identified segment of a population selected to be the most responsive to a promotional effort.

CHAPTER

13

Special Events

Gordon M. Nesbitt
Millersville University

Campus recreational sports facilities offer any number of event programs, ranging from intramurals and sport club games to fitness and aquatic classes. Special events can be distinguished from other events by the fact that they do not occur on a regular basis. They may also involve a larger scale than regularly scheduled events, but they can range from small activities (e.g., intramural poker tournament) to world-class events (e.g., the Olympics or the World Cup). Athletic facilities can also be used for concerts or professional speaking engagements.

Successful planning for special events requires specific knowledge, and a facility operator should be ready to handle any and all events that could possibly be held in his or her facility. With that end in mind, this chapter addresses the following topics: feasibility study, staffing, financial planning, rules and officials, risk and emergency plans, registration, facility scheduling, equipment, uniforms and supplies, awards and recognition, food service, transportation, housing, promotion, communication, and evaluation.

FEASIBILITY STUDY

A feasibility study should provide a justification for programs and facilities and a vision for the proposed solution; it is a valuable tool and a vital first step in implementing new or renovated facilities (National Intramural-Recreational Sports Association, 2009, p. 35). Anyone planning a special event needs to be confident that the event is feasible—that it can realistically be conducted within the parameters that are set forth. Is it realistic to expect a successful event in the available facility or facilities? A thorough analysis of the event's feasibility can provide much of the information you need for the remaining areas of planning.

Knell, Tellers, Bailey, and Bulseco (National Intramural-Recreational Sports Association, 2009) outline the following steps in the facility feasibility study process: mission and goals, existing facility assessment, needs assessment, benchmarking, programming, conceptual planning and budgeting, and the final planning report. These steps are addressed in the following paragraphs in terms of planning a special event.

Define the mission and goals for the special event at the beginning of the planning process. First, define the type of event you are considering and for whom you are planning it. Are you hosting a tournament for the university community, perhaps a homecoming event? Are you looking to host something for the surrounding community (e.g., a road race)? Then decide the event's size and scope. How many people do you hope to attract? Be realistic yet also plan for a showing that is larger than anticipated. Do you really think 300 college students will show up for a Wii tournament on a campus of 5,000 students? On the other hand, if your university is home to 30,000 students and you plan for only 25 students, what are you going to do when 300 appear?

The next step in conducting the feasibility study is to complete an **assessment** of facilities in which you might hold the event. Consider the size and scope of your event, as well as the date(s) and time(s) when it might take place. This information enables you to explore appropriate facilities that can be reserved when you need them. It is also worth exploring any other nearby events or activities occurring at or around the same time as your event to minimize competition.

A needs assessment should be thorough and unrushed. A facility needs assessment identifies all possible uses of or needs for the facility. With a special event, the need for the event should be assessed in order to help you determine whether the event would be successful. The first step is to determine what competition will affect your event. Are similar events being run nearby on that day at the same time as your event? What other activities might draw participants away from your event? What might potential participants be doing instead? Once you have analyzed the potential competition, determine how many people would be interested in attending your event. Simple surveys or polls can help you gather this information. If this assessment indicates enough interest for the event to be successful, you can proceed with planning the event. If not, you can cancel it and look at creating a different event.

Your assessment should also address a few other concerns. For example, if the event is to be held outdoors, what will you do in the case of inclement weather? You must also consider the attitudes of the potential participants. Will the target audience wish to participate in your activity? Do you have community support for the event? Will members of the upper administration enthusiastically support your event, or will they deny your request to host it? The needs assessment should also provide the details that are required for the programming of the event like where the event should be held, when the event should be held, possible income and expenditures, and other events or activities that will compete for the attention of the target audience.

Benchmarking is important in any facility design or special event project. Talking with people who have run similar events can give you insight into issues and situations that you might not think of on your own. Other administrators are usually fairly cooperative in sharing information about events they have held, and they can also provide you with much of the framework for the needs assessment. It is helpful to talk with them by phone, since real-time verbal conversation can lead to follow-up questions that might not arise in an e-mail exchange.

One of the most important areas to consider in the feasibility assessment is the budget. A thorough needs assessment should make it fairly easy to associate a cost with all areas of the special event. In developing the budget, think about sponsorship. For small one-time events, the department can usually cover the costs, thus easily taking care of the budget. If the department is unable to cover the costs, then you need to decide whether you are going to search out other sponsorships or pass the cost of the event on to the participant—or both. Your answer hinges in part on whether you expect the event to make money or just break even. More generally, a clear and well-outlined budget makes it easy to decide whether to move ahead with the event as planned, modify it, or shelve it.

After completing these steps, it is time to draft a final planning report. If the feasibility assessment indicates that the project is infeasible, whether due to lack of facilities or funding or some other factor, then the report does not have to be very long. If the project is deemed feasible, then the report's length and content should be determined by the individual to whom it will be submitted. For example, if upper administration has requested that you investigate the possibility of hosting a special event, you need to complete a thorough report that outlines either what the event requires or why it is not feasible. On the other hand, for a smaller event that is clearly financially feasible from the beginning, the report need not be extensive.

A comprehensive feasibility study should do the following:

- Recommend the exact date(s) and time(s) for the event.
- Propose a location for the event, unless a venue was already specified before the feasibility study was conducted.
- Give the event a carefully selected name, if requested.
- Outline and arrange a schedule of event elements, if requested.
- Formulate a thorough budget.
- Spell out start-up needs and next steps.
- Identify target audiences.
- Provide a reasonably complete marketing plan.
- Include a fairly detailed strategy for eliciting sponsorships.
- List sources or suppliers for such needs as tents, portable generators, and walkie-talkies.
- Suggest the most logical organizational pattern for such aspects as management, committees, and volunteers.
- Project where the event should go in the next 5 or 10 years in terms of factors such as attendance, budget, theme, organization, and staff.

FINANCIAL PLANNING

The feasibility study should give you a good idea of the costs involved in staging the event and of the revenue it might generate. Use this cost and income analysis to create a realistic budget for the event. The budget should include all possible forms of income, including registration fees, sponsorships, donations, spectator fees, parking fees, and advertising fees. Depending on the size and scope of the event, your costs may include ticket printing, facility rental fees, equipment and trophy purchases, personnel costs, maintenance costs, lighting (if necessary), permits required by local authorities, security, emergency personnel, athletic trainers, food, and perhaps merchandise for sale. Carefully planning the costs and potential income helps you ensure that the event stays within budget.

Always develop a conservative budget; it is much better to use a conservative budget and bring in more money than you spend than it is to go over budget. Your feasibility study should

Photo courtesy of Colorado State University.

Large events may require a very detailed accounting of income and expenses.

have outlined all expenses and areas of income. Using this information as a start, you should be able to develop a sound budget and then stick to it. If this is the first time you have implemented the event, be especially conservative, since you never know what emergencies might arise. If this is a repeated event, you should already have a good indication of where money will come from and where it will be spent.

Once you have established the budget, it is time to develop procedures for managing income. If the event carries a registration fee, how will participants pay it? Once the fees are paid, how will the checks, cash, or credit card numbers be secured and deposited? If cashiers are involved in accepting money, procedures need to be implemented to ensure that the cashiers are accountable for money they receive. Any time people handle cash, the possibility exists that some of it will be taken, and the event manager must put procedures in place to account for and secure the money coming in. If tickets are sold, keep count of the number of tickets sold and reconcile the cash on hand with the number of tickets sold to help ensure that all the money is deposited appropriately. When a large amount of money is taken in, establish a safe place to keep it until it can be taken to the bank; one way to do this is to locate a safe on the premises. Always have two persons deposit money to the safe or bank in order to reduce the risk that some of the money will disappear. Overall, then, putting proper accounting procedures into place helps make the event financially successful.

According to Mull, Bayless, Ross, and Jamieson (1987, pp. 244–246), responsibility for fee collection involves the following aspects:

- Training and supervising collection personnel
- Conducting financial transactions with participants and performing necessary cash register functions (sales, rentals, charges, voids, and refunds)
- Interpreting and enforcing policies, including those that govern fee scheduling, waivers, refunds, service charges, eligibility, and payment methods
- Securing collected funds, making safety deposits, preparing end-of-shift reports, and reconciling differences
- Issuing tickets, permits, identification cards, hand stamps, badges, and receipts
- Checking users' eligibility
- Performing bookkeeping that records, posts, and files daily income receipts
- Providing feedback and receiving and channeling comments regarding fees, charge policies, supplies, and procedures

A solid financial plan serves as the cornerstone for any successful event. It is worth your time and energy to organize your financial plan before initiating any other areas of planning for the event.

STAFFING PLANS

Proper staffing is crucial to a successful special event. Its importance has been emphasized by the American Sport Education Program (ASEP; 1996, p. 49):

> *A common mistake of less experienced athletic administrators and directors is failing to staff adequately and being reluctant to ask others for help, leaving an inordinate work load for themselves. The consequence often is that these directors are so busy performing various functions that they neglect their major responsibility—the coordinating and supervising of the other staff. If you are in charge of a large event, the importance of surrounding yourself with competent people cannot be underestimated because delegating responsibility is paramount to running this type of event. Recognize that staffing is not only recruiting the right people but also training, communicating with, motivating, supervising, evaluating, paying, and recognizing those who work with you to conduct the event.*

ASEP also outlined the following steps for creating staffing plans (1996, pp. 49–52):

1. Determine the staff required to conduct the event.
2. Recruit the volunteers needed.
3. Hire the employees needed.
4. Make assignments to all staff.
5. Provide orientation and training.
6. Plan the communication system with the staff.
7. Plan for the supervision of the staff.
8. Plan for the payment and/or recognition of your staff.

From the feasibility study, you should have a good indication of the scope of the event and the number of volunteers or staff you need in order to make the event successful. Do not underestimate the number of staff necessary. If the event director ends up being too busy managing less important areas of the event, he or she will not have time to plan and manage the more crucial areas. Once you have identified the number of staff required, it is time to recruit volunteers or hire staff, or both. You are likely to have little trouble recruiting volunteers for larger, more attractive events; in fact, in these cases you may have to do nothing more than announce the need for volunteers. Sawyer, Hypes, and Hypes (2004, p. 235) identified the following guidelines for working with volunteers:

- The 25 percent rule states that 25 percent of volunteers will do nearly all that is asked of them.
- The 20 percent rule refers to individuals who are truly effective—the real producers and result getters.
- Volunteers have feelings, so make them feel valuable and wanted. Treat them with respect and provide them with special privileges to reward them for their contributions.
- Volunteers have wants and needs. Satisfy them.
- Volunteers have suggestions. Seek their input.
- Volunteers have specific interests. Provide options and alternatives for them.
- Volunteers have specific competences. Recognize these skills and do not attempt to place square pegs in round holes.
- Volunteers are individuals working with other individuals. Encourage them to work as a team, not as competing individuals.
- Volunteers are not (usually) professionals in the organization or profession. Treat them with special understanding and empathy.
- Volunteers are not paid staff. Try not to include them in staff politics.
- Volunteers want to be of assistance. Let them know how they are doing (feedback), answer their questions, and provide good two-way communication.
- Volunteers have the potential to be excellent recruiters, especially through networking, of other potentially helpful volunteers.
- Volunteers can be educated to assume a variety of roles within the fundraising process.
- Volunteers are able to grow in professional competence with appropriate and timely training, motivation, and opportunity (p. 235).

Once you have your volunteers and staff in place, make sure that they understand their roles and responsibilities. Sawyer (2009, p. 17) outlines several pitfalls in designing an in-service education program:

- Feeding too much information at one time
- Telling without demonstrating
- Lacking patience
- Lacking preparation
- Failing to build in feedback
- Failing to reduce tension in the audience

Make sure that you plan your training program well. If you train your volunteers and staff properly, you will feel more comfortable with delegating authority to them and therefore will have more time for the supervision role that you should be performing.

The first step in volunteer and staff training is to develop a policies and procedures manual that outlines exactly what must be done and under what conditions it must be done. By setting clear expectations, the manual helps employees perform at their best. Staff training sessions can be conducted to clearly demonstrate the policies and procedures and to discuss the reasoning behind them. Volunteers and staff are more likely to enforce policies and procedures if they have a clear understanding of why they were put in place. You can now move on to activities, such as role playing and game situations, that reinforce the policies and allow management to see how the volunteers and staff perform under event-like conditions.

RULES AND OFFICIALS PLANS

Most sport events involve some type of rules, and developing clear rules in the beginning prevents problems later on. If rules and procedures are ambiguous, you will encounter problems, and people will protest. Depending on the event, rules may already be established and officials provided. For example, at a state soccer championship, the rules have already been established, and the state governing body provides the officials. If the event is not sponsored by a state or collegiate governing body, you may need to develop rules on your own; however, if the activity is a standard event, generic rules are probably available on the web. Preview all rules and establish exceptions or additional rules as needed to suit the type or location of your event. Also give some thought to eligibility rules for the event. Will you allow the general public to participate (e.g., in a road race), or will you restrict participation to current students, faculty, and staff (e.g., in a weekend basketball tournament)? Clearly stated eligibility rules help the event run smoothly.

Next, it is time to recruit the officiating crews and other staff (e.g., scorekeepers). If the event is sponsored by another group, it may have already taken care of the officials; otherwise, you will need to recruit and train them. Officials for campus recreational sports special events can generally be recruited from current intramural officiating staff if the activity is similar to events or leagues already organized on campus. If not, officials used for other activities might serve well for this event too. Allocate time to train the officials in any special rules for the event; officials who are unclear about rules hinder participants' enjoyment of the activity.

Generally, you can expect some problems with officiating, so it is worth considering ahead of time how you will handle protests of officials' calls or rule interpretations. If the event is short (e.g., 1 day), you may not have time for elaborate protest procedures. In these situations, it is important to have a supervisor on-site to make instant decisions about protests; this way, even if the decision goes against the protesting team, at least its members had a chance to voice their concerns.

Your event is also likely to be affected by the presence or absence of good sporting behavior. To minimize problems, establish policies and guidelines before the event and ensure that all staff know how to deal with participants and spectators who behave in an unsporting fashion. Security staff should also know what procedures to follow if a participant or spectator needs to be removed from the facility.

Each event you stage will have rules to be followed by either the participants or the spectators. Careful thought and planning must be put into these rules to ensure that the activity is enjoyable for everyone involved.

RISK, EMERGENCY, AND CRISIS PLANS

Every event planner needs to understand risk management techniques and develop emergency or crisis plans. According to Mull, Bayless, Ross, and Jamieson (1987), "Risk management is simply common sense and a feeling of ownership in your organization's safety program. The goal of a risk management program is to provide a safe environment for visitors and employees." (p. 327). Contingency plans should be developed for all possible situations that might arise during the event. ASEP (1996) has identified the following components of a risk management plan: "inspection of facilities, equipment housing areas, and all transportation aspects of the event; the presence of properly trained and educated coaches, officials, volunteers, and participants; as well as proper supervision over all aspects of the event" (p. 14). Follow the checklist shown in figure 13.1 for a good start in planning for event safety.

Emergency or crisis action plans are important components of risk management plans. As stated by Spengler, Anderson, Connaughton, and Baker (2009), one "essential risk management function is to prepare, communicate, and practice an emergency action plan (EAP) specific to one's sport program or facility. A properly planned and rehearsed EAP can help an organization reduce the amount of time it takes to respond to a medical emergency and respond in a manner that results in the best possible provision of care to an injured person" (p. 60). In preparing an emergency action plan, be creative and think about all the possible emergencies that might occur during the event. Be aware that crises are "large in scope, negative, and disruptive, and they can threaten an organization's mission and reputation. During a crisis, the mission of the organization is usually placed on hold until the crisis is resolved. Examples of crises are catastrophic weather events, fires, and terrorist events" (Spengler et al., p. 63).

Another part of a risk management plan is to prepare for handling injuries during the event. Sharp, Moorman, and Claussen (2007) identify "two major issues . . . associated with the provision of emergency medical care to participants: (1) making sure that qualified personnel are available to render emergency first aid and CPR; and (2) ensuring that there is a protocol to get outside medical personnel to the site as quickly as possible" (p. 489). Injuries will happen, and you need to have a plan for responding when they do. A good first step is to have qualified staff onsite—athletic trainers or at least someone with first aid and CPR certification. Depending on

CHECKLIST OF EVENT RISKS

Identify the risks in conducting this event by answering yes or no to the following questions:
Have you ensured . . .

	Yes	No
Proper supervision in all areas used by the event?		
A plan for occurrence of adverse weather conditions?		
Safety checks for playing areas?		
Checks for defective or unsafe equipment?		
Facility maintenance before and during the event?		
Plans for emergencies affecting all in attendance (spectators, workers, participants)?		
Plans for attending to participants' first aid or medical emergencies?		
Injury report plans?		
The presence of appropriate medical personnel and supplies?		
Fair and equitable opportunities for all participants?		
Qualified officials and other event personnel?		
Proper spectator facilities?		
Protected areas for spectators?		
A system for warning spectators of any possible risks?		
Proof of insurance for any drivers providing transportation?		

Figure 13.1 Sample checklist of event risks.

Reprinted, by permission, from R. Martens, 1996, *Event management for sport directors* (Champaign, IL: Human Kinetics), 68.

the event, it may also be necessary to place an ambulance with emergency medical technicians (EMTs) on-site, since transporting a seriously injured person immediately to a hospital can mean the difference between life and death.

Popke (2010) outlines 10 important steps to follow before, during, and after a critical incident:

1. Be prepared.
2. Cater to the victim's needs first.
3. Call an EMS (emergency medical services) crew.
4. Effectively handle bystanders.
5. Secure the facility.
6. Notify supervisors.
7. Hold a staff debriefing session.
8. Keep the media at bay.
9. Fill out all related paperwork.
10. Hold another staff debriefing session.

These important steps are proposed for a pool-related emergency but make a good checklist for any emergency plan for event management.

Another safety area to be concerned about is crowd management. If your event is going to attract a large audience, you will need to devote considerable time to planning how to manage all of those people. In the world of sports today, it is almost a given that somebody will get out of control at a large event, which puts pressure on management to respond appropriately. As Van der Smissen (1990) stated, "It is clear . . . that management does owe a duty to protect a spectator from unreasonable risk of harm from other spectators" (p. 15.12). Components of good crowd management include a trained and competent staff, effective procedures and policies, good signage, services for people with disabilities, and an effective communication system.

No matter how small the event may be, good planning for crowd management can ensure that everyone has an enjoyable experience. Sharp, Moorman, and Claussen (2007) give this advice: "Develop crowd control plans based on factors specific to a contest, such as whether there is a rivalry, whether there has been prior violence, whether alcohol will be served, and what the demographics of the contest are likely to be. Use all information available to determine what crowd behaviors may be foreseeable" (p. 522). If the competitors are known for an intense rivalry that can generate problems, you should arrange for extra security and plan your crowd-control strategy. Whenever alcohol is involved in an activity (whether sold at the event or as a part of pregame tailgating), you should plan extra security to deal with alcohol-related problems.

You can never plan too much for emergencies and crises. Being creative and thinking through any and all possibilities helps ensure that when something does happen, you are ready.

REGISTRATION PLANS

The first step in making registration plans is to determine who is eligible to register. Are you hosting an on-campus event for students only? Are you opening the event to the public? Are varsity or professional athletes eligible to participate? Determining your eligibility policies helps target your audience for your marketing plan.

Next, decide what type of information you need to request on the registration form. At a minimum, of course, you need the participant's name and contact information. If you are developing different levels of competition, you may also need to know something about his or her ability, age, or gender. For a road race, participants are usually categorized by age and gender so that you can determine a winner in each of various categories. For a sporting event, you might want to establish competitive and recreational brackets. If you are staging a team event, you will need the names of all members of each team.

Another important aspect of registration is determining the procedures that participants must follow in order to register. Where should they submit the registration form? By what date? Will you accept late registration forms? If the event carries a fee and you are going to accept late registrations, you may want to increase the fee for entries received after the deadline. Once the registration forms have been received, what will you do with them? Do you have a computer database set up to store the information? How will you organize the information on the day of the event? Answering these questions helps you ensure that the event is well organized and well run.

SCHEDULING FACILITIES

The facilities needed for your event should have been identified in the feasibility study. Reserving the proper facilities is one of the most important steps in event management. Without the facility, there is no event. Thus it is always important to check and double-check that the facility is reserved for your event. Make sure that you reserve enough time to set up, tear down, and clean up after your event. Once the facility has been reserved, make plans for facility access and preparation. Do you need special keys for the staff to access the facility for the event? Do you need to complete any forms to have the facility set up appropriately for the event? Are there any extra maintenance requirements for the event? Planning for the event will probably require you to contact the manager in charge of custodial services, as well as facility security.

EQUIPMENT, UNIFORMS, AND SUPPLIES

It is essential to have appropriate and well-functioning equipment in place for the event. Uniforms are also important. Depending on the event, you may be responsible for uniforms, and you should also think about uniforms for the staff. Dressing staff in an easily identifiable uniform helps greatly in any emergency and when participants have questions. The size of the event determines whether you should use different uniforms for different positions. For instance, at a major event such as the Olympics or World Cup, you would expect different uniforms for people who occupy various levels in the chain of command. Different uniforms help everyone identify who they should go to with questions. Are you going to have ushers? If so, do they have a uniform? What about ticket takers and concessions workers? It is also important to ensure adequate stock of supplies—if you run out of toilet paper or hand towels, that is what people will remember about your event.

Follow these steps provided by the American Sport Education Program (2006, pp. 27–29) to ensure that people remember the event and not a lack of equipment, uniforms, or supplies:

1. Inventory what is available.
2. Determine what is needed for the event.
3. Purchase what is needed.
4. Inventory new purchases.
5. Distribute the equipment, uniforms, and supplies.
6. Plan for storage and security.
7. Inspect and maintain the equipment.

AWARDS

For any large event, you will want to give awards and recognition. Are you planning an event with a champion? If so, you need a trophy (or trophies, for a team event). Or will you provide ribbons to the top finishers? Such questions must be answered well in advance of the event so that everything will arrive in plenty of time. It is also important to recognize volunteers, staff, and sponsors. Most people want recognition for what they have done to help out. Plan some time during the event to recognize people; most of us like to hear our name linked with praise, so make time to acknowledge the staff, especially volunteers. Make sure that the awards are properly stored and ready for distribution at the end of the event. For smaller events, you can use a microphone to call up the champions and recognize volunteers and staff. For larger events, you may hold an awards ceremony. For any event, plan well in advance for distributing awards.

FOOD SERVICE PLANS

Food service plans for a special event can include everything from concessions management to working with outside food contractors to preparing meals for celebrities, participants, or possibly staff. If you are bringing in celebrities for your events, you need to plan for meals while they are in town, which can be as simple as ordering fast food or contracting with campus dining services to provide meals. Food for participants may also be a necessity. For example, if you host a long-distance race, the participants need food along the way and at the end of the race to replenish their energy, as well as drinks to replace lost fluids and thus prevent dehydration. Depending on the length and scope of your event, you may also provide meals to staff and volunteers.

Sawyer (2009) outlines the following operations that a concession stand operator should understand: "(1) how to serve good food at a reasonable price, (2) development of marketing strategy, (3) financial management, (4) business planning, (5) purchasing, (6) inventory management, (7) business law, (8) health codes, (9) OSHA regulations, (10) selection of insurance, (11) how to advertise, (12) selection of personnel, (13) stocking the concession area, (14) maintaining the equipment, (15) housekeeping requirements, (16) how to establish price, and (17) convenience foods" (p. 120). Knowing what food will be popular is important for the financial success of the operation—large quantities of food that attendees don't want will not generate much profit.

Complying with health codes is critical in concession stand management. Any establishment selling food is subject to local health codes, and you must understand what is required. If the event is small and all you are selling is prepackaged candy purchased wholesale, your sales may not be affected by codes. For larger events, however, especially those requiring special preparation, you need to be cognizant of local codes and regulations and investigate the need for insurance. When conducting an event on campus, university food services can be a helpful asset for food preparation and sales.

TRANSPORTATION PLANS

Transportation may also be an issue for your event. Sawyer (2009, p. 210) notes that a special event may affect the community by bringing more traffic onto its roads even as it may reduce road capacity due to special event staging arrangement. "The first step toward achieving an accurate prediction of event-generated travel demand and potential transportation system capacity constraints involves gaining an understanding of the event characteristics and how these characteristics affect transportation operations. In turn, practitioners can classify the planned special event in order to draw comparisons between the subject event and similar historical events to shape travel forecasts and gauge transportation impacts" (Sawyer, p. 210). Does your facility have adequate parking for the number of people who may attend the event? How will you control foot traffic into and out of the facility? How will you control vehicular traffic to and from the facility? If your event is conducted on a street or road, have you contacted local law enforcement agencies to restrict use of the roads during the event?

Berlonghi identifies the following concerns regarding event traffic control (as cited in Walker & Stotler, 1997, p. 112):

> *As with every type of plan, the various traffic control groups (campus, city, county, and state) must provide input to the traffic plan. The intersections that have higher-than-normal accident rates must be identified, and extra personnel should assist out-of-town fans through these problem areas. Posting adequate signs on major thoroughfares to direct and inform spectators also decreases problems. Altering the duration of signal lights during ingress and egress assists vehicular traffic through most congested areas. Also, by providing bus lanes, alternative methods of transportation decrease the number of vehicles parking at your event. In addition, notifying local residents and businesses of game-day traffic plans helps community relations. Finally, by establishing emergency routes for police, fire, and medical personnel, dangerous situations may be quickly and safely overcome.*

Parking is also an important component of event traffic plans. "To create a smooth transition, parking must be [handled by means of] a coordinated effort between law enforcement officials and employees in your facility's parking lots. Since your parking employees are the first

The University of Texas at San Antonio, Department of Campus Recreation.

Staff and signage are needed to ensure the safety of event participants who use roads.

individuals with whom spectators come in[to] contact, first impressions are extremely important. These individuals must establish the 'tone' as to the proper behavior condoned by facility management (Antee and Swinburn, as cited in Walker & Stotler, 1997, p. 113). Graham, Goldblatt, and Delpy (1995) note that "a spectator's first impression of your event may be through the automobile windshield upon arrival in your parking lot. The last impression most certainly will be of your parking facility and traffic control" (p. 53). Graham et al. (p. 53) offer the following questions regarding positive parking interaction:

- Do you have a jumper cable service in your lot to assist stranded drivers?
- Do you have adequate lighting, signage, and parking hosts that help guests feel secure while reducing the likelihood of crime?
- Should you provide a parking shuttle from a satellite parking lot to the front gate to assist your guests and reduce parking congestion?
- Should you work closely with a municipal transportation agency to encourage spectators to use mass transit by offering an incentive, such as discounted admission or a sponsored ad gift specialty?

As Graham, Goldblatt, and Delpy (1995) note, "The goal of any successful arrival and departure is to ensure a safe, easy, and fun experience for the spectator" (p. 53).

Stedman, Goldblatt, and Delpy (1995) sought to inspire effective transportation management with the following thought exercise:

> *In order to make transporting guests a fun experience, put yourself in the position of the guest who has had the worst possible time prior to arriving at your parking facility. Perhaps they traveled halfway to the venue and then discovered that they didn't have their tickets and had to return home. Or perhaps the guest ran out of gas and had to walk the rest of the way. What can you do as a sport event management professional to transform their unpleasant experience into a surprisingly positive one? The answer you design will control their behavior and improve their perception and appreciation of your event (p. 54).*

Going all out to make the event as pleasant and enjoyable as possible increases the chance that it will not be just a one-and-done but an event that endures year after year.

HOUSING PLANS

If your event will attract participants or spectators from out of town, it is a good idea to make housing plans. These plans may be as simple as including a list of hotels or accommodations in the registration packet. If you are bringing in special participants or officials, however, it may be your responsibility to make and pay for their housing arrangements. For on-campus activities limited to students, faculty, or staff, there will probably be no housing arrangements that concern you.

PROMOTION PLANS

Any event worth holding is also worth promoting. It is crucial to identify the target audience and determine how to reach it. No matter how well the event is planned, if you don't reach people who will participate, your event will fail due to poor attendance. Today's technology allows you to spread the word in many different ways—for example, e-mail, text message, websites, and Facebook—in addition to tried-and-true approaches such as placing posters in dining halls and writing information on sidewalks with chalk. The downside is that information overload may cause messages to be overlooked or discarded by members of the target audience; thus it is worth your time to consult with members of the target audience regarding the best way to reach them. At the end of the event, let the community know what happened. Publicizing winners or results in media outlets gives extra recognition to participants, staff, and volunteers. Posting pictures of the activity on a website can also provide a good mechanism for marketing future events.

COMMUNICATION PLANS

During an event, communication with staff is critical. The American Sport Education Program (1996) has discussed the importance of making communication plans: "So often we see technically well-organized events break down because of communication problems. Don't assume anything with communication—others can't read your mind. In developing your event plans, don't forget the importance of good communication among yourself, your staff, your participants, and others" (p. 45). ASEP identifies the following people for whom you need a communication plan: staff, participants and coaches, spectators, members of the media, and representatives of the sport's governing body (pp. 45–46).

Communication with staff is critical. All staff members should be in constant contact with each other. They should also be kept informed about what is going on and about any appropriate responses. For smaller events, this may be accomplished by simply walking around and talking to staff members throughout the event. For larger events, or events held in multiple venues, good communication may involve using two-way radios or cell phones. Text messaging should be avoided, or limited, since it may take time for the text message to reach the recipient, and thus it may arrive too late. Text messages may arrive late due to excessive traffic on the service provider or inattention by the recipient. At least with a phone call you know that the recipient did not receive the call.

Participants and coaches need to know when to arrive for the event, what equipment to bring, and how to get there. All rules, policies, and procedures should be communicated to participants well in advance so that everyone understands what is supposed to happen and what is required of them. Sometimes a dispute arises due to a participant's failure to read instructions, but putting instructions in writing and providing them to participants allows the staff to point out policies and procedures as needed.

Some type of public address system should be available in case of emergency. For everyone's safety, you need to be able to relay specific emergency directions to staff, participants, and spectators. Letting everyone know what to do in an emergency can save valuable time and possibly lives.

EVENT EVALUATION PLAN

Any event worth doing is worth evaluating. Wever (as cited in Boucher & Weese, 1991, p.

321) identifies the following reasons for conducting an evaluation:

- Assessing the value, legitimacy, or worth of a program
- Obtaining evidence that will assess and demonstrate the effectiveness and efficiency of the overall campus recreational sports program or areas within the general program
- Comparing the effect of various program methods or approaches
- Determining the strengths, weaknesses, successes, and failures of a program
- Judging the quality of a program
- Determining program expansion
- Examining a specific program, process, service, or facility provided by a campus recreational sports department
- Determining whether or not a program is moving in the right direction
- Determining whether the program meets the needs for which it is designed
- Justifying past or projected expenditures to determine program costs in terms of money, human effort, or both
- Acquiring evidence to satisfy someone who has demanded evidence of effect
- Collecting information from different databases that can later be used to undertake further research on program performance
- Providing a means for linking the university community, administration, and campus recreational sports staff in the tasks of planning and delivering program services
- Justifying the present personnel who administer the program, as well as providing evidence to justify realigning the present personnel structure, support the present personnel structure, or support the inclusion of additional personnel to lead new program areas
- Determining viability of present recreational facilities if there is a need to renovate or expand facilities to properly accommodate new or existing programs

You can always do better, but you don't know what to change unless you conduct thorough evaluations. ASEP (1996, pp. 47–48) has offered the following steps for developing an event evaluation plan: Determine the system (or tool) to be used for evaluation, prepare the evaluation questionnaire and have it completed by those who have been selected to evaluate the event, and review and summarize the evaluation comments. Evaluations can be conducted through surveys, one-on-one interviews, focus groups, or any of a variety of other avenues. Members of every group participating in the event—athletes, spectators, employees, volunteers, and sponsors—should be contacted for their input on possible improvements for the event.

Develop an evaluation form well in advance of the event and distribute it widely. When you have gathered all of the information, review it and compile a list of improvements that can be made for the next time the event is conducted. Keep in mind that some people like to complain, so you need to do some investigation to determine whether the complaint is legitimate or just someone complaining for the sake of complaining.

In addition to evaluating the event, you should also evaluate the event staff. Sawyer (2009, p. 18) proposes the following purposes for staff performance evaluations:

- Provide employees with an idea of how they are doing.
- Identify promotable employees or those who should be demoted.
- Administer the salary program.
- Provide a basis for supervisor–employer communication.
- Assist supervisors in knowing their workers better.
- Identify training needs.
- Help with proper employee placement within the organization.
- Identify employees for layoff or recall.
- Validate the selection process and evaluate other personnel activities (e.g., training programs, psychological tests, physical examinations).

- Improve departmental employee effectiveness.
- Determine special talent.
- Ascertain progress at the end of probationary periods for employees with performance difficulties.
- Furnish inputs to other personnel programs.
- Supply information for use in grievance interviews.

Conducting evaluations of programs and staff can take considerable time, but it is well worth the effort since it helps you identify necessary changes for future success.

SUMMARY

A positive result from a feasibility study signals the start for planning a successful event. Along the way, many pitfalls can negatively affect the event's potential. Sawyer (2009) presents some of these pitfalls: "'But we've always done it that way!'; lack of creativity and innovation; uninspired marketing; poorly selected and [poorly] trained personnel; too much; too often; not enough money; timing! timing! timing!; event of poor quality; and poor physical conditions (e.g., insufficient parking, poor traffic control, lack of signage)" (p. 243). Careful planning in the areas outlined in this chapter helps you avoid pitfalls and make your special event a success. A comprehensive feasibility study will have the important details of the event worked out so that the pitfalls can be avoided. Developing excitement about the event will increase creativity and innovation and lead to inspired marketing. Selection criteria and training of personnel should be thoroughly developed before proceeding with the event. Other pitfalls can also be avoided by extensive pre-event planning.

Glossary

assessment—Evaluation of programs to determine whether they are effectively doing what they are supposed to do.

benchmarking—Process of contacting others with similar programs or facilities to see how they run their programs or operate their facilities.

References

American Sport Education Program. (1996). *Event management for sport directors*. Champaign, IL: Human Kinetics.

Boucher, R.L., & Weese, J.W. (1991). *Management of recreational sports in higher education*. Dubuque, IA: Brown.

Graham, S., Goldblatt, J., & Delpy, L. (1995). *The ultimate guide to sport event management and marketing*. New York: McGraw-Hill.

Mull, R.F., Bayless, K.G., Ross, C.M., & Jamieson, L.M. (1997). *Recreational sport management* (3rd ed.). Champaign, IL: Human Kinetics.

National Intramural-Recreational Sports Association. (2009). *Campus recreational sports facilities: Planning, design, and construction guidelines*. Champaign, IL: Human Kinetics.

Popke. (2010, July). 10 Steps to Managing Critical Incidents at Commercial Pools. http://athleticbusiness.com/articles/article.aspx?articleid=3577&zoneid=33.

Sawyer, T.H. (2009). *Facility management for physical activity and sport*. Champaign, IL: Sagamore.

Sawyer, T.H., Hypes, M., & Hypes, J.A. (2004). *Financing the sport enterprise*. Champaign, IL: Sagamore.

Sharp, L.A., Moorman, A.M., & Claussen, C.L. (2007). *Sport law: A managerial approach*. Scottsdale, AZ: Holcomb Hathaway.

Spengler, J.O., Anderson, P.M., Connaughton, D.P., & Baker, T.A. (2009). *Introduction to sport law*. Champaign, IL: Human Kinetics.

Van der Smissen, B. (1990). *Legal liability and risk management for public and private entities*. Cincinnati: Anderson.

Walker, M.L., & Stotlar, D.K. (1997). *Sport facility management*. Sudbury, MA: Jones and Bartlett.

Index

Note: The italicized *f* and *t* following page numbers refer to figures and tables, respectively.

A

AAHPERD (American Alliance for Health, Physical Education, Recreation and Dance) 41, 62, 112
Abacus Sports Installations 211
ABCD method 190, 191*t*
accountability 4-5, 55, 66, 110
accreditation agencies 107-108, 111-112
ACCT (Association for Challenge Course Technology) 34*t*
ACE (American Council on Exercise) 34*t*, 42, 62, 112, 161, 180
ACPA (American College Personnel Association) 5, 41-42, 107
ACSM (American College of Sports Medicine) 34*t*, 43, 62, 112, 180, 203
ACSM's Health/Fitness Facility Standards and Guidelines 203
active learning 189
active shooter plan 133-134
ADA Accessibility Guidelines for Recreation Facilities 206
adaptive programs 3
administration and support 55
adventure challenge programs 201
AED (automated external defibrillator) certification 34*t*, 129, 161, 179
AEE (Association for Experiential Education) 34*t*, 42
Aerobics and Fitness Association of America (AFAA) 34*t*, 42-43, 62, 112, 161, 180
aerobics classes 200
AFAA (Aerobics and Fitness Association of America) 34*t*, 42-43, 62, 112, 161, 180
affective learning 192
AHA (American Heart Association) 34*t*, 179
alcohol 238
alumni memberships 218
American Alliance for Health, Physical Education, Recreation and Dance (AAHPERD) 41, 62, 112
American Association for Health, Physical Education and Recreation 11, 12
American Association for Higher Education 4
American College of Sports Medicine (ACSM) 34*t*, 43, 62, 112, 180, 203
American College Personnel Association (ACPA) 5, 41-42, 107
American Council on Exercise (ACE) 34*t*, 42, 62, 112, 161, 180
American Heart Association (AHA) 34*t*, 179
American Mountain Guide Association 112
American National Standards Institute (ANSI) 203
American Physical Education Association 11
American Red Cross (ARC) 34*t*, 112, 129, 179, 180
American Society of Testing and Materials International (ASTM) 203
American Sport Education Program (ASEP) 234-235, 239, 242
Americans with Disabilities Act 13, 206-207
Amherst College 8, 9, 10
ANSI (American National Standards Institute) 203
anthropometrical measurement 9
AORE (Association of Outdoor Recreation and Education) 35, 42, 62, 112
aquatics 2, 13
- aquatic facilities 202-203
- careers in 26, 30*f*
- certifications 34*t*, 180
- equipment 156
- learning outcomes in 190-191

ARC (American Red Cross) 34*t*, 112, 129, 179, 180
architects, facility 205
ASEP (American Sport Education Program) 234-235, 239, 242
assessment
- about 105-106
- accountability and 55, 110
- benchmarking 112-113
- budget 110, 115
- departments 115
- dissemination of information 106, 117-118
- economics of 109-110
- ethics and 110
- facilities 113-114
- focus of 106-108
- methodology and research design 115-117, 117*t*
- personnel 106, 114
- professional organizations for 112
- program 113
- program planning 194, 195
- research in 106, 116
- resources for 118
- special events 231-233, 242-244
- standards of comparison 111-113
- student learning outcomes 108-109, 109*t*
- transparency in 106, 110-111
- types and areas of 113-115
- web-based 161

assistant directors 28, 30*f*
associate directors 28, 29*f*
Association for Challenge Course Technology (ACCT) 34*t*
Association for Experiential Education (AEE) 34*t*, 42
Association of Outdoor Recreation and Education (AORE) 35, 42, 62, 112
assumption of risk 124
Astin, Alexander 33
ASTM (American Society of Testing and Materials International) 203
athletic training services 229
audits 80
automated external defibrillator (AED) certification 34*t*, 129, 161, 179
awards 239

B

babysitting services 227
badminton 199
Barry University 5
baseball 201
basketball 199
behavioral learning 192
benchmarking 112-113, 209
biohazardous material 139
blog 157
bonding insurance 80
Boston, McKinley 5
bottom-up budgeting 66
Bowdoin College 8, 10
Bowling Green State University 164, 178*f*
branding
- about 2, 96-97
- components of 97-98
- defining phase 99-101
- delivery phase 103
- design phase 101-102, 101*f*, 102*f*
- development phase 102-103
- discovery phase 98-99

breach 125
Brown University 6, 8
budgets and controls
- about 65
- adjustment 75
- budget development 66-72, 66*f*, 69*t*-70*t*
- budget execution 72-75
- budget review 75-79, 76*t*, 77*t*, 78*t*
- budget submission and approval 72
- capital budgets 65-66
- components 67-68
- costs 72
- financial statements 69-71, 69*t*, 70*t*, 76-77, 76*t*, 77*t*, 78*t*
- internal controls 79-81, 80*f*
- operating budgets 65
- pricing decisions 71-72
- special events financial planning 233-234
- subcodes 74
- types 66-67

Bunker, Kent 15

business procedures 32*t*
business services department 55

C

Campus Labs 116
Campus Recreation: Essentials for the Professional (Franklin & Hardin) 33
campus recreational sports
 benefits 3
 defining 1-4
 evolution of 5-13
 fees 17-18
 financial challenges 17-18
 intramural movement 10-12
 issues and trends 16-18
 organizational fit 14-15
 organizational position 15, 185
 organizational purpose 3-4
 partnerships 13
 professionalization 12-13
 professional preparation 17
 program and facility elements 2-3
campus recreational sports careers
 academic preparation for 32*t*, 33-35, 34*t*
 attaining professional skills via 35-39
 competencies and skills needed 31
 degree programs for 33-35, 34*t*
 graduate work experiences 36-38
 growth of profession 25-26
 internships in 38-39
 job titles and responsibilities 28, 29*f*, 30*f*
 philosophical foundations 31-33, 32*t*
 principles of 43-44
 professional body of knowledge 31
 professional development opportunities 39-43
 professional preparation 28-33
 specializations within 26-28
 undergraduate work experiences 35-36
cardio equipment 154-155
cardiopulmonary resuscitation (CPR) certification 34*t*, 129, 161, 179
CAS (Council for the Advancement of Standards in Higher Education) 4, 13, 55, 62, 108, 111, 187-188, 189*t*
causation 125
CCSSE (Community College Survey of Student Engagement) 59
certifications, specialty 34-35, 34*t*, 112, 127, 128, 129, 161, 177-180. *See also* training staff
CHEMA (Council of Higher Education Management Associations) 4
Chickering, Arthur 33, 186-187
child care services 226-227
CIRP (Cooperative Institutional Research Program) 59
Cleveland State University 3
Club Natural High (Univ. of Southern Mississippi) 92
cognitive learning 192
College of William and Mary 6
Collegiate Recreational Sports Facilities Construction Report 2010-2015 (NIRSA) 17
colonial colleges 6, 7
Columbia University 6
Commission on the Future of Higher Education (U.S. Dept. of Education Secretary) 4
Committee on Women's Athletics 11
Community College Survey of Student Engagement (CCSSE) 59
community programs 3
community relationships 60-61
comparative statement 69, 70*t*
Competencies of Sport Managers Instrument 17
Connolly, Frank 161
consent 125-126
constructivism 5, 18
contributory negligence 125
Cooperative Institutional Research Program (CIRP) 59
coordinators 28
Corbett, John 11
Council for the Advancement of Standards in Higher Education (CAS) 4, 13, 55, 62, 108, 111, 187-188, 189*t*
Council of Higher Education Management Associations (CHEMA) 4
Covey, Stephen 48
CPR (cardiopulmonary resuscitation) certification 34*t*, 129, 161, 179
Craver, Forrest 3, 11
crisis management. *See* emergency response plan
crowd control 238
customer interaction chart 90*f*
customer service 173
cycle of intentionality 183

D

damages 125
Dartmouth College 6, 8, 13
Darwin, Charles 5
data collection 116-117, 117*t*
degree programs 33-35, 34*t*
DePaul University 223*t*
Dewey, John 4
Dickinson College 3, 11
directors 28, 55
diversity 13
documentation 140
duty to act 125

E

Education and Identity (Chickering) 186-187
Ellis & Associates 34*t*
e-mail communication 171
e-marketing 88, 96, 103, 156-158
emergency medical technicians (EMTs) 238
emergency response plan 127, 128*t*, 129-131, 131*f*, 173, 237-238
emergency response protocols 128*t*, 129-135, 130*t*, 131*f*
Emerging Recreational Sports Leaders 62
employee emergency procedures 131-132
employees. *See* human resources
encumbrance 77*t*
equipment
 asset management 137-138
 buying or leasing 73-74
 cardio equipment 154-155
 checkout 221-222, 222*t*
 competency 32*t*
 exercise and fitness equipment 154-155
 inspection checklist 138*t*
 rental to users 222-223
 replacement plan 138
 retail sales of 223*t*
 risk management 137-139, 138*t*
 for special events 239
 sports equipment 155-156
 strength equipment 155
 technology and 154-156
Erikson, Erik 33, 187
ethics 110
events. *See* special events
evolution 5
executive directors 55
exercise and fitness equipment 154-155
exergaming 155
experiential learning 4
 certifications 34*t*

F

facilities and facility management. *See also* risk management
 access control 135, 151-152
 Americans with Disabilities Act 206-207
 aquatic facilities 202-203
 assessment 113-114
 certifications 34*t*
 degrees for 32*t*
 design 204-206
 fabric structures 208
 facility operations 26, 55, 151-153
 future trends 207-208
 ice rinks 201-202
 indoor facilities 199-200
 maintenance 153, 210-213
 management software systems 149-151
 multi-use design 208
 outdoor facilities 200-201
 policies 135-136
 risk management 135-137
 scheduling 152-153, 208-209, 239
 security 136-137
 staffing 209-210
 standards 203-207
 technology in 148-153
 types 199-203
faculty 57
field hockey 201
fields, athletic 200-201
finances. *See* budgets and controls
financial statements 69-71, 69*t*, 70*t*, 76-77, 76*t*, 77*t*, 78*t*
fire emergency plan 132-133
first aid certification 34*t*, 129, 161, 179
First-Year Adventure trip (Kent State Univ.) 13
fitness, wellness, and exercise science organizations 42-43
fitness and wellness careers 26, 32*t*
fitness certifications 34*t*, 180
fitness programs 2
flooring 210, 211-213
Florida International University 15
Florida State University 2
focus groups 116
Follen, Karl 8
food services 227-229, 239-240
football 8, 201
formal learning 192-193

G

General and Specialty Standards for Collegiate Recreational Sports (NIRSA) 187
Georgia Southern University 2
GI Bill 11-12, 13
Girl Scouts 10
Good Samaritan laws 126
governance 32*t*
graduate assistantships 36, 44, 164-165
graduate work experiences 36-38
Graydon, Alexander 7
group exercise certifications 180
group relationships 52-53
gymnasiums 7-8

H

handball 199
Harper, William Rainey 11
Harper Wallace Harding planning model 184-195, 184*f*
Harvard Boat Club 8
Harvard University 6, 7, 8, 10
hazardous material management 139
hazards 124
higher education organizations 41-42
hiring. *See also* human resources
  interviewing 170-171
  job descriptions 166-167, 168*f*
  organizational charts 167, 169*f*
  recruitment 167
  references 169-170
  résumé review 169
Hiss, Anna 25
Hitchcock, Edward 9
holistic wellness 44
human resources. *See also* certifications, specialty; training staff
  assessment and 106
  certification of staff 177-188
  employee emergency procedures 131-132
  employee evaluation 174, 175*f*-177*f*
  full-time professional staff 163-164
  graduate assistants 164-165
  hiring 166-171, 168*f*, 169*f*
  interns 165-166
  motivation 174-177, 178*f*
  part-time professional staff 164
  personnel assessment 106, 114
  special events staff evaluations 243-244
  staff meetings 171-172
  staff supervision 209-210
  student employees 164
  types of employees 163-166
  volunteer staff 166

I

ICE (Institute for Credentialing Excellence) 112
ice rinks 201-202
IDEA Health and Fitness Association 41, 43
IFMA (International Facilities Management Association) 34*t*
implied consent 126
incremental budgeting 66
Indiana State University 17
informal learning 193
informal recreation 3
informed consent 125-126
inherent risk 125
injury response protocols 130*t*, 237-238
Institute for Credentialing Excellence (ICE) 112
instructional programs 3, 26-27
insurance 80, 240
Integrated Postsecondary Education Data System (IPEDS) 111
intercollegiate athletics 8, 10, 58
internal controls 79-81, 80*f*
International Facilities Management Association (IFMA) 34*t*
Internet marketing 88, 96, 103, 156-158
internships 165-166
Intramural Athletics (Mitchell) 11, 25
intramural clubs 2
intramural movement 3, 10-12
intramural sport 44, 192
intramural sport careers 26
intramural sport certifications 34*t*
Intramurals: Programming and Administration (Mueller) 5
IPEDS (Integrated Postsecondary Education Data System) 111

J

James Madison University 190
Jefferson, Thomas 7-8
Jeffries, John 9
job descriptions 28, 44, 166-167, 168*f*
Junior Club (Univ. of Pennsylvania) 8

K

Kansas State University 15
Kent State University 13
Kuh, George 33

L

lacrosse 201
laundry 224-225
leadership development 32*t*, 35, 52, 161
Lead On Conferences 35, 41, 62
learning
  and accountability 4-5
  active learning 189
  affective learning 192
  behavioral learning 192
  cocurricular units 57-58
  cognitive learning 192
  experiential learning 4
  formal learning 192-193
  informal learning 193
  learning outcomes 44, 106, 108-109, 109*t*, 190-194, 191*t*
  passive learning 189
Learning Reconsidered (ACPA et al.) 4-5, 13, 58, 107, 108, 112, 115
Learning Reconsidered 2: A Practical Guide to Implementing a Campus-Wide Focus on the Student Experience (ACPA et al.) 5, 58, 107, 108, 111, 112
LEED certification 154
leisure theory 33
Les Mills company 112
lifeguard certification 180
locker rooms 212-213, 224
Londono, Edward 15

M

maintenance, facility 153, 210-213
management 32*t*
management by walking around 172
Maple Flooring Manufacturers Association 211
marketing
  advertising 88
  audience 87
  banners 87
  branding 2, 96-103, 101*f*, 102*f*
  careers in 27
  e-marketing 88, 96
  marketing plan 88-92, 90*f*, 91*t*
  market research 93
  PEST analysis 86-87
  planning cycle 86*f*
  press releases 88
  print materials 87
  program promotion 85-88, 86*f*
  promotional strategies 87-88
  publicity 88
  signage 87, 88
  special events promotion 242
  sponsorship solicitation 92-95
  SWOT analysis 86
  technology use in 156-158
  vending machines 87-88
martial arts 200
massage services 230
membership services
  about 27, 215-216, 220-221
  alumni membership 218
  community membership 219
  dependents and children 218-219
  faculty/staff membership 218
  identifying users 216
  pricing 219-220, 221*t*
  student membership 216-218
methicillin-resistant staphylococcus aureus (MRSA) 213
Michigan State University 2
microblogging 157
Miller, Harvey 3
missing person plan 134-135
Mitchell, Elmer 3, 11, 17, 25
morality 9
MRSA (methicillin-resistant staphylococcus aureus) 213
muscular Christianity 10, 18

N

NASPA (National Association of Student Personnel Administrators) 5, 41, 107
NASSM (North American Society for Sport Management) 41
National Association of Student Personnel Administrators (NASPA) 5, 41, 107
National Coalition for Campus Children's Centers 227
National College of Physical Education Association for Men 11
National Commission for Certifying Agencies (NCCA) 112
National Commission on Accountability in Higher Education 4
National Commission on the Future of Higher Education 110
National Federation of State High School Associations (NFHS) 34*t*, 161
National Intramural Association (NIA) 12, 17, 26, 39
National Intramural-Recreational Sports Association (NIRSA) 3, 4, 12, 17, 35, 39-41, 40*f*, 62, 112
National Intramural Sports Council 12

National Outdoor Leadership School (NOLS) 42
National Recreation and Park Association (NRPA) 34*t*, 41, 112
National School of Recreational Sports Management 35, 41, 62
National Strength and Conditioning Association (NSCA) 34*t*
National Survey of Student Engagement (NSSE) 59, 116
National Swimming Pool Foundation (NSPF) 34*t*
NCCA (National Commission for Certifying Agencies) 112
negligence 123
networking 44
New Adventures trip (Ohio Univ.) 13
New Foundations course (Dartmouth College) 13
NFHS (National Federation of State High School Associations) 34*t*, 161
NIA (National Intramural Association) 12, 17, 26, 39
NIRSA (National Intramural-Recreational Sports Association) 3, 4, 12, 17, 35, 39-41, 40*f*, 62, 112
Noel-Levitz Student Satisfaction Inventory survey 116
NOLS (National Outdoor Leadership School) 42
North American Society for Sport Management (NASSM) 41
Northern Arizona University 2
NRPA (National Recreation and Park Association) 34*t*, 41, 112
NSCA (National Strength and Conditioning Association) 34*t*
NSPF (National Swimming Pool Foundation) 34*t*
NSSE (National Survey of Student Engagement) 59, 116

O

Oberlin College Recreation Center 2
Occupational Safety and Health Administration (OSHA) 139, 203
officials 236
Ohio State University 2, 11, 25
Ohio University 2, 11, 13, 16
Oklahoma State University 15
Oregon State University 11
organizational charts 167, 169*f*
OSHA (Occupational Safety and Health Administration) 139, 203
outdoor and adventure certifications 34*t*
outdoor and adventure recreation 3, 13, 27, 156, 190
outdoor recreation organizations 42
outrage and risk 124

P

participant development 31, 32*t*, 44
Pascarella, Ernest 33
passive learning 189
personality profiles 161
personal trainer certifications 34*t*, 35, 161, 180
personnel. *See* human resources
personnel assessment 106, 114
Phillips University 15
philosophical foundations 31-33, 32*t*
physical culture 6, 7, 18
"Physical Culture, the Result of Moral Obligation" (Jeffries) 9
physical education movement 9-10
physical training theories 7
physiology 32*t*
play theory 33
podcasts 157
pool operator certification 180
power 52
Powerful Partnerships: A Shared Responsibility for Learning (AAHE et al.) 58
Princeton University 6, 10
professional development. *See also* training staff
- about 39, 173
- engagement in field 61-62
- National Intramural-Recreational Sports Association 39-41, 40*f*
- professional organizations 41-43, 112
- regional, state, and provincial organizations for 39-41, 40*f*
- workshops and symposia 41

profit and loss statement 69*t*, 76*t*
pro forma statement 69*t*
program administration 55
programming 32*t*
program planning
- about 183-184
- assessment 195
- conduct initiatives and interventions 194-195
- develop initiatives and interventions 192-193, 193*t*
- develop outcomes 188-192, 189*t*, 191*t*
- measurable outcomes 194
- mission 184-185
- prioritization 184-188, 186*t*
- revision 195
- standards 187-188

projected statement 69*t*, 78*t*
psychographics 93
psychosocial theories 186-187
Purdue University 25-26

Q

Quayle, Bill 15

R

racquetball 199
Rationale for Independent Administration of Collegiate Recreational Sports Programs (NIRSA) 15
recreational facilities
- common types 3
- construction and renovation 16-17

Recreational Sports Directory 165
Recreational Sports Journal 33, 62
recreation and sport organizations 41
Recreation Management magazine 211
refusal of care 126
Registry of Collegiate Recreational Sports Professionals 60, 110
relationships
- community 60-61
- with faculty 57
- group work 52-53
- interdepartmental and intrainstitutional 55-59, 56*f*
- interpersonal 47-54
- intradepartmental 54-55
- organizational 52
- professional 61-62
- workplace 48-50, 49*f*, 53-54

releases from liability 124
religious-based colleges 6
Rensselaer Polytechnic Institute 6
research 32*t*, 106, 116
response protocols 128*t*, 129-135, 130*t*, 131*f*
retail sales 223*t*
risk management. *See also* facilities and facility management
- active shooter plan 133-134
- degree programs for 32*t*
- documentation 140
- employee emergency procedures 131-132
- environmental factors 135-137
- equipment 137-139, 138*t*
- fire emergency plan 132-133
- hazardous material management 139
- injury response protocols 130*t*
- managing risk 126-127, 127*f*
- missing person plan 134-135
- natural disaster procedure 132
- principles of 123-126
- response protocols 128*t*, 129-135, 130*t*, 131*f*
- risk assessment 79-80, 80*f*
- special events 236-237, 237*f*
- technology 147
- terrorist attack plan 133-134
- training protocols 127-129

Robel, Raydon 15
Roosevelt, Theodore 10
ropes courses 201
Rutgers University 6

S

SACSCOC (Southern Association of Colleges and Schools Commission on Colleges) 108, 111
safety and accident prevention 32*t*. *See also* risk management
SAHEC (Student Affairs in Higher Education Consortium) 4
Sandman, Peter 124
Sanford, Nevitt 33
Sargent, Dudley Alan 9, 10, 11
scalar chain 49, 52
scheduling 152-153, 208-209, 234-236, 239
services
- about 215
- athletic training 229
- child care 226-227
- equipment checkout 221-222, 222*t*
- equipment rental 222-223, 222*t*
- food services 227-229
- lockers 224
- massage 230
- membership 215-220, 221*t*
- retail sales 223*t*
- towels 224-225

seven vectors 186-187
sexual harassment 172-173
skating, in-line 200
Slippery Rock University 164
smartphones 156
soccer 201
soccer, indoor 200

social networking 157
softball 201
software
assessment 118
membership management 218
scheduling systems 152-153
software, assessment 119*t*
Southern Association of Colleges and Schools Commission on Colleges (SACSCOC) 108, 111
Space Planning Guidelines for Campus Recreational Sport Facilities (NIRSA) 203-204
special events
awards 239
communication plans 242
emergency plans 237-238
equipment and supplies 239
evaluation plans 242-244
feasibility studies 231-233
financial planning 233-234
food service plans 239-240
housing plans 242
promotion plans 242
registration plans 238-239
risk management 236-237, 237*f*
rules and officials plans 236
scheduling 239
staffing planning 234-236
transportation plans 240-241
special populations programming 27
sponsorship solicitation 92-95
sport 2
sport clubs 2, 27, 192
sport psychology 32*t*
sports equipment 155-156
sports official training 161
squash 199
staff. *See* human resources
staff development. *See* professional development; training staff
staff scheduling. *See* scheduling
Stagg, Amos Alonzo 11
standards 4, 13, 55, 62, 108, 111, 186-187, 189*t*, 203-207
Stone Recreational Center at Alma College 2
strength equipment 155
Student Affairs Administrators in Higher Education 41, 112
student affairs departments 14
Student Affairs in Higher Education Consortium (SAHEC) 4, 112. *See also* National Association of Student Personnel Administrators (NASPA)
student development careers 27
student development theories 31, 44, 186-187
student learning 32*t*
Student Learning Imperative, The: Implications for Student Affairs (ACPA) 58
students
administration involvement 3-4
campus involvement 164
college student development theory 186-187
control of interclass and intercollegiate athletics 8
employment of 114
graduate assistantships 36, 44, 164-165
graduate work experiences 36-38
internships 165-166
involvement in recreation 6-7
student employees 164
student learning outcomes 108-109, 109*t*
undergraduate work experiences 35-36
volunteer staff 166, 235
working with, in transition 50-52
StudentVoice 116
supervision 209-210, 234
surveys 116, 117*t*
sustainability initiatives 13
synthetic field surfaces 155-156

T

taglines 2
tax regulations 60-61, 220
teacher certification 180
technology
access control systems 151-152
compatibility 146-147
determining need 145-146
exercise and fitness equipment 154-155
facility management and 148-153
facility operations and 151-153
factors to consider 146
maintenance 147
marketing 156-158
membership management software 218
objectives for 146
personnel and 147
price 146
recreation equipment 156
risk management 147
scheduling systems 152-153
selecting 145-148
sports equipment 155-156
staff development and 158-161
technology services department 55, 59
terrorist attack plan 133-134
Texas Higher Education Coordinating Board (THECB) 113
THECB (Texas Higher Education Coordinating Board) 113
ticket sales 234
Title IX 13, 215
top-down budgeting 66
tort 125
traffic control 240-241
training rooms 229
training staff. *See also* human resources; professional development
blogs 160
chat rooms 160
communication 171-172
customer service 173
emergency procedures 173
online modules 159-160
professional development 173
risk management of 127-129
sexual harassment 172-173
special events 235-236
technology in 158-161
technology systems 147
video gaming 160
videos 160
web-based 161
transparency 106, 110-111

U

ultimate 201
unfair business practices 60
university department relations 57-59
University of Buffalo 15
University of California, Davis 2
University of Idaho 2
University of Illinois 2, 11, 12
University of Maryland 164
University of Michigan 2, 11, 25
University of North Carolina 2
University of Pennsylvania 6, 7, 10
University of Southern Mississippi 92
University of South Florida 2
University of Texas 11, 14
University of Virginia 7-8
University of West Georgia 5
University of Wisconsin 3
unrelated business income tax (UBIT) 60-61

V

Vedder, Richard K. 16
veterans, military 11-12
volleyball 199
volunteer staff 166, 235

W

waivers 124
Wasson, William 12
water polo 202
water safety instructor certification 180
water slides 202
WEA (Wilderness Education Association) 42
Web 2.0 157-158
web analytics 103
websites 103
wellness programs 2, 13
Western Athletic Conference 11, 17
Western Washington University 2
Wilderness Education Association (WEA) 42
Wilderness Medical Associates (WMA) 34*t*
Williams College 8
Wingspread Group 106
Wittenauer, Jim 17
WMA (Wilderness Medical Associates) 34*t*
workplace relationships 48-50, 49*f*, 53-54
wrestling 200

Y

Yale Boat Club 8
Yale University 6, 8, 10-11
YMCA (Young Men's Christian Association) 10
Young Men's Christian Association (YMCA) 10
Young Women's Christian Association (YWCA) 10
youth programming careers 27
YWCA (Young Women's Christian Association) 10

Z

zero-based budgeting 66

About NIRSA: Leaders in Collegiate Recreation

NIRSA is the premier association of leaders in collegiate recreation who transform lives and facilitate the development of healthy communities worldwide. By providing opportunities for learning and growth, supporting and sharing meaningful research, and fostering networking among our member community, NIRSA is a leader in higher education and champion for the advancement of recreation, sport, and wellness. Since its foundation in 1950, NIRSA membership has grown to comprise nearly 4,000 dedicated professionals, students, and associates, serving an estimated 7.7 million students. Supported by the National Center team, based in Corvallis, Oregon, NIRSA is governed by volunteer leaders from across North America.

About the Contributors

William F. Canning, MA, has served as director of recreational sports at the University of Michigan since September 2000. Bill is a nationally recognized expert in facility and business operations for collegiate recreational sport programs. He is a partner in Canning Gonsoulin & Associates, LLC, a firm that has assisted more than 20 university clients. Bill also is an owner of Centers, LLC, a firm that manages recreational sport facilities and programs for colleges.

Bill served as the associate vice president for business operations and associate dean of student affairs at Tulane University, director of cultural and recreational affairs and athletic facilities at UCLA, and associate director of facilities and finance at the University of Michigan.

Jennifer R. de-Vries, MS, has over 20 years of experience in collegiate recreation and serves as the associate director for business and facility operations with instructional responsibilities at Oregon State University. She was on the faculty of the National School of Recreational Sports Management from 2010 to 2012, served as NIRSA vice president for Region VI from 2005 to 2007, and received the 2012 Region VI Award of Merit. She was the associate director at the University of Oregon physical education and recreation department and the director of campus recreation and leadership at Elon College.

Douglas Franklin, PhD, has 35 years of experience in higher education and currently serves as the assistant dean of students for planning, assessment, and research at Ohio University. He is the NIRSA director on the board of the Council for the Advancement of Standards in Higher Education (CAS) and a commissioner for the Registry of Collegiate Recreational Sports Professionals. He has given numerous presentations on assessment, learning outcomes, and student employees. Franklin is coauthor of *Philosophical and Theoretical Foundations of Campus Recreation: Crossroads of Theory* and *Campus Recreation Career* and *Professional Standards, in Campus Recreation: Essentials for the Professional.*

Robert L. Frye, MA, is the director of recreation services at Florida International University (FIU) in Miami and has over 30 years of professional experience in campus recreation. He is a four-term editorial board member of *Recreational Sports Journal*, has chaired or served on NIRSA technology work teams, presented on technology in campus recreation, and served as a faculty member and chair of the NIRSA School of Recreational Sports Management. Frye has taught technology in recreation and sports in two university recreation and sport management departments.

Jose H. Gonzalez, EdD, has worked as a full-time faculty member and administrator of higher education programs for over 10 years. As the former director of campus recreation at Plymouth State University, he integrated technology into staff training and marketing for on-campus programs. He continues to teach online as an adjunct faculty for the health and human performance department. He has been a presenter on staff development, online training, and curriculum development. Currently Dr. Gonzalez serves as the manager for the Southern California region of REI's Outdoor School.

Evelyn Kwan Green, MBA, MS, is an instructor in the department of casino, hospitality, and tourism management at the University of Southern Mississippi. Green was one of the first full-time marketing professionals hired by a campus recreation department. For 10 years she served as the director of marketing, public relations, and sales in the division of recreational sports at the University of Southern Mississippi. She initiated and presented NIRSA's first preconference marketing workshop in 1999 and developed the inaugural marketing symposium the following year. For her contribution to recreational sports marketing she received NIRSA's National Service Award in 2000.

Jacqueline R. Hamilton, EdD, has served as the recreational sports director at Texas A & M University–Corpus Christi since 2002. She is an adjunct instructor in the College of Education teaching introductory research for graduate students. She has been a member of the NIRSA Research and Assessment Committee, the ACHA Healthy Campus 2020 writing team, educational content work team, and NIRSA board of directors.

Sarah E. Hardin, PhD, serves as associate director of Campus Recreation Centers, LLC, at DePaul University and the 2010-2013 Region III representative to the NIRSA Member Network. Her interest in career development is exemplified through her work as chair and faculty member of the NIRSA School of Recreational Sports Management, coordination of the Student Professional Development Pre-Conference Workshop and Career Opportunities Center, research, and presentations. In higher education she has worked as an academic adviser, faculty member in recreation administration, and policy analyst with the Florida State Board of Community Colleges.

Aaron Hill, MS, is a part-time faculty member for the urban policy and management programs at the New School in New York City. He holds a bachelor of arts degree in speech communication from the University of Southern Mississippi. He worked in campus recreation as a professional marketing manager and was the director of marketing for NIRSA from 2000 to 2003.

Bradley Hunt, MS, is the marketing and communications director of recreational sports at the University of Minnesota in the Twin Cities. He is an active member of NIRSA and most recently presented *Making Your Marketing Message Stick: The Process of Branding in Campus Recreation* at the 2010 NIRSA Annual Conference and Recreational Sports Exposition. He has provided marketing services for several conference planning committees, including the 2007 NIRSA Region III Lead On and the 2009 Association of Outdoor Recreation and Education (AORE) National Conference. Since 2007 his marketing and communications staff have been nominated for six NIRSA Creative Excellence Awards.

Stephen Kampf, PhD, has 20 years of experience in higher education. He serves as the assistant vice president and director of recreation and wellness at Bowling Green State University. He has worked on numerous NIRSA committees and served as the NIRSA state director for New York and Pennsylvania. A frequent presenter, he has spoken on assessment, hiring practices in collegiate recreation, and ethics. Kampf has authored or coauthored many articles on topics such as legal liability, sportsmanship, and impact of college recreation centers.

Maureen McGonagle, MBA, CRSS, has 23 years of professional experience in collegiate recreation. She works for Centers, LLC, as the director of campus recreation at DePaul University. She operates an award-winning recreation facility, and her department is responsible for generating over $3 million annually in revenue from non-student fees. Maureen has been an active NIRSA member, including service on the NIRSA Board of Directors, the NIRSA Services Corporation Board, the NIRSA Foundation Board, the Governance Commission, and the Commission for Sustainable Communities. She is a frequent presenter on leadership, business and management techniques, and student and staff development.

Gordon M. Nesbitt, PhD, has been involved in campus recreation since 1983 when he joined the staff at the University of Illinois at Urbana-Champaign as a graduate assistant. After graduating from Illinois, Dr. Nesbitt accepted a full-time position at Purdue University, where he served for 12 years and also completed his PhD. In 1997 Dr. Nesbitt accepted the position of assistant professor and director of the campus recreation program at Millersville University of Pennsylvania. Dr. Nesbitt has been a member of NIRSA since 1983 and has served on numerous committees and presented at state, regional, and national conferences.

Jeff Sessine, MS, is currently the senior vice president of Centers, LLC, where he oversees the management of collegiate recreation facilities and personnel at several universities in the United States. He earned a master's degree in higher education administration from Purdue University and a master's degree in athletic administration from Ohio University and has been an active member of NIRSA since 1990.

Julia Wallace Carr, EdD, has 20 years of experience in campus recreation as a senior associate director for programming and coordinator of fitness, group fitness, and wellness programs at James Madison University. She is an associate professor in the School of Hospitality, Sport and Recreation Management, where she is responsible for the master's degree program in campus recreation leadership. Dr. Wallace Carr is a presenter on learning outcomes and program planning at the NIRSA National Conference, a faculty member of NIRSA School of Recreational Sport Management, and a trainer and consultant for campus recreation programs on using the principles of LR2, program planning, and developing learning outcomes.